What others are saying about
Stories of Faith and Courage from the War in Iraq & Afghanistan

"This book will be a true comfort to me while my son is deployed and a reminder to me that no matter what happens, our loving God is in control and carries him in the palm of his mighty hands."

Susan Rowley, Blue Star Mom

"Our memories of the news accounts from the battlefield often dim with time, but these stories of our modern-day heroes of the faith will be carried for years in our hearts and shared long into the future with our loved ones."

Victor Primeaux, CDR, USCG (ret)
CMF's Director of Ministries to Coast Guard Forces and Families
Christian Military Fellowship (CMF)

"Anyone who wants to see God's love and power at work during times of war should read this powerful book. The stories are real, unvarnished, and vividly capture the full spectrum of human emotions and experiences from cradle to grave. It's much like reading Psalms in a modern-day context."

Chaplain (Col.) Scott McChrystal,
USA Ret., Assemblies of God Chaplaincy Ministries

"The stories, while brief enough to reach the hearts of those with hectic schedules, are both compelling and authentic, getting to the heart of the matter right away. No built up façade, no literary hype, simply stories of men and women who showed incredible courage in the face of the unexpected. These stories touch me in a deeply personal way because of our family's military service, and I know that many will be able to relate to the process of recognizing the hand of God, even in the midst of tragedy. I know that hearts will be touched in a special way."

Rebekah Benimoff, Army wife, contributor to
Faith Deployed: Daily Encouragement for Military Wives

"A compelling read, *Stories of Faith and Courage from the War in Iraq & Afghanistan* highlights hope in the m‌‌‌‌‌‌‌‌‌‌‌‌‌‌‌‌‌‌‌‌‌‌‌‌ inspiring compilation of firsthand account‌‌‌‌‌‌‌‌‌‌‌‌‌‌‌‌‌‌‌‌‌‌ ted by the war on terrorism."

Roger Benimoff, co-author of *Fait‌‌‌‌‌‌‌‌‌‌‌‌‌‌‌‌‌‌‌‌ emoir*

"*Stories of Faith and Courage from th‌‌‌‌‌‌‌‌‌‌‌‌‌‌‌‌‌‌‌‌‌‌‌‌‌‌‌ Afghanistan* chronicles the events from September 11th through the wars in Iraq and Afghanistan. Each devotional draws on firsthand experiences from those closest to the toughest moments of our country's recent history. These vignettes draw strength from Scripture that allows readers to understand that they can never let their current circumstances determine the presence of God—He is always with us."

Capt. Chris Plekenpol, author, *Faith in the Fog of War*

Stories OF Faith AND Courage
FROM THE THE WAR IN
IRAQ & AFGHANISTAN

JANE HAMPTON COOK
JOCELYN GREEN
JOHN CROUSHORN

GOD & COUNTRY
PRESS

ISBN 978-0-89957041-9
First printing—October 2009
Cover designed by Mike Meyers at Meyers Design, Kingwood, Texas
Interior design and typesetting by Reider Publishing Services, West Hollywood, California
Edited and proofread by Dan Penwell and Rick Steele

Printed in the United States of America
17 16 15 14 13 12 –W–9 8 7 6 5 4

Dedicated to those who have lived loudly for liberty
in Iraq and Afghanistan and their families.

White House Run

Jane Hampton Cook, Former White House Deputy Director of Internet News Services

TAKE OFF YOUR shoes and run," the security officer called to me.

I'll never forget that moment on September 11, 2001. Hundreds of my White House colleagues and I were evacuating the Eisenhower Executive Office Building (EEOB), the grand Victorian building next door to the West Wing.

At less than five feet tall, I don't have the leg length to run quickly, but I ran as fast I could to exit the White House complex. I remember the sick feeling I had when I learned that two planes had attacked the World Trade Center and a third plane had just hit the Pentagon. The possibility of a fourth plane striking the White House was very real.

> "They will lift you up in their hands, so that you will not strike your foot against a stone." (Psalm 91:11–12)

On that unforgettable date, my job responsibility was developing and designing the content for the official White House website. I was working on a new page focusing on President George W. Bush's educational initiative, but that page never was posted. Instead we created new postings, highlighting America's multi-front response: diplomatic efforts, military attacks, financial blocking of terrorist financing, and humanitarian aid.

When I think about September 11, I remember two things: the *courage* of those first responders, many who lost their lives, and America's strength, resilience, and commitment to *freedom*. A few days after the terrorist attacks, my mother had shared with me Psalms 91, a biblical passage that strengthened me during this difficult time. I found it fascinating that Psalm 91:1 (9-1-1) brought such as powerful message. *"He who dwells in the shelter of the Most High will rest in the shadow of the Almighty"* and in verse 11, *"he will command his angels concerning you."*

When the security officer called out to me to "take off my shoes and run" on that trying day, he was acting as an angel from God to guard me in all my ways.

Prayer:
Thank you for bringing guidance in times of extreme need.

A Life-Saving Latte

Chaplain, Maj. Gen. (Ret.), Charles C. Baldwin, former Chief of Chaplains, United States Air Force

W E'VE BEEN bombed," a guard hollered into the cafeteria where retired Major General Charles Baldwin, a longtime leader of chaplains, was sitting and drinking a latte.

The announcement didn't make sense to Baldwin. He hadn't heard an explosion, and after more than thirty years in the Air Force, Baldwin knew what a bomb sounded like.

Although he was a General and a senior administrative leader, going to the Pentagon was a normal part of Baldwin's daily routine. Stationed at nearby Bolling Air Force Base, he came to the Pentagon that morning to attend his first senior staff meeting as the new deputy chief of chaplains for the Air Force. He soon realized that nothing about September 11, 2001 would be routine.

"The meeting started at nine o'clock," Baldwin said. Led by the Secretary of the Air Force, the meeting took place in the basement of building eight.

> "But I have raised you up for this very purpose, that I might show you my power and that my name might be proclaimed in all the earth." (Exodus 9:16)

"We were about twenty minutes into the daily slide briefing, when someone interrupted. We turned our attention to the television and watched the second plane fly into the World Trade Center Tower," Baldwin recalled. Shocked, "we immediately adjourned."

"I had a ten o'clock meeting on other side of the Pentagon, but stopped to get a latte in the cafeteria" Baldwin said.

"Shortly after I got my latte, a guard ordered an evacuation." We immediately exited the building," Baldwin said. "That's when we saw the huge fireball on the other side of the Pentagon."

Baldwin then realized that his ten o'clock meeting was located at the site of the black billowing smoke. Had he proceeded to his meeting earlier and not stopped to get a latte, he would have been in the wedge when it was hit.

The Pentagon had turned from an office building into the burning aftermath of a battlefield. Having served as a chaplain in Desert Storm a decade earlier and as a rescue pilot in Vietnam, Baldwin knew what to do.

"I went to the Sheraton hotel across from the Pentagon where they were bringing in the wounded. At that point I turned into a chaplain and went from couch to couch." Baldwin spoke words of comfort to the patients triaged in the hotel before going to local hospitals. After about an hour, Baldwin decided to return to Ground Zero at the Pentagon. But it wasn't smoke or shock that drew him there. He wanted to be with the people who were hurting the most. His life's purpose led him in that moment to step in and simply be ready to face the tragedy head on.

Prayer:
Almighty God, you have given my life purpose and meaning.
May I embrace the service you desire for me.

JANUARY 3

More Chaplains than Normal

Chaplain, Maj. Gen. (Ret.), Charles C. Baldwin, former Chief of Chaplains, United States Air Force

ON AN AVERAGE day there are normally five or six chaplains in the Pentagon," Chaplain Charlie Baldwin explained, "but on September 11, 2001, it was really an amazing thing. There were about thirty-five chaplains in the building."

These chaplains were at the Pentagon that morning for various meetings. After the evacuation, they gathered at the casualty collections points to minister to those in need. Unlike local pastors who also arrived, these military chaplains had clearance to the Pentagon, which enabled them to help find survivors.

With all three chiefs of chaplains out of town, retired chaplain, Major General Baldwin and two other deputy chief of chaplains (Army and Navy) developed a plan. "We realized we needed to organize this pastoral care moment, because this was not going to be short term. So we claimed some tent space and then sent many chaplains as far as they could go into the building to look for survivors. Then we developed a plan to organize the chaplains on site as the wounded came out," Baldwin explained.

Many of these chaplains were senior officers with administrative responsibilities and no longer involved in day-to-day chaplain duties, but they all returned to their roots.

"We all became the chaplains who were present to help the injured. We went to the casualty collection points and just did, what any chaplain would do, what any pastor would do," Baldwin explained. "I stepped in and out of the role of organizing the chaplain ministries and just being one."

One gentleman came up to Baldwin, pointing to the gaping hole and said, "My wife's in that room right there. I need to get in there."

Baldwin talked to him throughout the day, encouraging him not to give up hope. It was possible she could have been away from her office. The good news didn't come, but Baldwin knew from experience that a chaplain's job was to not to give a magic answer but to be a hopeful presence during this trial. The ministry of the site was profound. Some might wonder if those chaplains wanted to be there. "Why wouldn't you want to be there? If you're a military chaplain, that is where you belong," stated Baldwin. "That is exactly the purpose for which you were trained—to be present with people during difficult times, not to have the magic answers, but to be present."

> "He heals the broken-hearted and binds up their wounds."
> (Psalm 147:3)

The presence of six times the normal number of chaplains at the Pentagon on September 11, 2001, was truly an amazing preparation for the immediate aftermath. For many hurting people that day, chaplains were God's instruments of hope and peace.

Prayer:
You are a great God. Thank you for putting an extra number of chaplains on site at the Pentagon that day.

JANUARY 4

The Day Rank Disappeared

Chaplain, Maj. Gen. (Ret.), Charles C. Baldwin, former Chief of Chaplains, United States Air Force

RANK DISAPPEARED on September 11, 2001. Everyone wanted to do whatever they could to help. About four o'clock in the afternoon, the fire chief in charge of the recovery process made an announcement at Ground Zero.

"We need volunteers to put on masks and gloves and be willing to do a sweep through the Pentagon. Any volunteers?" he asked.

"People ran to get a place in line," recalled retired Major General Baldwin, Air Force deputy chief of chaplains.

"So here we were in line. Next to me was a two-star general, and I was a one-star general. We're standing in our blues. We stepped forward, put on gloves, put on the masks. They gave us the instructions to stay together in rows, and we were going to sweep through the building and walk through the clouds of fire, dust and all that. And just before he said, 'Okay, this line step forward,' a brigade from Arlington Cemetery pulled up in buses."

Because this brigade was trained and ready to do a sweep, the fire chief released the volunteers.

"I looked around and saw the field full of people who were willing to step into the fiery furnace to see if somebody else could be pulled out. So we stepped away and went back to the areas where we could be helpful, be the pastors present."

> "And we know that in all things God works for the good of those who love him, who have been called according to his purpose" (Romans 8:28).

Two experiences prepared Baldwin to lead chaplains on that unforgettable day. He was a rescue helicopter pilot in Vietnam, where he witnessed death, carnage, and many other terrible things. Years later as a lieutenant colonel in Desert Storm, he was in charge of chapel services at the base in Saudi Arabia. "We preached every Sunday in the war zone and saw people die. Body bags were brought back to our base to process before sending them back home," he explained.

He learned his role was to be a calm, encouraging presence in the midst of the tragedy. "You don't have to be a military chaplain to have the theology of hope that says 'God is present in the midst of terrible things.' Military chaplains have the type of experience that says, 'God is present on the battlefield, not to help people kill people but to help them through the tragedies and consequences of sin. They don't bless the bombs, they just pray that God would be present with those who are the instruments, even we would say the instruments of peace. It's an amazing thing."

Prayer:
*Thank you God for your promise to be present
with me no matter what.*

Where was God on 9/11?

Chaplain, Maj. Gen. (Ret.), Charles C. Baldwin, former Chief of Chaplains, United States Air Force

"WHERE WAS GOD on the morning of September 11," a CNN reporter asked Chaplain Charlie Baldwin in an on-camera interview in his office not long after the terrorist attacks.

"It wasn't something I had to make up. It was obvious to me that he was present in the midst of the terror. He revealed himself through the angels of mercy who were present," Baldwin recalled.

Baldwin saw many moments of mercy at the Pentagon that day. "One second lieutenant, a young lady, came running over to me, asking, 'Chaplain, what can I do to help?'"

"Go to that tent and just wipe their brows, and you will be helping."

She went to one of the collection tents where victims were being brought. There she set up cots, and did whatever needed to be done.

> "Where can I go from your Spirit? Where can I flee from your presence? If I go up to the heavens, you are there; if I make my bed in the depths, you are there." (Psalm 139:7–8)

Right beside her was a two-star general doing the same thing. "I want to help. What else can I do?" Knowing the man was a Christian, Baldwin added, "Tell them not to be afraid. Tell them God is here. He will take care of them."

Baldwin mentioned that chaplains offer the same message to troops on the ground, "so they can be assured that God is with them; that they might know that they are not alone."

"These people weren't the preachers," Baldwin decreed. "They were just people who cared. They were God's hands, his instruments of love and comfort, saying 'God is with you, and he will be with you through this whole thing.'"

Baldwin was asked several times by reporters, "Where was God on 9-1-1?"

"The answer was, 'He was present.'"

"He worked through that second lieutenant, brand new to the Air Force. She probably didn't think she would experience something like this so early in her military career. But she just jumped into the middle of it all, carrying stretchers, taking bandages. If the nurses needed an orderly, he or she was that person." God was everywhere. He made his presence known through the least of these.

"He was in the building when the terrorists struck. He offered healing to those who received it. He offered comfort to those who were dying. And God's presence was overwhelming and even miraculous in some cases," Baldwin replied.

Prayer:
Thank you for using the "least of these" to provide hope to those in need on the battlefield. Thank you for being a presence among your people.

Chemistry Class

Maj. Brandon Reid, United States Air Force

I WAS HOLDING *and inspecting my chemical mask!*

Though I had been in the Air Force for five years and was on my second deployment to Southwest Asia where the threat and enemy were near, I had never before been concerned about my chemical gear. I now realized I should have paid more attention during my annual chemical defense classes, one of my requirements as an Air Force navigator on C–130's. Recalling how to put all the gear on was easy, but my worse case scenario was: I don all my gear and simply worry about dehydration. However, remembering where to inject the large needle from my gear into my hip without jamming it into my sciatic nerve was gaining prevalence on my list of important things to know.

It was fall 2002. Discussions of an invasion of Iraq gained fervor on television and on our base in Oman.

My crew and I had grown accustomed to flying into Pakistan and Afghanistan after September 11, 2001. Original fears of unknown operating areas and first-time combat operations had led to many prayers and self-reflection, but we had replaced them with card games and reading. With the exception of occasional small arms fire or a lucky rocket propelled grenade launch, threats to our C–130 aircraft were minimal. The walk many of us had taken with God to get through earlier tough times had been replaced by repetition.

7

This normalcy was broken that day when our commanders ordered us into a tent for a chemical gear refresher course. As they spread us apart to make sure we had enough room to inspect and manipulate our individual equipment, I noticed a difference. The more experienced master sergeant, not the young senior airman, was teaching the course. I suddenly realized this was for real. Something was about to happen. That moment brought the confrontation of war to the forefront of my thoughts.

> "I lie down and sleep; I wake again, because the LORD sustains me." (Psalm 3:5)

Much like repetitive life back home, we pray more during challenges than seasons of ease. Whether we're in the comfort zone or combat zone, God sustains us. If we routinely see life from an altitude of thirty thousand feet or fly through our day with our feet on the ground, *God is there.* He is with us when the sun goes down and when it rises, whether over the sands of a Middle East desert or an American suburb's sidewalks.

Prayer:
You are the maker of sunsets and sunrises.
Thank you for this day you have given me.

JANUARY 7

Preflight Prayer

Maj. Brandon Reid, United States Air Force

SO HERE I was about to fly into harm's way as a member of a crew that'd been flying together for two and a half months. We had flown more than twenty-five flights together and were well seasoned by Air Force standards. We knew each other's weaknesses, strengths, and limitations, though we'd never discussed religion. Now here we were in the cargo compartment of a C-130 aircraft getting our final briefing from our aircraft commander

Having gotten our mission for our first flight of the Iraq war, we went through our typical pre-flight intelligence and mission briefing. I decided to walk to the plane instead of riding in the crew bus to get my mind in the right place. For whatever reason I kept thinking of my father who served in Vietnam on an AC-130 gunship; he survived being shot down in enemy territory. Upon arriving at the C-130, I ran through my checklist, paying special attention to the defensive equipment controls. It was then that our aircraft commander asked me to lead in a word of prayer.

"Brandon, would you lead us in a prayer?"

While the request caught me off guard, it felt correct and needed. We came together as a crew and formed a circle. I said a prayer asking God to watch over us and our fellow brothers in the coming armed struggle. As proud members of the Air Force, we had chosen to join military service and sworn an oath leading us all to this destiny. I said some words of thanks and praise and asked God

> "The One enthroned in heaven laughs; the Lord scoffs at them (the kings who take their stand against him)." (Psalm 2:4)

to protect us. If we weren't meant to come back, we had accepted that and were at peace with it.

We'd never discussed our relationships with God before and perhaps many of these men had been separated from any type of relationship with God for years. However, his unshakeable presence and grace was upon each man on that plane and delivered a sense of calmness—all fear behind now, just get the job done.

Prayer:
Even though some on this earth have rejected you, I thank you that you are a God who welcomes us as we humble ourselves before you.

Parachute

Maj. Brandon Reid, United States Air Force

I DID SOMETHING I normally didn't do during that first flight into Iraq—I wore my parachute.

My father was a member of an AC-130 gunship crew in Vietnam that was hit by a SA-7 surface to air missile (SAM) in June 1972.* He was one of only three survivors. To hear him tell the story, he's not sure why he lived while others died. Of all the details of his survival, the one I find most amazing is that after standing up in his aircraft, he remembers an explosion and confusion all around him. It was then that he regained consciousness in mid-air. That presence of mind gave him the ability to engage his parachute. Thanks to his parachute, he survived that day, and I was born two years later.

Fast-forward twenty-nine years to my first flight into Iraq. I'm the one flying into harm's way, not my father. Although I had become accustomed to flying into Afghanistan's dangerous air space, it was not procedure for C-130 aircrew to wear parachutes. However, on that first flight, I felt compelled to wear a parachute like my father.

As a navigator, I'd reflected on my father's shoot-down many times over the years. I've always concluded that the parachute and a bit of luck saved his life. As we prepared for flights into Iraq, the intelligence we received painted a bleak picture for a C-130 aircraft, so I thought it best to don my parachute for that first flight, incase a SAM (surface to air missle) found us.

> "Defend my cause and redeem me; preserve my life according to your promise."
> (Psalm 119:154)

Not until I returned to Kuwait and prepared for a second flight into Iraq did I realize the truth. Perhaps my commander's request that I lead the crew in prayer steered my thoughts. It wasn't timing, luck, or a parachute that saved my father. It was God's will. God saved my father that day because he had work yet to be done. My own life was part of God's plan. After concluding this, I tossed my parachute in the back of the plane. I geared up for the next flight following normal sans-parachute procedure. I looked to God as my saving grace, not some piece of equipment.

Truth be told on that first flight into Iraq; the parachute was bulky and very uncomfortable. However, on all flights since with God on my shoulder, the weight has been lifted.

Prayer:
Lord, you are the great life-preserver.
Preserve my life according to your plan.

* Vic Reid's story is featured on p. 338 in *Stories of Faith and Courage from the Revolutionary War.*

had finally come. Because of the dust no one, including the enemy, would be moving tonight, so we thought.

Prayer:
Father, though the wind sometimes howls and dust hinders my visibility, I put my trust in you.

Night Watch

Corp. Will Brandon, United States Marine Corps

A COUPLE HOURS into that night, the dust storm began to let up. As visibility became completely clear, we were shocked to see an enemy convoy about four kilometers to our direct front. Lacking our night vision capability, the enemy used very dim headlights to maneuver. Although these headlights were about half as bright as regular automobile headlights, they were very visible from our position. We were astonished. The Iraqi convoy stretched from one end of the horizon to the other. It was just sitting there, not moving.

All I could think about was what a great opportunity for an air mission. The chatter over the radio suggested it was going to be a target for the artillery. We used the artillery quite often, and the round of choice was Improved Conventional Munitions. The ICM is a big bullet that bursts open and drops a bunch of little bombs that are designed to take out tanks. They could blow a two-foot hole in packed dirt so precisely that you could drop a soda can down the opening.

"Watchman, what is left of the night? Watchman, what is left of the night"? (Isaiah 21:11b)

Finally, after what must have been more than an hour of staring at this massive enemy convoy, we heard the sound of Marine artillery guns way off in the distance to our four o'clock. Five seconds later, we heard the burst, followed by the crackle of hundreds of mini bombs impacting. Unfortunately, all of the shells hit way to the left or right. Nothing hit any of the enemy vehicles to our direct front. The bomb had one effect. The enemy immediately turned off their lights.

"Great," we all thought. "We didn't hit any of them and now we can't even see them."

As I sat behind the driver's station where Lance Corporal Mejia watched the thermal driving screen, I switched between binoculars and night vision goggles trying to get a glimpse of something out there. Finally we saw movement. More than a dozen large dust signatures were barely visible in the air. Only one thing could throw a dust plume that high—a tank! Our twenty-six ton tracks are no match for a forty or sixty-ton standard battle tank. A .50 caliber machine gun could chew us up, let alone a round from the main gun of a tank.

All we could do was watch and wait for help as we stared into the darkness with a giant enemy in front of us.

Prayer:
Heavenly Father, be my watchman throughout my day and night today.

JANUARY 12

Chatter

Corp. Will Brandon, United States Marine Corps

AS WE STARED into the inky darkness, knowing an Iraqi tank convoy covered the horizon directly to our front, the radio chatter keyed up.

"We needed help out here and fast," we pleaded.

We had no tanks with us at that moment; they had all gone to refuel—a big problem. The only thing we had was several shoulder-fired AT-4s, rockets which are only good out to three hundred meters in the daytime. The Iraqi tanks would make easy targets of our highly silhouetted tracks long before that.

Our platoon sergeant, "the Gunny," began calling our commander over the comm, the communications network.

"Colgate, this is Iceman," we heard come across the net. "Why don't we have any tanks out here?"

"The tanks say they're not coming until they refuel, Iceman." Colgate responded.

"What do you mean they aren't coming till they refuel? We are going to be in some serious trouble here real soon!" Gunny exclaimed. "What about CAT?"

CAT is a Humvee with a TOW missile on top of it.

"CAT can't make it out to us," was the response. "Ground is too rough."

"All right everybody listen up. This is Iceman. Everybody start your vehicles now. We are getting out of here as soon as the first shot is fired." Everyone immediately started their trucks.

"No one is going anywhere. Shut your vehicles down now," Colgate shouted over the net; the anger quite apparent in his voice. Just as fast as we started them, we shut the trucks off.

Mejia and I went into the troop compartment and unstrapped the AT-4s. We jumped out of the back of the truck, and called over to an infantry squad leader, a corporal, who had ridden with us.

> "...a chattering fool comes to ruin."
> (Proverbs 10:10b)

"What's going on, what's up with you guys?" he asked.

"There are fifteen tanks coming this way, you guys need to get these ready," Mejia said handing him the rockets.

After Mejia and I returned to the Amtrak, the wind picked up. Everything looked hazy as dust filled the air again. This was worrisome because now we couldn't see the tanks anymore, only the dust. The whole world around us lit up once again into a Mars-like amber glow. It was as if a streetlight suddenly turned on over a dark foggy street.

Chatter is often useless, leading us nowhere. Babbling was no substitute for real action, real decision-making.

Prayer:
Weed out the fruitless noise and chatter in my mind and heart today. Fill it with the substance of you and the promises of your word for righteousness.

Bible in a Zip-lock Bag

Corp. Will Brandon, United States Marine Corps

TO OUR HORROR, the corporal to whom we had given the AT-4 fired off an illumination round from his M203 grenade launcher, but because of the wind, the round drifted back toward us. Its tiny parachute carried it back to the ground, completely giving away our position.

"*We were dead for sure now,*" I thought. I just knew the enemy tanks would loom out of the dust and darkness at any moment.

"What are you doing," I blasted. "The tanks are going to know we are here for sure now!"

"Where are they, we can't see them?" the corporal replied, not seeming to care that a lance corporal had yelled at him.

"They're out there. Straight ahead of us, about 1500–2000 meters. Don't fire another one of those flares," I begged.

I got back into the track and climbed up to the troop commander's station, behind the driver.

"Can you see anything?" I asked.

"No, nothing yet, too much dust," Mejia replied. "Take a break. I'll wake you if anything happens."

"I think it's going to be easier than it sounds, sleep that is," I responded as I climbed into the troop compartment.

Sitting on the center bench seat and leaning against the ramp at the very back of the vehicle, I lit a cigarette and tried to relax. Dirt cigarettes we called them—the ones the Iraqis tried to sell from the side of the road.

"How can I sleep at a time like this?" I thought.

I pulled a small zip-lock bag from my uniform's left breast pocket. Here I kept a pocket-size Bible the USO (United Service Organizations) distributed at Aviano Air Force base in Italy, where we stopped en route to Kuwait. Also in the bag was a plastic wallet-size picture holder with photographs of my girlfriend in Ohio and my family back home in Manitoba, Canada.

> "I lie down and sleep; I wake again, because the LORD sustains me. I will not fear the tens of thousands drawn up against me on every side." (Psalm 3:5–6)

After reading several versus from the Psalms, I returned the Bible to the bag and looked at the photo album. In my mind I said goodbye to everyone I loved. Then I returned the pictures to the bag and prayed. I thanked God for the life he had given me, my parents, and the people I loved. I asked God to take my life into his hands and do with me what he willed. When I was finished, I closed my eyes, laid down on the bench, and miraculously fell asleep.

Prayer:
Lord, you're in control. Thank you for sustaining
when I sleep and when I rise.

16

Armor of Light

Corp. Will Brandon, United States Marine Corps

I FELL ASLEEP for a period time, even though it felt like only a few minutes. Before then, I had been surviving on two hours of sleep a night. But a strange thing happened when I woke. Daylight was streaming through the driver's hatch where Mejia was still sitting. The darkness was over.

"What's going on up there, man?" I asked.

"Nothing, you missed it," Mejia replied. "It cleared up enough. Air was called in."

"I didn't hear anything," I exclaimed.

"I don't know how you missed it: it was kind of loud," he chuckled.

I was surprised Mejia didn't wake me when the Marine air strike destroyed the tanks, but grateful for the peace that came with sleep.

I was told later those Iraqi tanks were T-72s, the most modern tanks the Iraqis had. These were former Soviet vehicles weighing at least forty-one tons. Those T-72s would have made short work of us easily if they could have seen us. I was also told the tanks had closed within 1,400 meters of our line; almost well within the range of their main guns. If it hadn't been for that last dust storm, those tanks may have very well rolled close enough to see us, and our armament coil of smaller vehicles would have made easy targets.

> "The night is nearly over; the day is almost here. So let us put aside the deeds of darkness and put on the armor of light."
> (Romans 13:12)

As I think about that night in Iraq, I can't help but reflect in wonder and awe. I might have fallen asleep and missed the "air show," but I didn't miss God's hand. He used a dust storm to turn daylight into the darkest pitch I'd ever seen. He sustained us despite the missed location of the ICM, the chatter over the radio, and the mistaken illumination round fired by the corporal.

After that night we pushed on toward Baghdad. We were ambushed multiple times. On April 4th we attacked the West side of Baghdad and controlled the city within a week. We stayed as a reinforcement unit until President Bush announced the conclusion of combat operations.

We were some of the first Marines to come home and received a true hero's welcome.

I believe God answered many prayers that night and sent a final dust storm to spare us. I'm grateful to him for providing me assurance from his Psalms and allowing me to give him thanks for my life and those I love. He was the fresh air of hope in a dust storm.

Prayer:
God, thank you for your armor of light and
bringing us out of the darkness.

JANUARY 15

Operation Preparation

Cdr. Rob Thomson, United States Navy

GOD GAVE NOAH only seven days to pack the ark. Navy Commander Rob Thomson faced a similar challenge—loading the *USS Boxer*, a helicopter carrier, in a week's time in anticipation of the United States invasion of Iraq.

"We got word in late December 2002 that we would be shipping out to Iraq to prepare for a possible confrontation with Saddam Hussein," Thomson said.

Normally it takes months to prepare for this kind of deployment. Not only did they compress the loading operation into one week, but it was also the week between Christmas and New Year's Day. Crewmembers had to suddenly give up their leave and vacation plans.

As Operations Officer, Thomson was responsible for anything that involved planning and executing, such as moving helicopters and crafts, troops, and supplies aboard ship.

"We loaded our 2,000 Marines and 900 Navy crew and all of their gear between Christmas and New Year's Day, then set sail the first week of January 2003," Thomson explained.

Pressing utmost on Thomson's mind was his family he couldn't take with him or care for while he was gone.

"I was leaving behind Kinuko, my Japanese wife, in what to her was a 'foreign country' and Alex, my three-year-old autistic son, for her to care for alone in our San Diego home. No one from her family lived within

10,000 miles, and my family was 3,000 miles away in Pittsburgh."

Thomson and Kinuko had married nine years earlier, living mostly in Japan where Thomson served three tours of duty. Kinuko, the daughter of a rice farmer, grew up in a Japanese town that was so remote most of its residents had never seen a foreigner until Thomson came to meet her family. "Everyone stopped and stared," he noted.

Moving to San Diego had been a huge adjustment for the Thomsons but with a significant benefit. For the first time they were able to plug into a church and not simply attend chapel services. Although the church was small, their hearts were huge—ark-like.

"The church we attended only had about fifty or sixty members, but the love of Christ dwelt in each one," Thomson said.

When these church members learned about Rob's sudden deployment, they offered to help Kinuko and Alex, which gave Thomson tremendous peace of mind as he embarked on a deployment that would take him into a combat zone for the first time of his sixteen years in the Navy.

While Commander Thomson oversaw the practical preparations and operations for loading the *USS Boxer* and its 2,900 crewmembers, he also looked to the Great Shepherd and a loving community to care for the wife and son he was leaving behind.

Prayer:
Thank you for your practical provisions for my most basic needs.

JANUARY 16

Praying by Name

Cdr. Rob Thomson, United States Navy

SEVERAL EVENTS occurred between February and June 2003, while I was in and around Iraq that brought home to me the awesome power of God and how he works through his people," Commander Rob Thomson explained of his deployment to Iraq.

The *USS Boxer* arrived in the North Arabian Gulf the third week of February 2003. Thomson spent the next month preparing for battle in Iraq by pre-staging equipment and supplies in Kuwait. No one knew when the war would start, but they had to be ready when the call came. The plan was to send the Marines aboard the *USS Boxer* into Iraq through helicopters aboard the ship. Thomson's job was to plan and execute operations. Electronic communications proved invaluable.

"We did a lot of coordinating in chat rooms. I never experienced that way of operating before. Each area of operations had a chat room. So I would pull up about four to six chat rooms and watch as the operation's logistics unfolded in near real time," he said.

Although not useful for developing battle plans, chat rooms proved highly effective for executing operations "because it allowed a large volume of information to pass easily and quickly and bypass rigid command structure. Information just went out," he said.

Electronic communication also allowed Thomson to keep up with his family in San Diego. Through emails, Thomson learned how his wife Kinuko was doing. One day after taking Alex to therapy, Kinuko came home and found dinner on her doorstep. Ladies from their church supplied her with meals nearly every day during Thomson's absence. One church member with a knack as a handyman consistently offered his services, which gave Kinuko peace of mind if something broke at the house.

> "He makes me lie down in green pastures, he leads me beside quiet waters, he restores my soul. He guides me in paths of righteousness for his name's sake." (Psalm 23:2–3)

However, even in a world brought closer through instant communication, snail mail brought some of the most soothing words of support.

"I received countless cards and letters from friends and relatives all over the world."

What stood out to Thomson was how personal these letters were. He received cards and letters from relatives he hadn't seen in years, members of their churches, and people he didn't know. He received church bulletins with his name printed in them. People weren't just promising to pray for the troops. They were praying for him by *name*.

"This was tremendously uplifting. I received an indescribable peace in the midst of the chaos of war knowing that thousands of people were praying for me by name. It was a comforting feeling knowing that all of those people were lifting me up to the Almighty God."

Prayer:
Thank you for guiding me and embracing me by name. Direct me to the name of a service member so I may pray for them by name.

Floating Mines

Cdr. Rob Thomson, United States Navy

WHEN THE INVASION began, helicopters from the *USS Boxer* carried hundreds of Marines into Southern Iraq. Navy Commander Rob Thomson's job was to oversee the planning and executing of operations, particularly supplies. Helicopters would fly food, water, and equipment from the ship to ever-expanding places on the ground in Iraq. While these operations unfolded in a relatively orderly manner, one intelligence report proved to be particularly disruptive.

"Shortly after the war started as we were bringing supplies from the waters of the Northern Arabian Gulf, we got word that small Iraqi patrol boats had been sighted sowing mines in the waters near us," Thomson explained.

An inspection of these captured Iraqi patrol boats revealed disturbing information. Although many mines were on board these boats, there were also empty spaces, indicating missing mines. Most likely these mines had been dropped into the sea. Floating mines aren't anchored and can go anywhere. Even if the captured Iraqis had been willing to tell where they had dropped the mines, they couldn't possibly know where the mines had drifted.

Floating mines are spherical objects, about four to five feet in length, with little horns. When broken by making contact with an object, such as a ship, the horns set off a chemical reaction causing the sphere to explode. One mine could sink an entire ship. Mines can float in the water for years. A floating mine struck the *USS Tripoli* in the same waters in 1991.

> "Even though I walk through the valley of the shadow of death, I will fear no evil, for you are with me; your rod and your staff, they comfort me."
> (Psalm 23:4)

"Even with all our modern technology, floating mines are virtually undetectable. So I knew from that point on, that my ship could strike a mine in the middle of the night and it could be my last night on earth." The thought most pressing on Thomson's mind was simply: "Who would take care of my family?"

Because the information was classified, Thomson couldn't talk about it with his wife.

"Then it hit me. The One who was taking care of my family now during this present crisis would continue to take care of them whether I returned or not. God is faithful," Thomson reflected.

Psalm 23 was particularly comforting to Thomson during this time. Knowing that he was walking "or sailing" through the valley of the shadow of death, he chose not to fear evil and turned to God's rod and staff—the Scriptures—for guidance.

Prayer:
You are faithful. I need you to be my strength and comfort today.

Smash and Grab

Cdr. Rob Thomson, United States Navy

ABOUT ONE HUNDRED, mostly senior leadership, of the 2,900 military personnel assigned to the *USS Boxer* were aware of the classified intelligence reports of the floating mines. Navy Commander Rob Thomson, however, soon found himself participating in a mission so secret, only a handful knew about it. Not even the ship's admiral was aware of it until it was over. This operation was the rescue of Private Jessica Lynch.

Nineteen-year-old Jessica Lynch was a supply clerk with the United States Army's 507th Maintenance Company. After making a wrong turn into enemy territory, her convoy was ambushed near Nasiriyah, northwest of Basra, on March 23, 2003. Eleven of the soldiers died, and five were later rescued. Iraqis captured the injured Lynch and took her to a nearby hospital.

> "You prepare a table before me in the presence of my enemies. You anoint my head with oil; my cup overflows." (Psalm 23:5)

Thomson first heard about the attack through intelligence reports. The whole world, however, soon learned about her captivity through video shown on Al Jazeera. Like many others, Thomson wondered what it would be like to be that young and alone in a hospital in a hostile country.

"I thought of that poor young woman, alone and afraid, and was glad that I got to participate in the planning and execution of her rescue. I imagined her losing hope as she lay there broken in body and spirit and prayed for God to be with her," Thomson explained.

When Thomson learned they were going to plan the rescue operation, his sense of urgency increased for this dangerous "smash and grab" mission. The helicopters took off from the *USS Boxer*, picked up Special Forces on the ground, took them to the hospital, where the forces broke in, grabbed Lynch, and took her back to the helicopters and into safety.

Thomson noted the mission was done at night, which is always dangerous because of sandstorms and other visibility hazards. The helicopters had to fly low enough to stay under Iraqi radar but high enough to avoid deadly power lines.

"A few hours later on April 2, 2003, we got the word that the rescue had been successful. She was safe. There was a feeling of great joy and satisfaction among all of us who played a part."

Although the mission started as a secret, the whole world soon learned Jessica Lynch was safe. Many cups were overflowing with joy that day.

Prayer:
*Thank you for the abundant joy that comes with a
victory and a successful mission.*

JANUARY 19

Permanency of God

Cdr. Rob Thomson, United States Navy

"THE FINAL EVENT during the war that brought the presence of God close for me was in April 2003," Commander Rob Thomson explained. "Our Marines had pushed through Southern Iraq and were now approaching Baghdad. It had become impossible to properly supply them with food, water, and ammunition from the sea, so we needed to set up a supply depot ashore. I flew by helicopter with a few others to a place called Jalibah that is in the desert west-northwest of Basrah."

Because Jalibah was mostly just abandoned buildings, it was a good location for a supply depot. After surveying the area, Thomson and the others began to plan the logistics of getting supplies there and coordinating their dissemination. One of the most obvious challenges was the sand itself.

"There is a difference between the desert there and those here in the United States. The sand in Iraq is very fine. There's always sand in the air, and at night the sky can be pitch black," Thomson observed.

Because of the United States invasion, lights were out in Iraq and electricity was spotty. As Thomson took stock of the sand and the pitch-black horizon with only the stars and moon providing light, he realized how similar these primitive conditions must have been when Abraham lived in the same region.

"As I lay there at night on my cot in my tent, I thought to myself, 'I wonder if Abraham slept here?' We were very close to where archaeologists believe was once Ur of the Chaldeans, the original home of Abraham," he said.

God's omniscience and omnipresence took on a new meaning for Thomson in that moment. "It struck me that the same unchanging, all-powerful God who had watched over Abraham in this very spot 4,000 years before was now watching over me."

"Surely goodness and love will follow me all the days of my life, and I will dwell in the house of the LORD forever." (Psalm 23:6)

And he slept soundly that night in the dark desert taking comfort in God's permanent hand. A tent may have been his temporary shelter, but Thomson knew his ultimate dwelling was in the eternal house of the Lord.

Thomson left the Middle East in June 2003. He became a physics professor at the Naval Academy and retired in September 2007 after twenty years of service in the Navy.

Prayer:
May I dwell in you today. Your permanency throughout generations gives me hope for eternal life with you.

Going Forward

Lt. Sean McDougal, United States Navy

LIEUTENANT SEAN McDougal started 2003 expecting to retire from the Navy. "I was up for PCS—a permanent change of station—and going into what we call retirement orders," McDougal explained.

When he enlisted, McDougal began as a nuclear powered machinist mate working on a submarine nuclear power plant. He then went through an officer-training program to become a Surface Warfare Officer.

"I was a jack of all trades, master of none. We're tasked with everything—Intel, antisubmarine warfare, antiterrorism, pretty much everything," he explained. He was in Hawaii directing a Navy Schoolhouse training program. In the summer of 2001, they enacted anti-terrorism and force protection courses, "the very thing we needed for the war in Iraq, so I knew a lot about that going into 2003," he continued.

Operating under his orders to begin March 1, 2003, McDougal moved his family to Pensacola, Florida, in February. But at the last minute, during the final week of February, McDougal received new orders.

"It's funny because orders, once you execute them, you have to get other orders to negate them. It all had to do with timing. I had volunteered for anything going forward. No one knew for sure if there was going to be a war (in Iraq), we just knew something was coming up," McDougal said.

Then he received new, overriding orders to go to Tampa, the location of United States Central Command, which was led by General Tommy Franks. McDougal arrived in Tampa on March 1, 2003.

"From there I was immediately told that I was going forward. I had no idea at the time what 'forward' was. What they meant was that I was going to Qatar to be part of the Central Command (CENTCOM) unit that was going to physically fight the war. But I didn't know that at the time. All I knew was that I was going forward."

> "He changes times and seasons; he sets up kings and deposes them." (Daniel 2:21a)

He was only in Tampa a few days.

"And I got more shots, more vaccinations than anyone could imagine. Eight in one day. Anthrax, really hurt the most. Three days later, and I was on an airplane going to Qatar—going forward finally had a destination. It wasn't time for me to end my Navy career. God had another plan."

Prayer:
May I develop a flexible heart, one that is able to nimbly adjust to changes in timing and seasons and new directions.

American Freedoms

Lt. Sean McDougal, United States Navy

I ARRIVED IN Qatar March 11, 2003," Navy Lieutenant Sean McDougal noted. His job there at CENTCOM was to take night watch at the Navy desk, which meant anything dealing with Navy assets and friendly forces.

"Someone would turn to me and say 'Navy desk, tell this country to send this ship here,' or 'what is the status of that ship there?' That sort of thing," he said.

McDougal became friends with Major Randolph Winge called "Troll," who had the same job at the Air Force desk. And because they shared the same twelve hour shifts, they spent a lot of time together, especially mealtime. They had something in common; both prayed before eating.

> "He gives wisdom to the wise and knowledge to the discerning." (Daniel 2:21b)

"Didn't make a big deal of it," McDougal said of his low-key approach. He simply bowed head and said grace silently.

"I noticed that when Troll and I would start praying, other people who sat down with us, they would pray also."

The habit caught on, an unexpected leading by example. But the custom also brought out cultural differences with America's allies. A British captain told McDougal he would never fit into the British Army because they "don't display such things in public."

The openness of Americans verses the privacy of Britons was soon strikingly apparent. At the beginning of the war, an American reporter gave away a location of troops on LIVE television. Something similar happened with a British reporter regarding an amphibious landing.

"The British put that reporter in a fighter jet and flew him out. They told their newspapers they couldn't print some stuff," McDougal said, noting that the Brits don't truly have freedom of speech and press the way Americans do.

"If a helicopter goes down, we (United States military) are trained to give away information immediately. If we don't know the answer, we say we're working on it. The Brits won't tell you anything until they have the whole story. They hold everything until they have all the facts," McDougal said.

McDougal learned from a British watch officer that because Britain is so small in landmass, that one newspaper in Britain can reach a tenth of the population there. "That was the beauty of working with foreign governments and foreign people on what we call a deck plate or grass roots level. I now understand why other countries do what they do."

Little did he know that taking stock of these seemingly small cultural differences—praying before meals and freedom of speech—was preparing him for a moment requiring courage. He was building crucial relationships with the Brits that would enable him to stand firm in the future.

Prayer:
Keep me from being so self absorbed today that I miss discerning the needs of those around me.

Bad News

Lt. Sean McDougal, United States Navy

NAVY LIEUTENANT Sean McDougal was serving as a United States liaison officer as part of the British version of the Joint Operations Center at CENTCOM in Qatar on March 23, 2003. McDougal was watching the overhead 52-inch television screen when he and numerous Britons in the room saw a news report of an American service member who killed his commanding officer with a grenade. The incident took place at Camp Pennsylvania that was set up in Kuwait in a triangle formation with Camps New York and New Jersey.

> "Praise be to the name of God forever and ever; wisdom and power are his."
> (Daniel 2:20)

Colonel Snider, the guy in charge of British forces, turned to me and said, "Sean, where is the camp's location?" Colonel Snider sat at the corner of the room with his back to the wall so that no one could read his computer screen.

"I had the authority and training to know what I could and could not declassify to a foreign military such as Britain. I disclosed what I could."

Five minutes later, a British air operations officer announced that a Tornado, a British jet, was missing. It was flying from Camp New York to Camp New Jersey.

McDougal put the pieces together. He had just viewed classified information that indicated the firing of a patriot missile from Camp New Jersey toward Camp New York, the opposite direction of the Tornado.

"I wrote a buddy of mine and asked, 'Can the patriot shoot down an airplane?'" McDougal relayed that the answer was "yes."

"I'll never forget calling over the British colonel. 'I hate saying this, but I think we shot down your plane,'" McDougal recounted.

"That was heinous. That was the worst day of the war for me," McDougal said, "but, looking back, I've concluded that God gave me wisdom to put together what seemed to be two totally unrelated acts and figure out the truth about their missing plane. I was scared to death that I would say something wrong or embarrass our nation but I knew our ally had to know."

The information was soon confirmed and relayed in the official briefing later that day. Further investigation revealed mistakes on both sides.

"Although I can't prove it I know God was grooming me for other situations where I would have to give bad information to large groups and then stand fast."

Prayer:
God, you are might in power and wisdom. You give courage in the most trying times, when we need it most.

JANUARY 23

From Fishing Villages to Palaces

Lt. Sean McDougal, United States Navy

WHEN THE INVASION phase of the war in Iraq ended in May 2003, many with CENTCOM returned to the United States. Others, such as Navy Lieutenant Sean McDougal and Air Force Major Randolph Winge (Troll) were given different tasks.

"My job was to help the Third Infantry Division take over the Navy portion of Iraq that is the port of Umm Qsar," McDougal said. Umm Qsar is a fishing village that served as Iraq's main naval base under Saddam Hussein's regime.

When internal military politics prevented that plan from going as expected, McDougal decided to keep busy and productive by doing what he could. He employed his engineering and electrical skills. His diligence soon caught the attention of those in suits.

"What I ended up doing was sleeping in this giant building that needed a lot of repairs. I went around fixing swamp coolers—giant five-foot diameter fans that rely on garden hoses to moisten and cool the air," he explained.

"One night at 2 a.m. this gentleman came up to me. He wasn't wearing a uniform, but a business suit. He asked me what I was doing," McDougal said, explaining that he was fixing refrigerators that weren't cooling properly.

"How do you know that?" the man asked.

"Sir, I'm in the Navy; my job is to do damage control."

"Well, what's that?"

"Sir, for example, if a bomb were to hit the corner of this building, my job would be to reroute the electricity, plumbing, air conditioning, and everything, put in temporary fixes, and then fix everything back up to normal specifications," McDougal explained.

> "Do you see a man skilled in his work? He will serve before kings; he will not serve before obscure men."
> (Proverbs 22:29)

The next day, McDougal saw the man in the business suit walking and talking with his skipper at chow time. They spoke again.

The next day his skipper gave McDougal the news, "Sean, you and Troll are going to Baghdad."

"Excuse me, what do you mean?" McDougal asked.

"Well, the ambassador asked for you."

"What ambassador and what are you talking about?"

"Well, the ambassador you spoke with last night and today."

The ambassador was Walter Slocum and he wanted McDougal and his buddy Troll to go into Baghdad and help fix up the palaces.

"The whole reason I went to Baghdad was because I was bored late one night and decided to help out the guys in the Third ID by fixing a refrigerator that wasn't cooling their water bottles," McDougal explained.

Diligence and hard work opened the door for McDougal to a new opportunity. He became part of the Iraqi Ministry of Defense, led by Slocum.

Prayer:
*Thank you for the blessing you provide as
the result of diligence and hard work.*

Palaces and Mass Graves

Lt. Sean McDougal, United States Navy

MY COLLATERAL DUTIES ended up being the major part of my job," Navy Lieutenant Sean McDougal explained about his work in Baghdad in 2003.

McDougal's Iraq experience was common. Often collateral or "side jobs" took precedence over designated responsibilities. McDougal described collateral duties this way: "If your main duty is to be a dad, your collateral duty might be taking out garbage."

"My job was to fix up Uday Hussein's palaces, mansions," McDougal noted. However, because he had LIVE weapons training and had set up antiterrorism force protection for the Navy as the director for Schoolhouse training in Hawaii, he took on hefty collateral duties. He provided security for teams that "went out of the wire" and into Baghdad searching for evidence of embargo violations by Saddam Hussein. They were seeking proof that he had misused oil money.

> "He reveals deep and hidden things; he knows what lies in darkness, and light dwells with him."
> (Daniel 2:22)

One of McDougal's collateral duties took him to a site he never imagined he would ever see: mass graves. They were looking for evidence of abuses.

What made these graves so secret was not the style of burying. These weren't deep holes with mounds of bodies covered by several feet of dirt. Saddam chose distance, not depth, to bury evidence of his dastardly deeds. He picked remote locations in the desert, such as the site that McDougal visited about an hour outside of Bagdad, to hide his evil. Saddam had Iraqi soldiers buried in mass graves to hide the number of casualties in Iraq's war with Iran. He or his sons also ordered thousands of Iraqis killed.

These graves were very shallow. Sand thinly covers the skulls and bones that remain. From a distance, these graves look like dimpled sand dunes against an otherwise smooth terrain.

Small signs, as crude as a typical handmade yard sale sign in America, mark the graves. With Saddam dead, Iraqis felt free to the mass graves. They hoped to find even just a remnant—such as the sole of shoe—of their loved one, and carry it home as a reminder of the one lost.

The uncovering of these mass graves revealed that in the end, Saddam's evil could not be kept a secret. The evidence was obvious to all who visited these remote desert dunes.

Prayer:
Thank you that you are a God of justice who knows all things.

Bricks and Lions

Lt. Sean McDougal, United States Navy

I TOOK THOUSANDS of pictures in Iraq, especially of my tour of Babylon. I have very visible proof that there are four ages of Babylon. The wear and tear on the bricks show all four ages perfectly," Navy Lieutenant Sean McDougal noted.

McDougal also took pictures of the Saddam Hussein bricks. Saddam ordered workers to reconstruct King Nebuchadnezzar II's massive palace. One brick in the center of each wall was inscribed with praises of Nebuchadnezzar. Saddam also had a brick placed in the center of each wall. These bricks proclaimed him as the fourth emperor of Babylon and a descendant of Nebuchadnezzar. By some accounts Saddam used as many as sixty million bricks to rebuild Babylon.

> "The king was overjoyed and gave orders to lift Daniel out of the den. And when Daniel was lifted from the den, no wound was found on him, because he had trusted in his God." (Daniel 6:23)

"Saddam saw himself as the fourth person to rebuild Babylon. All that made me see Daniel Chapter 2 in a whole new light."

Daniel interprets a dream for Nebuchadnezzar and details the four emperors of Babylon. The fourth kingdom had feet made of iron mixed with clay. "As iron is strong but brittle and does not mix with clay, the fourth emperor will fall quickly and the nation of Babylon will not be united and will split up."

That is exactly what Saddam tried to do and he fell quickly. McDougal visited Basra's underground prison, which many Iraqis claim as the lion's den where Daniel was held.

"The tour guide told us of the story of Babylon and how the Nazis came in WWII, and took everything. The only statue left was what they call the Lion of Babylon, or to some, the Lion of Daniel," McDougal said. The guide's account seemed ripped from an *Indiana Jones* movie.

The tour guide claimed that the statue is the only statue of a human and lion in which one is not trying to kill the other. "The Lion of Daniel" shows a lion standing over a man as if protecting him.

Whether or not the Basra prison was the site of Daniel's imprisonment, there's no doubt that this prison was a dark, dark place under Saddam's rule. Many service members have taken pictures and heard stories that document the maze of evil.

The Bible refers to lions nearly 120 times, proving the presence of lions in the ancient Middle East. Lions are now extinct in Iraq. And thanks to the bravery of United States service members such as Sean McDougal—Saddam Hussein's evil reign is also extinct.

Prayer:
Father, thank you for breaking the chains of evil.

JANUARY 26

Whatever Providence Brings

Lt. Daniel Nichols, United States Navy Chaplain

(A reservist goodbye email to his United States Department of Labor colleagues before joining Operation Iraqi Freedom in March 2003)

WHATEVER PROVIDENCE brings, I can claim to have found such meaning and satisfaction in my employ among all of you.

I am one of thousands. Just one among tens of thousands (reservists) called-up in the past weeks and months, and one of countless thousands for whom the oath we swore, to protect the United States Constitution from enemies foreign and domestic, takes on harsh new reality.

> "You will increase my honor and comfort me once again."
> (Psalm 71:21)

I follow in the steps of far greater men— men and women sent from these shores to carry freedom's torch to places where liberty's light wanes dim. And when I return, I will bear a title I shall cherish more than any other I have yet attained: United States Veteran.

I suppose it is the right of those afforded such honor to offer a departing word, and if not, your forbearance is requested. You should know that we who go, and those who've gone before, are ordinary people. We do not share a single color of skin, an ethnic origin, or a common creed—save that of leaving no fallen behind.

Beneath each helmet and uniform stands a brother, a sister, a father, a mother, a son, a daughter, or a friend. As a chaplain, I have shared in their common stories and walked beyond the thin line of bravado to see the human being beneath. But though these are ordinary people, they are not common. In my experience, I have seen no hereditary trait that presupposes a person toward bravery. And these are courageous people, not for staring death in the face, but for embracing duty when called and struggling forward against all odds for the sake of a few intangible values. Values such as liberty and human dignity, values without which life on earth would bear no worth at all.

I know that all of you will strive with diligence and dignity in your various tasks. There is but one thing I would request before trading my coat and tie for boots and a pack: honor the veterans among you and among the people you serve. Honor them not simply with a smile or a clap on the back, but with sensible policy and mindful execution of your duties. The cost of service to country is often very high and with lasting consequences for those who go and loved ones who remain.

I wish all of you tremendous success and look forward with hope to the privilege of serving with you again.

Prayer:
Thank you for those veterans who have served this nation.

JANUARY 27

Keep It Simple

Lt. Daniel Nichols, United States Navy Chaplain

(A devotional given to members of the Navy and Marine Corps in June 2003, during Operation Iraqi Freedom.)

JESUS OF NAZARETH understood people, and he certainly understood me very well: I need things to be plain and simple. Mind you, this doesn't make a person any less of an intellectual. Indeed, many *intellectuals* have a suspicious habit of convoluting their discussion with wise sounding phrases and fancy words.

But there is a difference between polish and power.

We in this Navy and Marine Corps team have our moments of polish and shine; but not without having earned it first. Indeed, there is something to be said for our shared habit of being succinct that surpasses concepts like *efficiency* and finds itself rooted in the example set by Jesus so many centuries ago.

That is the difference between polish and power.

Think back, if you will, to the days preceding your coming here, preceding the war.

> "Love the Lord your God with all your heart and with all your soul and with all your mind. This is the first and greatest commandment. And the second is like it: Love your neighbor as yourself. All the Law and the Prophets hang on these two commandments."
> (Matthew 22:37–40)

Apart from the jitter in your gut, most likely there was a sense of tradition, of history, of feeling part of something larger than yourself. If I'm wrong just try to follow me, but I'm thinking many of you had visions of yourselves accomplishing heroic deeds and winning much acclaim for family, God, country, and corps—for the majority of Marines out there.

Those imaginings were not based upon arrogant presumptions. They were based upon discipline, training, and courage—all enhanced by experience. My guess is, you weren't thinking about accomplishing whatever tasks might be set before you using complex formulas or grand schemes.

You kept it plain and simple.

Pilots would fly. Gunners would shoot. Mechanics would fix. Docs would heal. All of the years of training, dreaming, sweating, studying, thinking, hoping, and praying were summarized with the same succinct, but informed assurance with which Jesus answered those who questioned him.

When you know what you are about, when you know where you are from, when you take hold of those virtues which are greater than yourself, when you focus your abilities upon the task at hand, and act, THEN—regardless of your success—you surpass the impotent polish of childishness and begin to live in the power that springs from maturity.

All of you have grown through this experience and will continue to grow and mature as this mission presses forward. Not because of polish, but because of perseverance.

Continue to keep it simple Marines and Sailors, by handling one task at a time and one day as it comes to you. Let us, together, weave yet another red stripe on Old Glory.

Prayer:
Eternal God, thank you for the simplicity of handling life one day at a time. Amen

Jesus Loves the Little Children...

Lt. Daniel Nichols, United States Navy Chaplain

IT WAS LATE June, 2003, my first opportunity to walk among the people of Iraq. The children especially swarmed around our small group as we made our way through the ancient pathways of a small village just south of Babylon. Dark haired, bright-eyed faces swarmed all around, waving, clapping, and sticking their hands out for a handshake, and it was all accompanied by little voices vying for attention.

> "Then little children were brought to Jesus for him to place his hands on them and pray for them. But the disciples rebuked those who brought them."
> (Matthew 19:13)

"Meestar meestar!" was the frequent call that came to my ear. Perhaps it was my six-foot-five frame, or that I was wearing the garb of a chaplain—a different uniform than those with whom I traveled, but it was more than likely the fact that I was not carrying a weapon of any kind. A few begged, for money, some begged for food, or for shoes to wear on their calloused feet as they jogged along the hot tile-paved alleyways. But more than that they wanted to be around the excitement and to be touched by these strangers in their midst.

My gaze shifted frequently from this boisterous throng to the adults, who paused in their shops or as they traveled, staring at us in uncomfortable silence. Yet, many of these offered a smile and a wave, likely those who had returned to gainful employment.

One thought still echoes through my mind as I reflect upon that experience. For many of these children, their first memory of life will be clapping and cheering for American soldiers as endless convoys drive past their agrarian homes. I wonder what their next memory will be. I hope it will be one of freedom, of joy, of hope.

As people of faith, ours is the burden, not only to hope for good, but to do it. Likewise, as heirs to a heavenly and eternal inheritance, as children of the living God, it is not enough for us to speak of prayer and how prayer changes lives. We are to be people of prayer, people who communicate with the Creator and Redeemer of all people.

Prayer:
Thank you for prayer and the privilege to pray for others around the world.

All the Children of the World...

Lt. Daniel Nichols, United States Navy Chaplain

THE TIME PASSED quickly that day, my first walk outside of the confines of a protective convoy in a village just south of Baghdad in early July, 2003. And our business finished, we were about to depart when a young boy appeared before me, standing quietly and looking up at me through large bright eyes. His red shirt was tattered and dirty, but his smile and his countenance were as untarnished as a cloudless sky. Another boy who had been harrying me for money and attention received a quick elbow to the ribs in the way that young boys do, and moved off to other interests.

Thus, this young child, a boy of perhaps ten years of age watched me for a moment before saying in strongly accented English, "Thank you for freedom." "America, I thank you." "Mr. Bush" he kissed his curled finger in a sign meaning prayer and blessing and lifted it upward. "Thank you."

"You're welcome," I replied and held out my hand to shake his. He had a strong grip for a small child. For a moment we simply studied one another as smiles blossomed on our faces. He pointed to the nametag on my uniform, which had my English name written in Arabic script.

> "But Jesus called the children to him and said, "Let the little children come to me, and do not hinder them, for the kingdom of God belongs to such as these." (Luke 18:16)

"Schlonek," he said, curiously, not sure what to make of my name.

Apparently the seamstress had sewn the letters from left to right as we read them in English. He read right to left.

"Nichols," I corrected him and patted my chest. He then pointed again to the insignia below my name and read off the English letters one by one.

"LT, CHC, USNR— United States it means. You are of United States," he said, grinning at his newfound comprehension.

He smiled broad and wide. "Yes," I smiled in return, reminded of my four children and wife back at home.

Again he repeated, "Thank you for freedom."

And then I am whisked away, my mind fogging with the images, the smells, the poverty, and yet some small tangible sense that hope has been seeded into the next generation. These children represent the future of Iraq. They will grow up remembering the great changes brought to their nation. I shall pray for that hope, and I shall pray for the Iraqi people.

Prayer:
Thank you for the precious gift of children and the hope you give through them and for them.

JANUARY 30

Greetings Marines

Lt. Daniel Nichols, United States Navy Chaplain

HAVE YOU STOPPED recently to consider what it is that you've accomplished? I'm not certain if many of you have been able to witness new-born liberty, but just a few miles north of us, hundreds upon hundreds of thousands of people are experiencing what we take for granted every day—for the very first time. Let me relate an experience shared with me only a few weeks ago. I'll do my best to give the telling it's due.

> "A generous man will himself be blessed, for he shares his food with the poor."
> (Proverbs 22:9)

A corporal with Division had been on a routine soda run, and like other times, a small crowd of children gathered around to watch. As was his normal routine, the young marine offered candy to the delight of those gathering nearby. Upon completing his purchases, the marine turned to find an older Iraqi man standing before him holding a broken cross. Puzzled, the corporal asked if he needed some help, all the time mindful and somewhat intimidated by the growing numbers around them.

"I am a Christian," said the man, holding up the broken cross, trying to connect with the young man. The marine smiled, nodded, and moved to the side to be on his way, but the man insisted in his broken English. "I am a Christian, you are American; I thank you."

The marine turned, puzzled by the exchange, offered another smile. "I could probably fix that cross for you if you like," he replied.

The older man smiled, clearly not understanding. "Never could I carry such a thing before, not in public, would kill me." He made a distinct motion with his hand, crossing it over his throat. "You, American Marine, saved me, wife, and children."

Again, the marine nodded. "You're welcome," he managed after a long pause. Then he turned, climbed back in his truck, and looked back one last time at the man.

"I pray for you ... for Marines!" shouted the man over the din of the motor.

Then he lifted the cross and declared, "Freedom!"

Marines, no matter how tedious your tasks may seem, you have brought freedom to a people long oppressed, and their gratitude to you will last for generations. Perhaps you will never know exactly how it is that you have changed the lives of these people, but you have and continue to do so every day, with every flight hour, every shift, every turned bolt, every floor swept, every report printed. Few else can claim the same.

Prayer:
Eternal God, give us courage to labor as your servant people,
healing broken people and rebuilding devastated communities,
providing safety for the weak and hope to those who have none.
Position us among the poor with words and deeds of freedom.

JANUARY 31

When He Wakes Up

Maj. Janis Dashner, Chaplain, United States Air Force

AFTER A CONVOY on a reconnaissance mission was ambushed, the injured soldiers came to the emergency medical unit in Baghdad where Dashner was serving as an Air Force chaplain. Chaplain Janis Dashner wrote in her journal about the night of December 4, 2003: "Dr. K did all he could to save Bruce's leg but it was too badly damaged. Only a few hours have passed and he is already on the plane heading for Germany."

Bruce's platoon Sergeant, Tommy, was also injured. He had several shrapnel wounds in his legs plus three gunshot wounds—one in his upper arm and two in his chest. Unlike Bruce, he was stable enough to wait until the next day for an airlift to the United States military hospital in Germany. Dashner quickly realized that Tommy was more concerned about Bruce than himself.

"Tommy is extremely worried about Bruce's ability to cope with the loss of his leg. Bruce was orphaned at age seven, grew up in foster homes, doesn't have a girl friend, and makes friends with great difficulty. He considers the Army unit he is assigned to as his family. Tommy told me that Bruce begged him while they were on the side of the road not to let 'them' which is actually 'us' take his leg off. He said he would rather die than to have that happen," she wrote.

> "A man of many companions may come to ruin, but there is a friend who sticks closer than a brother." (Proverbs 18:24)

Dashner waited all night with Tommy. When Dr. K came and talked to him about his own injuries, Tommy made an interesting request.

"Now Tommy is in a race to get to Germany before Bruce wakes up too much. He wants to be with him when he has to learn this news," Dashner wrote.

The medical team called the hospital in Germany. The staff there made sure Tommy would occupy the space next to Bruce.

The Sergeant's concern for Bruce revealed true servant leadership. Despite suffering from three gunshot wounds, Tommy wanted to continue to be a leader and friend to Bruce.

Four years later, Dashner watched the State of the Union Address on TV. When President George W. Bush introduced a young soldier sitting with Mrs. Bush in the gallery, Dashner began to cry.

"The young, tall, healthy Tommy stood up to acknowledge the applause. My tears are ones of joy," Dashner journaled that night.

Army Sergeant Tommy Rieman of Independence, Kentucky, was awarded the Silver Star for his bravery in Iraq in December 2003.

Prayer:
*Father, thank you for using friendship in such a
powerful way. Open my eyes to the needs of my friends.
May I be a friend who sticks closer to a brother.*

Hope of Spring

Maj. Janis Dashner, Chaplain, United States Air Force

THE NEWS TELLS us of the cold weather that is coming over the United States. We on the other hand are having some spring time experiences. After all the rain from last week, we have grass! It is growing in and around cracks and in between the C wire. It is soft bright green grass. I know it is soft because I stopped to pet it, it's a simple pleasure," Chaplain Janis Dashner wrote in her journal on December 12, 2003.

The moment reminded her of Song of Solomon 2:11–12 "For lo, the winter is past, the rain is over and gone. The flowers appear on the earth." And in this case, grass.

"I'm sure our winter isn't over just yet. But it is nice to have a preview of the spring to come. I'm sure the winter for the Iraqi people isn't over either... but spring will come," she continued.

Dashner served at a Mobile Aeromedical Staging Facility in Baghdad. The television show, *M*A*S*H*, depicted doctors and nurses rushing to helicopters to retrieve wounded patients. MASFs are a modern version but with a key difference. Military medical staff stabilize wounded patients at a MASF and then load them onto a plane that takes them to a hospital. The MASF is mobile and usually used at the beginning of a war. When the situation is stabilized, a Contingency Aeromedical Staging Facility takes over. Dashner witnessed this transformation.

> "See! The winter is past; the rains are over and gone. Flowers appear on the earth; the season of singing has come, the cooing of doves is heard in our land." (Song of Solomon 2:11–12)

"The MASF has grown into a CASF which is a larger facility with the capability to hold patients for longer periods of time. This is the place where patients are 'collected' from various treatment areas, field hospitals, and surgical hospitals; they stay with us until airlift is ready to fly them, usually to Germany," she wrote in her journal, noting that loading patients onto planes is often heavy work.

And while spring had not fully come to the people of Iraq, the transformation of the MASF to a CASF was a hopeful indicator of a more stable Iraq, a little green grass growing under the barbed wire. The day after

Dashner wrote about the hopeful signs of spring, United States soldiers captured Sadaam Hussein. Hope was on the horizon.

Prayer:
*Father, thank you for the hopeful signs you give of new life to come, of the change of seasons that electrify the earth.
I pray for continued hope for the people of Iraq.*

FEBRUARY 2

May I See a Mirror?

Maj. Janis Dashner, Chaplain, United States Air Force

FOUR PATIENTS wounded from the same building explosion arrived at the CASF where Chaplain Janis Dashner served. One of them was named Chuck. He had lost one eye and had extensive shrapnel facial wounds. The morphine left him confused.

"While in the convoy from the hospital in the Green Zone to us he got disoriented. He shared that ride with a soldier from Pakistan. Hearing the foreign language confused Chuck; I don't think he realized he was in United States hands," she wrote on December 12, 2003.

The medical staff asked Dashner to watch him.

"When I took his hand to introduce myself, he held on and didn't let go. His 'good' eye was swollen shut and he couldn't

> "A man finds joy in giving an apt reply— and how good is a timely word!" (Proverbs 15:23)

see. My ministry last night was to talk with Chuck, to calm him down, to wash his arms and legs off so we could see what wounds needed dressings and what were just scratches from crawling through the debris," she wrote, noting he soon fell asleep.

Chuck woke up two hours later.

"I noticed him as he reached up to touch his face. He was feeling the stitches that had been put in place to piece together his face. Then he asked the question I don't think any of us expected. Chuck asked if he could have a mirror. As his nurse found one for him, I told him what he was going to see. When he looked at himself, through one blurred eye, he asked me. 'Do you think my children will kiss me when they see me?'"

As a chaplain, Dashner knew her job was not to have magic answers but provide hope. And although she gave an apt reply, the moment pulled on her heart.

"Wow. Try to stay upbeat and reassuring with that question," she wrote of the difficulty.

While they loaded Chuck and the others onto the plane, bombs exploded nearby.

"All I could think was how scary it would be to be blind, tied to a litter, and then, on top of all that, hear explosions going off not too far away. Tonight this group will be in Germany, safe from further harm," she wrote.

As she journaled about Chuck, a mortuary staffer called, asking her to conduct a memorial service.

"In the midst of this job, I am doing all stuff other normal pastors around the world are doing (preaching on Sunday, preparing Bible studies). I am reminded of my seminary professor's words: 'that Sunday mornings come with amazing regularity.'"

Prayer:
Remove callousness from my heart. Give me the tenderness of a chaplain and the courage to speak reassuring words to those in need.

FEBRUARY 3

Buddies

Maj. Janis Dashner, Chaplain, United States Air Force

"IS HE GOING to be alright?' That was the first question Joe asked when I walked up to his bed side," Chaplain Janis Dashner wrote in her journal on March 3, 2004.

He had been watching me as I stood at the bedside of a patient directly across from him. Both of them had just come by helicopter to the CASF, and both had been injured in the same mortar attack, though they didn't know each other. Now, a common experience bonded Joe to the guy across the aisle from him,

Joe had serious injuries to both of his legs, which were held together with pins. As he wiggled his toes, he couldn't believe that he still had his legs. The guy in the other bed was worse. Shrapnel had torn apart his body armor and helmet. The equipment had saved his life, but a piece of shrapnel got in, up under the front of the Kevlar helmet."

The man had undergone head surgery but was very confused. Joe was touched by the other man's condition.

"Joe told me that they had been put in the same vehicle after the attack, but didn't know what to do for him. Joe kept talking to him 'Hang on buddy, we've got you. You're going to be alright.' Now, as Joe was talking to me, that life affirming declaration became a question. 'Is he going to be alright?'" Dashner recorded.

Although she had heard similar questions over the years, she never quite got used to them. Her heart remained tender.

"I never know the answers to these questions, none of us do, not the doctors, nor nurses, nor the medical technicians who work tirelessly to save lives. God knows that answer," Chaplain Dashner wrote.

Dashner's experience had taught that friendship was essential in the recovery process. She focused on this truth as she concluded her journal that night.

> "A friend loves at all times, and a brother is born for adversity." (Proverbs 17:17)

"I know that Joe and his buddy are alive and heading to Germany tonight. I know that Joe is still watching over a friend who has been through a life-altering event with him. I know they both have a chance to live beyond these events, a chance that others do not have. I know that without a buddy like Joe it would be a hard and lonely recovery for one soldier."

Prayer:
Thank you for the strength that friendship provides.
Enable me to be a better friend to someone today.

FEBRUARY 4

Are We Sure?

Gina Elliott Kim, daughter of Larry and Jean Elliott, missionaries to Iraq, 2004

AFTER MUCH prayer, we now knew where the Lord wanted to lead us, so we accepted a position in Baghdad, Iraq," was the sentiment if not the exact words of that astounding email my parents sent about their decision.

"Whew!" I said, sitting at my computer in my home in Houston, Texas. My two brothers and I had witnessed my parents, missionaries for twenty-six years in Honduras, daily read the word of God, pray, and diligently seek his will for their lives.

Knowing they were wholly yielded to the Lord, I could only put my faith into action as I replied to their email. I assured them I trusted God.

For years my dad had built water purification systems. In fact, he had made eighty water wells available to Hondurans, along with starting twelve Baptist churches, and establishing ninety-two mission points there. He wanted to take this system to Iraq and give people clean water to drink, build relationships with them, and ultimately share Christ with them in a friendship-way. The missionary guideline for the Muslim world is not to engage in direct pulpit evangelism but to share the Christian faith when asked about it directly and, above all, show love through service.

When my parents came through Houston on their way to Iraq, they shared this story with my Sunday School class at church. Mom had asked Dad if they were sure the only reason they were going to Iraq was because the Lord was leading them and not for any other reason. My father reassured her and offered to pray, asking God to speak to them.

> "If I rise on the wings of the dawn, if I settle on the far side of the sea, even there your hand will guide me, your right hand will hold me fast." (Psalm 139:9–10)

They got on their knees, letting their Bible fall on their bed. It opened to Psalm 139:7–10: "Where can I go from your Spirit? Where can I flee from your presence? If I go up to the heavens, you are there; if I make my bed in the depths, you are there. If I rise on the wings of the dawn, if I settle on the far side of the sea, even there your hand will guide me, your right hand will hold me fast."

And to the Elliotts, the far side of the sea meant Iraq and it was confirmation that they were indeed to go to the far side of the sea.

Prayer:
Lord, thank you for your promise to be with me
today wherever my path may take me.

Life Given in Love

Gina Elliott Kim, daughter of Larry and Jean Elliott,
missionaries to Iraq, 2004

MY PARENTS, Larry and Jean Elliott, were killed March 15, 2004, in a drive-by shooting in Mosul, Iraq, where they were scouting sites for a water purification plant. Gunmen fired AK-47 assault weapons on their vehicle. Their coworkers, Karen Watson and David McDonnall, also died. Carrie McDonnall survived. My parents were fully aware of the dangers of Iraq and with their whole hearts they knew they were in the center of God's will.

A young Christian Kurd, who had survived a chemical weapons attack ordered by Saddam Hussein, traveled with my parents. He noticed that Mom and Dad meticulously documented the names of each village they visited and listed ways they could help meet needs. My dad repeated, "I love this project; this is what I've lived my life for."

My mom emailed me that she was determined to learn the Arabic language and then teach Dad. How she loved these people and wanted to tell them about the love of Jesus.

> "They did not love their lives so much as to shrink from death."
> (Revelation 12:11b)

In an email she told me she had asked their driver to share with her numerous Arabic phrases and expressions. Then she wrote them down twice—phonetically and with the right spelling.

When the FBI returned their belongings to us, we discovered a sheet of paper folded up with all those words written down in her own handwriting, just as she had emailed me. It was only an 8-1/2 x 11 inch sheet of white paper folded in two and then in two again and again. There was one bullet hole through the middle. When we unfolded it, the paper resembled one of those snowflakes that you cut out in kindergarten. One bullet had made eight holes.

This unique, bullet-created snowflake on paper decorated with handwritten Arabic phrases was such a literal example of how my parents lived their lives. They were wholly committed to sharing God's love even at the risk of their own lives. Like that paper snowflake, their lives were unique. When their legacy is full opened in heaven, their snowflake will be something beautiful and intricate, decorated with stories of the lives they touched and the light they shared.

"Years ago Larry and Jean died to self. They lived for the needs of others and the glory of God. Larry and Jean discovered long ago there was a cause worth living for and a cause worth dying for," said Jerry Rankin, International Mission Board President.

Prayer:
God I thank you that your cause is worth dying for,
because Christ first died on the cross for me.

Does My Help Come From?

Gina Elliott Kim, daughter of Larry and Jean Elliott,
missionaries to Iraq, 2004

I WAS NOT ready to attend another funeral. Mom and Dad had died only five months earlier. But my good friend's brother died tragically. She had helped me so much through my grief, and I needed to go. With a few other friends, I flew to Oklahoma. When we got to the church, they could tell I needed a few moments alone. I sat in the car with my cell phone in one hand and a small Bible in the other.

> "I lift up my eyes to the hills—where does my help come from? My help comes from the LORD, the Maker of heaven and earth." (Psalm 121:1–2)

With tears streaming, I cried out, saying, "Lord, now is the time I would call Mom and Dad and say, 'Please pray for me right now. I am having a difficult time.' But I can't do that! I need you to talk to me, to be REAL to me. I am going to open up my Bible and ask you to please speak to me!"

I opened up my Bible to Psalm 121:1–2, "I lift up my eyes to the hills—where does my help come from? My help comes from the Lord, the Maker of heaven and earth."

I wondered why he didn't reveal something more "profound", but I thanked him for being my helper, trusting that passage was what he wanted me to read. I regained my composure, went inside, and greeted the family. As I waited in the pew, I wondered what the pastor would say, praying for God to give him the right words.

"You know, I didn't know what I would say today," the pastor confessed as he addressed the congregation. "What do you say to the family when a tragedy like this happens to a loved one? I asked the Lord and He showed me. I want to read to you a passage from Psalm 121:1–2."

I sat back with such awe as he read that SAME passage. It was as if the Lord reached down from Heaven, put his loving arms around me and said, "I am your Helper! Look to me and I will take care of you! I will never leave you!" I thanked him for being so REAL to me! To maintain my composure, I focused on the cross hanging behind the pastor. On reflection, I realized the only way my family and I would get through this difficult time was to focus on the cross and let him be our Helper.

Prayer:
Lord, please help me to lift my eyes to YOU and to realize that my help indeed comes from you, the maker of heaven and earth!

FEBRUARY 7

Daddy's Last Words

Gina Elliott Kim, daughter of Larry and Jean Elliott, missionaries to Iraq, 2004

"MOM, WHAT were the last words your Daddy said to you before he died?" my daughter asked out of the blue.

We were driving one morning a few years after my parents' death. Her question caught me off guard. I pondered a minute to think about my answer. I had thought about so many things since my parents' tragic death in Iraq in March 2004—my father's hearty laugh, my mother's radiant smile, their fearless commitment to their faith, and simply that people wanted to follow them. For some reason, I had never thought about that one specific question. It only took me a second to remember, though.

"Love you!" Dad had written in his last email to me.

It was a short, sweet one-sentence email that he wrote to me after sending a group email to the rest of our family. They had written they were happy to be in Iraq and believed that no matter what happened, they were in God's hands. They were where they should be.

"Hey Sweetheart, we are fine, just have not had access to the internet. Love you! Dad."

I know my Daddy did not know those would be the last words he'd ever say to his only daughter this side of Heaven. Once more, I thought how God had blessed me even in this difficult time by taking care of so many details—just like this one. I thanked the Lord for letting the last words from my father be that he loves me, especially since my "love language" is words of encouragement above the other languages of time, gifts, service, or affection defined by relationship expert Gary Chapman.

> "A word aptly spoken is like apples of gold in settings of silver."
> (Proverbs 25:11)

But then I realized that my father could have died at almost any time and his last words to me would have been ones of love and encouragement. You see, my Dad was so good about using words to encourage people. During this time of indescribable grief and pain, I have remembered the numerous times he put his hand on my shoulder and said things like, "Do you know how proud I am of you?" and then, repeating, "Do you really know?"

I have wondered what my last words will be to those I love. I want to live each day, blessing others with my words, for like my Dad, I will never know when my last words will be.

Prayer:
Lord, may my words bring you glory each and every day.
May I be a blessing to those with whom I come into
contact every day. Make my mouth a vessel of your love.

FEBRUARY 8

Primer 1: The Quartermaster

Capt. Mark Braswell, United States Army

OF THE THREE J's behind this book—John, Jocelyn, and Jane (me), I'm the one without military experience. Dr. John Croushorn is author of *A Walk in the Sand*—an army doctor who served in Iraq.

Jocelyn Green has first-hand experience on the front lines of military family life and has written *Faith Deployed: Daily Encouragement for Military Wives*.

Working for President George W. Bush in the White House for two years has given me insight into government and political perspectives. My previous books, including one in this Battlefields and Blessings series, *Stories of Faith and Courage from the Revolutionary War*, have given me a strong historical perspective. Good stuff, but not a substitute for military know-how.

But what I do bring are questions, because I'm not totally familiar with military terms, such as, "When you say the *net* do you mean *communications network?*"

"Yes," the Marine replied.

What I needed was a military primer, and that's what I received in April 2008, when I traveled to San Antonio for a speaking engagement. While checking my luggage to fly back, I suddenly realized I was surrounded by Army Reservists. I told one of them about this book, and he pointed to an Army Captain.

"See the patch on his arm? He's been to Iraq. Talk to him."

When I got to the gate, I introduced myself, explaining my mission of seeking stories for this book. Our plane was delayed an hour. Perfect timing. He suggested we get coffee. As we sat down, I got to know Captain Mark Braswell. As it turns out, we are the same age. Although we attended different Texas universities, we had a few friends in common. He gave me a primer on Iraq. He defined terms and even drew me a map, explaining locations and the challenges he and his company faced during their service there.

> "Our barns will be filled with every kind of provision." (Psalm 133:13a)

Capt. Braswell's job was infrastructure, which made him the perfect person to issue an impromptu primer. He commanded the 340th Quartermaster Company in the United States Army Reserve, based out of Fort Sam Houston. Their mission was to provide shower, laundry, and clothing renovation services to soldiers. One can't get more basic than showers and clothing.

Sometimes you have to turn to the basics in life to get started on a new path, to learn something new. God gave me a primer through someone well equipped in equipping. The meeting was a reminder to me of God's provision for this book.

Prayer:
Thank you for your provision of wisdom and knowledge at just the right time.

Primer 2: MOS and Flexicute

Capt. Mark Braswell, United States Army

I HAD THE opportunity to talk with Captain Mark Braswell at the San Antonio airport in April 2008. He commanded the 340th Quartermaster Company, under the United States Army Reserve Command from January 2004 to October 2006, including a one year deployment for Operation Iraqi Freedom from October 2004 to October 2005. Captain Braswell gave me a primer on Iraq and the military to explain some of the basics.

One term he discussed is the MOS, Military Occupational Specialty. The Army and Marine Corps use the MOS to classify general and specific jobs for military personnel. One of the challenges Iraq presented was job expectations in contrast to job realities. Soldiers were trained for a specialty, but because of the changing needs and harsh conditions in Iraq, they often ended up doing something else.

Braswell deployed to Iraq in October 2004. His job was to lead 127 men and women who helped establish shower, laundry, and clothing renovation services at various locations across Iraq. However, a government contractor was in place and already doing much of the work they were trained to do. Seventy-seven of them ended up doing something else—providing security for the contractors. They learned to conduct "gun truck" missions in a combat zone. Gun trucks are armored vehicles with crews who escort and protect supply convoys from insurgent attacks.

> "Whatever your hand finds to do, do it with all your might."
> (Ecclesiastes 9:10a)

"They operated .50 caliber machine guns and Mark-19 automatic grenade launchers. They learned to use frequency hopping radios and a Movement Tracking System to call-in and email Casualty Evacuation and Improvised Explosive Device reports. They navigated across Iraq on rugged back roads or alternate supply routes," Braswell explained.

These soldiers became technically and tactically proficient combat soldiers, eventually mentoring active component units. The 340th lived-up to two mottos, their own motto: *Proud and Ready* and the Army Reserve's motto: *Twice the citizen—Twice the soldier.*

Hence, their MOS didn't hold up as expected. That's when Braswell told me the real mode of operation in Iraq is *flexicuting*. "You have to flexicute, that is, execute but remain flexible."

Braswell's explanation fit right in with an interview I had recently conducted with a lieutenant. He also found that most of his work in Iraq had little to do with his MOS and more to do with what was needed.

Braswell explained that the diversity of Army Reserve soldiers came in handy for such sliding job descriptions. Army Reserve soldiers have additional skills and know-how thanks to their civilian jobs. Because he's an attorney, Braswell was accustomed to holding another job. Being an Army Reservist had an added benefit of being flexible in the field.

Flexicute applies no matter the job. For whatever the work of our hands, God calls us to employ a flexible attitude as well.

Prayer:
*May I work with diligence and might at whatever work
you bring to my hands and may my heart maintain a
flexible attitude to the changes around me.*

FEBRUARY 10

Primer 3: From Base to Outpost

Capt. Mark Braswell, United States Army

CAPTAIN MARK Braswell provided me with a primer on base structures, from the well-developed Air Base and Camp to the rough and tumble Forward Operating Base (FOB) and Combat Outpost (COP). Air Bases have sophisticated buildings, amenities, and fortifications.

"For example, air bases are developed with paved roads, reliable electricity, hard buildings, multiple dining facilities operated by Kellogg, Brown & Root (KBR) with televisions and next-day laundry service by KBR, shower trailers, and flushing toilets. Sometimes they are isolated from urban areas," Braswell explained.

Camps are the next step down from an Air Base. Rudimentary Combat Outposts are located in insecure territory with no services provided by KBR, fewer life support services and facilities, no showers, and only burn-out latrines like those used in the Vietnam War.

"There are no fixed buildings or Hesco barriers, which are folding mesh-metal barriers that are set-up and filled with sand for protection, or concrete T-walls," Braswell said. Outposts move with the battle.

Led by Braswell, the 340th Quartermaster Company established field services for six FOBs in Iraq, mostly stretching in the dangerous western Al Anbar Province. Built in secured locations, FOBs had an aid station rather than a hospital and a helicopter landing zone rather than an airstrip. Soldiers prepare and serve only two meals a day without a luxurious KBR dining facility. FOBs support tactical operations of COPs. FOBs are highly beneficial because they reduce reaction time for medics treating injured soldiers and for Quick Reaction Forces to respond to soldiers in combat.

In its most basic form, FOBs include triple strands of concertina wire surrounding them, interlocking fields of fire for crew served weapons, guard posts, and heavily guarded entry control points.

> "May there be peace within your walls and security within your citadels." (Psalm 122:7)

"More advanced FOBs feature additional protections such as Hesco barriers and amenities such as telephone and Internet cafes, portajohns, and perhaps a Hajji store where soldiers can shop," Braswell added.

Many life changes take us out of our comfort zone and into a "forward operating base." College students rely on the support of home while the university gives them a semi-permanent stop on the road of life. Getting a new job and moving to a new town requires new infrastructures, such as new doctors and schools. While not the same as combat, life's transitions rely on everyday courage until the forward operating position becomes a permanent home base.

Prayer:
Father, thank you for carrying me through life's transitions, for those forward operating bases that give me enough support and security to get to the next stage in life.

FEBRUARY 11

Primer 4: METT-TC

Capt. Mark Braswell, United States Army

THE 340TH Quartermaster Company found itself serving during one of the most difficult phases of the war. They came to Iraq in October

2004, months after the successful 2003 invasion but years before the successful surge.

"Anti-Coalition forces attacked the 340th with mortars, rockets, rocket propelled grenades, Improvised Explosive Devices (IED), daisy-chained IEDs that the 340th called 'convoy killers,' snipers, and small arms fire. Incoming mortars came so close that they hit the shower and laundry tents at Camp Habbiniyah and FOB Corrigedor in Ar Ramadi," recounted Captain Mark Braswell, commander of the 340th Quartermaster Company that provided crew members with gun trucks, and provided supplies as they outfitted Forward Operating Bases.

What they faced was an ever smarter enemy. Braswell shared about a battlefield formula known as *METT-TC*: Mission, Enemy, Time, Terrain, Troops available and Civilians on the battlefields. This formula was crucial to making decisions about fighting an ever smarter enemy. Evaluating the elements of METT-TC led to changes in daily operations, such as timing.

"The mission of providing Shower, Laundry and Clothing Renovation (SLCR) services was often affected by enemy activity. During major offensive operations, the soldiers closed down the shower tent in order to guard detainees in Ramadi. Also, the hours of the day or night (when the SLCR services were provided) changed based on missions and enemy activity."

The greatest threat to the gun truckers of the 340th Quartermaster Company was traveling in combat logistics patrols. Early on, the enemy figured out how to create IEDs that are often made with high explosive artillery shells. They placed IEDs on road curbs or other hidden locations and waited to detonate them until vehicles or pedestrians passed by. Then the enemy expanded on IEDs by using EFPs or explosively formed projectiles. EFOs are mortar or artillery rounds and rockets that aim and propel the explosion into vehicles. They are designed to penetrate armor from a distance. The METT-TC gave decision makers a guideline for evaluating dangerous terrain.

> "I'm giving you thirty sterling principles—tested guidelines to live by. Believe me—these are truths that work, and will keep you accountable to those who sent you."
> (Proverbs 22:17)

"Sometimes, roads were closed due to attacks. Soldiers had to wait for Route Clearance teams to clear roads of any IEDs before traveling on the road," Braswell noted. When main roads were blocked because of combat, soldiers were forced to take back roads and alternate routes and travel at unexpected times. That's what good guidelines do: provide principles and boundaries to live by.

Prayer:
*Thank you for providing practical operating guidelines
in your word, and wisdom to keep my path straight.*

Primer 5: Medals

Capt. Mark Braswell, United States Army

CAPTAIN MARK Braswell went into Iraq in 2004 with two main prayers: that all 127 men and women under his leadership would come home alive. He also prayed that he would come home to be a husband to his wife and a dad to his two newly adopted daughters.

After spending a year providing shower, laundry, and clothing renovation services at Forward Operating Bases in some of the most remote and dangerous places in Iraq and performing gun truck missions supplying and supporting military bases, the soldiers in the 340th lived up to their mottos: *Proud and Ready!* and *Twice the citizen—Twice the soldier!*

Several of the 127 soldiers serving in the 340th Quartermaster Company were wounded and two had serious head or neck injuries from IEDs. "These two were very close calls. One soldier received an emergency field tracheotomy from a Navy Corpsman that saved his life," Braswell explained. "Some returned by medevac and all the rest returned in October 2005. All came home alive."

Braswell was proud of the medals his company earned. Ten of the wounded soldiers earned Purple Heart Medals and seven received Bronze Star Medals. One of the 340th soldiers rescued some Marines who

> "Thus, by their fruit you will recognize them."
> (Matthew 7:20)

were injured by double stacked landmines in an IED kill-zone for which he was awarded an Army Commendation Medal with "V" device for Valor and thanked by the Commandant of the United States Marine Corps.

Some soldiers earned the new coveted Combat Action Badge for their experience in combat. "Every soldier earned a distinguishing shoulder sleeve insignia for their wartime service, or as soldiers simply call it a 'combat patch' that they proudly wear on their right shoulder," Braswell proudly reported.

No mission was too tough. The soldiers got the job done. Every time, they adapted and overcame the challenges. For their service in Iraq, all of the soldiers in the 340th also received the Armed Forces Reserve Medal with the "M" Mobilization device, the Iraq Campaign Medal, the Global War on Terrorism—Expeditionary Medal, the Global War on Terrorism—Service Medal, and the Overseas Training ribbon.

Although medals and recognition are important, the greater satisfaction for Braswell was knowing that every soldier came home alive; and that he had the opportunity to continue being a father to his daughters and a husband to his wife.

Prayer:
Thank you for the medals and rewards that recognize achievement.
Thank you also for the greater blessing of family and friendships.

Heart of a Child

Col. Mark Troutman and Sandy Troutman,
United States Army

GOING TO THE United States Army War College is an honorable and desirable assignment. Located in Carlisle, Pennsylvania, the War College has a one-year master's program that is setup in two semesters. The students and their families arrive in the summer for a year of get-togethers and classroom learning.

"During Mark's first semester, the Senior Leadership Branch contacted him (along with eight others) about going to Iraq in December. It is unheard of to pull students from the War College. So this was a big deal," Sandy Troutman explained of her husband's one-year deployment to Iraq. The students would finish the following year.

Some children "keep their own counsel." One day Sandy took her children, Anna and Nathan, to Boyds Bears near Gettysburg, Pennsylvania. There they could build bears by stuffing them with meaningful colored beans: yellow for laughter, green for imagination, blue for friendship, red for love, and purple for bravery.

"I was helping Nathan fill the bear, thinking he might want a full rainbow of beans," Sandy said. Nathan only wanted two colors: red and purple.

"Mom, this bear is for Dad. I want it filled with love so that Dad is filled with love. So he knows God loves him, we love him and that he has all the love he needs. Dad needs a lot of courage right now, so the rest is for courage," Nathan said quietly with earnest eyes.

"I managed to choke out something along the lines of 'his bear being just perfect.' Needless to say, we did not fill the bear with many of the other colors."

"As I carry this story in my heart, I realized that for all of my *expertise* in the human heart, Nathan knew with the simplicity of a child what was needful and really counted. *His* words expressed a love so pure that it hurt in its blinding brilliance."

Nathan named the bear—*Mark Bear*. It stayed with him for a long time, quietly going where we went, and in Nathan's arms

> "For out of the overflow of his heart his mouth speaks." (Luke 6:45b)

every night. Anna and Nathan also sent a tiny bear to Mark from Boyds Bears that day as a symbol of the bears waiting at home for him. When Mark returned in October 2005, Mark Bear faded onto the shelf of beloved but no longer necessary toys. The bears took Mark and Nathan to the other side of a very long year.

Prayer:
Thank you for speaking to the heart in remarkable ways.

FEBRUARY 14

Letting Go

Capt. Amy Malugani, United States Marine Corps

ONE OF THE hardest moments for Captain Amy Malugani was the day she had to let her Marines go forward to their assigned units. Her public affairs team separated and spread throughout two Marine infantry regiments in November 2004 to clear the booby-trapped city of Fallujah that had been under complete insurgent control after the first attempt to take the city had stalled in April 2004.

"We had synergy. Our personalities matched—our work ethics and motivations. It was an amazing team," Malugani explained.

In the early months of her first tour (August 2004 to March 2005) Malugani served as the public affairs officer for the 1st Force Service Support Group (1st FSSG), which provided logistical support for more than 25,000 Marines and Sailors in al Anbar province. The job of Malugani's team was to tell their story: internally through documentation and externally through reporters.

In October 2004 Malugani received the call from higher headquarters. Her team would push with the infantry unit into Fallujah. They spread throughout Regimental Combat Team 7 (RCT-7) and RCT-1 to assist about forty embedded reporters covering the battle. The insurgents had grossly inflated the number of civilian casualties during the stalled April push. Getting an accurate story out to the Iraqis and the rest of the world was even more important the second time around.

"I wanted to go and be with those Marines, my team, but I had to let them go and trust, all would be well," Malugani said, noting that she watched battalion and unit movements from RCT-7 headquarters on the skirts of the city. And while she kept her eye closely on the situation reports that documented the names of casualties, Malugani stayed focus on doing her job with excellence.

> "But to each one of us grace has been given as Christ apportioned it." (Ephesians 4:7)

"I admired how well the public affairs team seamlessly integrated into all these different facets of the Marine Corps —ground, aviation, logistics—operating with generals in one moment and then with little notice operating on the front lines with infantry lance corporals."

The battle was block-by-block fighting—Marines kicking in doors. One block might be filled with smoke from a full-scale battle while at the same time another might be calm, filled with Marines distributing food. Although it was hard letting her team go, the situation was beyond her control. She had to trust.

"You do your part and there's just a higher power, a divine order. There is enough grace to deal with whatever comes next."

Prayer:
*Thank you for giving us the measure of grace
we need, moment by moment.*

Realities

Capt. Amy Malugani, United States Marine Corps

ONE OF THE greatest challenges for Captain Amy Malugani was mentally preparing for high alert situations. "Knowing that I had the capacity to do whatever it took to keep myself and someone else alive was difficult. I did have to provide security, but I didn't have to fire my weapon personally, even though there were some close calls. Everyone has that instinct to protect themselves and those around them. Your defense mechanism kicks in," she noted.

Battlefield realities reveal humanity's primal state. Everyone wants to get out alive. Surprisingly, reality was sometimes better than expectations. "As my vehicle moved deeper into the city, I expected the stench to be overwhelming based on the death totals but to my dismay it was bearable."

Sometimes reality was simply a matter of logistics and innovation. When the Marines raised the Iraqi and American flags in the city of Fallujah, there wasn't a single investigative reporter around to capture the significant moment. A lieutenant used his mini DVD camera to film it. Unit by unit, they handed the recording back through the city in a wrapper from a ready-made-meal.

> "Therefore we do not lose heart. Though outwardly we are wasting away, yet inwardly we are being renewed day by day."
> (2 Corinthians 4:16)

"Marines moved it from the center of the city to the logistics channel; I got it from the edge of the city and into headquarters. They used it in the press conference that night, and media outlets broadcasted it around the world."

Sometimes the news media was abuzz with a different reality. A *Los Angeles Times* photographer captured a striking close-up of a Marine smoking a cigarette—reminiscent of the Marlboro man commercials from decades past. Everyone wanted to know his name.

"This was a big deal back in the states. I was getting called to put a name with the famous face. It may appear simple; however reality proved otherwise in the midst of a battle with Marines on the move."

"At other times reality was worse than expectations. Your brain doesn't allow you to prepare for some things, such as suddenly being overwhelmed by a swarm of flies or a dog gnawing on a dead insurgent's remains.

"You don't allow yourself to imagine some of the sites you're going to see. I'm a believer in being in the moment, being in the present. There's always enough grace in the moment. It's when I go into the past or into the future that anxiety or fear sets in. The grace is in the moment. I tapped into that a lot for strength and peace."

Prayer:
Father, renew my heart. Help me to live in the present tense, trusting you for strength for whatever comes my way today.

FEBRUARY 16

Scared When You Least Expected It

Capt. Amy Malugani, United States Marine Corps

THE TIMES I was scared—they were the times I didn't think I would be. The times I was relaxed were times people would think that I'd be scared." These were the upside-down expectations that Captain Malugani had during the Battle of Fallujah in 2004.

She expected to be scared when she went on jump teams into Fallujah during the taking of the city, but she found calmness instead. "If I had to be any place, I would want to be with an infantry regiment. I was surrounded by a regimental combat team, hundreds of Marines. I felt very safe, protected. I felt surrendered to their expertise." She also found strength in the experience of those around her.

"My colonel had more than twenty years in the military. I was with a gunner that had more than twenty years and a sergeant major who had more than twenty years. I had sixty years of experience with me every single day. With all that was going on in Iraq, it was not a safe place to be. But now with these three experienced Marines, I was in the safest place I could be.

"Early in my deployment, my mom asked me, 'Are you safe?'"

"Well, it's kind of relative, Mom. I'm in Iraq."

During the Battle of Fallujah, Malugani found that she felt less safe during times of isolation in a tent that the Marines used for transient

> "About noon the following day as they were on their journey and approaching the city, Peter went up on the roof to pray." (Acts 10:9)

needs. "They put me in there because I was the only female with them. They were concerned for me, making sure I had space in a secure area. With no electricity and often rain beating down on the fifty-man tent, being alone was accompanied by irrefutable fear."

She often longed to talk with her father, who had served as an Air Force paratroop rescuer in Vietnam because he would understand the things she was going through. Her grandfather served in the Army during World War II. Their service inspired Amy to join the military. Although she couldn't always talk to her earthly fathers, she knew she could instantly turn to her heavenly father.

"When I would see things that were really challenging, I would remind myself that this is the now. I knew I would have an opportunity later, when there was time, to process what I was seeing as well as pray. I would remind myself that my expectations weren't matching my reality and that was okay."

Prayer:
Thank you for being a Father who is available to listen 24-7.

FEBRUARY 17

Surrender and Freedom

Capt. Amy Malugani, United States Marine Corps

DURING THE Battle of Fallujah in November 2004, Captain Malugani's lieutenant had moved through with an infantry battalion. On a day-trip into the city with her commanding officer, unexpectedly she was within walking distance to the lieutenant's operation's center.

"A reporter came up to me and said, 'I want to tell you, I wouldn't have gone through this city if it hadn't been for your lieutenant. We were all scared to death, but his bravery convinced us to go with him.'"

The battlefield is a primal place. Everyone wants to get out alive, yet so much is beyond one's control, such as incoming fire. News of casualties hit hard, such as the death of Sergeant Peralta who, while mortally injured, grabbed a grenade thrown by insurgents and saved the lives of the four Marines with him.

"The reporters who went in with us had to trust that we were going to take care of them. Everybody at some point has to surrender, to trust something bigger than self: the person next to them, the equipment, or God. But each individual had to learn to trust."

"In my own life I just felt so free and surrendered. It's like the serenity prayer: *Change the things I can and accept the things I can't.* I tried to the best of my ability to change the things I could by overseeing public affairs in the very best way. Surrendering to the divine order, I'm doing my part, and the outcome is not really up to me."

> "If I give all I possess to the poor and surrender my body to the flames, but have not love, I gain nothing."
> (1 Corinthians 13:3)

Captain Malugani found freedom in surrender. "Free in the sense of *free to* not *free from.* I was free to choose the way I was going to look at it, whether I was going to see grace, chaos, or both. I was free to be present or to shut down and suppress."

"What I did witness out there was those who believed in a divine order and surrendered to it, had a calmness and contentment about them. Those who didn't have a belief in a heavenly being tended to be upset. Many days I missed my family and wanted to go home; however, when I chose to put my trust in the divine order, I had the openness to process what I was seeing and experiencing."

Prayer:
*Thank you for the gift of brotherly love that is
willing to make the greatest of sacrifices.*

Preparation

Capt. Amy Malugani, United States Marine Corps

IN THE MIDST of chaos there is also tremendous grace each moment. That is what I took with me into Fallujah. Serving with RCT-7, was one of the greatest experiences in my life," Captain Amy Malugani explained.

Malugani came home from her first Iraq deployment in March 2005. She returned for her second deployment in July 2005. "God is always preparing us for something."

Two years earlier Malugani was sent to the Philippines for an exercise that prepared her for Iraq. "While in the Philippines, I served with an infantry battalion —thirteen hundred guys and two women. I was the only female officer. I couldn't figure out why I was selected to accompany the unit at the time, but concluded that God was preparing me for something.

"That's something I love about the Marine Corps. Unexpected situations and circumstances challenge an officer, we grow—sometimes seamlessly and sometimes unwillingly—with each experience. Each incident came in a different light allowing me to experience something new or to share my knowledge with someone in need.

"During my second tour in Iraq, my Marines went out west, while I remained at the headquarters with the commanding officer. The command element anxiously watched the operations unfold, praying our battalion would come back intact. This was not the case. I was devastated to learn that we had lost nine Marines. One casualty was a fellow officer, a great man with a smile that inspired everyone," Malugani explained, noting that her faith upheld her when her friend was killed.

> "For physical training is of some value, but godliness has value for all things, holding promise for both the present life and the life to come." (1 Timothy 4:8)

Throughout her deployments, Malugani took religious education courses for confirmation in her church. Her faith proved a safe place for her to be, even allowing her to cry during the time of loss. The Marines under Malugani turned to her for strength. She wondered if they felt more comfortable to let their guard down and cry in front of her because she was a female.

When the Marines came back from operations in western Iraq, they said "Hey, Ma'am, can I see you outside?" Many opened up to her. Maybe they thought that she *had it,* and thus, they could talk to her. Often words weren't spoken.

Chaos and grace coexist. "These are opportunities to see that faith is enough. I get so easily distracted; sometimes I forget that faith is enough."

Prayer:
Thank you for using my past experiences for a good purpose in the future.

63

It Is What It Was

Capt. Amy Malugani, United States Marine Corps

(Excerpt from an email Malugani sent January 1, 2006)

IT IS WHAT IT IS. Some laugh when I say this, some look like they are going to smack me, and some simply wonder if life can really be that simple. I say it because I need to hear it. It's a good reminder that asking *why* is usually just a waste of time. The real question is *how*. This short little phrase is about acceptance and the precursor to action.

Recently I incorporated this little phrase back into my life. I forgot how much peace and simplicity it brought me. Perhaps it's because I am on my way home and craving the simple life so much. Or perhaps after two combat tours in one year I have learned what's trivial and what's important.

Last night a friend and I discussed the book I am reading, *The Great Divorce*, by C. S. Lewis. The book is mostly about decisions and surrender. As the conversation progressed, it led to stories and analogies about letting go and letting God. We both kept coming back to the same point: it has to be a decision we make every day. Surrender is something that is done one day at a time; the more we let go the more freedom we experience.

> "We were therefore buried with him through baptism into death in order that, just as Christ was raised from the dead through the glory of the Father, we too may live a new life." (Romans 6:4)

Towards the end of our conversation, my friend looked at me and said, "Amy, it was what it was." The exchange was a moment of clarity for me.

What a simple phrase yet such a profound effect, well at least on this girl. Sometimes we hold onto old habits, people, places, and things because at some point in our life we needed them or so we thought to survive or succeed. However, there comes a point at which the spirit can no longer grow because there is not room for it to stretch out and expand. We have to make a decision to make room for the new; we have to make a decision to let go of the old. The simplest way to let go is to know and accept that it "was what it was" and now my life "is what it is."

Change isn't bad. Sometimes it's not good but most of the time it just "is." My hope for all of you is that you will live life one day at a time and embrace the blessings God has for you each day.

Prayer:
Father, thank you for the new life I can have in you each day.

Marine Club

Todd Akin, United States Congressman, Missouri and father of Lt. Perry Akin, United States Marine Corps

GOD PUT IN Perry's heart the service of the Marine Corps," Congressman Todd Akin (R-Missouri) explained of his son's life-long desire to be a Marine.

Akin passed down a principle found in Ephesians 2:10 to his six children. "For we are God's workmanship, created in Christ Jesus to do good works, which God prepared in advance for us to do."

"What most people know intuitively is that God made us unique. That's a very common thought. But the other part of this verse says 'from the beginning of time, before the ages, God had a job that every single one of us are called and prepared to do for him,'" Akin explained.

That desire to find a purpose in life begins early. Adults often ask children what they want to do when they grow up. Children may answer "be a fireman" or "be a doctor" but they often aren't sure. What children do know is this: they want to do *something*.

"Most people don't really know what they want to do at an early age but there's something inside that's guiding and pulling them in certain directions, so they try this or that. My belief is that every one of us has a sort of a destiny—something we were created to do for the Lord."

Akin witnessed this guiding and pulling in his son. As a boy, Perry started a Marine club with his brothers and friends. They bought used uniforms and little wooden rifles from an army surplus store to use in their club.

"They stood at attention in line. They raised the American flag on the flag pole. They tied pieces of clothes line to the top of trees. They took big steel pulleys and slid down the line, crashing into the ground. But they were tough and didn't cry because the Marines don't cry," he reflected with a laugh.

It was no surprise to Akin when Perry entered the Naval Academy. Perry's decision to become a Marine was the workmanship of God, manifested in childhood.

> "For we are God's workmanship, created in Christ Jesus to do good works, which God prepared in advance for us to do."
> (Ephesians 2:10)

"And so it takes courage, a great deal of courage to chase the dream that God puts in your heart. Yet you can do it because you know the Lord is with you. And so that's something that I taught to my children," Akin explained.

It's never too late to seek God's purpose for your life. It simply takes faith to ask God for direction and courage to follow where he leads.

Prayer:
Lord, give me the courage to pursue the
dreams you have put in my heart.

Challenge to Trust in God

Todd Akin, United States Congressman, Missouri and
father of Lt. Perry Akin, United States Marine Corps

WHILE AT THE Naval Academy, Perry Akin followed the dreams God placed in his heart. His senior year and subsequent training brought a few news-worthy moments to his dad, Congressman Todd Akin.

"Father I would like to have permission to enter into courtship with your scheduler," Perry requested. The young scheduler was Amanda, a member of Akin's staff.

"Not my scheduler?" the stunned congressman replied. "She's seven years older than you are."

"Well, Dad, she's a godly woman, and she'd make a really good wife even though she's seven years older," Perry responded.

Congressman Akin agreed. His scheduler eventually became his daughter-in-law. After finishing the Naval Academy, Perry entered the United States Marine Corps.

"He went through basic training, contracted mononucleosis somehow, was sicker than a dog, and finished his training in spite of it. He was still recovering from mono when he went to Camp Lejeune. Even being under the weather, Perry succeeded in passing the Marine life-saving training. (Because this experience is so hard, a small percentage of people ever pass the test.) He's very self-disciplined," Akin described with fatherly pride.

As the ranking Republican on the Armed Services Subcommittee on Oversight and Investigations, Congressman Akin was well-briefed on Iraq. "Then in January 2005 came the biggest news of all: Perry was being shipped to Fallujah. His mother and I were concerned because we kept reading in the newspaper about Marines who had died while there."

Perry's maturity was evident as he reassured his parents of his faith in God and reminded them to acknowledge the Lord in all circumstances. "You know, my days on this earth are exactly as long as the Lord allows them to be. Nothing I can do can make them grow shorter or longer. It is all in the Lord's hands."

> "Trust in the LORD with all your heart and lean not on your own understanding; in all your ways acknowledge him, and he will make your paths straight." (Proverbs 3:5–6)

"So we put our trust in God. Perry reminded his mother and me of the Lord's direction as he went to serve," Akin said of his resolution to trust God while his son was in Iraq.

From the choices we make to the uncontrollable conditions we face, God reminds us to trust in him and not in our own understanding.

Prayer:
Thank you for reminding me to turn to you in trust and faith, especially when life brings surprising news.

Work Left to Do

Todd Akin, United States Congressman, Missouri, and father of Lt. Perry Akin, United States Marine Corps

LT. PERRY AKIN's first great challenge came within days of arriving in Fallujah in January 2005. One responsibility was looking for IEDs.

Perry just about found one in a puddle on a road in the rainy season, but he looked at it and concluded that it wasn't an IED. A short time later, a Humvee drove over the road, and to the dismay of Perry, there was an IED in that puddle. It destroyed the Humvee, but fortunately, did not kill the driver.

"It was a place where an enemy was sitting with a detonator; he could have easily pushed the button when he saw Perry standing and looking at that puddle," Akin noted of the close call.

The next great challenge came a few months later when Perry was promoted from second lieutenant to first lieutenant. About this time Congressman Akin was part of a Congressional delegation to Baghdad. Akin received permission to meet with Perry while in Fallujah, his gunny sergeant, the major and lieutenant colonel in charge.

Less than twenty hours later, Akin was on a plane returning to the United States. About the same time, Perry and his men were constructing a roadside guard station. Suddenly mortar rounds started coming in; numerous troops were struck with shrapnel. Perry ran for cover with his gunny when a 120mm mortar round landed ten feet from them. That mortar was the size of a cantaloupe, Akin said, using his hands to illustrate the size by making a circle.

"If it had gone off, I would have been in tiny little pieces, but the round was a dud," Perry said. Perry's own words "that his days on earth were exactly as long as the Lord allows them to be" brought comfort. They allowed Congressman Akin to make sense of the miracle.

> "Many are the plans in a man's heart, but it is the LORD's purpose that prevails."
> (Proverbs 19:21)

"It wasn't God's time to take Perry. My son had a sense that God had a purpose and a time for all things," Akin said, reflecting on Ephesians 2:10.

Survival is a mystery. Why do some die while others survive? It's the question and mystery of the ages. Yet God reminds the living that he has work for them yet to do.

Prayer:

I praise you for those miracles, the blessings of the battlefield. May they remind me of my own purpose, the one you have given especially to me.

A Congressman's Question

Todd Akin, United States Congressman, Missouri and father of Lt. Perry Akin, United States Marine Corps

WHEN CONGRESSMAN Akin visited his son, Lt. Perry Akin, in Fallujah in March 2005, he asked many questions about the leadership in Iraq. One answer shocked him.

When I talked to the major in Fallujah I asked, "Now, if there were one or two things that I could do to help you, what would they be?"

"I'd like more up-armored Humvees," the major replied.

"You got to be kidding me? We've had this controversy for two years. We are shipping up-armored Humvees into this place (Iraq) like it's going to sink," Akin said in disbelief.

"What do you mean you need up-armored Humvees?" Akin asked, astonished.

"Well, we don't have enough, Sir. We don't have as many as we need," the major replied.

As the ranking Republican on the Armed Services Subcommittee on Oversight and Investigations, Akin was quite familiar with the up-armored Humvee controversy. Because of the enemy's increasing use of IEDs and mortar attacks, Humvees needed additional armored protection.

> "God is mighty, but does not despise men; he is mighty, and firm in his purpose." (Job 36:5)

"So I go back here (Washington, D.C.) and have the staffers do some digging. We discover that the up-armored Humvees are going to areas around Iraq where there's almost no violence, but the Marines in Fallujah were getting a limited amount of the up-armored Humvees. So we changed where the up-armored Humvees were going. Within a month or two, up-armored Humvees were flowing into Fallujah," Akin said.

Akin didn't know at the time that his "good work" would soon affect someone close to his son. Congressman Akin was visiting Perry at Camp Lejeune about a year after he'd been in Fallujah. Perry's best friend from the Naval Academy walked out the front door of this little bungalow where second lieutenants live at Camp Lejeune and greeted Congressman Akin.

"Congressman Akin thank you for saving my life. I was driving one of those up-armored Humvees and hit an IED. It totally destroyed the Humvee but I walked away from it," the Marine explained.

"That was one of those special moments for me when the Lord made this connection and ended up saving the life of this young man," Akin said.

Whether serving in Congress or the community center, you are God's workmanship, created in Christ Jesus in advance to do good works (see Eph. 2:10). Even when you don't see the fruits of your labor, you can trust in God's might and firmness in his purpose for your life.

Prayer:
Bring to me confirmation of the work you have for me.
Remind me of what is truly important today.

FEBRUARY 25

Why We Fight

Todd Akin, United States Congressman, Missouri and father of Lt. Perry Akin, United States Marine Corps

A QUESTION THAT reporters often ask Congressman Akin is this: How did having a son in Iraq impact your decisions as a lawmaker?

"It would be nice if I had a flashy story to relate. I grew up in the Vietnam era. I saw the Mel Gibson movie—*We Were Soldiers*—that accurately summarized my sense that there wasn't good civilian leadership when our troops were at war (in Vietnam)," Akin said.

"So as a member of Congress I have a passionate belief that it's not a light matter to send people to war. When we send men and women to war, we must tell them to win. Don't send them into a no-win situation. Give them the best equipment possible. Make sure they can whip whoever they face, and get it done."

"Having my own children in the military didn't change my mind about anything, because I always felt like all those kids were my kids. You put a name on them, it's more personal. It's scarier."

Akin's foundations and principles are set. His beliefs in liberty are well grounded.

"I believe there are some principles you are willing to die for. I'll die for my Creator. I will also die fighting to protect the liberties and freedoms that we inherited in this country. That's what generations of Americans have been willing to do when their nation called. Their sons and daughters have responded throughout history because we have a creed we believe in," he said of the principles found in the Declaration of Independence. "We hold these truths to be self evident..."

"There's a God who gives basic rights to people. The job of government is to protect those rights. To boil it down to a formula: God gives basic rights to people. The job of the government is to be a servant, a protector of those God-given rights," Akin said.

"So what's the big deal about us fighting terrorists? Terrorists kill innocent people to make a political statement. Terrorists want to terrorize you and me to take away our liberty. We believe life is a gift from God—the exact opposite point of view. We've always fought people who are polar opposites of ourselves. That's what my children were brought up to believe. That's what I believe. That's what I do. My work is that I fight the war of ideas rather than bullets," Congressman Akin explained.

Life is a gift from an everlasting God who created each human heart with a desire for freedom.

> "God blessed them and said to them, 'Be fruitful and increase in number; fill the earth and subdue it. Rule over the fish of the sea and the birds of the air and over every living creature that moves on the ground." (Genesis 1:28)

Prayer:
Thank you for creating me, for giving me liberty and basic rights.
I pray for our government leaders, for their commitment
to protect the rights you have given me.

FEBRUARY 26

Congressman's Hat

Todd Akin, United States Congressman, Missouri and
father of Lt. Perry Akin, United States Marine Corps

I LOOK AT MY job in a number of different ways. Sometimes I think God loaned me a hat that says *United States Congress*. My job is to think how many innovative ways can I find to use my hat today," Congressman Akin expressed about his governmental role.

"Our lives in Congress are not too much different than anybody else's. We have just a certain number of people that we talk to, circulate around, and do things. We don't have much power. Because there are four hundred and thirty-five of us, it's difficult to get an agreement. Unless there's a pretty good consensus, many things just don't happen."

"Part of wearing my hat means I must take other ways of looking at my job. After graduating from engineering school, I began selling computers for IBM. Now God has called me to sell something else—the principles of Scripture that make people free and prosperous. I look for opportunities to sell his ideas."

Akin spoke to 250 international students who were visiting Washington, D.C. to study American government in the spring of 2008. They were curious.

"What type of government do we have in America and how was it founded?" Akin relayed. He asked them where the idea of separation of church and state came from. They weren't sure. "The founders got the idea from the Bible."

> "Be imitators of God, therefore, as dearly loved children and live a life of love, just as Christ loved us and gave himself up for us as a fragrant offering and sacrifice to God." (Ephesians 5:1–2)

He explained the influence of a 1580s-era Scotch theologian, who saw a pattern in the Old Testament of separating civil government from church government. Adopting this idea, the Pilgrims founded America based on the new principle of separating these two governments.

"The Supreme Court has incorrectly understood the First Amendment. It was never the founders' intent to take God out of civil government, because we believe God is the source of all human rights. How can you take God out of government if you believe he is the source of inalienable rights?" Akin asked.

Akin sees his role as explaining the founding principles of our nation to others. He feels that that's part of his job—to sell God's ideas.

"I have no power of enforcement. But I have the power to persuade, and that's how I look at it."

Regardless of what hat you wear or what skills you possess, God is the source of your inalienable rights, a reason to celebrate life and share your freedom with others.

Prayer:
Thank you for the founding principles of our nation and those who came to the United States to establish a new nation built on the idea that you designed both civil and church government.

Blueprint

Todd Akin, United States Congressman, Missouri and Father of Lt. Perry Akin, United States Marine Corps

THE THING that makes me tick is 2 Timothy 3:16–17: 'So that the man of God may be fully equipped for every good work,'" Congressman Todd Akin said, explaining that the Bible provides a blueprint for anything believers need in order to fulfill the tasks God has given them to do.

"You won't find the details of calculus or some scientific thing in the Bible, but you will find all the principles for life. Now if I were to make a statement to the majority of evangelical churches: 'the Bible is the blueprint for all of life,' they would say 'of course we believe that,' but their actions suggest that they don't believe that at all."

> "All Scripture is God-breathed and is useful for teaching, rebuking, correcting and training in righteousness, so that the man of God may be thoroughly equipped for every good work."
> (2 Timothy 3:16–17)

The Bible, the way the founders looked at it, was much more of a blueprint for all aspects of society. As they read it, they discovered the idea of establishing a civil government based on a covenant between groups of people as found in the New Testament church. As a result, the founders replaced the idea of the divine right of kings with a covenantal view of civil government.

"This was a completely new technology built on biblical principles. They believed that if they followed the principles in Scripture, they could build a better civilization. They had the optimism and zeal to go forward and build a new country because they didn't believe the world was getting worse. By using the principles of God's Word they believed they could build the "shining city on a hill, a light to the nations."

"So—with this perspective—when a person goes to Sunday School class, it's not 'if you have enough faith, you can pray for a Cadillac?' but rather, 'what does the Bible say about socialism? What does the Bible say about the use of firearms for defending your family? What does the Bible have to say about government?'" Akin asked.

"We should be taking the Bible seriously and applying it to all practical issues, but we're just not doing that. God has laid this on my heart—

to see what the Bible has to say about everyday practical matters. The founders viewed the Bible as a gold mine of truth. They believed that society could continue to improve their conditions by building on the blueprint. Today's populace has barely scratched the surface of what's there to find," he said.

Prayer:
Thank you for the blueprint of your word, your Scripture that is my map, my foundation for understanding your plan for life.

FEBRUARY 28

Work Ethic

Todd Akin, United States Congressman, Missouri and Father of Lt. Perry Akin, United States Marine Corps

MAINTAINING A strong work ethic, no matter the job or challenges, was the prevailing view among the nation's founders.

"The Puritans believed people had a job to do with their lives. Why should one person look down on another if they were doing what God prepared them to do? So how can I look down at another person for their occupation?" Congressman Akin expressed when it came to his viewpoint of work.

> "Rejoice in the Lord always. I will say it again: Rejoice!"
> (Philippians 4:4)

"The one person the Puritans looked down on was the individual who wouldn't work at all, because he wasn't doing what God called him to do. They developed what is called the Puritan work ethic, which included the idea of a classless society because every person is a child of God doing his work," Akin elaborated.

"In ancient Judaism, work was expected of even the highest ranking in a home. A wealthy woman was expected to at least spin wool, even if she had servants. For Americans of the founding era, labor was a reflection of one's calling, benefiting both the individual and society. All of these concepts have contributed to America's prosperity over the years.

"One of the things that a soldier runs into in Iraq, particularly as it gets to be summertime, is that it's not a very pleasant environment. Lots of sand, but not enough beaches to go with it. He wears heavy equipment

74

and armor that contributes to his continuous sweating condition because of the high temperatures," Akin noted.

The men and women serving in Iraq work round the clock, often 24/7 under strenuous and unimaginable conditions.

Although he's not worked in the uncomfortable conditions found in Iraq, Akin understands the challenge of thankfulness.

"All of us have unpleasant circumstances in our lives. I got cancer seven years ago and that's not something I would have chosen on my own, but we're supposed to be thankful in all circumstances regardless," he continued, explaining how music, particularly songs of praise, uplifts him. Akin continually referred to the challenge of Philippians 4:4, "which calls us to rejoice in the Lord always."

A strong work ethic combined with a joyful heart and a gracious, thankful, attitude honors God, blesses others, and even prospers a nation.

Prayer:
Thank you for the blessing of work. No matter my circumstance, may I find ways to praise you and rejoice in you.

Lt. Perry Akin and his father, Congressman Todd Akin, Missouri

The Blessing

Todd Akin, United States Congressman, Missouri and Father of Lt. Perry Akin, United States Marine Corps

PERRY WAS in Fallujah because his nation called him to defend what he believed in. He was convinced that God gave basic rights to people. Where do those rights come from? Is that something the founders just invented or is there a biblical basis for the fact that God gave us life?" Congressman Akin asked, referring to the principles for which his son, Lt. Perry Akin, fought for in Iraq.

"I now ask people to picture this. Adam and Eve are standing in the garden. They've been created by God in the image of God. There's no sin yet. They're hardwired with all the things that we feel as human beings. Adam is looking out. He sees his gorgeous wife looking at the garden. He's shaking with anticipation," Akin describes of the scene.

"What does God say to him? He says, 'Adam the way you feel is the way I made you. It's okay. Be fruitful and multiply. Build a bridge. Put the barn and the orchard over there. It's okay. That's what I made you to do: to work the soil, to love your wife, and to make children that the earth can be filled,'" Akin continued.

"You see God called Adam to do what was in his heart to do all along. This was more than a *creation mandate*; it was the gift of freedom. The Bible says it was a blessing,"

Dictionaries define a mandate as command, but blessings are different, something prosperous, glorifying, and honoring.

> "God blessed them and said to them, "Be fruitful and increase in number; fill the earth and subdue it."
> (Genesis 1:28a)

The Declaration of Independence reflects the blessing of Genesis. "Creator" signals the origin of the blessing when God gave humanity freedom. "We hold these truths to be self-evident that all men are created equal, that they are endowed by their Creator with certain unalienable Rights."

"It was at that point that humans received their freedom under God. That's why we fight to protect our God-given freedom," Akin said. "What is the blessing? Isn't that what we've been fighting for? Isn't that what the terrorists want to undue?"

And indeed, many have fought for the blessing of life over the years and are defending it today. The blessing is God's gift to us.

Prayer:
God, what a blessing you have given me, the blessing of freedom, the gift of prosperity and hope for the future.

Likelihoods

Sgt. Michael Huntley, United States Marine Corps

"YOU GUYS are the next on the list," recalled Sergeant Michael Huntley of his deployment to Iraq in 2005. Huntley, a Marine canine handler, had begun training his new dog, Keve, the previous February. "In November 2005, it came time for us to go. Of course my family and friends were worried. People put me on their prayer list. My father told everybody at McLean Bible Church in Virginia, and they were really supportive through their thoughts and prayers."

Huntley wasn't too worried. From what he knew, he would likely be stationed at a well-protected, sizable air base such as Al Asad. The worries began when he and the other teams joined up at Camp Lejeune, North Carolina, two weeks before deploying.

"As we were arriving, we learned a dog team was coming home from Iraq because the handler had been shot through the arm. He wasn't hurt too bad, but he was still coming home," Huntley said.

Because the dogs are so effective at detecting IEDs, insurgents put a higher bounty on dogs and their handlers than

> "I eagerly expect and hope that I will in no way be ashamed, but will have sufficient courage so that now as always Christ will be exalted in my body, whether by life or by death."
> (Philippians 1:20)

other soldiers and Marines. Snipers were on the hunt. When the injured handler arrived at Camp Lejeune, the deploying handlers peppered him with questions.

"He was at this place called *combat outpost*. It's not really a working base, just a large post. It was called the wild west because all this stuff was

78

breaking out there," Huntley recalled. "If you liked to be in gun fights, get blown up, or get shot at, then combat outpost was the place to go."

As he anticipated his assignment, Huntley took comfort in what he knew. (The dogs and their handlers normally rotate in and out of Iraq with each originating from different bases.) The Marine Corps was now sending dogs and their handlers for only two-week rotations into combat outposts because it was so dangerous.

When he arrived at Al Asad, he got his assignment. "Huntley, you're going to combat outpost."

That was not the only shock. The military had stopped the two-week rotation. Huntley was going to be there for seven months.

Huntley was thinking, *Okay, we just had a handler leave there because he was shot and now things are blowing up there.* Suddenly the likelihoods had changed. He was going to need more courage than he ever expected.

Prayer:
You are the source of courage when life takes an unexpected turn.

MARCH 3

Wild West

Sgt. Michael Huntley, United States Marine Corps

I DIDN'T TELL my parents," Marine Sergeant Huntley said of his assignment to the combat outpost. "I tried to make it as comfortable as possible for them."

The United States Army had just taken over an agricultural college in Ramadi after a fierce firefight when Huntley arrived there in November 2005. They had turned the college grounds into a combat outpost. The place was a web of generators and strung out power lines. A village with many boarded up windows surrounded the outpost. Because the buildings sat above the outpost, insurgents could just take pot shots into the post from different buildings.

I arrived during a blackout at 4 a.m. The other dog handlers came out and grabbed me and said. "Hey, follow us." They had us sit down.

"We just got attacked yesterday; gun fights are here and there." And within the hour they were attacked again.

"The enemy launched about seven or eight mortars, large rockets, into the base. Then they just started shooting," Huntley recalled. "This was the first night I was there. I was already firing back at random things and shooting large machines guns, something I hadn't done since target training. Now all of a sudden I'm shooting at people, shadows, or silhouettes of where I think the fire is coming from."

The firefight lasted about thirty minutes.

Huntley soon learned why this place was so hot. They were in the enemy's backyard.

"Ramadi was where all these fighters lived. They would travel to Fallujah and Al Asad to fight. Then they'd go home at the end of the day to Ramadi. So we were fighting pretty much in their backyard. That's the reason they were so aggressive and why it was so dangerous at that point in time," Huntley explained.

> "Then he gave the commanders of units of a hundred the spears and the large and small shields that had belonged to King David and that were in the temple of God."
> (2 Chronicles 23:9)

Fighting the enemy in his own backyard was not was Huntley expected, but like the others, he responded the best way possible: with prudence and practicality.

"We had to wear our Kevlar vests and helmets at all times," he said.

Prayer:

Thank you for providing protection in practical ways, from seat belts to bullet proof vests. I pray for those in the military, men and women who need your protection today.

MARCH 4

Surprises in the Roughness

Sgt. Michael Huntley, United States Marine Corps

THE FIRST THREE months, we got mortared four or five times a week. You could set your watches by it. Because the enemy knew there would be a large gathering of people at the chow hall, that's when they'd launch their mortars, at breakfast, lunch, or dinner," Marine Sergeant Huntley recounted about the combat outpost in Ramadi in late 2005.

The enemy used religion as a cover. "They often launched an attack after their prayers; the biggest time was right before sundown. They'd go to their mosque and get preached at with hate towards the Americans. Once the prayer and preaching ended, they would attack," he explained, noting that not everyone in Iraq was the enemy.)

"I saw that religion was the only saving grace they had over there. If you were to go into their mosques, they're very beautiful with granite walls, very holy and sacred. Their religious beliefs are extremely strong. It's one of the things that they hold on to. But if you were to go into their houses, they're very dirty, third world country-ish—like mud huts," he said.

Despite the fighting, Huntley and others went on peacekeeping excursions. Every couple of weeks they'd go on peacekeeping missions where they weren't necessarily hunting for anybody. When they arrived at a house, they'd say, "Hey we're not here to hurt you guys, we're trying to help."

It was surprising that most people were trying to help get their country back to some sort of civilized structure. Huntley was under the impression that when they went out on a peacekeeping mission that they would meet heavy resistance. Instead, people welcomed them into their homes. They gave them food and drink, and then let them rest for the time being. They also knew that if the extremists found out, they would be killed.

> "I will lead the blind by ways they have not known, along unfamiliar paths I will guide them; I will turn the darkness into light before them and make the rough places smooth. These are the things I will do; I will not forsake them." (Isaiah 42:16)

Keve stood out on these peacekeeping visits. Dog are not pets in Iraq but dirty pack animals. Most people looked at Huntley in a strange way, because he had a dog that was very pristine, on a leash, and was there to help. They were intrigued. Most had never seen a trained dog, so he showed them some funny little tricks, making her sit, lie down.

In the midst of extremist warfare, these peacekeeping moments were among the most surprising. They were smooth places along the roughest terrain.

Prayer:
*Thank you for life's surprising moments, where something
or someone turns out much better than I expected.*

Keve

Sgt. Michael Huntley, United States Marine Corps

THE ATTACKS at the combat outpost in Ramadi didn't stop Sergeant Huntley or his dog, Keve, from fulfilling their mission of detecting explosives.

"I would have the dog out searching for explosives. It would be my determination whether or not Keve was on to something based on her cues," Huntley said.

By the time he went to Iraq, Huntley had trained thirteen dogs for the Marines in seven years. Dog training requires a lot of time and attention with the dog. One can't just get anybody to go and look at a dog and say, "You know what? That dog is taking a lot of interesting in something. It's all about their body, what they do, and their reaction to different things. I'm just there to determine if this dog is on to something or not," he explained.

Huntley and Keve went on numerous raids and cache sweeps. They'd go along the Euphrates River, that's where the enemy liked to hide a lot of their stuff. Keve's biggest find was an acetylene torch tank packed with approximately 250 pounds of high explosives. The terrorists would ignite the container allowing it to shoot large molten steel able to penetrate any kind of military armor and kill anything in sight. Keve 's important find was able to get that explosive off the street."

> "I guide you in the way of wisdom and lead you along straight paths." (Proverbs 4:11)

Keve was also able to find explosives in unsuspecting places. "We were doing a scouting mission, and she started pulling me. It looked like a rock with bushes around it. Turns out it was an actual IED, what is called a daisy chain. It was a 155mm mortar that was rigged seven more times in daisy chains along the road. The engineers dug it up and saw one line going to another rock and then another and so on," he explained.

Dogs like Keve begin their training when they are about a year old. The United States military often procures German Shepherds or Belgium Malinois as working dogs. They spend three months training in patrol work, such as fighting and chasing after bad guys and three months in the detection field learning how to detect either explosives or narcotics. The dogs emerge as dual purpose—attack and detection.

During her deployment Keve found quite a few pounds of raw explosives, several thousand rounds of ammunition, and numerous rifles and rocket launchers.

"She should take all the credit, she's the one who found all the stuff, I was just the one holding the leash at the time," Huntley said.

Prayer:
Thank you for giving dogs amazing senses and for using them in such a remarkable way, to detect the plans of evil and make roadways safe and clear.

Motivation

Sgt. Michael Huntley, United States Marine Corps

MOTIVATION IS the primary tool in working with explosive-detecting canines. "Everything in their training is considered a game to them. It all depends on their reward, whether they're going to work for it or not. What's their drive like? One dog might like a squeaky toy, and another dog might like a rubber kong—Keve's favorite," Huntley explained.

"The hardest thing about training a dog is the way you approach the training. Not every dog is the same. Some learn quickly, some don't. So you have to look at this dog and figure out if the dog is responding to your first method of training. If not, you've got to go to something else, sometimes to the point where you want to pull your hair out. Finally you stop and try something totally off the wall and all of sudden it starts working and you say 'WOW,'" Huntley said, noting that Keve was a difficult dog to train.

The reward of a rubber kong may motivate a dog, but it usually takes something deeper to motivate humans. Complexity and new challenges are what drive humans to work and gives them hope for the future.

"It's the greatest job I've ever done. I never have the same day twice. In dog training there's always something different that I'll learn or see every single day. I guarantee that if I pull my dog out one day and do some sorts of training with him or her, and then the next day I do the exact same training scenario, the dog will respond differently."

Motivation alone is not nearly enough to get me through days of intense mortar attacks and the risks associated with detecting explosives. Sergeant Huntley found that his faith strengthened his courage: "It made me a stronger believer in God—in his master plan. That brought me a lot of comfort. If something was going to happen to me, it was going to happen to me, and there was nothing I could do about it. I wasn't as scared anymore."

> "My God is my rock, in whom I take refuge, my shield and the horn of my salvation. He is my stronghold, my refuge and my savior— from violent men you save me." (2 Samuel 22:3)

Although he was definitely nervous at times, his faith helped him to block out the jitters. "My faith helped me to stay focused on the mission at hand; I wasn't focused on being scared," Huntley reflected.

After serving in Iraq for seven months, an uninjured Huntley safely returned to the United States.

Prayer:
Father: Thank you for giving us inner strength for the times we need it the most.

MARCH 7

Cleaning Things Up

Maj. Jim Lively, United States Marine Corps

I THINK EVERY piece of trash in this neighborhood is dumped on the street. Some piles are higher than the homes!" I stated curiously to an Iraqi Army officer during my initial patrol through Ramadi.

The sight and smell of hundreds of trash piles spread throughout Ramadi was one of the most overwhelming things I'd ever experienced. Years of fighting had forced the city government to shut down trash collection services and prevented citizens from safely moving the garbage to local dumps outside the city. The people literally lived among the trash. They would collect it in their homes, walk outside, and dump it on the street. Some neighborhoods did become large collection sites. The worst was a twenty-foot high wall of trash that lined the outside of a school.

During our first several months there, the fighting was too intense to initiate cleanup projects.

The trash piles remained ever present reminders of the insurgency. The enemy loved the trash pile. They were experts at hiding the infamous improvised explosive devices, or IEDs, among the trash. Iraqi soldiers, Marines and often Iraqi citizens were attacked by these hidden dangers, which became symbolic of the evils of Al Qaeda.

The Iraqi citizens obviously did not like the trash piles, but they could do little to correct the situation. Any local leader who protested was often harshly dealt with by insurgent forces. The enemy liked it dirty, because when people saw the oppression and filth, they figured they would taunt us saying, "See, your government and the American Forces are weak. They can't even pick up the trash! How can they possibly fight us?"

Those trash piles have made me think about how often I've let trash pile up in my "spiritual neighborhood" cluttering my life, testimony, and spiritual growth. Satan, like the insurgents, loves trash—the places where I hide my deceit, pride, arrogance, lust and selfishness. If I ignore my time with the Lord through prayer and scripture reading (which is my daily garbage clean up), it's then that I find trash piling up in my life. Only God's grace, through the power of the Holy Spirit, can provide a routine clean up.

"Search me, O God, and know my heart; test me and know my anxious thoughts. See if there is any offensive way in me, and lead me in the way everlasting." (Psalm 139:23–24)

For the Iraqi people, we were finally able to organize huge cleanup efforts that created jobs and returned some normalcy to Ramadi. The Iraqi soldiers found large dump trucks and bulldozers hidden by the enemy and subsequently used them to clean up the neighborhoods. The trucks became something to cheer, not to fear. Hundreds of Iraqi men accepted clean-up jobs. The entire project grew into a phenomenal cleanup effort that brought much joy and pride back to the Iraqi citizens.

Routine cleanups are a good path to peace in life.

Prayer:
*God, thank you for the joy and peace that comes
when my heart and spiritual life are clean.*

A Simple Prayer

Maj. Jim Lively, United States Marine Corps

THERE WERE NO congratulations when my close friend took command of a rifle company in Iraq. This is unusual because taking command is the premier goal of every Marine infantry officer. Unfortunately, his move into that billet didn't come with normal fanfare or military formations, but rather with the specter of loss, frustration, and battlefield confusion. My friend's new role came suddenly. An IED had struck the military vehicle of the previous company commander, killing him instantly.

When I saw my friend's solemn countenance, I knew he had just been given the unwelcome task of both taking command of a company who'd just lost its commander and leading a recovery effort to locate his remains. The emotional, physical, and spiritual challenges of this assignment are among the most difficult a Marine can ever experience. In a period of two hours he went from standing as the battalion's watch officer at a relatively benign post to leading a company that was still in contact with the enemy. As he was packing and preparing for the unwelcome task, I asked him if he needed anything before he left. He chuckled and said, "Yea, I think I might need a map!"

> "Let your conversation be always full of grace, seasoned with salt, so that you may know how to answer everyone." (Colossians 4:6)

We had a rare moment of levity. I grabbed a map I didn't use often, and then asked if I could pray with him. As we prayed, I felt the Lord's hand on us both. He went out that day and did a phenomenal job in a very challenging situation. Looking back, I'm so thankful the Lord gave me a chance to lift my friend up in prayer and encourage him.

The opportunity to minister to others is an important responsibility for Christians. In this case, a fellow Marine needed encouragement and hope. He was visibly calmer after we prayed and earnestly thanked me for it. I believe I could have offered him a million tidbits of advice about taking command, but none of them would have meant as much to him as that simple prayer. I've done this several times during my career, including praying with a family member of a wounded soldier.

Sometimes in life you don't know what to say, which is a good signal that maybe it's time to get on your knees and pray. The act of yielding a situation to God is a simple roadmap to bring encouragement, express faith, and share the gospel. Prayer goes a long way to restore hope.

Prayer:

Father, give me an opportunity to offer to pray with someone who needs encouragement. May the words of the Holy Spirit fill my voice as I lift them up. Lord hear my prayer.

MARCH 9

Being Ready to Serve

Maj. Jim Lively, United States Marine Corps

OUR HEADQUARTERS radio buzzed an amazing message one night in Ramadi: "An Iraqi Army medic just helped deliver a baby!"

The only response I could muster was, "Say again!" This was our procedural response meaning, "Are you kidding me?"

Incredibly enough it was true. Although the birth of a baby is common place, this delivery was astonishing for several reasons. First, Ramadi was still a dangerous place in December 2006. Any movement by civilians at night was completely unauthorized because insurgents would often attack our forces under the cover of darkness. Consequently, the Iraqi was unable to take his wife to the hospital to deliver her baby that night. The family managed to get word to the nearest Iraqi Army unit. That's when this amazing Iraqi Army medic made himself available.

Second, childbirth in Muslim countries is completely the purview of females. Men are not involved at all. To circumvent strong cultural taboos, the Iraqi medic stood outside the make-shift delivery room and shouted instructions to the women who were with the pregnant woman. He coached them through the process to safely deliver a healthy baby boy.

This surreal event occurred at the height of the fighting in Ramadi. Not only did the birth bring joy to the family but it also gave the Iraqi soldiers and our advisory team, who were so frequently exposed to death and destruction, an opportunity to celebrate a life-giving moment. This simple act of compassion also earned the Iraqi Army a great deal of respect from the locals, who for decades had viewed them only as a treacherous arm of an evil dictator.

What's most amazing to me is that in spite of several understandable reasons to decline the request, the Iraqi medic simply made himself available. He accepted the risk of attack and left his base to answer the family's call. He then used creativity to avoid cultural taboos. His story has made me wonder how often do I extend myself this way? God calls me to consider others first—to be available and poured out. The risks may be different, but to make myself completely available I have to put the needs of others ahead of my own. I may never know the full measure of what my simple acts of service accomplish, but that's irrelevant in light of God's call for my obedience.

> "I hope in the Lord Jesus to send Timothy to you soon, that I also may be cheered when I receive news about you. I have no one else like him, who takes a genuine interest in your welfare. For everyone looks out for his own interests, not those of Jesus Christ."
> (Philippians 2:19–21)

For one Ramadi family, an Iraqi soldier's unselfish act in a precarious, war-torn neighborhood resulted in a precious addition to their family and a great source of hope.

Prayer:
Lord hear my prayer, that I may not look out for my own interests, but will make myself available to answer the call of service you ask of me today.

MARCH 10

The Wedding

Maj. Jim Lively, United States Marine Corps

Wow, God's certainly going to have to work a miracle here."

Those were my fiancée's words on June 9, 2006, after I told her I was deploying to Iraq three months earlier than expected. We had planned on getting married at the end of August with the idea of having a few months together as a married couple before I deployed. Faced with this new timeline, we decided to move the wedding date. And move it, we did. We married three weeks later.

The twenty days in between June 9 and July 1 were a blur of phone calls, emails, and some incredible support from our friends and family. Originally the wedding was going to be in Dallas, Texas. The new location was Norfolk, Virginia, on the very busy July 4th weekend. The first thing my wife and I did was pray and commit our decision to God. Our primary goal was to not let anxiety about any single aspect of the wedding cause friction between us or our families. We wanted the event to be a celebration. We also pledged to not try to replicate in twenty days what we had initially planned for the Texas wedding.

God answered our prayers abundantly. The wedding was amazing. There was not a single detail that did not work our perfectly. All of the original wedding party was able to attend. Even our close family members made it to Virginia. The result was a wedding that honored God, a true demonstration of his love. God reminded us that no matter where a wedding takes place or the details of which bakery bakes the cake, the purpose of a wedding is to celebrate the love God gives between man and woman. We honestly believe that we did not miss a thing by not having a larger wedding in Texas—and we certainly saved some money.

> "'For I know the plans I have for you,' declares the LORD, 'plans to prosper you and not to harm you, plans to give you hope and a future.'" (Jeremiah 29:11)

God also taught us a great deal about our faith and each other as we worked to pull all of the details together without any anxiety and frustration. His early blessing of our marriage under those circumstances was a foreshadowing of how he would get us through my twelve-month deployment to Iraq. I learned that my wife was a mighty prayer warrior, unflappable in the face of the pressures of planning a wedding in twenty days. Even though it was not the wedding we had originally planned, God did an incredible work, and the wedding was a precious celebration. Our wedding will always be a reminder to us of the sovereignty of his timing and his plan—not our own. He showed us that a change in plans resulted in a more abundant celebration of his love.

Prayer:

*Thank you for the plans you have for me, plans to prosper
me and give me hope. Thank you for times you give
us to celebrate life in abundance.*

The Separation

Maj. Jim Lively, United States Marine Corps

SEPTEMBER 29, 2006, was one of the hardest days of my life, one I'll never forget. I watched my wife of just three months standing in the driveway alone as I drove away to catch my flight to Iraq. Even as a ten-year veteran of the Marine Corps with a previous deployment to Iraq under my belt, I was completely unprepared for the emotions I felt that day. The idea of leaving my new wife while I entered a war zone was gut-wrenching. The entire day was really quite miserable. As we laughed, cried, and prayed throughout the day, it was very difficult to find much joy in the situation. We both were struggling with accepting this long separation.

As a newlywed couple who had barely had time to experience married life, we were suddenly faced with a year-long separation—with me in near constant threat of physical injury. These were abnormal circumstances for the first year of marriage, to say the least. Normally we should have been figuring out how each other prefers to squeeze the toothpaste tube. Instead, she was going to sleep while I was waking up. The time zone difference alone made communication difficult.

> "Do not be anxious about anything, but in everything, by prayer and petition, with thanksgiving, present your requests to God."
> (Philippians 4:6)

While I faced the uncertainties of a war zone, she faced the challenges of making decisions about our future. During that year she would have to sell our house, move us to our next duty station, and attend to a myriad of issues that normally we would have accomplished together. Needless to say, the situation was ripe for doubt, fear, frustration, and disobedience.

As the deployment progressed, my wife and I learned a great deal about each other. We learned the importance of communicating in whatever form available. By God's grace alone, she and I were able to encourage and nurture each other through prayer, letters, emails, and phone calls. We found amazing strength that God brought to each of us as we lived our lives with our hearts united, but our physical beings separated by oceans, continents, and time zones.

In a situation cultivated for struggle, God gave us an enormous peace. We learned how to trust our relationship to him. Only his divine control over our lives helped us endure the long, trying separation. We returned to each other with an emotional and spiritual strength that will benefit our marriage petitioning God through prayer for years to come because we submitted to his will and trusted in him. We learned that no matter the circumstance, whether it's the emotions of loneliness or the practicalities of renting an apartment, we bridged our separation and strengthened our hearts by petitioning God through prayer.

Prayer:
Thank you for the ability to petition you no matter what time zone I live in or what zone of life I'm in.

Courage in the Night

Debbie Lee, Gold Star Mother of Marc Alan Lee, First Navy SEAL Killed in Iraq

IT WAS A warm August evening in Surprise, Arizona and my Bible study was gathered, as we celebrated my birthday. One of my friends had given me one of the Willow Tree Angels named "Courage." She told me that it reminded her of me. To her I was a Woman of Courage.

None of us knew at that moment just how much courage would be required for me to survive what was about to happen, which would change my life forever.

As we were finishing cake and ice cream I received what would be the most devastating phone call of my life. My oldest son, Kristofer, called asking where I was and how long it would take me to get home. When I questioned why he said, "You just need to come home." I had a sick feeling in my stomach, and I knew what faced me ahead. I knew that when I arrived home I would be informed that my youngest son Marc had died—the first Navy SEAL killed in Iraq.

Something inside of me knew when Marc left my home in March of 2006 that he wouldn't be returning and that would be the last time I would see him. I'm not a fearful, worrisome type of person, and I didn't dwell on that while he was deployed, but somehow I knew. I immediately left and asked my friends to pray. As I drove home a song came to me.

I put my hope in you, Oh Lord, trusting you I will not be shaken, knowing that you will see me through I put my hope in you. I sang it over and over as I drove home.

I expected to see a black sedan sitting in front of my house, but there wasn't one. I guess I've seen too many movies. Instead I saw Kris pacing in the street.

"Mom, the Navy's here," he said, confirming the news—Marc was dead.

My friends, prayed, cried, and com-

> "Be strong and very courageous."
> (Joshua 1:7)

forted me. God provided friends that night and insights on courage to prepare me, knowing how much I would need to trust him to face the days ahead.

Prayer:
Thank you for the gift of courage.

A Hero's Courage

Debbie Lee, Mother of Marc Alan Lee,
First Navy SEAL Killed in Iraq

IN THE EARLY morning hours my house had emptied after receiving the tragic news my son had died. I wondered how I would survive. I knew where my strength would come from so I opened my Bible to Psalm 27 (NKJV). "The LORD is my light and my salvation; Whom shall I fear? The LORD is the strength of my life; Of whom shall I be afraid? When the wicked came against me to eat up my flesh, my enemies and foes, they stumbled and fell."

Through this passage, God confirmed to me Marc wasn't afraid. I learned more about Marc's final act of courage in the following days. On August 2, 2006, in Ramadi in 120-degree temperature, Marc carried the additional weight of a 150 pound M60 without a sling. His teammates were absolutely amazed at his strength.

It was the biggest battle since the war began. They had been in a firefight for two hours when Marc single handedly stood in the direct line of fire and shot off more than one hundred rounds of ammunition. Three times that day Marc would stand in the direct line of fire to defend his buddies, for you, for me, and for this nation.

Marc was a young man who selflessly gave his life because he valued other lives as more important than his own.

That evening God comforted me with Psalm 27 and I knew I needed to read it at Marc's funeral to encourage others and give them hope.

"Lord, how can I do that? I'm sure I'll be weeping and who knows, I might faint." Again I felt God nudging me.

> "Though an army may encamp against me, my heart shall not fear; though war may rise against me, in this I will be confident."
> (Psalm 27:3, NKJV)

I read Psalms 27 at Marc's funeral without crying or breaking down. God gave me amazing strength as I applied each verse to our hearts. I had no clue where God would "deploy me" in the days to come, but I had hope and was confident he would see me through.

Prayer:

Thank you for providing strength during extraordinary circumstances. Thank you for the courage of Marc Alan Lee and others who have sacrificed their lives for me.

MARCH 14

Father to the Fatherless

Debbie Lee, Mother of Marc Alan Lee, First Navy SEAL Killed in Iraq

WHEN MARC left my home in March of 2006, somehow I knew it would be the last time I would see him. I'm not a worrier, not a fretter, that's just not who I am. But I sensed God preparing my heart.

When my second husband died twelve years earlier, the same thing happened. We had just buried my grandmother, and I remember sitting in church when a thought crossed my mind: *you're going to need to prepare for another funeral.* Days later I received the news my husband had died tragically.

After his death, I remember reading "God's a husband to the widow and a father the fatherless." Realistically, how does that work?

Try me, I sensed God saying.

So I tried him. I discussed an important decision I was facing and waited for his response. Nothing. I started to cry, facing the reality— *There's nobody there. I'm all alone. I've got to make all of these decisions myself.*

Then I remembered I hadn't had my quiet time. My scheduled reading for the day was 2 Kings 20:5, "I have seen your tears, and I have heard your prayers and I will answer."

I realized that's exactly how a husband would respond to his wife: validating her concern, comforting her, and telling her he would take care of it.

"Lord you're serious," I realized about his promise. That was just the beginning.

> "A father to the fatherless, a defender of widows, is God in his holy dwelling." (Psalm 68:5)

God proved himself over and over developing in me a deep and confidence in who he is. When my children would come to me seeking answers they would often hear me tell them "Go ask your Daddy." They knew I meant to be in God's word, praying, and asking for his wisdom.

So it's no surprise that Marc followed in his Daddy's footsteps and laid down his life. Marc knew who is true father was. God laid down his life for us in Christ for our freedom in eternity. Marc laid down his life for our freedoms on earth. I'm so very proud of him.

Prayer:
Thank you for being a father to the fatherless and a husband to the widow, for the practical provisions of life and drawing me closer to you.

MARCH 15

Letter to the President

Debbie Lee, Mother of Marc Alan Lee,
First Navy SEAL Killed in Iraq

I MET CONGRESSMAN Greg Walden at Marc's memorial service in Hood River. Even though I had lost my son, I explained how much I still believed in what we're doing in Iraq, and how proud I was of President Bush, and maybe one day I could thank him.

On September 11, Congressman Walden called and said, "I'm having dinner with President Bush on Wednesday, and I will hand deliver your letter if you have it to me in an hour."

At the beginning stages of grief, I was numb. I couldn't even write a letter to my best friend, yet alone the President of the United States.

I had stayed in Hood River to repair an empty rental. I had no computer and no paper. I had found Marc's writing tablet the day before under the house. As I wrote the date September 11, memories from 2001 flooded my heart. I had two sons and a son-in-law serving in the military. I knew then this was going to be a personal war, but I had no idea just how personal.

The letter that followed was inspired by God!

Hours after the President received my letter he hand-wrote me an amazing letter saying he would be honored to meet me. Arrangements were made to meet in October.

President Bush walked into the room with tears in his eyes and hugged me and said, "I'm so sorry, mom." He picked up his big chair that had been set about eight feet from mine and set it down two inches from mine and said, "This is where I want to sit, next to a hero's mother."

> "But I pray to you, O LORD, in the time of your favor; in your great love, O God, answer me with your sure salvation." (Psalm 69:13)

He held my hand and said, "How you doing mama? You're going to need to rely on the Lord."

He was sincere, so compassionate. I knew he had a plane to catch, a bill to sign, yet people would have thought I was the only person in the world for that thirty-five minutes.

God's creativity never ceases to amaze me—those he uses, his timing, and the tools he provides. His favor fell on me in my greatest time of need, and he provided me an opportunity to meet President Bush.

Prayer:
Thank you for using ordinary things to orchestrate your favor and blessings in life.

Courage

Debbie Lee, Mother of Marc Alan Lee,
First Navy SEAL Killed in Iraq

I ENVISION EVERY morning, in heaven, a briefing between God and Marc, "Okay, where are we going to put mom today?"

Iraq. Eighteen months after my son's death.

My third tour with "Move America Forward" ended with the news I would be able to deliver 226,000 Christmas Cards to the troops in Iraq.

> "Be strong, take heart all you who hope in the Lord." (Psalm 31:24)

It took courage to decide to travel to the war zone where my son gave his life—courage God gave me.

Courage was my companion the night I boarded the C-130 bound for Baghdad. My flight made the craziest cork-screw landing that I could imagine to avoid being shot down by terrorists. Courage dressed me in body armor and Kevlar to go out on patrol in Baghdad and walk the streets with the 1-4 Cavalry. Courage to board the Blackhawk in the middle of the night on a secret flight to Camp Marc Lee, the base in western Iraq named in my son's memory. Courage to walk where Marc walked his last steps, spent his last night, to smell what he smelled, and embrace what he embraced.

Yet that night at Camp Marc Lee, I was reminded of what real courage is. Real courage is what our troops, my heroes face every day. Real courage is being willing to give up your right to everything you want for your future to make a better place for others. Real courage is facing the enemy and being willing to pay the ultimate price with your life because you value others' lives more than your own. Real courage is using your voice and actions to make a difference in the world. Real courage is selfless, noble, true, humble, right, and honorable. That is the description of our men and women serving in Iraq.

My Angel of Courage sits on my desk, her arms lifted high and fists clenched in victory, as if to say, YES! As a nation founded on God's principles we need to raise our hands high and thank the one who created us and blessed us to be born in America.

Prayer:
Thank you for this amazing nation. Thank you for the courage you have given the members of the military. May I show courage to them by saying thank you with my voice, pocketbook, and voting.

Fly on the Commanding General's Wall

Multinational Force-Iraq Command Chaplain, (Col.) Mike Hoyt, United States Army

A COMMAND CHAPLAIN enjoys a special relationship with his commanding general. Multinational Force-Iraq Command Chaplain, CH Colonel Mike Hoyt was one of a few colonels who attended meetings led by General George Casey and then, General David Petraeus.

"We have access that most other colonels don't have because of that relationship," Hoyt said. "I saw my role not as a religious expert, because we had a lot of Ph.D's and political advisers, but I was the top credentialed clergyman on the staff. I was the only one who could interpret religion as a doer of religion," said Hoyt, who didn't talk statistics, comparing the percentages of Shi'i to Sunni. "Part of my role was to talk about the religious lifestyle decision-making that people would use to interpret coalition actions such as a curfew during Ramadan."

These "fly on the wall" moments included daily briefings and the "meeting of the wizards" as Hoyt called the Effects Assessment Synchronization Board that met every six weeks. All general officers from the theater along with coalition commanders, the ambassador, and embassy staff attended this day-long meeting to review the strategic campaign plan—the document approved by the president and implemented by MNFI and the ambassador.

> "Men listened to me expectantly, waiting in silence for my counsel. After I had spoken, they spoke no more; my words fell gently on their ears."
> (Job 29:21–22)

Hoyt was one of three listening "flies on the wall." They didn't record the meetings but watched, listened, and offered "what if" questions. They analyzed who said what and to whom as well as the high points and off track moments.

It was Hoyt's job to try to interpret the spiritual psyche as he saw it as a clergyman. And hopefully through a restatement of that, he could offer the leadership an approach to a solution that would make it more inclusive of the Iraqi civilian on the ground who was trying to practice his faith in the midst of a violent environment, fifty percent of which we were creating.

If Hoyt heard something he was apprehensive about in a meeting, he would write it on a 3 x 5 card and pass it to a nearby general. Sometimes Hoyt was asked to share his concern with the group or sometimes they would discuss it later. Either way, this listening method proved an effective leadership tool.

"When I presented myself as a leader who was willing to learn from everybody and anybody, then I was able to uncover ideas that people would never have brought up," Hoyt stated.

Prayer:
Thank you, Father, for the gift of listening, for the gift of wise counsel.
May I listen today, and if I speak, may I speak with wisdom.

MARCH 18

Risk

Multinational Force-Iraq Command Chaplain,
(Col.) Mike Hoyt, United States Army

COURAGE DOESN'T disappear with responsibility, it rises with rank. The soldier on the ground routinely reveals raw courage, while generals continually muster moral courage. As Multinational Force-Iraq Command Chaplain, Hoyt had the opportunity to observe such moral leadership first hand.

One of the things that's always going around in the back of their minds (general officers) is "what is the appropriate level of risk?" It's not risk to their careers as some people would like to say. For the four star billets, it's the risk to the country. And they are obsessed with getting it right for the sake of America.

"My two MNF-I CGs are men of incredible intellect, valor, and purpose. It is an honor to pray for them" Hoyt said.

Generals must keep open the broadest number of options for America. A general officer is exercising the military might of the United States. That's serious business. That's life and death. If you make a strategic decision to clean up Ramadi, then that decision will get people killed. That's all there is to it. It can't be done nicely.

With 3,500 civilian deaths a month, Iraq was peaking in "Iraqi on Iraqi violence" in 2006. Violent Iraqis justified their crimes through the idea that someone had it coming to them because of their sense of loss. Revenge often stemmed from centuries-old conflicts. Hoyt saw similarities with his deployment to Bosnia.

The difference in Iraq was that it was being manipulated by Al Qaeda and covered with religious verbiage that created a mirage for the poor and disenfranchised that said, "If you really want to be religious, this is what you have to do." So they took advantage of chaos and leveraged it to their side.

To respond, the generals had to weigh the right thing to do given the risk involved. They knew that extending tours of duty or increasing the number of troops through a surge would increase risk.

> "So the three mighty men... drew water from the well…and carried it back to David. But he refused to drink it; instead, he poured it out before the LORD. 'Far be it from me, O LORD, to do this!' he said. 'Is it not the blood of men who went at the risk of their lives?' And David would not drink it." (2 Samuel 23:16–17)

"The problem when you get up into the higher echelons of decision-making is that black and white is rarely available. You often have to choose between bad choices in an ambiguous environment. Then you choose as wisely as possible. War rarely presents a lot of good choices. Implementing national policy on foreign soil and conducting theater level war is volatile and unpredictable," Hoyt said.

Rising in the ranks requires moral courage and risks for the right reasons.

Prayer:
God, thank you for the courage it takes to be a leader.
I pray for those generals as they weigh the risk and
costs to America. Give them wisdom.

Listening to the Troops

Multinational Force-Iraq Command Chaplain, (Col.) Mike Hoyt, United States Army

ONCE YOU'RE empowered by the four star, you're empowered. 'Poof' you go out and execute. If you stay within the commander's intent then you don't have anything to worry about," Multinational Force-Iraq Command Chaplain Hoyt, United States Army explained.

When a command chaplain comes into the theater, he has thirty days to figure out and present his plan to the commanding general in the "sit down." It's the one chance to tell the CG what you can do for his organization, and how you plan to do it. Then you listen to what he thinks.

In his sit down with General Casey, and later with General Petraeus, Hoyt presented his plan. They responded the way general officers usually respond: "Get out there and be with the troops, tell me what they're thinking, what they're going through and what difference it makes."

> "Even now my witness is in heaven; my advocate is on high." (Job 16:19)

Commanding generals want their chaplains to be independent observers, whether at staff meetings or with troops in the field. They want feedback from someone who is going to tell them the *way it is* from the carefully guarded heart level of the soldier. Chaplains are not "command spies;" they are pastoral advocates for all.

"I'm the chaplain. I'm supposed to tell the truth. Commanders and soldiers are free to talk with the chaplain unencumbered with the concerns of climbing the ladder of success. The chaplain protects that honesty and communicates the feedback that the decision maker needs in order to understand the impacts of war planning and execution. I'm not going to tell the CG all the 'raw raw whoop-ity whoop stuff,'" Hoyt explained. "I'm going to tell him what I see."

For example: "These guys down here are sucking wind, boss. It's tough. There are quality of life issues with isolation, water supplies, hot chow, and intermittent mail call. Sometimes there is a real slug fest going on for control of an area. Anxiety levels are high. Leadership is challenged. Perceptions of contributing and sacrifice and loss are an issue. Other times the worse it got, the more unbeatable the team became. The resilience of the force is truly amazing.'" Hoyt indicated. "I could always depend on the CG to decide how to deal with issues in the most positive of ways."

Command chaplains become eyes and ears for all ranks. It's an important part of mission.

Prayer:
Abba Father, thank you for leaders who listen to the needs of others.

Welcomed Visits

Multinational Force-Iraq Command Chaplain, (Col.) Mike Hoyt, United States Army

M Y PRIMARY objective in going out into the field was to communicate to the soldiers their part in the big scheme of what America was doing in Iraq," explained Multinational Force-Iraq Command Chaplain Hoyt.

Hoyt traveled throughout Iraq several times a week. His mission was to encourage the force spiritually and deliver the theater commander's message to the troops by telling them what they were up against. Hoyt traveled anyway he could: by helicopter or by Humvee; it didn't matter. After having traveled in two hundred convoys, he stopped counting the number he'd been in.

"I'd travel out and talk with chaplains first. I would lay out for them the role of Multinational Force-Iraq and show them all the different players that were involved in making this great effort work," he explained. "I would build that backwards down to their level, where they were at and where their division was—their brigade and battalion. Sometimes I would consider what their company was doing. I'd try to work that all the way back up and how that affected the strategic outcomes of the country."

Hoyt went as the direct representative of the theater commander. People would notice his patches, the cross on his right and the colonel's eagle in middle. His visits were well received.

People were always willing to be engaged at a spiritual level. And that's not a tribute just to Hoyt, but that's a tribute to all the fine chaplains out there who are and were authentic in their faith.

Sometimes Hoyt arrived after a catastrophe occurred, even one affecting the convoy he was in.

"As mad as the guys were about the losses they'd sustained and as confused as they were about whether or not it was worth it, they were always willing for a chaplain to be with them. It was okay not to have the answer. It was okay not to know, and it was okay to be mad at the time. And to be all that in front of the chaplain, that was okay and, in fact, sometimes it was welcomed," he said.

"Then when the body bag was zipped up and the dust was gone, stuff would get back to whatever was normal in an abnormal environment, then we'd work out the details," Hoyt reflected. "I came across that a lot. That always was a sacred time for me, being able to be a minister in the mess of the moment."

> "The islanders showed us unusual kindness. They built a fire and welcomed us all because it was raining and cold." (Acts 28:2)

Prayer:
You are the great host, the one who welcomes all who come to you with over-flowing kindness even under challenging circumstances.

Religious Conference

Multinational Force-Iraq Command Chaplain, (Col.) Mike Hoyt, United States Army

NOT EVERY problem in Iraq is religious but every enduring solution requires a religious accommodation," explained Multinational Force-Iraq Command Chaplain Hoyt of the signature event he's most proud of: the Iraq Inter-Religious Conference.

This council brought together leading clerics for Sunni, Shi'i, Christian, and Yezdi on a national level for a dialogue on reconciliation.

The point was to interrupt this cycle of violence that was spinning out of control and destroying the fabric of Iraq along religious lines. This was an attempt to engage at the clergy level. The conflict in Iraq is religious. It's criminal, mercenary, and Al Qaeda as well. It has an unmistakable religious quotient to it that when you don't deal with it, it escalates out of control. That is exactly what happened in 2006.

It took sixteen months, but the first meeting took place in June 2007 with the approval of Iraqi Prime Minister Nouri al Maliki. The conference was the broadest representation of religious leaders (by sect and geography) held in Iraq in thirty-seven years. After intense discussions, the leaders signed a final statement denouncing violence and terrorism and demonstrating support for democratic principles and the Iraqi Constitution. They pledged to actively work to reduce violence as well as to protect and restore holy religious sites. Most importantly, the accord was the first religious document publicly renouncing Al Qaeda by name and declaring the spread of arms and unauthorized weapons as criminal acts.

> "If it is possible, as far as it depends on you, live at peace with everyone."
> (Romans 12:18)

Canon Andrew White was the central figure of the effort. Appointed by the Archbishop of Canterbury as the Anglican Bishop for Baghdad in 1998, he is the best known Western minister in the Middle East. Although threatened and beaten near death, Canon White survived the Saddam Hussein regime. He founded the Foundation for Reconciliation in the Middle-East.

"Because of White's tenacity in Iraq, he became the best connected Western cleric in the Middle East. The guy's contacts were amazing. There isn't any head of state in the Middle East that he doesn't know. He is known and accepted by the senior religious leaders at the highest levels," Hoyt said.

Andrew was saying all along this was a religious problem. If you don't address the religious malfeasance that's going on there, it's just going to get worse.

The Iraq Inter-Religious Conference was a key to reducing violence that took place in the months following the meeting.

Prayer:
Father, you smile when humanity seeks to live in peace.

BUA Prayer:
Word from the Chaplain

Multinational Force-Iraq Command Chaplain,
(Col.) Mike Hoyt, United States Army

SOLDIERS ON the ground are not the only ones who benefit from chaplain support. General officers do as well. In fact, because generals make high-stakes decisions, they need the ethical and spiritual encouragement a chaplain can provide.

From June 2006 to September 2007, CH Colonel Mike Hoyt served as command chaplain for the theater in Iraq, which meant he was the senior chaplain coordinating all religious support for all branches of the United States Armed Services in Iraq. He was also the personal staff chaplain to the commanding general for MNF-I, Multinational Forces-Iraq. He first served General George Casey and then, General David Petraeus.

"Often in recurring staff meetings like the BUA, the leadership looks to include a word from the chaplain. Generally, the chaplain's role is to provide some level of refreshment for the audience either through humor, or through an uplifting verse or an ethical challenge," Hoyt explained.

The *Battle Update Assessment* was one such meeting. This daily briefing provided an update on everything that had happened in the past twenty-four hours and projected operations over the next seventy-two to ninety-six hours for the commanding general's staff. Usually coalition nation members, Embassy personnel, the Iraqi government representatives, and sometimes the Secretary of Defense or the CENTCOM commander participated in these meetings through video conferencing.

> "This I recall to my mind, therefore I have hope. The LORD'S loving-kindnesses indeed never cease. For His compassions never fail. They are new every morning; Great is Your faithfulness!" (Lamentations 3:21–23 NASB)

Hoyt or the Multinational Corps-Iraq Command Chaplain brought a sixty-second message of encouragement at the BUA each week.

It provided a spiritual and ethical outlook on soldiers, on lifestyle, on professional ethics, on the uplifting things of life so that you aren't drug down in the monotony and the routine and the gore of what's going on day to day. It's that one moment to take a break and reflect.

After reading Lamentations 3:21–23, Hoyt offered up this prayer at the BUA on July 2, 2006.

"We thank You for the Mercy shown to us in delivering our forces through many missions. We appeal to Your loving Presence for those hurt by the thrust of evil. In this sad time of war, grant us a portion of Your strength of character and Spirit that we may not grow weary in well doing. Keep us humble in our successes, diligent in our duties, and bring forth the fruits of righteousness so that evil may be silenced and we may join the chorus of Your message—*Joy to the world, and on earth, Peace to all men of goodwill with whom You are pleased. Amen.*"

Prayer:
Father, your loving kindnesses indeed never cease. Your compassions never fail, and you provide ways to encourage the great and the small.

MARCH 23

BUA Prayer: Do Not Lose Heart

Multinational Force-Iraq Command Chaplain, (Col.) Mike Hoyt, United States Army

THE UNITED States military leadership in Iraq had a responsibility to provide spiritual and ethical encouragement to the American military force and its leadership, who were making indescribable decisions. This proved delicate because America was leading a large coalition of religiously diverse nations and assisting a new government in Iraq, where religion influenced the conflict.

"We have to be true to our religious integrity as Americans. We are not a non-religious nation. Just because we don't want to offend anybody doesn't mean we need to reduce ourselves to no belief. That was one of the challenges," Multinational Force-Iraq Command Chaplain, Colonel Mike Hoyt explained of the discussions he had with the commanding general's chief of staff about how to approach the word from the chaplain at meetings such as the *Battle Update Assessment* or BUA.

They concluded that a weekly prayer was an appropriate measure of encouragement at these meetings. The prayer had to be as inclusive as possible. It couldn't tick anybody off and had to also encourage our Iraqi and coalition audience from a variety of faiths or no faith. However, because prayer is a method all faiths share, these simple BUA prayers proved a welcomed path for encouraging the war weary hearts of people.

Here's Hoyt's BUA prayer from Nov. 19, 2006: "We thank You this day Lord, for leaving the windows of heaven open to us through the gift of prayer. We confess to You our world's experience sometimes dwarfs our awareness of You and things appear insurmountable.

"But You have set eternity in our heart and planted wisdom in our innermost being and given understanding to the mind.

> "Now He was telling them a parable to show that at all times they ought to pray, and to not lose heart."
> (Luke 18:1)

"We pray for insight into the illusive goals of peace so we may cease the perplexities of war. We pray for a graceful approach with each other so we may practice the lessons of love. We pray for Your enduring mercy and comfort so our wounded may be relieved from the suffering we cannot touch.

"And we pray to You, the God of our Universe, so our vision will exceed the horizon of the here and now and our heart will, in purpose and in faith, be lifted to hope in You. Keep us in prayer this week so we may hear Your voice of triumph in the tasks before us each day. Amen."

Prayer:
Thank you for prayer and its power to encourage and keep us from losing heart.

BUA Prayer: Not By Might

Multinational Force-Iraq Command Chaplain, (Col.) Mike Hoyt, United States Army

THE ENEMY often accused Americans of being religious crusaders. But such false rhetoric did not erase the need for people of all ranks to receive ethical and spiritual encouragement. The challenge of the commanding general's chaplain was to find a way to provide that nourishment despite the enemy's provocations.

Discussions about having a prayer at the BUA, the daily Battle Update Assessment, inevitably led to questions about whether or not America is a Christian nation. As plain as he could, Hoyt made the case that America was expecting the Iraqis to be what they are: Muslim. They expected America to be what America is, a place embracing freedom of worship.

"We at least espouse Christ-like principles. And we allow Christianity to occur unfettered and unbothered and their view of us (the Iraqi) is that we are a Christian nation. So I don't think it's wise for us to stop being Christian while we are the lead nation for this coalition. We ought not to deny our heritage or our history when we're expecting everybody else to step up to the plate and be what they are. Let's continue to be what we are," Hoyt said, adding that he sought to be as inclusive as he could with the theology that he owned.

Here's the BUA prayer Hoyt offered on July 28, 2007. "Lord God, we are in that most difficult of jobs—to win a war without loving it. We do not shirk the battle. We ask wisdom to keep our balance. Teach us O Lord, to live both of these truths. We serve

> "It is not by might, nor by power, but by my Spirit says the Lord of hosts." (Zechariah 4:6)

in Iraq leaving behind our 'real life' so we can work in the 'real life' mission we are trained to conduct. We pursue our craft with a genuine selfless attitude, yet we do not overlook Your ceaseless Grace.

"We reenlist with commitment to our job, but postpone reviving our hearts in relationship with You for the days ahead. We are consumed with what we do; and we are prone to forget what You have done. Thank You Lord for Your eternal patience and still, small voice that tells us life is not meant to be a series of trade offs, but a triumph of faith. Help us to exchange in faith that which we cannot keep in order to gain that which we cannot lose."

Prayer:
Thank you for reminding me that above power and might,
you move through the spirit.

107

BUA Prayer:
They Looked Forward to It

Multinational Force-Iraq Command Chaplain,
(Col.) Mike Hoyt, United States Army

WE GOT MANY, many requests for the prayers and many compliments from other nations routinely asking for them. The couple of Sundays that the BUA prayer didn't happen, the commanding general was personally asked by other members of the staff and coalition, "Where was the prayer today?" They looked forward to it.

Whatever the chaplain said at the BUA, he had to make it brief. Time was a factor. As a result, Hoyt composed only a few lines at time, something that could be read in less than a minute. Here's the BUA prayer from April 7, 2007 with an introduction from Scripture:

"Pilate said to them, 'You have a guard; go, make it as secure as you know how' (Matthew 27:65) but "I am God, and there is no one like Me, declaring the end from the beginning and from ancient times things which have not been done, Saying 'My purpose will be established, and I will accomplish all My good pleasure'" (Isaiah 46:9–10).

> "My purpose will be established, and I will accomplish all My good pleasure."
> (Isaiah 46:10)

"Thank You God we do not own the final solution. Even when we think we have all things carefully wrapped up in our plans and means, truly we are the ones shrouded in the mystery of life eternal under Your conditions. Nothing is final with You until You declare it so. Even at the consummation of the Age it is Your Holy and unstoppable purpose to make all things new.

"You make fresh Your mercies for us each day. You interfere upon our designs with a loving deliverance that remakes our hearts and redeems a soul even after we have long buried the idea of a second chance! Nothing unravels the weight of guilt and the sepulchers of excuses like Your Holy forgiveness. Nothing resurrects a new horizon to a lost vision like Your promise that all things are possible in faith. And nothing heals our wounded bodies, comrades, relationships like the bona fide example of a living God who makes death a by word, and suffering a benediction in the vocabulary of victory.

"Remind us of the strength of an unbreakable and immortal promise in You. Lead us in our worship to the rendezvous with your Almighty power. And bring to us this week those unexpected, unthought of appearances from You that sets our hearts aflame with the joyful news nothing is final until it is complete in You. Amen."

Prayer:
Thank you for firmly establishing your purpose. Show your purpose for me today. May I live my life fully in your will.

MARCH 26

BUA Prayer: September 11, 2006

Multinational Force-Iraq Command Chaplain, (Col.) Mike Hoyt, United States Army

THE ANNIVERSARY of September 11, 2006, brought an opportunity for Multinational Force-Iraq Command Chaplain, CH Colonel Mike Hoyt to deliver a special prayer during the commemorative ceremony in the Green Zone at the temporary U.S. Embassy in Baghdad.

"Almighty and Everlasting God, We gather today in the shade of Your enduring love to mark terrible moments in our past and express convictions of hope for our future. We acknowledge Your Majesty holds all of our experience in the grip of Your Eternity. Nothing we remember or endeavor to achieve removes us from Your Sovereignty, even when events seem to distance us from Your Love. **You do not change.** We come in prayer relying upon Your constancy of character, eternal purpose, and abiding love to be our guide."

"We will not and cannot forget the acts of terror thrust upon our world September 11, 2001. Neither will we become a part of terror's bitter cycle. So we come, in the posture of prayer, humbling our hearts first as we remember the *triumph* of good over evil.

"We humbly ask You to carry our prayer of compassion towards those friends and families who face each day bereaved of a loved one killed in this battle against evil. Comfort them in Your Holy hug as the God of this Universe and help us to remember the outcomes of our labor keep sacred their loving sacrifice.

"We beseech Your miracles of healing upon the maimed and wounded bodies of those smashed in the vice of terror. Restore their confidence in the good works of humanity and grant them a zeal for life.

"We pray for our enemies . . . we do not know how. We cannot excuse their conduct or negotiate with their evil. We freely admit their actions are beyond our reach but well within Yours. Let justice roll down like waters and righteousness like an ever flowing stream. Show us paths of reconciliation and guard us from the self made tyranny that fails to see the beam in our own eye so that we may walk the road of redemption with integrity.

> "Let justice roll down like waters and righteousness like an ever flowing stream." (Amos 5:24)

"Inspire in us, through Your works of Grace, a forgiving spirit. Equip us in the duty of justice to remember mercy. Protect us from the deceptions of might and power so we may see Your works and hear Your still, small voice.

"Finally, Great and Merciful God—You who exact the destinies of nations from the character of its citizens—we pray for our future. Remove the stumbling blocks of international strife and bring to our leaders the strength and wisdom from above. So that one day we may 'beat our swords into plowshares and each man may dwell in safety under his vine and his fig tree'. Amen."

Prayer:
Thank you for sending your justice and righteousness like a flowing stream—with consistency and power.

Operation Bandanas

Mary Bass Gray, Operation Bandanas,
www.operationbandanas.org

MARY BASS GRAY of Fayetteville, North Carolina, did what many mothers of deployed soldiers do as her two sons made numerous trips to the Middle East. She prayed continuously. She also turned to Psalm 91, often known as the soldier's Psalm, and prayed its inspiring verses for her sons.

"One of my sons did night missions. As I read the scripture 'you shall not be afraid of the terror by night or the arrows that flies by day' (Psalm 91:5), I pray courage for my son as well," Gray explained.

When Gray found a website selling camouflage bandanas imprinted with Psalm 91 in November 2006, she knew immediately what she had to do. She decided to find a way to get a bandana into the hands of every soldier at Fort Bragg, North Carolina. As a result, Operation Bandanas for Fort Bragg was born.

Mary began collecting donations to buy the Psalm 91 bandanas, which cost three dollars each. Volunteers from her church began getting together to fold the bandanas and stuff them into plastic zip-lock bags along with printed notes. Cases of the folded bandanas were shipped to Fort Bragg soldiers.

> "He who dwells in the shelter of the Most High shall abide under the shadow of the Almighty." (Psalm 91:1)

The effort grew beyond Fort Bragg as other churches and communities learned about the bandanas. Today, the bandanas are going to military personnel in a variety of places.

Verse 3 in Psalm 91 stood out to Mary, "Surely he will save you from the fowler's snare."

"I think of our troops being under the attack of the enemy over there—who is the fowler and the traps that are laid for them through these IEDs and roadside bombs. And I pray for each and every one of them that God will deliver them from the snare of the fowler. So it's a beautiful Psalm that anyone can read but a soldier specifically will get encouragement from it," Mary explained.

Bandanas serve a practical purpose. Soldiers use them for a variety of purposes, a face shield from sand storms, a sweat band, and even a tourniquet. Mary noted that God's Word is an offensive weapon—not a defensive weapon, in God's armor.

"So I believe that as our soldiers suit up for battle, we should also be able to give them a piece of the armor of God to give them protection, deliverance, courage, encouragement, and comfort," Mary said.

The terrorist attacks of September 11, 2001 ignited the war on terror. The coincidence of the numerical reference of Psalm 91:1 makes this passage of Scripture an even more comforting source of strength to military personnel and their families.

Prayer:
*Almighty God, I pray your protection over our military members,
that you will keep them from the fowler's snare and
that they may abide under your shadow.*

Receiving Bandanas

Mary Bass Gray, Operation Bandanas, www.operationbandanas.org

WHEN MARY Bass Gray of Fayetteville, North Carolina, began Operation Bandanas in November 2006, she turned to chaplains for help. As a result, chaplains became the primary distributors of these donated camouflage bandanas imprinted with Psalm 91. By June 2008, Operation Bandanas had provided more than 55,000 bandanas to members of the military. How did military personnel receive them? They received them with much appreciation!

Multinational Force-Iraq Command Chaplain, CH Colonel Mike Hoyt, who served as senior chaplain for all United States forces in Iraq (2006–07), explained the impact of these bandanas on Soldiers, Sailors, Airmen, and Marines.

> "He will cover you with his feathers, and under his wings you will find refuge; his faithfulness will be your shield and rampart." (Psalm 91:4)

"The conversation stops when I pull one of these out. I tell that this is being presented to you by citizens of the United States of America, from Christians who specifically have you in mind in prayer. They have spent their money and their time to be sure these are delivered to you guys, to let you know that they support you and are behind your personal spiritual life," he said.

Hoyt explained that when he pulled out the bandanas from their ziplock bags and handed them to members of the military, many asked him pray over them right then and there.

"Everyone looks at me right in the eye and says thanks," Hoyt noted. No one just stuffed a bandana into their pocket as if it were just another token.

"Man, what a powerful thing that is for soldiers. The bandana sort of becomes a hallowed relic right there," Hoyt said.

The bandanas have been used in many ways. Some soldiers who received the bandanas before deploying had their children write a message on the back of the bandana, as a continual reminder of those back home. A sergeant suffered a severe leg wound from a rocket attack in Iraq. Those who were with him grabbed whatever they could find. They tied two of these bandanas together and wrapped them around his leg. The bandanas not only saved his leg, but possibly his life.

The bandanas have also played a role as men and women return home.

One tradition you may or may not be aware of that's developed on the part of some soldiers is having their fellow soldiers/friends 'sign' these bandanas as a keepsake before heading home to remind them of God's protection and those who shared it with them," wrote Jeff Hawkins, 2ND Brigade Combat Team Chaplain, 82nd ABN, Camp Taji, Iraq.

These bandanas have become tactile, visible reminders of God's Word and his divine attributes of comfort and protection.

Prayer:
Thank you for using a simple piece of cloth, something a little heavier than a feather, as a reminder of your shield and protection.

Swiffer

Maj. Brad Head, United States Air Force

ONE OF THE hottest commodities in the PX is a Swiffer. When a new shipment arrives, word spreads like wild fire and these mop-like wonders are gone in minutes," Air Force Major Brad Head fired off in an email to his wife Meredith shortly after arriving in Taji, an air base twelve miles north of Bagdad, in February 2007.

Having developed policy and programs for the U.S. Air Force Academy while stationed at the Pentagon, Major Head volunteered to come to Iraq and develop curriculum for the Iraqi Air Force Training School. He and twelve other United States Air Force members from around the world were charged with the task of building the training pipeline necessary to resurrect the Iraqi Air Force which had been disbanded early in the war.

Besides the fact that we are a very small island of Air Force blue in a very large sea of Army green, the best way to describe Taji is MUDDY. This place is ridiculous! There are literally hundreds of construction projects going on all over the place and the last thing they are worried about is using concrete for the roads."

Head's mission was a critical piece of President George W. Bush's National Strategy for Victory in Iraq. The primary tenant of this new strategy was to get a large number of coalition troops out of Iraq in order to re-establish the Iraqi military.

It would take a lot more than a Swiffer, however, to clean up the mess threatening Head's mission. Setting up his 10x10 feet room alone proved a challenge. Head and his roommate each received a wall locker, night stand, and mattress, and spent the better part of their first twenty-four hours trying to piece the IKEA-like furniture together with the help of a single leatherman hand tool. Realizing parts were missing from the furniture that they were to assemble, they bought used items from a contractor and searched for furniture in warehouses filled with old stuff from the Soviets and French. Worse than their personal living quarters, the twenty-seven buildings designated to house the new training school were in complete shambles. They were far from usable with less than two months to go before they were scheduled to be open for business.

"How broken and shattered is the hammer of the whole earth! How desolate is Babylon among the nations!" (Jeremiah 50:23)

"They haven't even started construction, or secured funding on what should be a multi-million project," Head explained after his initial tour of the school property.

"Needless to say, I seriously doubt we will be ready for students in April, but we'll see. It doesn't matter what we are all supposed to be doing here in the long term—in the short term we'll all be picking up hammers, brooms, and paint brushes and using some serious elbow grease to get this place going," Head conveyed.

Prayer:
Father, give me the fortitude and tools I need to clean up the mud and messes facing my life or the life of someone close to me today.

Standing Up Something from Nothing

Maj. Brad Head, United States Air Force

THE BIG PROBLEM is that our headquarters is in Baghdad and most of the military leadership has no idea where we are working or what we are working with. They are driving a timeline to start on April 1, 2007, based on political and general officer demands, not the reality on the ground," Major Brad Head explained of the challenges facing their mission to begin a training program for the Iraqi Air Force.

Air Force staff at headquarters in Baghdad thought the renovation of the designated Iraqi Air Force training buildings at Taji was complete. They were mistaken. The facilities were in shambles, with no electricity, functioning sewage, or water.

"It could take months to secure the funding and then who knows how long it will take the Iraqi contractor to actually renovate our facilities. In the meantime we don't have a single vehicle, computer, printer, phone, or any office space to place equipment, if we did manage to get our hands on the tools we needed," Head explained.

Because the United States Army was in control of Taji, Head and his team often took their supply requests to the Army. They found themselves navigating key differences between the Army and Air Force, such as the number of officers to enlisted men. The Army at Taji had thirty enlisted men/women to each officer. The Air Force had a smaller ratio, with six enlisted for every ten officers. When an Army colonel offered to supply Head, a Major, with one of his office chairs, he was surprised when Head picked up the chair himself instead of asking the Air Force Captain with him to move it.

> "He is our father in the sight of God, in whom he believed—the God who gives life to the dead and calls things that are not as though they were."
> (Romans 4:17b)

The cultural differences between military branches were nothing compared with the cultural differences with the Iraqis. Iraqis think in terms of decades and centuries while Americans tend to think in terms of days and weeks. The Iraqis wanted a three-year program to commission their new officers; too long by U.S. military standards for standing up the Iraqi Air Force.

The U.S. military convinced the Iraqis to begin with a special fifteen-week senior term at the Iraqi Military Academy in Rustamiyah specifically tailored for cadets indentified to come into the Iraqi Air Force. However, these different approaches made it difficult to know how to guide the curriculum. What should an Iraqi Air Force lieutenant fresh out of the Academy know and be able to do?

"We literally have nothing," Head explained.

Their true mission was to make something out of nothing. And that requires resourcefulness and faith.

Prayer:
Thank you for the abundant resources you have given me and for your faithfulness to make something out of the nothings in my life and in others.

The Confrontation

Maj. Brad Head, United States Air Force

WHILE THE chaplain was preaching the one thing that kept popping into my mind was that the previous three weeks had been a test of my character, and I'd failed miserably," Major Brad Head emailed his wife after attending a worship service at the base in Taji.

The battlefield is not immune to personnel conflicts. If anything, the increased life or death tension combined with scarce resources only worsens such problems. Head had observed that his commander was content to "sit back and let things unfold," failing to be more proactive. Another was frustrated that he had not received the commander's role. All of these threatened their mission of standing up the Iraqi Air Force. The chaplain's message that day encouraged Head to boldly face these personnel challenges.

"I committed to myself that I would confront him and let him know. That night we were in the office trying to put the finishing touches on our request for funding and he was basically saying there was no need to keep my position on the books because he didn't see what my replacement would be doing. I couldn't swallow it any more and I expressed my frustration to him in pretty plain language," Head explained, knowing such frankness normally wouldn't go over so well when addressing a superior.

Their shared faith, however, played a role in resolving the conflict. "He is a Christian, also, and apologized for offending me. I apologized for not coming to him sooner. The commander joined in and apologized for not taking a more active leadership role and not addressing the brewing discontent earlier. He was convinced that God had sent him there for a reason," Head indicated.

His commander then started crying, saying that when God grabs a hold of his heart it comes out of his eyes.

"Next thing you know, two hours later we were all praying together," Head said. "I won't say everything is now magically perfect in my life, but the air is clear and I've opened a channel of communication with both bosses."

> "The speech of a good person clears the air; the words of the wicked pollute it." (Proverbs 10:32; THE MESSAGE)

Head was thrilled at what clearing the air did. He was able to provide some guidance to the funding process for the renovations they so desperately needed to get the school going. The resolution also had a ripple effect on the other team members.

"People are starting to notice a difference and morale seems to be improving across the board."

Prayer:
Thank you for the sweet relief that comes by resolving
a conflict and setting paths straight.

Chaplain (Capt.) Matt Hamrick (April 21) conducting a baptism service in Iraq

Iraqi Air Force

Maj. Brad Head, United States Air Force

WHEN THE Iraqi Air Force members are at work, they typically eat and sleep at the base because military members are regularly targeted for assassination," Major Brad Head revealed in an email to his wife.

An Iraqi Air staff deputy director had been recently kidnapped and killed. Most Iraqi Air staff didn't tell anyone they were in the Iraqi Air Force. As a result, members didn't like to stay at work very long so they could "show up" in their neighborhood every few days to keep people from asking questions. The commander of one of the Iraqi flying bases went so far as to put up a taxi cab sign on his car to disguise his real job.

Despite facing overwhelming odds, Head and his teammates managed to start the Iraqi Air Force program with twenty-three students on schedule in April 2007. They solved their renovation woes by securing temporary digs in a building they labeled "the Alamo" until the renovation of their permanent facility known as the "White Castle" was complete.

Head and his team finalized the curriculum, customizing it to reflect the subtle nuances of Iraqi culture and taking into consideration the unique roles, mission, and equipment fielded by the new Iraqi Air Force.

> "I write these things to you who believe in the name of the Son of God so that you may know that you have eternal life." (1 John 5:13)

"In spite of the complete failure of our staff to plan for our arrival, we are doing the best we can with what we've got. I've resigned myself to the fact that successes for the original team will be to lay a solid foundation for those who will follow in our footsteps," Head explained, noting they were effectively re-creating the Iraqi Air Force from scratch.

"When I call headquarters in Baghdad for guidance, they respond that no one knows better than I do; so just do what I think makes the most sense. I regularly find myself creating policies that will drive the creation of the Iraqi Air Force for years to come," Head noted.

Head identified disconnects between the number of Iraqi military personnel on the books and what the Iraqi military was supposed to look like by calendar year's end. Taking space limitations into consideration, he mapped a plan that flowed the majority of people possible into the most critical career fields. As he made something out of nothing, he was doing general's work—well above his pay grade.

"In the U.S. Air Force, the person who makes those types of decisions is the four-star general in charge of Air Education and Training Command. Here I am a newly pinned Major sitting in a trailer in Taji (with little to no input from Iraqi military or anyone in the coalition) and effectively making that same level of decisions. Another Major is doing something similar. Surreal," he wrote.

Head's experience was about to become even more *surreal*. General Allardice, commander of the Coalition Air Force Transition Team (who also happened to be his boss from his time on the Air Staff in the Pentagon), asked Head to accept a new responsibility and move to headquarters in Bagdad. He was about to find himself doing work he never dreamed he would get to do.

Prayer:
Father, you are the giver of surreal moments in life, and I praise you for the gift of your Son, whose promise of eternal life will one day take me to Heaven, the greatest place beyond earthly reality.

APRIL 2

Watermelon

Maj. Brad Head, United States Air Force

COULD A watermelon mishap—a seedy mistake—take down plans for building up the Iraqi Air Force?

"I took a piece of watermelon and then froze as I pondered what the proper etiquette was for dealing with seeds in Iraq," Major Brad Head emailed his wife.

The meeting was one of the most—if not *the* most—important meeting of Head's deployment. He had come to Iraq with the mission of rebuilding the Iraqi Air Force by establishing their accessions and training pipeline. Scarce resources nearly killed the mission, but they had somehow managed to start the program on time. After moving from Taji to Baghdad, Head arranged several meetings with key players to obtain "buy in" for the long-term acceptance of one key element of the Iraqi Air Force training program. One important person not yet on board was the Iraqi Minister of Defense. Then the call came. Head was asked to grab his slides because he and General Allardice had been invited to brief the Iraqi defense minister.

When they arrived, the defense minister invited them to a traditional Iraqi lunch of roast lamb, rice, kabobs, and flat bread. Desert was watermelons and oranges. That's when Head's "near international incident" over watermelon took place. How do Iraqis handle the seeds?

"I fell back on some basic etiquette classes we received that said, 'when in doubt just do what your host is doing.' I looked down the enormous conference table (it could easily seat 25) just in time to see the minister lean forward and let several seeds dribble out of his mouth. Relieved that I wouldn't cause an international incident, I chowed down on my piece of watermelon, happily spitting my seeds on the plate."

After dinner the minister excused his other guests and settled down on one of his six leather couches to hear the Americans' pitch for creating a new interim Iraqi Air Force Academy. The briefing was short and to the point. All of the prep work they had done, including a letter Head had helped to draft that was signed by General Dempsey (Commander of Multi-National Security Transition Command-Iraq) paid off. The minister approved the program and offered whatever support he could provide to help rebuild the Iraqi Air Force Academy.

> "Do you see a man skilled in his work? He will serve before kings; he will not serve before obscure men."
> (Proverbs 22:29)

"General Allardice was almost skipping as we left," Head shared, "This was a huge victory for us!"

"I'll say it again for the millionth time. This has been one of the most surreal experiences in my entire life. I never dreamed I would have the opportunity to engage at the level I've been working to accomplish some of the things we are getting done. We are building the Iraqi Air Force, as Gen. Allardice likes to say, 'one brick at a time.'"

Prayer:
*Thank you for the times in life when hard
work brings a tangible reward.*

A Sweaty Rhino

Maj. Brad Head, United States Air Force

BEFORE I left for this deployment, I swore up and down to my wife, Meredith, that I was going to ride in a helicopter one time from Baghdad to Taji; stay there the entire six months and take a helicopter ride back to the airport; and finally, fly home. By no means was I ever, ever, ever going to ride in a convoy. We had an understanding," Major Brad Head emailed to his friends, noting things didn't exactly work out as planned.

Gen. Allardice invited Major Head to take a new position at headquarters and then move to Bagdad. This assignment involved traveling regularly from his office at Phoenix Base in the International Zone to the Victory Base Complex across town. Unable to catch a helicopter one day, Head had to ride in a Rhino, part of a convoy or "carpool" as he told his wife.

For those who've never heard of a Rhino, it's a heavily armored bus that looks like something out of a Mad Max movie. Several times a day a Rhino and several armored Humvees make the twelve mile trip from the safety and security of the IZ through the appropriately named 'Red Zone'

> "True intelligence is a spring of fresh water, while fools sweat it out the hard way." (Proverbs 16:22; THE MESSAGE)

then through the heart of downtown Baghdad and over to Victory.

It was very hot that day—116 degrees. "While the air conditioner was making noise, I think that was about all it was doing. The 'sweatbox' (as Rhinos are affectionately called) was living up to its name. Did I mention that when you ride you have to wear your body armor, helmet, and Nomex gloves (just in case it catches on fire)? Miserably hot as we were, we were at least making progress, that is, until just after we entered the IZ."

Suddenly the Rhino died. All efforts to restart the vehicle failed. A lieutenant colonel's loud coaching did more to frustrate the poor driver and flood the Rhino than to get it started again. The second lieutenant in charge of the convoy tried to jumpstart it by pushing it with his Humvee. Failure. Next option? Towing.

"Now these are up-armored Humvees that already have an extra two thousand pounds of armor plating on the doors. A Rhino weighs about thirteen tons. I'm not sure what towing capacity a Humvee has, but I'm pretty sure we were way over it. Did I mention it was hot? When the Rhino died so did the barely functioning air conditioner. My body began to sweat in places I'd never felt sweat before. (Did you ever feel sweat dripping off your shins?)" Head retorted sarcastically.

The crew eventually hooked the Rhino up to a Humvee for an inch-by-inch towing through the IZ. When the ordeal was finally over, Head noted that even the outside's oven-warm breeze actually felt refreshing. He returned to his room, stripped off his drenched fatigues, and sat in his boxers to enjoy an ice-cold Dr. Pepper that never tasted so good.

But good humored Major Head made the most of the ordeal. He told his wife he loved her "more than all the sweat on all the soldiers in Iraq."

Prayer:
*Thank you God for humor, a gift to wipe away
sweat and unpleasantness in life.*

APRIL 4

Missing Piece

Maj. Brad Head, United States Air Force

A FUNNY THING happened on a trip back to Taji. First of all, when Major Head got off the helicopter, all his old friends started giving him a hard time saying things like, "Didn't we use to have a Major Head that worked here?" He related this of the quick return trip he made to Taji after taking a new role at headquarters with General. Allardice in Baghdad.

"I felt kind of like the guy on *Survivor* who chose to switch to the other tribe in the middle of game. I wasn't fully accepted as a member of my new tribe yet (it doesn't help that I worked for the General before and they all know it) but I was definitely not welcomed back with my old tribe," Head commented.

The ribbing he received was only just the beginning. On the return flight to Baghdad, he carried a backpack and two other large bags transporting his belongings he had left behind in Taji. After landing, they headed over to the General's vehicle when Head made a startling realization.

123

"As I loaded my bags in the car I caught my holster and it seemed a little light. That's when I noticed my 9mm pistol was not there. I quickly scanned the ground and seeing nothing started running back to the helicopter pad. As I rounded the corner, the helicopters took off for their next mission. Not sure if this seems like a big to deal to the civilians out there, but in the Army you can get in some serious trouble for losing your weapon. It's not like I can deny that it happened, my General and Colonel bosses were both standing there with me when I noticed it was missing," Head explained.

He also noted it was dark. The helicopter was loud and he wore earplugs, so he couldn't have heard the pistol drop.

"And I had on body amour and was carrying three heavy bags, so I wouldn't have felt it drop. I scurried over to the passenger terminal and told them I thought I left my pistol onboard. After they stopped laughing, they got on the phone and called ahead to the helicopter's destination. Sure enough it was back right where I'd been sitting," Head relayed with relief.

> "Prepare your shields, both large and small, and march out for battle!" (Jeremiah 46:3)

"The General wants to see you ASAP," General Allardice's executive assistant barked at Head the next morning when he arrived at work.

"You obviously need this more than I do. You can give it back when you get your own," Allardice said as he handed Head a pigtail, which is a lanyard soldiers sometimes use to keep guns attached to their belts in case it falls out of the harness.

"Everyone then had a good laugh at my expense," Head said.

Major Brad Head has a great sense of humor. He knows when to laugh, especially at himself.

Prayer:
*Father thank you for grace for those times in life when
I misplace or lose something of value. Give me a clear
mind and the ability to laugh at life's minor foibles.*

Rank

Maj. Brad Head, United States Air Force

A S I WALK around and eat in the chow hall, I'm very aware of the fact that I'm now a Major. I easily outrank at least 99 percent of the people I see every day. It's polar opposite from being a lowly Captain at the Pentagon, where 99 percent of the people I saw everyday outranked me—pretty surreal," Major Brad Head emailed shortly after arriving in Iraq.

Head experienced what officers often face: *silence.*

"When I sit down at a table in the chow hall, conversation typically comes to an awkwardly abrupt halt. I try to convince the soldiers to carry on. Sometimes they'll ask me a question about how I think things are going. It's strange to have young soldiers stop to hear what the major is going to say."

The questions gave him a reason to live up to his rank.

"I understood, for the first time in my career, the responsibility to give a positive but honest evaluation. I generally assure them that what they are doing is incredibly important. So many sources tell them every day that what they're doing is wrong and inevitably doomed to failure.

> "Brothers, pray for us."
> (1 Thessalonians 5:25)

These assessments are based on lies so it's hard to keep them from getting extremely cynical," Head explained.

Head also discovered some hard realities. He met one soldier who occasionally was tasked with suicide watch. Head immediately thought the soldier meant guarding a post targeted by insurgents. Instead suicide watch was staying awake all night with a fellow soldier who was suicidal to prevent that person from injuring himself.

"When people at home say they support the troops, they just don't support the war—that is garbage. That is not a distinction you can make. That's like saying, 'I hate schools and everything they stand for but I support the teachers,'" Head continued.

All the political talk at chow time led Head to observe the reason they fight.

"Never fear, these soldiers aren't fighting for the administration or even their military leadership. At the most basic level, they are fighting for each other. When bullets start flying, you can be assured no one is thinking about politics. They are fighting for the soldier on their right and left.

"Please say a quick prayer for the young soldiers, Marines, and Airmen out there on the front lines every day. They are doing a hard job much of their country doesn't support, and losing their lives, limbs, friends, and innocence in the process," Head concluded.

Prayer:
*Heavenly Father, I pray for strength, encouragement, and discernment
for the men and women serving in the United States military.*

APRIL 6

Pray for the Iraqis

Maj. Brad Head, United States Air Force

WHEN AIR FORCE Major Head met with his Iraqi interpreters for the first time in the spring of 2007, he got a first-hand telling of Iraq's harsh realities, both past and present.

One interpreter's brother had recently been murdered by insurgents. Another had lied his way through a checkpoint, telling the insurgents he was Sunni when he was really a Shiite. He made up family names, an indicator of tribal heritage, to stay alive. Each interpreter used a pretend name to protect his identity. Zero's story was particularly heartfelt. He had joined the Army when Sadaam was in power, but left before completing basic training, staying only ten days.

> "What other nation is so great as to have their gods near them the way the LORD our God is near us whenever we pray to him?" (Deuteronomy 4:7)

"We'd only known this guy for thirty minutes. When we explained that we were going to be training Iraqi Air Force officers and enlisted Airmen, he passionately urged us to make sure we taught future officers to respect their enlisted troops. Apparently the reason he left Saddam's Army is that enlisted men were routinely raped by their officers as a form of punishment for not following orders," Head explained.

Despite his traumatic experiences, Zero had a great sense of humor.

"I asked if he had girlfriend and he assured me he was engaged to actress Angelina Jolie. He said they had talked about it last night and she agreed to leave Tom Cruise (he meant Brad Pitt) and move to Baghdad to

126

be with him. He then winked and told me it was only a dream but a 'good dream,'" Head wrote, noting if Iraq is going to succeed, it will be because people like Zero face their fears and do the right thing.

"Abraham Maslow's psychological hierarchy of needs says that people first need food, clothing, shelter, and security before they can be concerned about higher order needs like self-actualization. The Iraqis have spent so much time struggling for the basic order needs that they have never dreamed of moving up to the higher levels we so often take for granted.

"Please join me in praying for these and the millions of Iraqis like them who want nothing more than what the average American wants: to get married, have a family, a stable job that pays well, food on the table, a couple of kids, and a lasting sense of security and stability for themselves and their country," Head related.

Prayer:
Lord, I pray for Zero and the other interpreters in Iraq as they seek to rebuild their lives. Reveal yourself to them in remarkable ways.

APRIL 7

Recreation & Reflection

Maj. Brad Head, United States Air Force

I BOARDED AN Iraqi C-130 for the worst ride I've had in my fourteen years in the Air Force. It was hot and bumpy, I was cold and sweaty, and half-way through I started looking for a barf-bag. One of the Iraqis in my direct line of sight had already located a bag and was regularly using. Fortunately it was a short trip, and I managed to make it without puking—chewing gum and drinking lots of water help!" Major Brad Head wrote about flying to Ali base, where General Allardice had been invited as the guest speaker for a special celebration for the Airmen there, honoring the United States Air Force's 60th anniversary.

After the festivities, Head did what many service members did while visiting Ali base—tour two of Iraq's most historical sites: The Ziggurat and the House of Abraham.

The Ali base is located on the site of the ancient Sumerian city of Ur, the one mentioned in the Biblical account of Abraham. Over 4,000 years earlier King Shulgi ordered the construction of the brick Ziggurat (similar to the Egyptian pyramids).

While touring Head saw the oldest example of a free-standing arch in the known world; the oldest example of indoor plumbing; and script written into bricks which were placed more than two thousand years before the Romans ever existed. The House of Abraham was the last stop on their tour. Although no one can verify that it's actually Abraham's house, the Iraqis have long made the claim.

"It was incredible to think about walking in the same area (even if it is not exactly right, it has to be close) where Abraham walked. Like Jerusalem, all of the world's greatest religions (Judaism, Christianity, and Islam) can trace their roots to this one place," Head wrote, noting the Ziggurat is also supposedly perfectly aligned with the four corners pointing in the cardinal directions.

> "He also said to him, 'I am the LORD, who brought you out of Ur of the Chaldeans to give you this land to take possession of it.'" (Genesis 15:7)

Touring these sites was a welcome break from Iraq's severities, such as riding in full armor on a bus through Baghdad or experiencing the worst airplane ride ever. The sites were reminders of humanity's roots, particularly God's promise to Abraham to make his descendents more numerous than the stars.

One condition shared by the tourists with father Abraham was the heat. Head used his trademark humor to make the connection.

"The whole time we were walking around (in the 120 degree heat), all I could think of was that when God told Abraham to leave here and go to the place that I will show you, Abraham must have been thrilled!" Head observed with a grin.

Prayer:
Thank you for historical markers that show the greatness of the past and the promise you have made for our future.

Muddy Season

Lt. Col. Greg Rosenmerkel, United States Air Force

THE IRAQ rainy season isn't best defined by rainfall inches; it's unof-
ficially measured by how long the mud ponds last.

"We're right in the middle of the *rainy season,*" Air Force Lieutenant
Colonel Greg Rosenmerkel explained in a January 2007 email to his
friends after only a few weeks into his six-month deployment. "From what
I've seen so far, that statement may be a bit misleading. While it has rained
four to five days this month, up to 1.5 inches in a day, it's the lingering
ponds that keep one thinking it's a 'season.'"

Rosenmerkel commanded an Air Force team whose mission was to
oversee a number of engineering projects at the Logistics Support Area
Anaconda, collocated with Balad Air Base, about thirty miles from Baghdad. Rosenmerkel's team provided capabilities the Army needed but could-
n't provide from within.

"The base is flat. Storm sewer inlets are
few and far between. The soil is impermeable
silt clay, and the Iraqi irrigation canals surrounding us are higher elevation. Even in
wartime, we can't make water flow uphill.
Mud is everywhere," Rosenmerkel observed.

"All the mud really just adds to the
inconvenience. We're obviously in uniform

> "If anyone will not wel-
> come you or listen to
> your words, shake the
> dust off your feet when
> you leave that home or
> town." (Matthew 10:14)

all the time, so when you gotta go in the middle of the night, you get
dressed, schlep through the mud to the porta-potty, and try to get back in
bed without bringing the mud with you," he explained.

Mud clings to everything. It's consistency is not normal mud either—
it's slippery. It could be described as somewhere between a McDonald's
chocolate shake and baby poop. It's got a remarkable ability to track one
hundred feet down a hallway, then when it dries it just turns to dust and
finds its way into your coffee cup.

Boot scrapers dot all doorsteps. These boot brushes are everywhere,
but they really just serve to remove the big rocks and fling mud higher on
your pant leg or your buddy's.

The mud in Iraq is hard to get off because it's fine and silt-like. Understanding Middle East mud sheds new light on the Biblical phrase "shaking
the dust off your feet"—a response to an insult or inhospitable gesture.

Rosenmerkel's observation literally shows how hard it can be to "shake the dust from your feet."

Just as it's sometimes necessary to clean mud off your feet, so it's also important to let go of life's insults. Like mud, it's better to view them an inconvenience.

Prayer:
God, enable me to let go of the insults that sometimes come my way.
Keep them from becoming grudges. Instead, help me to have
the persistence to wash them off as mud from my feet.

APRIL 9

Gravel Job Conditions

Lt. Col. Greg Rosenmerkel, United States Air Force

TO BUILD ROADS, one needs asphalt. To make asphalt, one needs gravel. Sometimes getting gravel for engineering projects at Anaconda-Balad-Balad Air Base seemed as primitive as the cartoon celebrity, Fred Flinstone, operating a bronco crane at Bedrock's Slate Rock and Gravel Company.

After eighteen years in the Air Force, Lt. Col. Greg Rosenmerkel was used to having some discretionary funding authority. The United States military process in Iraq was very different. No matter your rank, all expenditures went all the way to the "corps" for approval.

> "He lifted me out of the slimy pit, out of the mud and mire; he set my feet on a rock and gave me a firm place to stand."
> (Psalm 40:2)

"One of our challenges has been getting construction work estimated, bid, and completed in an incredibly volatile market. In the past few weeks we've seen costs for gravel range between $200 and $400 per ton. For those of you that don't buy much bulk rock—that's about a factor of *x10+* off market rates in the states, which makes it hard to come close on estimates when it takes forty-five days for work to get funded," Rosenmerkel emailed his friends.

Gravel woes went beyond paperwork pushing and market drivers. They were gravely serious.

"The story goes that this week the quarry operator was taken hostage and the family had to pay a $500,000 ransom," Rosenmerkel wrote, adding the driver was beaten or worse. "Further, a *passage fee* must be paid to the village sheiks to use the roads, so in an industry where profit margins are generally around 3 percent, there ain't much left."

Getting gravel delivered also created security problems, which slowed the process. Because a truckload of gravel is a great place to hide a bomb, and the U.S. military try to give work to local contractors and suppliers, and getting material on base is quite an operation. First, the local contractors line up at the gate, often as far as the eye can see. One by one, they come in and dump their load for *dirty ops* where the material is screened. Once that's done, it's loaded into other trucks that are permitted on base as *clean ops*. Camping overnight in a line is something Americans do for concert tickets, not paychecks. Not so in Iraq. If their gravel truck didn't go through dirty ops early enough to ensure they would be out by 1700 hours, the Iraqi drivers would line outside the gate and camp overnight.

"It's a good reminder of the blessing of having regular work hours as most Americans do," Rosenmerkel concluded.

It's also a good reminder to pray for those in need.

Prayer:
Thank you for reminding me of the blessings you have given America. I pray that the Iraqis will soon overcome the challenges they face just to get a paycheck.

Baptism and Communion

Lt. Col. Greg Rosenmerkel, United States Air Force

A MUDDY PLACE in need of gravel for making asphalt no doubt had other rudimentary buildings. The Anaconda-Balad chapel was no exception. On the inside, this expandable shelter was lined with plywood. The outside had a traditional-looking bell tower topped with a pointy A-frame roof. However, the bells were far from traditional—they were empty 105mm shells.

What proved to be time-honored, however, was the role friendship and faith played in giving Rosenmerkel perspective and inspiration in Iraq.

"Early in the deployment, my team and I all sat down and discussed our goals for the next six months. One of Captain 'Donna's' goal was to get baptized. Yesterday at 1400 hours, we got to witness this great event, and it sure helped shift focus on the present and future," Lt. Col. Greg Rosenmerkel emailed his friends.

The presiding chaplain offered this during the ceremony prep: "This is a historic region, especially for a Christian baptism. While Israel is the nation most often mentioned in the Bible, Iraq is mentioned second most often. The names used in the Bible are Babylon, Land of Shinar, and Mesopotamia. The word Mesopotamia means 'between the two rivers' more exactly between the Tigris and Euphrates Rivers. The name Iraq means 'country with deep roots,'" Rosenmerkel expressed, noting that Iraq is home to the ancient land of Assyria, land of Eden, Tower of Babel, Nineveh, Babylon, and Ur, Abraham's home.

"If you can mentally escape from the current situation, it's truly awesome to be here. The Tigris is on our base map."

Encouragement also came from casual conversations ending in poignancy.

> "And when your children ask you, 'What does this ceremony mean to you?' then tell them, 'It is the Passover sacrifice to the LORD, who passed over the houses of the Israelites in Egypt and spared our homes when he struck down the Egyptians.'" Then the people bowed down and worshiped." (Exodus 12:26–27)

Despite the chapel's rudimentary conditions and makeshift bell tower, Lieutenant Colonel Rosenmerkel found that what most mattered in a church is not its appearance, but those relationships and friendships that direct a heart toward God.

"Friendships and a re-kindled participation in church really helped us keep perspective," he observed.

Prayer:
Father: Thank you for those ceremonies, ministers, and people who direct me to your word and lead me to you.

Field Trips

Lt. Col. Greg Rosenmerkel, United States Air Force

"I THINK IT'S important to get out, take a break, meet some people, learn something new, see things that most take for granted or don't know exist," Lt. Col. Greg Rosenmerkel wrote about the weekly field trips he arranged for his Air Force engineering team.

One trip was to the CRAM operation at Anaconda-Balad Air Base, known as *Mortaritaville*. "CRAM stands for Counter Rocket, Artillery, Mortar—It's loud, and not a favorite alarm clock. The 'shooter' is a phalanx 20mm gun off Navy ships," he emailed. Rosenmerkel attached a photo showing their tour guide holding the rocket that had interrupted their physical training session earlier that morning. The mortar turned "our 'push-ups' into 'get downs.' CRAM system did its job. We were back at it in no time."

His team visited a number of places, including the reverse-osmosis water purification plant. The people were always more impressive than the process. The boss of the whole water production program is Eloy. Greg's favorite story of Eloy is from summer

> "I only know that in every city the Holy Spirit warns me that prison and hardships are facing me." (Acts 20:23)

2004. He was relaxing on the deck at 11 p.m., shirt off, cooling down, and watching the new *X-Men* movie in 3D when a mortar hit about fifteen feet away. Of course he was knocked out, woke up and thought, *how cool is THAT technology*. They pulled a chunk from his skull, left one in his shoulder, and he laughs about it. Incredible guy, loves his country, loves the military, and loves making water.

They also visited "Monster Garage Iraq," the contractor shop that assembles IED detection equipment and repairs battle-damaged rigs so they can return to safe-clearing supply routes.

"While the equipment provides great protection, we're still losing people as the bad guys figure out how to break stuff. Our technology is constantly improving, as is theirs. The repair shop guys are warriors, incredibly dedicated to keeping soldiers safe. Seeing the vehicles in the shop with holes in them where people used to sit is the most angering thing I've seen since we got here. I find it ironic how cowardly the insurgents are fighting the battle," Rosenmerkel emailed.

Rather than just stimulating their intellect, these field trips strengthened his team's resolve. Rosenmerkel's email after watching the president's State of the Union address summed up their determination. "I will say this: I believe we can fight here, or wait until they come back to the United States. It ain't pretty, so let's say we fight 'em here."

Prayer:
Thank you for using the stories of ordinary people who do difficult things to inspire others who are facing danger.

APRIL 12

Things I'll Miss

Lt. Col. Greg Rosenmerkel, United States Air Force

THURSDAY WAS huge—first, our replacements arrived, and second— we are now making asphalt on base. I know for most of you this is humdrum news, but for us civil engineers, it is a banner day. More pavements faster and cheaper," Lt. Col. Greg Rosenmerkel emailed his friends near the end of his deployment. His team celebrated with Mountain Dew.

As Rosenmerkel completed his six-month deployment to Iraq, he emailed his friends with a list of the things he would and wouldn't miss about Iraq. In addition to dust, mud, wind, heat, cold showers in the winter, and warm showers in the summer, here are some others he wouldn't miss:

> "A man can do nothing better than to eat and drink and find satisfaction in his work. This too, I see, is from the hand of God."
> (Ecclesiastes 2:24)

Getting dressed in the middle of the night to walk outside to the porta-john, wearing 40 lbs. of body armor and Kevlar helmet after a morning run with a 40-year-old back, the nauseating smoke from the burn pit, showering in a small, hot, crowded, stinky, muddy trailer with a dozen other guys, and waking up to the CRAM shooting down a mortar.

He also wouldn't miss the painful experience of attending memorial services, but all was not bad in Iraq. Rosenmerkel had a few things he would miss: bottled water everywhere and running into old friends from previous deployments and air bases. He'd also miss church in the expandable shelter because "everyone there wants to be there."

"This was possibly my last opportunity to be a commander of my Airmen, a group at the level in which I see them all every day. They were a joy and an inspiration to strive to be the kind of leader they deserve. New Army friends, a totally different culture—some of it I liked, most of it I respected. They were all deployed at least twelvemonths," he wrote.

There were two things he'd miss watching: F-16s take off in the dark with full afterburner (the sound of freedom) on the way home from the office and the incredible dedication of so many people.

Most importantly he'd miss feeling like a day's work will make someone's life better. And as the author of Ecclesiastes concludes, such satisfaction in one's work is from the hand of God.

Prayer:
Enable me to find inherent satisfaction in the work you have given me, knowing that the work of my hands comes from your hand.

Emergency Room

Mary Ebersole, wife of Lt. Dennis Ebersole

J OSH, JOSH, wake up!" I screamed.

I couldn't believe my eyes. My three-year-old son had lost consciousness.

It was July 4, 2007. Despite Dennis' absence, I had been determined to celebrate Independence Day with our three children. The plan was to play in the morning, nap in the afternoon, and watch the fireworks that night.

After Josh's nap, I noticed he was a little warm, but I didn't think much of it. I decided to put him in bed with me and snuggled him close. Within minutes of lying down, his arms, and legs shook. His eyes rolled back, something he'd never done before. I was shocked and scared. I screamed out to my mom, who, by the grace of God, was visiting us that day. She's an intensive care nurse. Her presence calmed me because I couldn't believe what was happening. I hoped to God I wasn't going to lose him.

We screamed his name over and over again. The seizure only lasted about thirty seconds, but it felt like hours. Joshua regained consciousness but moaned lethargically. I immediately called 911. An ambulance arrived within minutes. As they took us to the ER, I kept praying Josh would recover and for strength. I had to be strong. As the primary caretaker of three little ones, there was no room for crying. I cradled Josh in my arms, stroked his hair, and took in every detail of him, from the way he smelled to the feel of his hand in my hand, while we waited in the ER for the blood test results to come back.

> "For when I am weak, then I am strong."
> (2 Corinthians 12:10)

Two hours later, we got the news. He had a febrile seizure, set off by the sudden temperature spike. They told me to keep an eye on him overnight and call the pediatrician for follow-up care—such simple instructions compared to the myriad of problems he could have faced. Needless to say, we missed the fireworks, but thank God sweet Joshie was still with us.

"Am I really fit to do this?" I wondered for the thousandth time at my circumstances.

God reminded me that I was not alone. He provided my mom, the paramedics, and ER doctors. In that moment, he fulfilled my every need. For more than a decade, God had been growing and preparing me for Dennis's deployment. God was my strength while my husband served his country.

Prayer:
Thank you God for your promise to be our strength when we are weak.

APRIL 14

The Phone Call

Mary Ebersole, wife of Lt. Dennis Ebersole

RRRRIIIIIINNNNGGG!"
The telephone's sharp ringing interrupted a peaceful afternoon in 1999. Dennis and I were in the midst of planning our wedding that summer. On the phone was his commanding officer, who had called to notify

Dennis of an involuntary deployment of Navy reservists for Kosovo. The news took my breath away.

Countless military families have dealt with a loved one's mobilization, but not having been exposed to this before, I was frightened. A first generation American, I didn't grow up in a military family. My parents left Taiwan for educational and employment opportunities in the United States. Although I grew up in Rockville and Bethesda, Maryland, neighbors to Washington D.C., I never knew anyone who had been deployed.

After that phone call, I wondered if I could live with such uncertainty. When Dennis and I started dating in 1997, he told me he was in the Naval Reserves, but had not been called up during his ten-year tenure. As a result, I hadn't thought much about it. Ironically, if he hadn't been in the reserves, we might not have met. I was pursuing my doctorate at the University of Virginia, and Dennis was working in Phoenix, Arizona, when he came to DC for a two-week Navy Reserves trip. We met randomly and unexpectedly one Friday night while playing volleyball with mutual friends.

He asked me to go sailing with him the next day. I was attracted to his confidence, strength, honesty, listening skills, and patience. It also helped that he was attractive and very tall—six-foot-seven, especially compared to my petite height of five feet. We had a great date and maintained a long distance relationship until his day job transferred him to the East Coast.

> "By faith Abraham... obeyed and went, even though he did not know where he was going." (Hebrews 11:8)

But I will never forget that phone call in 1999. It was my first brush with the reality that Dennis could be called up. The thought of what he could face and what it could mean to our impending marriage was the most frightening possibility I had ever contemplated.

Thankfully, he was not involuntarily recalled then, giving me time to adjust my thinking. God was planting seeds for what was to come. Like Abraham, I had to move forward despite the uncertainty of mobilization in my marriage. Even though I didn't know where the road would take us, I realized that faith was the best map for such an unknown journey as deployment.

Prayer:
*Thank you for your promise to be with us where we
or our loved ones may go.*

White Crosses

Mary Ebersole, wife of Lt. Dennis Ebersole

I HAD DRIVEN by them many times—those orderly white crosses gracing the grounds of Arlington National Cemetery. I had never attended a funeral there. September 11, 2001 changed that.

Dennis knew three who died. Two were Boeing contractor colleagues who were on the plane that crashed into the Pentagon. His third colleague, Commander Dan Shanower, was killed while on duty at the Pentagon. Dennis had met Shanower during a naval exercise years earlier. His unit supported Shanower's.

While attending Shanower's funeral at Arlington Cemetery, I felt an immense sadness for his death, but also deep gratitude for his military service. I couldn't help but wonder, "What if this was Dennis and I was the grieving widow?" As I saw those white crosses, my breath was taken away again, just like the day the telephone rang in 1999 about Kosovo deployments.

After September 11, I knew Dennis could be mobilized, along with waves heading to Afghanistan. Sure enough, we received our second involuntary mobilization notification. The thought of having Dennis sent away during our young marriage was difficult, but we knew we would follow God's plan.

> "Love the Lord your God with all your heart and with all your soul and with all your mind." (Matthew 22:37)

Those white cross have a different meaning for me now than when I first saw them years ago. They represent the sacrifice of life for country, and to me, they also represent Christ's death on the cross. My parents, originally from Taiwan, didn't practice any religion when I was growing up. We exchanged Christmas gifts, but didn't embrace its religious meaning. I had some great high school friends who turned out to be Christians. They encouraged me to attend their church. As a result, I accepted Christ as my savior when I was seventeen. I didn't understand everything then, but God planted seeds of faith in me.

Dennis and I had been married a little over a year at the time of the September 11 attacks. We had found an amazing church that spurred our faith, helping us understand what it means to be "Jesus with skin on," as our pastor says.

We built friendships, studied the Bible, and led small groups with other young married couples. Although Dennis wasn't mobilized after September 11, God was working in our lives, growing a community of support that would later be a huge lifeline. Life often brings seasons for planting. This was our time to cultivate friendships, learn God's word, and sew love for him.

Prayer:
Thank you for the meaning behind the cross. Thank you for preparing us for the crosses we will bear in the future.

APRIL 16

Filial Piety

Mary Ebersole, wife of Lt. Dennis Ebersole

DAD, I'M over here!" I shouted for the third time to the elderly man descending from the plane. After living in Taiwan for two years, my father returned to the United States in December 2006. I barely recognized him. He walked with a slow gait. His stilted movements revealed his lost strength. His facial expressions were very limited. I knew that something was very, very wrong.

As he came toward me, I fought back tears. The Chinese virtue of filial piety has been passed on to me, and I knew I would one day care for my parents, but I never dreamed it would come this quickly.

Later that evening, my suspicions were confirmed. He was very weak and it was not just from the plane ride. Suddenly, the roles were reversed. I became the parent, helping him to undress, bathe, brush his teeth, and get into bed.

The floodgate of tears opened as Dennis and I talked about the situation. My parents were now divorced. My mother was balancing work and college courses and barely had time for herself. The rest of our extended family was out of town. We had three young children under the age of four, including a month-old baby. Plus, we had recently received a mobilization notification. Again, the possibility of deployment, especially in the throes of the Iraq war, took my breath away.

Dennis and I immediately agreed my father would stay with us. Within a few weeks, the situation proved to be even more challenging.

After a crash course in Medicare, secondary health insurance, and prescription drug coverage, along with a humongous number of visits to doctors, specialists, and labs. We heard the dreadful diagnosis—Prostate Cancer. Not just cancer now, but my father also had Parkinson's Disease.

> "Do not be anxious about anything, but in everything, by prayer and petition, with thanksgiving, present your requests to God." (Philippians 4:6)

Then, it happened. After several brushes with deployment, Dennis was mobilized in March 2007. A patriotic man, Dennis was eager to do his duty for our country, but I was not eager to see him go. The timing couldn't have been worse, so it seemed.

I didn't know how I was going to care for three children and my ailing father alone. After wrestling in my heart, I realized the best way to face the days ahead was to take them one day at a time, and most importantly, one prayer at time. Sometimes when it seems all we can do is pray, that is the best thing to do.

Prayer:
*Thank you for family and for the opportunity to care
for them no matter the circumstance.*

APRIL 17

Community of Strength

Mary Ebersole, wife of Lt. Dennis Ebersole

WHEN DENNIS left for his tour of duty to an undisclosed location in March 2007 (I didn't know where he was going), there was no choice for me but to jump in with both feet to care for my three children and father. Every incident, from the normal to the emergency, was ripe with opportunities to pray for strength.

Days were filled with driving my dad to medical appointments while also paying attention to my children's needs. Sometimes the only moments I had to myself were in the car. Once the kids were strapped in and watching a movie, I would pray. Other times, it wasn't until very late in the evening when I got on my knees to pray. The emergencies happened, too.

We visited the ER three times. God gave me strength to make it through those stitches and close calls, including Josh's febrile seizure.

God's strength also came from the friends we made early in our marriage through our church. When word got around of Dennis's mobilization, our community of Christian friends mobilized as well. They sustained us by preparing meals, sending us gift cards, and watching our children so I could take my father to the doctor.

God also showed me why he brought my father into my home during this inopportune time. Although ailing, my father was a source of strength by becoming a wonderful companion to my children. He entertained them, and they entertained him. My heart was also burdened for him spiritually. I discovered I didn't have to debate him, but could best witness by quietly living out my faith. I continued hosting a ladies Bible study in my home. My children said grace at dinner. My father constantly asked me about the generous women who regularly delivered meals. He was amazed at their support and love.

"And the God of all grace, who called you to his eternal glory in Christ, after you have suffered a little while, will himself restore you and make you strong, firm, and steadfast." (1 Peter 5:10)

Of course, I screamed, "Yahoooo!" when Dennis came home in October 2007. No one welcomes the refining fire of difficult circumstances that God had prepared for me. I had so much less responsibility—no children—when Dennis could have gone to Kosovo. Yet, God chose 2007 and not 1999. He had planted seeds of faith and friendship that grew over ten years to prepare me for Dennis's deployment. They ripened at the right time, giving me strength while my husband served our country. God's mobilization of sustaining grace was just what I needed during Dennis's mobilization.

Prayer:
Father thank you for planting seeds in my life and ripening them at just the right time when I need them most.

Much is Given

George W. Bush, Forty-third President of the United States

PRESIDENT GEORGE W. Bush is an avid athlete. He exercises daily and for many years, that meant a run, a good long jog. Then he took up cycling. He's so fast; he outpaces the secret service agents riding with him.

As much as the drive to exercise motivates him personally, something greater also drives him. While maintaining high respect for other religions, Bush has not hidden his faith. In extensive interviews with Brett Baier for the Fox News Channel in January 2008, President Bush revealed his core belief about stewardship.

> "From everyone who has been given much, much will be demanded; and from the one who has been entrusted with much, much more will be asked." (Luke 12:48b)

"I believe that to whom much is given much is required, and we've been given a lot," President George W. Bush explained.

This idea comes from Luke 12:48: "From everyone who has been given much, much will be demanded; and from the one who has been entrusted with much, much more will be asked." It's a verse that guards against selfishness and complacency.

"It's in our moral interest to help others. The enemy, those who kill the innocent to advance their political agenda, cannot recruit based upon their ideology. They can only recruit where there's hopelessness," Bush continued.

Bush believes that a key component in fighting terror is the need to combat poverty and diseases, such as AIDS, which affected 33 million globally. If a large portion of a nation's work force is ill, then the economy can't grow. Impoverished people are more apt to turn to an ideology of terror than those who have hope.

"Disease and hunger cause people to be hopeless. That's why our foreign policy is to help others live healthy lives. To help others live in a free society. It's the ultimate solution to protecting America," Bush explained.

Six months later, in July 2008, President Bush signed legislation that tripled the United States funding to fight AIDS, malaria, and tuberculosis around the world, particularly in Africa. Bush described the five-year, $48 billion program as "the largest commitment by any nation to combat a single disease in human history."

For a president of the United States, "much is given" means a responsibility of stewardship and decision-making in leading a nation. But "much is given" doesn't have to be measured on a continental scale. Much is given can mean many things. For a physician, "much is given" is about dispensing knowledge and prescriptions with mercy. For a mom, "much is given" is observing her children's needs and responding with an abundance of love.

Prayer:
Show me today the "much" you have given me, whether it's
my time, talent, or treasure. Lead me to an opportunity
to use my abundance selflessly.

Author of Life

George W. Bush, Forty-third President of the United States

DON'T LET shame keep you from getting tested or treated," President George W. Bush said to those with AIDS after signing legislation authorizing a $48 billion program to fight AIDS globally. "Your life is treasured by the people who love you. . . . It matters to the people of the United States."

Valuing life is one of President Bush's core beliefs. Fox News Channel's reporter Brett Baier interviewed President Bush in January 2008. Baier asked Bush whether he was an idealist or a realist. Bush's reply revealed his perspective on the author of life and freedom.

"I consider myself a combination of idealist and realist. I am idealistic because I believe in this fundamental truth: There is an Almighty. And a gift of that Almighty to every man, woman, and child on the face of the earth is liberty is freedom. I believe that with the very essence of my being, and am therefore am willing to act on that," he replied earnestly.

"Now if you believe, that (freedom is a gift from God) then it ought to make you an optimistic person because freedom yields peace. It's also a realistic way to defend America because ultimately the ideology of freedom must trump the hatred of the ideologues that kill to achieve their objectives. In the long term the only way to protect America is to spread liberty. Some say that is hopelessly idealistic. I say that it is idealistic but it has worked," Bush explained.

Baier asked Bush to size up whether he would be able to declare victory in Iraq before his term's end. Bush gave a realistic but optimistic reply.

"Victory in Iraq is going to be gradual. The security situation has certainly improved. The political situation is getting better and the economy is beginning to improve. It takes awhile to recover from a tyrannical situation. I think when I get out of here, I will have put Iraq in a position so that my successor, whoever that is, will be able to deal with the situation on the ground there. And I believe (the next president) will understand the strategic consequences of the emergence of this free society," he said.

> "The Lord God formed the man from the dust of the ground and breathed into his nostrils the breath of life, and the man became a living being." (Genesis 2:7)

Scripture explains that God took something lifeless—dust—and gave it life. No matter a person's ethnicity, religious heritage, or nationality, the desire for freedom is as natural as the air we breathe.

Prayer:
O giver of life, thank you for this most precious gift you have given me.

APRIL 20

Principles

George W. Bush, Forty-third President of the United States

THE 2008 PRESIDENTIAL campaign saw many moments where faith factored into the public discourse. Questions about candidates' core beliefs, religious affiliations, and their pastors infused an interesting dynamic into the media madness swarming the primaries. In a January 2008 interview, Fox News Channel's Brett Baier asked President George W. Bush about the "faith factor."

"How much do you think faith factors in to the Oval Office?" Baier asked.

"Having sat in that office now for seven years, I know how important it is to have a set of principles from which one will not vary. And your faith helps to develop a set of principles by which decisions should be made," Bush responded.

Among Bush's beliefs are the ideas "to much is given, much is required" and that life and freedom are gifts from God. Another guiding principle is the premium that Bush places on trust. He understands that personal relationships matter, which is one reason he occasionally invited heads of state to his ranch in Crawford, Texas, a place where leaders could speak their mind in the open air.

"I think the best way to conduct foreign policy is to establish kind of a level of trust. In other words, when you sit down with a person, they have got to trust you in the sense that you're going to tell them what's on your mind, and you'll do it in a way that is not judgmental necessarily and a not zero sum (for them), and a good place to start that is here on the ranch," he said.

"Was your faith ever shaken over these seven years?" Baier also asked.

"It's been strengthened. One's walk is (number) one, very personal, and two, is not always on the smooth road. No question the president gets tested, there's tests throughout all of life . . . that's just part of life," he explained.

> "Light is shed upon the righteous and joy on the upright in heart." (Psalm 97:11)

No president makes decisions and enacts policies without experiencing criticism and opposition. In fact, historically, presidents usually have bumpy rides, especially in their second terms. And as revered as George Washington was in his day, his second term was more challenging than his first. As several before him, Bush found strength in his faith during the rocky times.

"And faith helps bring joy in moments of trouble. It brings light in moments of darkness. Faith, for me, has been a very important part of appreciating the job of the president," he said.

Prayer:
Father, I thank you for bringing joy to my heart!

"Honor the Dead"

Chaplain (Capt.) Matt Hamrick, from Camp Liberty, Baghdad, Iraq

THAT WAS THE toughest time I'd ever had as an Army chaplain, stretching me beyond limits. I agreed to "cover down" my buddy's unit, which was part of the 2007 troop surge, while he went home on mid-tour leave. He had been in Iraq ten months and needed a break. He told me not to worry because the violence had subsided somewhat.

I was visiting some of my mechanics when my government cell phone did something it rarely does. It rang. Something was wrong. I learned some guys in my buddy's unit had been hit, resulting as: both "killed in action" and "walking wounded." I went to the Troop Medical Center immediately. Someone showed me the tent where the KIA would be placed—a sobering sight.

The radio call soon announced the convoy's arrival. As the hydraulic ramp lowered, I saw four body bags holding four brave warriors. They were taken one by one into the tent. Once the doctors and necessary personnel were present, I prayed over the soldiers. Mortuary affairs personnel unzipped the bags and located the soldiers' identification cards. This was the first time I had seen a soldier killed in combat—incredibly difficult. I kept imagining soldiers I knew being in the same situation. These brave warriors may not have been "my" soldiers, but because they were American soldiers, they were "my" soldiers.

> "My salvation and my honor depend on God; he is my mighty rock, my refuge." (Psalm 62:7)

After each was identified, I stood over them individually and prayed for their families, friends, and fellow soldiers who would walk through the valley of grief in the upcoming days, weeks, and years. Seeing these patriots made me truly realize the high price of freedom. I saw firsthand what freedom really costs. I don't think I will ever look at our flag the same way again. When I see the stars and stripes I now see the great sacrifice made to defend it.

The Army Chaplain Corps is charged with "nurturing the living, caring for the wounded, and honoring the dead." I always thought the only way for me to honor the dead was to lead a respectful memorial ceremony for fallen heroes. My opinion has changed. In that tent I honored those soldiers as best I could. I represented Christ in that moment and hope I represented him well. I am grateful I was able to do what I could to honor those brave warriors. They will forever be in my memory.

Prayer:
Lord, may I honor you today. Thank you for your sacrifice for me and for those who have given their all for the cause of freedom.

Humble Leaders

Lt. Gen. Robert L. Van Antwerp, United States Army

LT. GEN. ROBERT. L. Van Antwerp is taking the United States Army Corps of Engineers to a higher level using the framework of Jim Collins' book, *Good to Great*. Greatness for the Corps "can be boiled down to four standards," he explained. 1) They are "delivering superior performance every time; 2) setting the standards for our profession; 3) making a unique, positive contribution to our nation and other nations; 4) and building the Corps' team to last."

"You can't go to great without exceptional leadership throughout the organization," said Van Antwerp. "*Good to Great* details five levels of leadership based on Collins' research of publicly traded companies. Many reach the fourth level, but few get to level five. The two distinguishing characteristics of level five leaders might surprise you—humility and professional will. They are humble and have a burning desire for the organization to succeed."

"Humility is a characteristic that God looks for in those he holds in high regard. Isaiah 66:2 says, 'These are the ones I esteem, declares the Lord, those who are humble, contrite in spirit and tremble at my word.' For me, it means placing my confidence in him and not in my own strength."

Humility is not a quality often associated with leadership, but it is a distinctive characteristic of level five leaders. Godly principles work in a secular world. They're uncommon, but they work.

The Purpose Driven Life by Rick Warren describes humility as "not thinking less of yourself, but thinking of yourself less. Level five leaders know it's not about them."

147

Van Antwerp is contrite in spirit with respect to handling criticism. Often the Corps plays a role of intermediary as it works with the federal government, regulatory bodies, local authorities, and others.

"This puts us right in the middle, at times. If we've done something wrong or not delivered, we want to admit it. We want to be 'repentant' about it, and we want to use that as a stepping-stone to something better," he said, noting that trials and tribulations produce perseverance, which produces hope and proven character.

> "This is the one I esteem: He who is humble and contrite in spirit, and trembles at my word." (Isaiah 66:2)

"If you want to grow your character, you've got to be in the hunt, I tell people 'Don't shy away from the tough tasks. If you are out there, if you're swinging the bat, you're going to get criticized. But you'll learn from your mistakes, and you'll grow as a result,'" he concluded.

Prayer:
Allow me to think of myself less without thinking less of myself. Show me how to have a contrite heart.

Lt. Gen. Robert L. Van Antwerp is the Commander of the United States Army Corps of Engineers. His agency is responsible for executing diverse engineering, designing, contracting and construction missions for civil and military projects around the globe, including Iraq and Afghanistan. The thoughts expressed by him are his alone and in no way reflect those of the United States Government, Department of Defense, or the United States Army.

APRIL 23

Building Strong

Lt. Gen. Robert L. Van Antwerp, United States Army

THE UNITED STATES Army's motto "Army Strong" translates into "BUILDING STRONG" for the United States Army Corps of Engineers, which has about eight hundred civilians and two hundred military members deployed to the Middle East. In the Gulf Region Division, this framework has been further translated into "Building a Strong Foundation for Iraq."

Lt. Gen. Van Antwerp, USACE commander, explained some characteristics behind "BUILDING STRONG." He cited John Maxell's book,

Talent is Never Enough, that describes a number of successful qualities that are not considered talents. The book asserts that America's sidewalks are filled with people who have talent, but many of them don't succeed because they lack specific attributes, such as initiative.

"One attribute that I love is passion. I would take passion over skill, experience, and a lot of other things. Passion is what gets people up in the morning. Passion is what makes you want to stretch and go to the next level," Van Antwerp said.

"Another attribute is teamwork. In using a sports analogy, great players with great talent win games, but great teams win championships. That's the difference. We want to win a championship," he continued. "It's like iron sharpens iron. When you get a team together, you also receive better disciplined thoughts and accountability. These teams need team leaders, but it's about a team effort."

One USACE construction project is an example of passionate teamwork. "We're building a state-of-the art children's hospital in Basra," Van Antwerp related. "Project Hope has raised funds for the medical equipment, major corporations have donated and contributed, and the Iraqis are responsible for hiring and training eight hundred staff members."

"This is an example of something that can be done with incredible teamwork. Basra was a place where security was very, very challenging, making it difficult to get in and do the work. We've had a number of contractor personnel who were kidnapped and killed just trying to get to the worksite, but with teamwork we persevered for the greater good."

> "As iron sharpens iron, so one man sharpens another."
> (Proverbs 27:17)

The greater good is to make life better for those kids.

"If you walk into the resident office, you'll find pictures of Iraqis kids on the wall with the statement underneath, 'This is what it's all about.' It tugs at your heart. It isn't about the Corps of Engineers or who built it. It's about children having a chance at life as a result of this work. That will be reward enough for us."

Prayer:
*Thank you for reminding me of the value of teamwork and
the passion needed to complete a challenging project.
Enable me to "sharpen" someone else today.*

Advocate

Lt. Gen. Robert L. Van Antwerp, United States Army

FOR A GENERAL officer, advocacy often requires moral courage.

"I've got people on the front lines everyday working construction projects in Iraq, Afghanistan, and more than thirty other countries. I visit our team in the Middle East every three to four months to encourage them and learn of their challenges so I can be a better advocate. I have to have their best interest in mind and stand up for what's right. I'm their representative. I'm their advocate," explained Lt. Gen. Robert L. Van Antwerp, Commander of the United States Army Corps of Engineers.

On these visits Van Antwerp reviews programs, holds town hall meetings and listening sessions to make sure we're on track.

"A lot of it is cheerleading and encouraging the folks that we have over there," he noted.

The Corps designs, awards contracts, and supervises construction. In Iraq about 70 percent of their employees are Iraqi contractors and in Afghanistan, about 80 percent are Afghan contractors. The Corps hires them for construction management and oversight.

In the United States, the Corps is divided into eight divisions.

"In the Bible, God asks, 'who will stand in the gap for the people?'" said Van Antwerp. "The Lord is looking for advocates."

> "Then I heard the voice of the Lord saying, 'Whom shall I send? And who will go for us?' And I said, 'Here am I. Send me!'" (Isaiah 6:8)

Advocacy is another godly principle that works in a secular world. When a leader is humble and more concerned about others and the organization than himself, then he or she is free to be the best advocate possible.

"Before an order is given and while an issue is being discussed, we have to have the moral courage to stand up, be heard, and represent our folks," Van Antwerp said.

As a result, Van Antwerp is prayerful about the decisions he makes, especially the major ones. After seeing a presentation in his office, he often thanks the presenters and then tells them he wants to pray about it before giving them an answer, usually the next day.

"I'm sure that's a bit unusual for them. I want to make sure I have undergirded my decisions in prayer. That's how I do it," Antwerp said.

"My confidence is in him. If you're confidence is in God, you can accept the outcome because he is sovereign and is watching over the details."

Prayer:
Give me the courage to be an advocate for others.

Getting It Right . . . for Their Sake

Lt. Gen. Robert L. Van Antwerp, United States Army

THE BATTLEFIELD brings out a soldier's courage.

Scott Smiley was working for Lt. Gen. Robert L. Van Antwerp's son, Jeff, a company commander in Iraq. A terrorist with explosives in his car approached Smiley's vehicle in Mosul in 2005. When confronted, instead of surrendering the man committed suicide and exploded his car. Smiley was commanding the Stryker and had his head out of the commander's hatch. He took shrapnel in both eyes and the front part of his brain.

"I've seen his X-rays, the entry and exit wounds," Van Antwerp noted.

Doctors had to remove a portion of his frontal lobe that supposedly controls one's emotions. Yet, Smiley has made a remarkable recovery.

"I believe God rewired him. He's absolutely the same guy as before the injury, except that he can't see. When he was injured, it was pretty early in the war and we were trying to figure out the policies for handling wounded warriors. The Army hadn't really solidified what we were going to do with those injured this severely. Could he even stay in the Army?" Van Antwerp relayed.

The general became a personal advocate. "I called the Human Resources Command, requesting that they move Scott Smiley into my command. I told them I knew he could contribute and that I want to bring him in to watch over him as 'Support to Wounded Warriors' matured," Van Antwerp reflected.

Smiley and his wife moved to Fort Monroe, Virginia., where Van Antwerp was serving as commander of United States Army Accessions Command, responsible for recruiting and training thousands of young patriots. Smiley recruited for the Army, became an inspirational speaker, and took on life's challenges, giving God the glory for his recovery. After climbing Mount Rainier, Smiley received ESPN's 2008 ESPY and is an inspiration to us all.

> "And who knows but that you have come to royal position for such a time as this?" (Esther 4:14)

Van Antwerp also intervened to help Smiley reach his dream of teaching at the United States Military Academy. After contacting a longtime friend and dean at the Academy, the deal was done.

"I'm able to do some good things for others because of my position in the Army. In the case of Scotty, I was in a position to help," Van Antwerp explained.

Advocacy is much more than just advocating policies and positions. Moral leadership requires personal advocacy as well.

Prayer:
Provide me an opportunity to be an advocate on someone's behalf.

APRIL 26

Unseen Recovery

Lt. Gen. Robert L. Van Antwerp, United States Army

LT. GEN. ROBERT L. Van Antwerp's is the father of three sons and two daughters. All of his sons have served in the United States military.

"I'm so proud of them," Van Antwerp said, noting that one is a major and one just made the major's list. "For me, it is a family business. I want to get things right because of my boys, their friends, and all others who serve."

For about a month in 2005, all three of his sons were in Iraq at the same time.

"We were on our knees a lot," Van Antwerp said of how his family responded.

Van Antwerp's youngest son and namesake, Robbie, was injured while driving a Humvee in Iraq in 2005. The explosion threw all five soldiers from the vehicle and two were killed. Robbie spent thirteen months recovering at Walter Reed Army Medical Center in Washington, D.C. Recovering physically is one thing, but overcoming post traumatic stress syndrome and living with the loss of his soldier friends is a different kind of recovery.

Physical recovery is difficult, but the war within is often the tougher and more challenging part.

"We're just trying to be very faithful in helping and encouraging him," he said.

Churches are becoming more aware of the challenges facing soldiers, veterans, and their families. Van Antwerp cited Maj. Gen. (Ret.) Bob Dees's work with "Bridges to Healing Ministry," part of Campus Crusade for Christ's military ministry. Van Antwerp described their work as "a full court press to help counselors and churches minister in this hidden battle." The ministry has published a basic guide for churches, the "corps of compassion," to begin equipping them to understand and restore PTSD sufferers and their families.

> "My intercessor is my friend as my eyes pour out tears to God." (Job 16:20)

"You can talk about the power of positive thinking, but that does not do it. You have to come back to the idea that God does have a plan for your life. The essence is that God loves you. These momentary trials will work together for good to those who love Him and are called according to his purpose," Van Antwerp reflected, referencing Romans 8:38.

In the end many who have suffered in this way will be able to comfort others in the same manner that they've been comforted. This is "another godly principle" that works.

Prayer:
Father I pray for those wounded warriors, as they recover both physically and emotionally. Bring them complete healing that they may both comfort others and fulfill your plan for them.

Aura

Lt. Gen. Robert L. Van Antwerp, United States Army

WHY DO soldiers fight? Why do they risk everything?

"In the most basic sense, they do it for their fellow soldiers," Lt. Gen. Robert L. Van Antwerp said, noting the high-level of patriotism he has seen in soldiers since Sept. 11, 2001.

"In Accessions Command, we brought new soldiers into the Army. The Army has to recruit about 175,000 soldiers every year to maintain the strength. What is remarkable is that our young people have responded to the call knowing they're going to deploy," Van Antwerp explained. Prior to commanding the United States Army Corps of Engineers, Van Antwerp led United States Army Accessions Command, which is responsible for recruiting and training soldiers.

"Our obligation to these volunteers is to provide them the best training and equipment possible."

Getting it right means conducting drills in body armor and convoy live-fire training. It also means shifting away from a confrontational, adversarial drill sergeant mentality to a leader, mentor, and trainer role model. And that means: AURA, an easy-to-remember leadership principle for making the "Army Strong."

> "The watchman opens the gate for him, and the sheep listen to his voice. He calls his own sheep by name and leads them out."
> (John 10:3)

"You would know one of our soldiers because there's a special AURA about them. The letters mean something. The *A* means they know that they're accepted into the unit," Van Antwerp said.

"The *U* means they're understood. They're treated like people. We know their names. We know that they have a family. We know what they like to do for recreation. A good unit leader knows that about his people," Van Antwerp continued.

Getting to know them helps soldiers understand that they are cared for and are not just a number. Van Antwerp noted that Jesus' model of leadership was one that called people by name.

"The *R*, we recognize them for what they did well, very specifically," he explained. A leader's job was to identify things they did well and correct mistakes.

"If you're doing recognition to correction about five to one, you're getting it about the right way. The final letter is the *A*, appreciation. Our soldiers need to know that we appreciate them. I am grateful that they would volunteer to come into this army during a time of war."

Through great training and AURA—acceptance, understanding, recognition, and appreciation—we can change volunteers into soldiers.

Prayer:
Strengthen my desire to truly get to know the people in my circle of influence: To accept, understand, recognize, and appreciate them.

Remote Runway Homecoming and A New York Reunion in Texas

WHILE COMPILING stories for this book, I (Jane Cook) had the opportunity to travel from my home in the Washington D.C. area to Texas for speaking opportunities. Because I was sans family, I was not in my usual mom role on the plane. This freed me to do something I don't often do: Talk with the stranger sitting next to me.

On my mind was this book. My flight was two-legged, with a stop in Memphis before final wheels down in San Antonio.

Even though the plane was the same, my seats were different for each leg. Both times brought special opportunities. I was able to sit next to someone who had a loved one who had served in Iraq.

On the first jaunt, I sat next to a woman who was returning home to Memphis. As we talked, I learned she was soon expecting an even better homecoming. Her stepson was expected to arrive home from Iraq within the next week or two. She told me how proud she was of him, how much he had grown up through his service in the Marines.

"He was just a kid when he went over there the first time," she related.

Her stepson was not out of his teens when he went to Iraq as part of the invasion in 2003. She explained he had looked forward to returning in 2007, because he had grown up so much. Now in his early twenties, he wanted to share what he had learned with the guys who were young like he was when he first left.

Then she shared the frustration many military families experience. She and her husband knew he was coming home, but the window of his return was more than two weeks. Their son had contacted them, alerting them he was scheduled to return, but couldn't tell them when or where. He wasn't allowed to contact them any more until he was wheels down in the United States. They lived in an uncertain "hurry up and wait" mode.

> "My people will live in peaceful dwelling places, in secure homes, in undisturbed places of rest." (Isaiah 32:18)

When our plane landed in Memphis, she called her husband from the runway. He had wonderful news. Their son had just called him. He wasn't yet in Memphis, but was in Maine.

This woman, who was traveling with a group of her colleagues, started telling them he was on United States soil.

I won't forget the tears that welled in her eyes. She wasn't crying, but her deep blue eyes were simply moist. Moist with relief. Moist with comfort. Moist with peace that returning home can bring.

THE SECOND LEG of my trip from Washington D.C. to Texas in April 2008 brought yet another opportunity to witness a homecoming. I had about an hour in Memphis before flying to San Antonio. I pulled out a copy of my book, *Stories of Faith and Courage from the Revolutionary War*. I wanted to skim it, reflecting on my speech the next day.

The woman sitting next to me asked me about it. I explained the book was a devotional incorporating stories from the Revolutionary War. Not knowing her background, I simply shared that many of the stories have a connection to today's military families, who, like our founding fathers, have given up their quiet lives to live loudly for liberty.

She then shared her story. A hospital administrative clerk, she was from Buffalo, New York. She had four children, three boys now in their twenties and a twelve-year-old daughter, who was traveling with her. Then she told of her excitement. On her way to the airport, she stopped by her son's favorite pizza place. She bought him a New York style pizza and Buffalo wings. She wanted to make this reunion as special as possible.

She explained her son was in the Army and had been in Iraq. On his departure, he had prepared her the best way he could for his deployment.

"Mom, I know it's hard, but I'm going over there to relieve someone else, so they can come back to their family," he had said.

He returned from Iraq in 2007, but she hadn't seen him much since he first arrived. He had found a civilian job was going back to work for the military at Fort Sam Houston in San Antonio.

Her life had been affected by the war on terror in another way. She lived across the street from the former home of one of the Buffalo Six, a group of Yemeni-Americans who were convicted of providing support to al-Qaeda.

"I don't understand how people who were born in this country and grown up here can become so hateful," she said dismayed over her brush with terrorists in her own neighborhood.

We talked a little while longer. Later I had the opportunity to catch a glimpse of her reunion with her son. I didn't notice what she was wearing on the plane, but at the baggage claim I saw her taking pictures with her son. She and her daughter wore white T-shirts with big black letters that said, "I love New York."

With some buffalo wings, a New York-style pizza, and a T-shirt, this mom brought her son a little touch of his old home to his new home in San Antonio. She understood the value of a home-style gift, one from the heart.

Prayer:
Thank you for the meaning of gifts, and how they make special moments even more memorable. Show me how I can give a gift, even simple kindness, to someone today.

APRIL 29

Bring Your Courage!

Former General Counsel, Mary L. Walker, United States Department of the Air Force

IN THE PENTAGON a shield hangs on one of the doors of the Vice Chief of the Air Force with a motto that shouts—**Bring Your Courage!** *No kidding*, I thought, as I passed the motto.

It takes courage to see that evil has made inroads so deep that a global war must be waged to deal with it—and courage to step forward in a complacent world to wage that war. For a long time our citizens took for granted the security we provided them. After 9/11, some reacted by withdrawing into their homes and their communities.

As Christians we often react in the same manner to the spiritual battle, the war against evil for the souls of men and women. Some fear that evil, and retreat to their safe Christian communities—to their families, churches and Christian networks. But that is not what God has called us to do.

When Jesus gave his last words to his disciples, he did not say, "Wait and see"—or "stay together and comfort each other." In Matthew 10:16, he said, "Go . . ." He directed them to engage the enemy and gain ground. "Go and make disciples. He sent them into the world—"as sheep in the midst of wolves." When Jesus sent them out, into harm's way, he also reassured them that they wouldn't be alone when he said, "I am with you even to the end of the age."

The men and women I work with in the Air Force live with the possibility of death. Though they accept that they might die for the cause of freedom, they do not live without joy or happiness. But they live with this reality—that their lives are committed to a higher purpose.

As Christians we must remember that our purpose is to change lives—to offer hope to the fearful and the lost—to rescue men and women from eternal death, and to offer them true freedom in Christ. In this, we also need to live with the courage that moves forward in the face of danger.

> "I am sending you out like sheep among wolves. Therefore be as wise as serpents and as innocent as doves."
> (Matthew 10:16)

He has told us to "Go"—but he has also told us, that *he is with us*. If those who fight in our military can live courageously in the face of death for the sake of freedom, how much more should we live courageously who go with God.

Ask God what your part in His plan would be. *And* bring your courage!

Prayer:
*God, give me the courage to go and fulfill your
purpose of bringing others to you.*

Letters Home

Former General Counsel, Mary L. Walker,
United States Department of the Air Force

I WAS TRAVELING through America on Air Force business one morning and had a few minutes to gaze at the local paper over breakfast. I saw a two-page spread on "Letters Home" from those who had died in Afghanistan and Iraq. The pictures captivated me . . . uniformed young men and women smiling from the prime of life.

As I read their letters, I was struck by how many spoke of death. In the course of describing their challenges and how much they loved their families and missed them, they spoke of the important business that they were about in those faraway places. Their letters revealed that they did not regret their service. While they knew they might die, they wanted their loved ones to know they were ready. Many spoke of their faith in God and their assurance of salvation because of Jesus.

Not long after that, I was back in the Pentagon and happened to walk past the chapel that serves the men and women who work there. I reflected on how unusual it is to have a chapel in a government building, although I suppose it shouldn't be surprising for the Pentagon. The men and women who walk those corridors face death as a present reality no matter their age or health. And perhaps that is why so many of the young faces who looked up at me from the pages of the newspaper considered themselves ready to die.

The Bible tells us (Ecclesiastes 9:12) that none of us knows the day or the hour when our life will end. But do we think about what that would mean if it was today? And, what does "being ready" mean?

> "Moreover, no man knows when his hour will come: As fish are caught in a cruel net, or birds are taken in a snare, so men are trapped by evil times that fall unexpectedly upon them."
> (Ecclesiastes 9:12)

In their letters, those young people spoke of their faith. Because of their relationship with God, they could go and serve in defense of others' freedom. They risked their lives with the confidence that it was not in vain. They knew they might die—and some did. They counted the cost and were ready to make the sacrifice, knowing that God was behind them. What a great thing it is to have an eternal perspective. These young men and women had wisdom beyond their years and they gave their lives so others could be free. They could do so because they were certain of their eternal destiny. How many of us can say the same?

Prayer:

Father, open my heart to accept Jesus as my savior that I may be ready to face eternity. Help me submit to your will and take delight in serving you as my God and Kiang.

The War at Home

Andrea Westfall, Oregon Army National Guard, Kuwait and Iraq (2002–2003)

WHEN ANDREA Westfall came home in May 2003 from her nine-month deployment to Kuwait and Iraq as a flight medic, she knew something had changed within her.

"I reacted to loud noises," she remembered. "I no longer felt safe and always watched doors. I didn't like to be around people—large crowds were awful for me. I thought I was going crazy, but it wasn't until a year after I got home that it was bad enough to get help. I was self-medicating, getting drunk every night. I was miserable, and I wanted to feel anything different than the hell I was in."

Westfall was diagnosed with *post-traumatic stress disorder* (PTSD) and went to the nearby VA Center for treatment, but she knew that wouldn't solve everything. For her nagging questions about God, she turned to a local church.

> "My spirit is broken."
> (Job 17:1a)

"Spiritually, we are the most vulnerable when we come home," she said. "We've been immersed in seeing death and destruction. There's a lot of woundedness."

Church services weren't easy for Westfall, either.

"How are you doing?" someone would ask.

"Actually, I can't sleep, I'm really struggling," Westfall would state.

"But you're seeing someone about that right? There's a book you really need to read."

No one seemed to understand that Westfall needed more than a pat answer or a best-selling book—she needed the body of Christ. "I didn't need a church with a full-blown military ministry," said Westfall. "But little things would have made a difference like someone coming over and mowing my lawn or fixing what was broken."

One day at work she was having a hard time dealing with a situation—anxiety was high. "What's your problem? You made it home alive," her boss told her.

Yeah, Westfall thought, *but I wish I'd died over there.*

It wasn't until the local newspaper ran an article about Westfall that the extent of her struggle with PTSD was fully told. The day after the story ran, a woman came sobbing to Westfall's mother: "I prayed for Andi every day when she was gone," she said. "When she came home I stopped praying because I thought she was safe. But that's when her war really started."

Those words travelled near and far, including up to the Pentagon chaplain.

Finally, somebody gets it, thought Westfall.

Prayer:
Lord, open my eyes to the hurting people around me;
show me how to lift them up with your strength.

Andrea Westfall in Kuwait

Andrea Westfall in Kuwait

God's Army

Andrea Westfall, Oregon Army National Guard, Kuwait and Iraq (2002–2003)

ONE WEEKEND in February 2007, Andrea Westfall stood outside Times Square Church in New York City, finishing a cigarette before bracing herself to go inside. Though she still believed in God, she had given up on going to church—but she made an exception on this particular day. Today, Westfall was asked to share her story with Times Square Church leadership.

God, prove to me that people love and serve and mean it, she prayed. *I have to see that a church has a heart for veterans.* She didn't think it was possible.

163

But as she listened to the leadership explain why they wanted to launch a military ministry, she noticed tears in the eyes of two senior pastors. "I got a glimpse into their hearts," Westfall recalled. "My body armor started to fall apart after that; the pieces started coming off. Friends were saying that at the end of that weekend, my whole countenance had changed."

Westfall returned to Times Square Church from her home in Texas for the Easter morning service and found herself fully engaged with the sermon's theme of being called into battle by God as the King and Commander in Chief.

"The pastor said that we're part of God's army," said Westfall. "I understood that. I started putting some pieces together that I was just missing: this belief in God is not a passive one, but faith is active and proactive, moving, growing. It means jumping in when needed, resting when it's time. It's like the army. I understood that. *I can do this*, I remember thinking, *I can put my whole heart into this*. And like that moment I first said my oath to join the army. For the first time in my life I made a public profession of faith and went forward for an altar call. That Easter Sunday was my birthday."

> "Now to the King eternal, immortal, invisible, the only God, be honor and glory forever and ever. Amen."
> (1 Timothy 1:17)

While she anticipated that she would stumble on this new spiritual journey, Westfall understood the connection of God as king, warrior, and Lord. Still experiencing symptoms of *post traumatic stress disorder* even as she grows in her faith, Westfall shares her story through the Military Ministry's Bridges to Healing program that educates churches about PTSD.

Prayer:
Lord, help me submit to your will and take delight in serving you.

MAY 3

PTSD in the Old Testament

Dr. Bill Butler, leader of Times Square Church's Military Ministry, New York City

THROUGHOUT the ages, countless soldiers, returning from battle, have suffered from what we now call *post-traumatic stress disorder* (PTSD), caused by exposure to constant traumatic events.

In 1 Samuel 30, David and his men, following a battle, were returning to the city of Ziklag, where their wives, children, homes, and possessions were. When they arrived, they found that the city had been ransacked and burned to the ground by the Amalekites. David and his men cried uncontrollably.

Brave and mighty warriors, in their right mind, would have quickly planned a pursuit of the enemy and fought for their loved ones who had been taken captive. Instead, these soldiers wept and discussed killing David.

David and his men were likely suffering from PTSD. Intense psychological distress with uncontrollable, uncharacteristic emotions, such as crying and depression, is classic in PTSD. Hopelessness, fear, and horror occur in the face of unfamiliar challenges. PTSD sufferers are unable to think rationally or process information properly in stressful situations. They can't deal with problems at hand, nor can they plan for the future. Displays of inappropriate, aggressive behavior, often against authority, can lead to crime and even murder.

> "For I the LORD thy God will hold thy right hand saying unto thee, Fear not; I will help thee."
> (Isaiah 41:13)

David, distraught from PTSD, "encouraged himself in the Lord his God" (1 Samuel 30:6). *Chazaq*, the Hebrew word for encourage, means to grow strong, firm, and secure by taking hold of the Lord. When David encouraged himself in the Lord, it was actually God taking hold of David, filling him with strength and security, and healing his affliction. This is what Jesus Christ does for us, when we passionately seek Him.

It was one man, David, who sought the Lord and the others were healed as well. He led them to regain what was lost in their lives. Each of us can be like David, if we desire Jesus Christ above all else. To minister to the military, we must passionately, unceasingly seek the Lord for more of His presence, His ways, and most importantly, His love.

Prayer:
Lord, help me to place you alone in my uppermost affections and to seek your healing for myself and for those around me.

Flight 77

Lt. Col. (Ret.) Brian Birdwell, U.S. Army and Mel Birdwell

LT. COL. BRIAN Birdwell was watching the news of the planes crashing into the World Trade Centers with two co-workers in his office at the Pentagon, Sandi Taylor and Cheryle Sincock, when the phone interrupted them.

"Mom, get out of the building." It was Sam, Sandi Taylor's daughter. She had a bad feeling that the Pentagon would be a sure target for another hijacked plane.

Surely they won't hit the Pentagon, Brian thought. *If they did that, they'd have the whole U.S. military after them."*

Moments later, Brian excused himself to use the men's restroom. "I'll be back in a moment," he told them. They would be the last words he spoke to the two women.

Stepping out of the men's restroom on the second floor, he started down the corridor when a deafening explosion blew him across the corridor. Even as a Gulf War veteran and an artillery officer for more than ten years during his seventeen-plus years of service with the U.S. Army, the sound that filled the air was louder than anything he'd ever heard.

> "My flesh and my heart may fail, but God is the strength of my heart and my portion forever." (Psalm 73:26)

In an instant, the corridor had gone from being well-lit with bright fluorescent lights to being pitch black. Walls of fire rushed at him from two directions—the site of the explosion and the elevator shaft—tearing the glasses of his face and throwing him to the ground. The building shook; debris from the walls and ceilings suddenly became dangerous projectiles flying through the air.

Brian could see nothing, except for a yellow orange haze with black around the periphery surrounding his body. That's when he realized he was on fire.

Meanwhile, Brian's wife, Mel, was at home working on a science experiment for home school with their twelve-year-old son Matt when their neighbor, Sara, called.

"Is your TV on? The Pentagon has been hit," she said, panic in her voice. Mel almost dropped the phone and ran to turn on the TV. The scene clearly showed Brian's office behind the helipad. Flames were coming out all the windows in that area.

"Mom, that's not Dad's side of the building," Matt kept saying, "It's not him." But Mel knew the truth.

Prayer:
Lord, when my flesh and heart fail, let my spirit still be strengthened by you.

Escape

Lt. Col. (Ret.) Brian Birdwell, U.S. Army and Mel Birdwell

EVERY NERVE in Brian's body screamed in pain. His arms, back, legs, face, and hair were all on fire. As he gasped for air, he swallowed thick black smoke and inhaled aerosolized jet fuel and heat so intense his lungs began to blister.

Disoriented and with damaged equilibrium from the concussion, his attempts to stand and escape failed repeatedly. Finally he collapsed and waited for his soul to depart from his body.

> "He will be the sure foundation for your times, a rich store of salvation and wisdom and knowledge; the fear of the Lord is the key to this treasure." (Isaiah 33:6)

But somehow, he had landed under one of the only working sprinklers in the corridor, and the cold water extinguished him. Suddenly he was reoriented and began stumbling forward. But with the point of impact behind him and a fire door closed in front of him, he was trapped.

Then out of nowhere, a locked door to the B-ring opened and Col. Roy Wallace entered followed by Lt. Col. Bill McKinnon who Brian recognized immediately.

"Call Mel! Tell her I'm alive!" he yelled. But McKinnon had no idea who the skinless, charred body in front of him was, even as the two officers carried Brian to safety with the help of two other men: Chuck Knoblauch and John Davies.

Most of Brian's skin was gone. What was left was charred black. Sixty percent of his body had been burned, 40 percent of which was third-degree. He was going into shock.

A fellow officer from the Pentagon commandeered Capt. Calvin Wineland's SUV in the parking lot to carry Brian, who was strapped to a body board, to Georgetown Hospital. Finally, someone got through to Mel and told her Brian was alive and on his way to Georgetown.

Mel's relief was overshadowed, however, when a nurse from Georgetown called her and said, "You've got to get here *now*. He is very, *very* serious."

Mel was completely unprepared for what she saw when she finally saw her husband in the ICU. He was so swollen, his head was almost as wide as his shoulders. The medical team had already scrubbed some skin off his face and put salve on him, so he looked white, almost transparent. Every place else was covered in bandages. It would be a long, agonizing road ahead.

Prayer:
Lord, when the world falls apart, be my sure foundation, my source of stability.

MAY 6

President's Salute

Lt. Col. (Ret.) Brian Birdwell, U.S. Army and Mel Birdwell

TWO DAYS later, Mel and Brian received special visitors: the President and First Lady.

"Colonel Birdwell, it's nice to meet you," said Mrs. Bush. "We're really proud of you. You're an American hero."

Mel interpreted for Brian, who either spelled words in the air with his fingers or mouthed things around the tubes in his mouth and nose. Mrs. Bush talked with the Birdwells for a few minutes before giving Mel a long hug and asking how she was doing.

The President walked into the room, looking haggard with bloodshot eyes. He stood at the foot of the hospital bed, said "Colonel Birdwell," and saluted Brian.

Brian tried to return the salute, and in raising his arm, revealed bright red muscle under the sterile towels draped over him. With tears in his eyes, President Bush stood still, holding his salute while Brian desperately tried to complete his. He made it three-quarters of the way before dropping his arm in pain.

"Colonel Birdwell, you are a great American, a hero, and we are going to get the guys who did this," the President said. "This will not go unanswered." Then he turned to Mel, gave her a hug and kiss and asked how she was doing. He asked if he and Mrs. Bush could pray for her family.

"When President Bush held his salute for me, I don't think he was doing that out of respect for a single person, that is me, but for all our men and women in uniform," said Brian.

> "He will guard the feet of his saints, but the wicked will be silenced in darkness. It is not by strength that one prevails." (1 Samuel 2:9)

Noticing Mel's Vacation Bible School T-shirt, which read, "Every day's a holiday with Jesus in your heart," President Bush asked, "Is every day a holiday with Jesus in your heart?"

"Yes. Some of them are not especially happy holidays, but every day is a holiday," Mel replied.

Soon the Bushes were gone.

"I had looked into the President's eyes and could see he understood the gravity of what lay before this country—that by standing in Brian's presence—a potentially dying soldier—he would soon be sending other soldiers to their deaths by the decisions he would make in the upcoming days," said Mel.

Prayer:
Lord, give us the courage to see past our
pain enough to still find delight in you.

Silent Agony

Lt. Col. (Ret.) Brian Birdwell, U.S. Army and Mel Birdwell

FOR THREE months, the pain was so unbearable—far worse even than the pain of being on fire—that Brian repeatedly asked God to take him home. Instead, he survived, enduring more than thirty excruciating surgeries, daily debridements, and torturous physical therapy.

Debriding involved strapping Brian to a hard rubber board and submerging him in a tank filled with a warm water-chlorine derivative-iodine mixture. They then either cut away dead tissue or scrubbed it off. "It felt as if they were using steel wool washcloths—on top of the stinging," said Brian. "They were wiping a washrag over open wounds where, in some cases, it was directly on straight muscle. It was absolutely agonizing." They even gave Brian amnesia medication, not to relieve the pain, but to help him not remember it. Sometimes the dosage wasn't enough, and the memories were terrifying, not to mention the anticipation of the next "tank session." The dressing changes and debriding in the tank took almost three hours daily.

"Be strong and very courageous."
(Joshua 1:7)

Skin grafts were another source of pain. The doctors used his own skin from his stomach and upper thighs (donor sites) for his fingers, elbows, face and arms. The rest of his body which would be grafted later was covered with cadaver or pig skin temporarily to prevent infection. As the pig or cadaver skin began to rot, the staff debrided it, cleaned the area and put more on, much like replacing soiled bandaids again and again.

"The skin grafts were exceedingly torturous," said Brian. "But the area that hurt the most after a grafting surgery was the donor site." Once the doctors shaved off the skin, to protect that donor site they would cover it with a substance that was glued and stapled on. Staples were removed (again, painfully) on the third day.

"Actually, there wasn't anything that didn't cause tremendous amounts of pain," said Brian. "If I don't recall something, it was because I was so often out of my mind with the pain."

Before every bath, dressing change and surgery, Mel prayed with Brian and read to him Joshua 1:9: "Have I not commanded you? Be strong and courageous. Do not be terrified; do not be discouraged, for the LORD your God will be with you wherever you go."

Prayer:
Lord, may I take courage in the confidence that you are with me no matter what.

Miracles in Hindsight

Lt. Col. (Ret.) Brian Birdwell, U.S. Army and Mel Birdwell

MANY PEOPLE ask, "Where was God on September 11?" The Birdwells can point to several examples of how God worked not only on that day but in the months leading up to it to keep the loss of life from being even greater than it was.

The wedge of the Pentagon that was hit had been newly renovated, with entire departments that had not moved back in yet, so it was the least-occupied area of the building.

One of the renovations was Kevlar coating on the windows, which likely saved lives by preventing glass from shattering and becoming projectiles.

> "Do you not know? Have you not heard? The LORD is the everlasting God, the Creator of the ends of the earth." (Isaiah 40:28)

Months prior to September 11, 2001, Pentagon officials conducted a mass casualty exercise to prepare a major emergency response. The scenario they created was a plane hitting the building. Because of that exercise, emergency medical supplies were provided to all medical personal in the Pentagon, saving Brian's life.

If Brian had gone to the restroom twenty seconds earlier or later, he would have been in the plane's path and died. If he had stayed at his desk, he would have died.

Brian survived the blast though he stood just two car-lengths from the point of impact, and suffered no puncture wounds or broken bones.

Those who rescued Brian had to swipe their badge at a powered door to reach him—and it worked, though power had been shut down to that part of the building.

Weeks prior to September 11, Brian insisted on buying leather Army shoes—a first for him. Those shoes protected his feet, allowing an IV and morphine shot to be administered there, which saved his life.

Brian was the only casualty taken to Georgetown Hospital because Sgt. Jill Hyson, who rode with him from the Pentagon, had worked there, and it was the only hospital she know how to get to. (Most other victims had been taken to Arlington Memorial Hospital.) Georgetown had cleared all non-life threatening patients from the hospital in order to respond to Pentagon casualties. Brian was the sole casualty there and received the entire staff's attention.

Brian has said that when people ask, "Where were you God?" it's only because they are not looking hard enough.

Prayer:
Lord, I praise you for being in complete control.

Facing the Fire

Lt. Col. (Ret.) Brian Birdwell, U.S. Army and Mel Birdwell

IN DECEMBER 2001, Brian was discharged from the hospital. At home, Mel was his caregiver.

After his physical therapy sessions at the hospital, Brian took a nap before Mel helped him work on getting better range of motion in his arms by bending and straightening them.

The two-hour after-dinner routine included Mel helping him shower, putting lotions and creams on his fragile grafted skin, dressing him, and massaging scars to help break up and loosen scar tissue.

For thirteen months, Brian also wore tight compression garments on his hands and

> "I will bring [them] into the fire; I will refine them like silver and test them like gold. They will call on my name and I will answer them; I will say, 'They are my people,'" and they will say, 'The LORD is our God.'" (Zechariah 13:9)

arms twenty-three hours a day to help reduce scarring and bumps as the skin healed, and to keep scars already there as flat as possible. He also wore a headband for his forehead.

"While I was carrying the burden of physical pain, Mel carried the burden of the emotional," said Brian. "I think the greatest strain was on her, and I don't say that because my job was easy."

On March 12, 2002, Brian returned to work at the Pentagon part-time. "Stepping back into the place that could have—that *should* have—been my murder scene was important to me," said Brian. "I stepped back a winner. I was a walking miracle, a testimony to what God did for me that day. We were winning; the terrorists weren't."

Brian and Mel have shared their story and their faith through *The Oprah Winfrey Show*, ABC's *Nightline*, CBN, CNN and FOX News Channel. They also authored *Refined by Fire* and created Face the Fire Ministries in 2003, through which they personally bring hope and encouragement to burn survivors and critically wounded military and their families nationwide (www.facethefire.org).

"It's exactly as 2 Corinthians tells us, to comfort others with the comfort we have received," said Brian. "It's very gratifying to be able to come alongside somebody and encourage them. We discuss the strength that carried us through this process, which was certainly our faith in Jesus Christ. As brutal as that experience was, the Lord had a better plan for us than what we knew, so here we are."

Prayer:
*Lord, use whatever trials I face in order to
reflect your goodness and grace.*

MAY 10

The Attack

Carrie McDonnall, Missionary to Iraq, 2004

MARCH 15, 2004. What started out as a day full of meaning and purpose, discovering how to meet the needs of a community in northern Iraq, turned into a surreal nightmare, the scars of which Carrie McDonnall will bear for the rest of her life.

Carrie and her husband of two years, David, were humanitarian aid workers doing an assessment at an Internally Displaced Peoples (IDP) camp on that spring day. With them for the day were visiting veteran aid workers Larry and Jean Elliot and Karen Watson, one of the first missionaries into Iraq.

The visit at the camp went well, but as the afternoon wore on, the team grew anxious about arriving at their destination for the evening (a protected Kurdish zone) before nightfall. Driving in Iraq in the dark was not safe, especially for Caucasians.

Hoping to save time, they chose the most direct route, which was to go straight through the city of Mosul—instead of around it. It was a calculated

risk, since Mosul was home to a dispropor-
tionate number of insurgents and angry
Islamic extremists.

> "O LORD my God, I take refuge in you; save and deliver me from all who pursue me." (Psalm 7:1)

It was still light as they approached
town, but Carrie's heart raced at the scene
ahead of them: traffic. Once downtown, the
traffic became gridlock, and the truck with five white Americans became
a sitting duck.

And then Carrie felt something sting the top of her ear. Clutching it,
she blacked out, coming to again only when she heard David's booming
voice: "Everybody get down!" But sitting in the backseat between the two
other women, there was nowhere to hide. The deafening staccato of automatic rifles filled the air.

Everything happened so fast it was impossible to make sense of it all.
One thing Carrie knew: they were under attack, and they were defenseless.

Prayer:
*Lord, help me turn to you instead of to my own
resources when I am under attack.*

MAY 11

No Way Out

Carrie McDonnall, Missionary to Iraq, 2004

IT WAS LIKE a nightmare, everything was in slow motion," Carrie
said. "All I could hear was gunfire, and all I could smell was gun-
powder—and blood." Six men with AK-47s and at least one Uzi sub-
machine gun surrounded the vehicle, their weapons were raised, and they
fired at will. "I felt pain everywhere," Carrie recalls. "Bullets and shrapnel were ricocheting off the walls and floor of the truck. There was no
way out."

Carrie couldn't move. She couldn't think. She could barely pray that
God would stop the bullets, and once she did, she blacked out again, only
to awaken later to an eerie silence. All the bustling people on the streets
had disappeared; even the traffic had disintegrated. All that was left was
the remains of the truck and the shattered humanity within it.

Carrie's limbs wouldn't move. Her left hand was missing fingers; bones were exposed. She couldn't breathe through her nose but couldn't figure out why.

Jean Elliot, slumped against Carrie, was dead. Moments later, Karen also breathed her last. Larry, in the front seat, was gone as well. Carrie started hollering for help in Arabic, but she could barely breathe and her voice was faint. Still, at the sound of Carrie's strained call, David sat upright in the driver's seat and sprang into action, moving as if he hadn't even been hit.

> "O righteous God, who searches minds and hearts, bring to an end the violence of the wicked and make the righteous secure." (Psalm 7:9)

Unbeknownst to David and Carrie, their attack was the start of the targeting of Non-Governmental Organizations (NGOs) in Iraq. In the next forty-eight hours, more news became available about American civilians who were killed, burned, and hung from a bridge in Fallujah. "Soft targeting" had officially begun.

Prayer:
Lord, search my mind and heart and help me achieve righteousness on this earth before you call me home.

Finding Help

Carrie McDonnall, Missionary to Iraq, 2004

AFTER LOOKING at his wife, who was covered in blood, dust, and shattered glass, David got out of the truck and began shouting for help in Arabic. Finally, three reluctant Iraqi men were recruited to help Carrie out of the truck. As they pulled her out, every nerve in her body seemed to shriek back to life with unspeakable pain. "I couldn't move because I had too many broken bones," she recalled. "I had been hit in the face, too."

The taxi ride to the hospital was agonizingly slow. Once inside the unsanitary facility, the McDonnalls were still not at ease. They weren't sure if the Iraqi doctors in Mosul—a known insurgent territory—would dutifully work for the Americans' recovery or dutifully push them over the brink toward death. They had to get to the American Army's Combat Support Hospital (CSH).

As Carrie fought to stay awake, she noticed that the doctors were focusing more on David, even though he appeared to be okay.

> "Be merciful to me, LORD, for I am faint; O LORD, heal me, for my bones are in agony." (Psalm 6:2)

Soon, armed American soldiers arrived to protect David and Carrie until the medics arrived, but precious minutes ticked by as the helicopters were shot at and unable to land. While they waited, two soldiers who professed to be Christians prayed over Carrie at her request.

At long last, the Army got the situation under control, and Carrie and David boarded two separate helicopters to the CSH unit. Once inside, Carrie heard David pray, "Jesus, we don't know what is happening. Just help us." Then, seeing Carrie across the hospital, he shouted out, "I love you! We're gonna make it through this, baby!"

Prayer:
Lord, when I find myself in unfamiliar territory,
be my guide and grant me peace.

MAY 13

Waking Up to Loss

Carrie McDonnall, Missionary to Iraq, 2004

AFTER BEING prepped for surgery, Carrie finally allowed herself to fall into the arms of a deep sleep. She awoke eight days later at Parkland Hospital in Dallas, Texas. Her mother, father, and sister were with her.

She had been hit twenty-two times by bullets and shrapnel. In the CSH unit, they immediately gave her a blood transfusion without first screening for antibodies, which is only done when the risk of death without the transfusion is extremely high.

For the first several days at Parkland Hospital, Carrie drifted in and out of consciousness, flooded by memories of the attack, a feeling of helplessness, and a longing to see her husband.

"Mama, where's David? Tell David to come in," she would say.

Finally, on the eighth day, when she was firmly lucid, her father spoke to her. "We have something to tell you," he said softly. "Baby, David didn't make it." The room spun as Carrie's mind and heart reeled at the shock of those words. She cried out in agony, but encased in casts and hooked to multiple tubes and wires, she couldn't even hug her mother, father, or sister Jennifer. It was the most alone she had ever felt.

> "I lie down and sleep; I wake again, because the LORD sustains me." (Psalm 3:5)

She discovered that David had gone into cardiac arrest in the helicopter on the way from Mosul to Baghdad, completely shocking even the surgeons. His internal injuries were more serious than anyone had imagined. He died the day after Carrie last saw him.

On the same day she learned of her husband's death, she discovered his funeral was being held in Colorado and that she could not travel to be there. Understanding the logic with her mind, her heart wept at not being able to share in the service that would honor and celebrate her husband's life.

Prayer:
*Lord, sustain me through my own moments of isolation
and give me the strength to face each new day.*

MAY 14

Slow Recovery

Carrie McDonnall, Missionary to Iraq, 2004

CARRIE STILL had to focus on recovering from her physical injuries. One bullet shattered her left tibia. Another bullet went through her upper left leg, and another scraped her right thigh. She lost all the fingers on her left hand except the middle finger and thumb. A shattered bone in her right arm and bullet to the joint in the left elbow rendered both arms useless for a while.

Bullets and shrapnel hit her right ear and face, breaking the septum in her nose and fracturing her mandible. Another bullet hit her in the right chest, broke her ribs, and exited beneath her left breast. Amazingly, only one small scar on her face gives any hint as to what she endured.

Years after the attack, Carrie said it still felt fresh. "My senses went into overdrive that day," she said. "I remember it all. I have never had to relive that experience in a dream because it's so vivid when I'm awake. I replay parts of it every day in my mind."

Even with her incredible losses, however, Carrie never was angry with God. "I did go through a time of questioning, and came to understand that even if I had answers to all those questions, I would still miss my husband and friend."

Carrie's heart for the Muslim people also remains unchanged. "I still love them and desire that they come to know Christ," she said. "They were a loving people. Not all Muslims are terrorists. This is just a fallen world."

> "He who began a good work in you will carry it on to completion until the day of Christ Jesus." (Philippians 1:6)

She continues to heal and recover in the States, but she doesn't rule out one day returning to Iraq. "I still want to be involved in missions," Carrie said. "I want to encourage believers to be obedient to God's Word and share the gospel. That's what I'm doing now. But if God should ever show me he wants me to go overseas again, I'll be obedient."

In the meantime, she has written her story in *Facing Terror* (along with Kristen Billerbeck) and founded Carry On Ministries. The nonprofit organization seeks to help awaken the church to God's global purpose, to help ease the burdens of those who are serving among the nations, and to mobilize God's people to unity so that we might "stand firm in one spirit, with one mind, working side by side for the faith of the gospel."

Prayer:
Lord, show me how to use my own trials and sufferings to further your kingdom and give you honor and glory.

MAY 15

Here Am I, Send Me

Capt. Daniel Gade, U.S. Army, Iraq (2004-2005)

I COULD TELL when my superiors approached me that day that something was up. I was right.

"We have to send a bunch of guys from Korea to Iraq," my boss told me. "We know you're scheduled to change command in a few days, but we want to know if you want to go with your soldiers to Iraq or go with your family back to the States."

It was just two days before my wife Wendy and two-year-old daughter Anna Grace were scheduled to leave Korea and get our house settled for the next chapter of our lives. After handing over command of my tank company, I was to join them a couple weeks later and start grad school at Syracuse University in order to teach at my alma mater, West Point.

Plans change.

"Here am I Lord," I replied, "send me."

It was clear to me then that God didn't give me all the skills and abilities in order to turn my back on seventy-five guys who were counting on me and seek my own comfort in the academic life. My duty was to my soldiers.

Wendy cancelled her flight immediately to stay in Korea with me for the next two and a half months of training. During that time, we all flew to Colorado for a family reunion before the deployment to Iraq.

My parents, who I had not seen in two years, are strong believers and were as confident that God had called me to this mission as I was. My father, who served in the Viet Nam war, pulled me aside at one point for a crucial piece of advice.

> "Some trust in chariots and some in horses, but we trust in the name of the LORD our God." (Psalm 20:7)

"I want you to make a decision that whatever happens, you will not be bitter," he said.

Did he have some premonition that I didn't have? Or had he just seen too many soldiers respond with bitterness to the blows war dealt them? Taking Dad's advice turned out to be providential. I had no idea what God had in store for me, but I deliberately chose to trust his sovereignty no matter what.

Prayer:
Lord, help me trust you so completely that I will not be tempted to grow bitter over my own trials.

Welcome to Ramadi

Capt. Daniel Gade, U.S. Army, Iraq (2004-2005)

HOLY COW, *this place is really, really dangerous.* We didn't need to say it out loud—at the same moment, we were all thinking it.

Seven days after we took over our sector in Ramadi, Iraq, we suffered our first casualty. My roommate, Tyler Brown, was killed by a sniper on Sept. 14, 2004. Inside, I was crushed—Tyler was an amazing man of God with a bright future ahead of him—but as company commander with 120 guys looking to me for leadership, I couldn't let my grief interfere with my job performance.

Fast forward to Nov. 10, 2004. In an instant, the soldier riding one arm's length to my left in our tank was killed when a rocket-propelled grenade hit him in the face.

In America, when somebody dies, we take time to mourn. In Iraq, we have a memorial service for the fallen, and those

> "Now I know in part; then I shall know fully, even as I am fully known.
> (1 Corinthians 13:12b)

who can attend do, but we literally wash the blood out of the vehicle they were killed in, pack up their gear, send it off to next of kin, and go about our mission because we must. Most of the time, we swallow our tears and keep going. It's surreal.

As a Christian, those traumatic experiences affected me much differently than those who don't have strong faith. My own trial (and I couldn't have known then the trauma waiting for me two months later) is one little brushstroke of a really big painting God is creating. Most people think their story, their circumstance IS the painting. So for those people, when something horrible happens, when someone is killed, they lose a leg, or a wife gets sick, they have a tough time putting it into perspective.

During the months and years ahead, Wendy and I knew our situation was ultimately not about us. It's about God's plan, and whatever way that circumstance works into God's plan it's not something I should be moping about. I should be honored that God is choosing me for a dramatic part of his plan, even though it's painful.

Prayer:
Lord, even when I can't see the bigger picture,
help me to trust in your sovereign plan.

Reality Check

Wendy Gade, wife of Capt. Daniel Gade

WHAT DO you mean? I don't understand!" I stood in the Costco parking lot with my cell phone pressed to my ear, shaking my head as if that would clear the confusion away. Daniel had just called from Iraq and told me his roommate Tyler had been killed in action.

"No, no, no," I kept repeating, "It just can't be."

But it was—and at Daniel's request, I drove to Atlanta, two hours from where I had been living in Birmingham with my sister, to take his condolences to Tyler's family. I arrived just hours after they heard the news.

Will they be angry? I wondered as I rang the doorbell.

Tyler's brother opened the door and graciously escorted me through the crowd of friends and family already filling the house and introduced me to his parents.

> "For from him and through him and to him are all things. To him be the glory forever! Amen." (Romans 11:36)

They took me into another room and gathered Tyler's siblings and their spouses. Mrs. Brown just held my hands as I haltingly shared with them Daniel's condolences and offered to try to answer their questions from my limited information.

"Was there anyone else?" They wanted to know.

"No, he was the only one killed that day," I had to tell them. It was so difficult. It's hard to know your loved one was singled out, yet you're glad that no one else was killed.

Looking into Mrs. Brown's tear-stained face, my eyes were opened to a terrifying possibility. I thought to myself, *God allowed Tyler to go home, and this was a Christian man with great potential. He was a great leader. He had an opportunity to do something much grander and safer, and he chose to be with his soldiers—and he lost his life. God doesn't love Tyler's parents any less than he loves me. So just because Daniel loves God and loves us, and I really, really, really want him to be my husband and Anna Grace's daddy, I don't have any guarantee that that is God's plan.* It sent the message to my heart that this was about God's glory, not about us.

Prayer:
*Lord, show me how to use my present circumstances
to reflect your glory to those around me.*

Are My Legs OK?

Capt. Daniel Gade, U.S. Army, Iraq (2004-2005)

THIS COULDN'T *feel more dangerous than it does right now,* I thought, squinting into the desert sun.

The road we were driving on was elevated and right alongside of it was an irrigation canal. We were visible for a long way, no trees or buildings obscuring the view. I felt exposed to unseen attacks—but this was the road we had to take to reach the next sheik who we hoped would give us information on Al Qaeda whereabouts. I was in the front passenger seat while my driver kept driving.

> "Why, you do not even know what will happen tomorrow. What is your life? You are a mist that appears for a little while and then vanishes." (James 4:14)

The next thing I knew was that I was on my back in a ditch—just waking up. Somebody was screaming. I tried to go to whoever it was, but my soldiers pushed me back down on a stretcher where I had been unconscious for a few minutes.

"Relax sir," my soldier said, "you're the only one." They were already treating very massive wounds.

I'm the only one WHAT? I wondered.

Then it hit me. *I'm the only casualty.* My mind was very foggy, my vision blurred. Everything looked bright but sounds seemed far away. I was in shock.

When I lifted my head and looked past my feet, I saw the Humvee I had been riding in still on the road with its door blown open. The guys were working on my leg, my body armor was blown open, and I thought at the time that I could actually see my intestines. As it turns out I couldn't quite—but almost. My battalion executive officer (XO) was holding my hand talking to me—it's what one does with casualties.

"Are my legs okay?" I asked.

"You're going to be fine," was the response.

If you've ever watched any war movies, you know that "You're going to be fine," means "You're in really serious trouble." It's what you tell someone who's dying because you don't want them to panic; that just complicates the medical situation. That's when I knew it was pretty bad.

Prayer:
Lord, help me make the most of every day you grant me on this earth.

Our Most Severe Category

Wendy Gade, wife of Capt. Daniel Gade

IT WAS Jan. 10, 2005. I was on my way out the door to run an errand and my mom, who had been visiting from Atlanta, was about to head home.

Then the phone rang.

"Hello?" I answered.

"Good morning ma'am, this is Captain _____ from Ft. Carson. I need to inform you that your husband has been injured. I have a report to read to you."

Daniel had been injured once before so I was not alarmed yet. I thought, *Well he'll call me as soon as he can; this is probably a little more serious.*

"Broken bones and lacerations," the captain continued. "He's very seriously injured . . . I'm sorry to tell you this is our most severe category."

So that's when I understood. Daniel was hanging on to his life.

After jotting down some phone numbers, I hung up the phone and somehow, through the tears, strung the words together to tell my mom what I just learned. She fell on her knees and started praying immediately. Both of us got our church prayer chains going and I asked Patton, Daniel's brother, to relay the information to Daniel's family. All I could do then was pray.

Daniel had a fractured skull, a broken bone in the neck, and a massive wound from his sternum, across his groin to the right knee. Sitting in the humvee, the explosion came through the bottom of his right leg and

> "There is a time for everything, and a season for every activity under heaven: a time to be born and a time to die . . ."
> (Ecclesiastes 3:1-2a)

out the top of the same leg. Two fists could fit in the gaping hole of his leg. The abdominal wall on the front was stripped away; the skin and flesh were pushed to the side. An ice cream scoop-size of tissue had been carved out from inside his left thigh.

But I wouldn't know any of this until many agonizing hours later. Thoughts of Tyler's death came to mind. I trusted God, but I was not convinced he would choose to save Daniel's life.

Prayer:
*Lord, give me the desire and discipline to become
an active prayer warrior even before crisis hits.*

A Series of Miracles

Capt. Daniel Gade, U.S. Army, Iraq (2004-2005)

MY LIFE HUNG in the balance. One wrong move, a delayed decision or action from those in charge of my care, would have made my wife a twenty-nine-year-old widow and my daughter fatherless.

But a series of coincidences (or maybe miracles) saved my life that day.

First, as we were getting ready to leave to visit the sheiks that day. My medic, Sergeant Krause, asked to tag along with our convoy.

"Hey sir, I know I normally don't go out on missions with you but I feel like I should today," he said.

Then one of my superiors, the battalion executive officer (XO), also asked to come.

"I haven't been out with you in a while, and I'm bored," Major Cotton said.

After the blast, the medic ran up to me, took one look and said, "We need to get this guy on a helicopter." If they had taken me to the base "aid station" five kilometers away (normal procedure), I would have died in transit.

> "For he will command his angels concerning you to guard you in all your ways." (Psalm 91:11)

Because of his higher rank, the XO was able to call for a helicopter on a higher priority radio frequency in order to divert a helicopter that had already been in flight. So a helicopter arrived at the scene in five minutes instead of the usual thirty.

When the man who dispatched the helicopter heard that I, a stranger to him, needed to be picked up and was in really bad shape, he immediately sent an email to his home church in California. So within five minutes of the injury, Christians in California were praying for me at a time when I needed it most.

In the meantime, Sergeant Krause reached into the wound and applied direct pressure on the severed artery and vein. A tourniquet would have slipped into the wound and I would have bled to death on the scene.

When I heard the blades of the helicopter chopping the air above me I thought, "Oh thank God I'm saved," passed out and woke up three weeks later—out of a medically-induced coma—at Walter Reed Army Medical Center in Washington, D.C.

Prayer:
Lord, when you bless me with your care and provision, help me recognize it as your providence and not just a lucky break.

Bond of the Holy Spirit

Wendy Gade, wife of Capt. Daniel Gade

WHEN DANIEL arrived at the tent hospital thirty miles from the scene of the attack, surgeon Lt. Cdr. Lowell Chambers rushed him to the operating room, bypassing the emergency room, for a nine-hour surgery. It was another critical decision that was the difference between life and death for Daniel Gade.

During the course of Captain Gade's recovery, he sent a letter to Dr. Chambers to thank him for saving his life. The excerpts below are taken from Dr. Chambers' reply:

Daniel,

It's great to hear from you! We have been praying for you, Wendy, and Anna Grace multiple times each day since we had the privilege of caring for you on January 10.

During the course of [the surgery] I noted feeling an unusually strong bond with you. I feel a special bond with all the warriors God has given me the opportunity to care for but I felt it particularly strong in this case. After learning you are a Christian, I came to understand this was likely the Holy Spirit bearing witness that you were a fellow believer. At one point after we had done all we could surgically and were just trying to get you stabilized enough to transport, you transiently dropped your blood pressure and had some cardiac arrhythmias. There was nothing more for me to do surgically and as I asked CDR Narine (our senior anesthesiologist who did your

185

case) to give you some Epinephrine. I was so afraid we were going to fail you and your family (I noticed your wedding band) that it overwhelmed me and I just put my head down on your shoulder and wept and prayed for you. By the grace of God your arrhythmias stabilized, your BP came back up, and we were then able to transport you. . . .

> "The Lord is near. . . with thanksgiving, present your requests to God."
> (Philippians 4: 5b, 6b)

Thank you for the great sacrifice you and your family have made for our nation. Your example of courage and strength are inspiring and are a great witness to our Lord and Savior Jesus Christ. We are praying for you daily as you face the ongoing trials of rehabilitation. I count it the highest of honors to have been able to care for you.

Prayer:
Lord, thank you for granting me will and intellect, but help me never forget to bring my requests to you instead of trying to solve all things myself.

MAY 22

Heroines in Flight

Wendy Gade, wife of Capt. Daniel Gade

WHY ARE *we doing this? Why are we doing this?* The nurse said over and over in her mind as she looked at her watch. She had been stationed outside the tent hospital as the hours crawled by, waiting until Daniel stabilized so they could transport him to the Army hospital in Baghdad. *We could be working with someone else that has a better chance of survival,* she thought.

At last, he was ready to be moved. Her time had come, and she sprang into action. Another nurse volunteered to join her for the journey even though it wasn't her turn, and they took off into the sky with Daniel's life now in their hands.

Not long after, the helicopter came under attack. The aircraft shook and jerked away from enemy fire while the two nurses did what they could to keep Daniel as stable as possible. The ventilator that was doing Daniel's breathing for him stopped working, so one nurse had to hand-ventilate him while the other continued to administer his medicine. I'm not sure what they were giving him, but I know he needed it. Without that second set of hands from the nurse who volunteered, Daniel's life would have been snuffed out in transit.

> "Whatever you do, work at it with all your heart, as working for the Lord, not for men." (Colossians 3:23)

"I don't feel a pulse," said one nurse, looking up at the other. "Do you?" Neither of them could find it. The helicopter continued to rock violently, the roar of the rotors making it difficult to hear. They really didn't know if he was alive.

I can't believe the nurses didn't give up; I truly can't. But they just kept performing their duties as if he were alive—one hand-ventilating him and the other giving him the medicine—because they couldn't be sure.

Finally, they landed at the hospital in Baghdad. When they turned him over to the Army, the nurse said, "We have worked very hard. Please, you need to understand what we've put into this man. Now it's your turn," and handed him into their care.

Prayer:
Lord, help me always do my job to the best of my ability, even if I can't be sure of the outcome.

MAY 23

This Is Where We Start

Wendy Gade, wife of Capt. Daniel Gade

MY HEART was pounding. Three days had passed since Daniel had been injured, and I was about to see him for the first time at Walter Reed. Daniel's brother, Patton, prayed with me before we entered surgical ICU together.

Machines filled the room, with tubes going in and out of Daniel's body. He had just been checked out by his doctors at Walter Reed, and since they had not re-bandaged him yet, I was able to get a good look at the magnitude of his injuries. They had opened up his belly; it was just wide open. I had never seen anything like it.

Okay, all right, this is where we start, I thought. *This is where we are, what we're going to move forward from.*

I had a job to do: to support my husband and be the leader of the family while he recovered. I had to rise now because he needed me. I wasn't going to look back on it with regret, I was going to do the best I could. So that's where we started.

And it was a long road ahead. In Korea, he spent all his free time working out and trained his men to push themselves beyond their physical limits, too. Some of the guys thought he was crazy, but when Daniel was hit, everyone could see how being in good shape really helped his body. He had additional muscle and more blood.

> "But he said to me, 'My grace is sufficient for you, for my power is made perfect in weakness.'"
> (2 Corinthians 12:9a)

The body ate up his muscle to get energy. He went from being really strong and muscular to being so thin he couldn't even keep a ring on his finger. His cheeks were concave, his eyes almost looked too big for his face. We had shaved his head to be able to keep it clean easier, and the resulting appearance reminded me of pictures I had seen of prisoners in Auschwitz.

He was unbelievably thin and weak. For the first time since I had known him, he was helpless, but I knew he was going to make it. And in the meantime, I braced myself for what would be required of me—calling on prayer and God's strength to be my support.

Prayer:
Lord, use my weaknesses to prove your strength and receive the glory.

Waking Up to Change

Capt. Daniel Gade, U.S. Army, Iraq (2004-2005)

WHEN I became conscious again, my leg was gone. But I was alive.

A week after the injury, my right leg was decomposing so quickly that my body had become septic and I was crashing. The doctor was terrified I was going to die so he made a decision: it was either my leg or my life.

As soon as they took my leg, my vitals began to improve. But I was in a precarious position for many weeks to come.

In the first two months following the injury, I had received more than one hundred and twenty units of blood (the human body has about ten to twelve units of blood), and I had undergone about thirty-five surgeries. Kidney and liver failure plagued me, too. I was so messed up that it took me a while before I was even ready to start physical therapy. My abdomen was still open for a long time—the doctors at the initial trauma station had opened it to visually inspect all the organs and make sure no little piece of shrapnel had nicked anything.

> "When times are good, be happy; but when times are bad, consider: God has made the one as well as the other."
> (Ecclesiastes 7:14)

So it was at least two months after I got hurt that I could even sit up. It took three people to move me to the chair with all the tubes and wires. I sat for ten minutes and was in total agony.

The recovery process seemed really drawn out, punctuated with ups and downs. At first I was just thrilled to be alive—thrilled that my genitals were intact, that I could still be a dad and a husband, be functional. So I went from that elation to trying to cope with the exact level of my disability. *How bad is it? How bad is it going to stay? How good is it going to get?*

Throughout the recovery process, my dad's advice came back to me. I had decided not to become bitter before I ever landed on Iraqi soil. I was determined to stay true to that resolve, to remember that my circumstance was just one brushstroke in a masterpiece God was creating.

Prayer:
Lord, grow my desire to glorify you so much that I will be content with both good times and bad as long as you are honored.

189

I Have Training to Do

Wendy Gade, wife of Capt. Daniel Gade

LET ME GET that for you," my father-in-law said as he reached to adjust the hospital bed for Daniel. We all wanted him to be as comfortable as possible while he was Walter Reed.

I'll never forget Daniel's response.

"No," he said, looking at each of us hovering over him. "Actually, you all need to leave. I have training to do." He was just determined to figure out how to do these things on his own, including operating his mechanical bed.

Another time, a nurse asked him, "What would you prefer, your head to be up or down, or your feet . . . ?"

And he said, "What is the optimal position for healing?" In other words, don't ask me what I want, tell me what is going to get me better and out of here. He was very determined that he was not going to be enabled. He was going to be Daniel.

We laugh at these stories in our family because it was such a relief to see his trademark "can-do" attitude shining through again. The insurgents could take his leg, but not his faith, his personality, his dry wit. He was going to continue.

> "Forgetting what is behind and straining toward what is ahead, I press on toward the goal to win the prize for which God has called me heavenward in Christ Jesus."
> (Philippians 3:13b, 14)

That's not to say there weren't hard days. There weren't lots of them in terms of being totally discouraged. There were a lot of painful days. I can only think of one day where the hope was truly needing to be replenished. For him, many of the days just felt like the movie, *Groundhog Day*—the same thing over and over again.

But, as Daniel has said: "I had a personal mission. I wanted to get on with my life, and I didn't feel like I had time to sit around moping. I don't ever wake up in the middle of the night and think, 'Wow I'm really glad that happened to me,' but I'm not feeling sorry for myself either. It's just what God's plan is for our family."

Prayer:
Lord, whatever task is ahead of me, give me the strength and determination to do it well.

A New Normal

Capt. Daniel Gade, U.S. Army, Iraq (2004–2005)

THE INSURGENT attack January 10, 2005, and the ensuing recovery period began a new chapter in the life of our family. All in all, I was an inpatient for four months, then spent another six months as an outpatient, learning to walk again with a prosthetic.

If you saw me today, you wouldn't see that I had lost a leg. You wouldn't see me running any marathons, but you'd see me cooking dinner while Wendy runs errands, or studying for my doctorate program at the University of Georgia as I prepare to return to West Point as a professor. You'd see Wendy and me juggling twins, born in June 2008 (on our ninth anniversary), or caring for Anna Grace, now six years old. This is our new normal day.

> "Everyone who is called by my name . . . I created for my glory." (Isaiah 43:7)

We have seen God work directly in our lives in ways that many people haven't had the opportunity to. This whole story is for a purpose, and the lesson is that life isn't about us, as individuals. God has a plan which will take place one way or another, and our lives are about trying to match our actions to his will. He will do whatever it takes to get us where he wants us to be. Self-pity has no part in the plan, nor does selfishness or arrogance; all those things are the result of not understanding where we fit in the plan.

Wendy had a sense from very early on in this story that God was going to use this experience to grow our faith. She thought certainly, that it would grow her faith, mine, and our family's—but God didn't stop there. For example, Patton had set up a web site to post updates on my condition and allow others to leave comments. By visiting that site, other people were being brought back into a desire to pray and to reconnect with God. God used the situation to witness to people across the world who we didn't even know. Seeing God work in such a direct and dramatic way has taught us that, essentially, our lives are to bring glory to God, not to ourselves.

Prayer:
Lord, use my life to bring you glory.

This Is My Calling

Deborah Johns, Blue Star Mom, Director of
Military Relations for Move Forward America

I WANTED MY seventeen-year-old son, William, to enroll in college—not the military. But he had other plans.

When I began getting phone calls from military recruiters, I was furious. They needed me to come to the recruiting office and sign a consent form, they said, because he wasn't eighteen yet.

"I don't want to discuss it," I told one recruiter on the phone, "and if you call me again I'll call my Congressman and report you!"

Months passed, and soon it was Christmas vacation. When William suggested we go for a drive together one day, I happily went.

Two and a half miles later, we were at the front door of the U.S. Marine Corps recruiting office. I was speechless. There was such silence between us you could cut it with a knife.

When we entered the office, the staff sergeant stood up and introduced himself to me. "Is there anything I can get you?" he asked me.

"A stiff drink would be nice." I was only half-joking.

The staff sergeant explained they needed my signature so William could be in a delayed entry program and put on the schedule so when he finished high school he would go to boot camp. I looked at my son, still so young.

> "Therefore put on the full armor of God, so that when the day of evil comes, you may be able to stand your ground."
> (Ephesians 6:13a)

"This is what I want to do; this is my calling," William said.

"You know if I sign you into the Marines, you are probably going to go to war."

"I know Mom, but I want to serve my country. This is what I want to do."

I signed him in. "But you're going into intelligence, not infantry," I said.

He signed up for infantry.

William graduated from boot camp as expert rifleman and was at the top of class. I was so proud of him. When you go to their graduation ceremony, it's indescribable the admiration you have for these young men.

This time I cried tears of joy, knowing my son was achieving something very special in order to serve our country.

Prayer:
*Lord, help me train and prepare myself for the
situations that lie ahead of me.*

Mother's Day Gift

*Deborah Johns, Blue Star Mom, Director of
Military Relations for Move Forward America*

NO SOONER did my son graduate from boot camp than we were notified he would be deployed to Iraq. I knew this moment was coming, but I still wasn't ready for it.

In early March, all the military moms and wives in our area got phone calls from our men.

"Pray for us," said William. "I don't know when we'll talk again."

About a week later, the war officially began. I'll never forget it—the war started on William's nineteenth birthday. Then it was four months—112 days—without any communication. I searched for every broadcast there might be, looking for a glimpse of my son or information about his unit. For long stretches of time I was just glued to the TV because I didn't want to miss something. It was so unbelievably difficult.

When the first casualties list came out on April 7, 2003, it was devastating. You grieve for the families who have lost their sons or daughters and plead with God you won't be next. It takes your breath away. You are literally gripped to see any pictures on TV, to get any news reports. You're starved for some assurance. You don't want to leave home

> "Trust in the LORD with all your heart and lean not on your own understanding."
> (Proverbs 3:5)

because you don't want to come back and see a black sedan waiting for you. Every time there's a knock on the door, your stomach drops to the floor.

Then Mother's Day came. And while I obviously would have preferred to have my son with me on that day, I did receive a very powerful gift. I was watching the right news broadcast at the right time.

193

"I just talked to a Marine who just had his nineteenth birthday the day the war started," the reporter said. My heart skipped a beat. "Just last year around this time he was going to his senior prom." While he didn't say his name and I never saw him on that television screen, it was enough. I knew that was William, and now I knew he was alive. My son was still okay.

Prayer:
Lord, help me not base my confidence on my own understanding when I should be trusting you instead.

Finding Support

Deborah Johns, Blue Star Mom, Director of Military Relations for Move Forward America

THERE WAS no local support group in place, so some other women and I started one for Marine moms. They came from all over to meet together. Everyone brought pictures of their sons and we made buttons with those pictures that we wore every day. We read letters from our sons, said the pledge, hugged, and cried together.

We had lunch at a restaurant situated on a river in Old Sacramento. At the end of lunch, we each took a yellow rose to the river bank as a way of remembering our sons in a special way.

"Corporal William Johns, Fallujah, Iraq: God bless you. I love you. Come home safe," I said, and threw the rose into the river. Each mother did the same thing, saying her son's name, where he was deployed, and said a little message. We did this for ourselves, but people at the restaurant stood up and applauded.

> "The God of all comfort . . . comforts us in all our troubles, so that we can comfort those in any trouble with the comfort we ourselves have received from God."
> (2 Corinthians 1:3b–4)

I also started a national group called Marine Moms that puts together a Condolence Book for every family who loses a loved one in the war. If someone from Idaho is killed, a Marine Mom from the area will collect cards from across the country, put them in the Condolence Book, and present it to the family at the funeral.

There's a special bond military families have—we understand each other in a way no one else can. We pray for one another every day and help the moms with kids about to go on their first deployments. We extend grace to each other. We know we can cry without having to explain why. We all know.

Besides the support of other military families, my faith in God has gotten me through so much. If God chose to redeploy William to heaven, that's God's choice, and not something I have control over. So God alone just gave me a lot of peace and comfort, knowing that whatever happened was God's decision. I know if he dies, we will see each other again in heaven. I just can't go through a day without thanking God for all he has done for me.

Prayer:
Father, help me use the trials in my life to counsel and comfort others.

MAY 30

Looking for William

Deborah Johns, Blue Star Mom, Director of Military Relations for Move Forward America

WHEN THE time came for William to come home, we decorated our car and made signs to celebrate: *Welcome home! We love you!* When the day finally arrived, my two younger sons and I drove to Camp Pendleton in San Diego to pick him up.

We watched with mounting excitement as a busload of Marines came in. Parade vehicles, flags, and yellow ribbons surrounded us. Marines reunited with their families as people cheered and cried with band music blaring in the background. Scanning the crowd over and over, we couldn't find William.

"Excuse me," I approached a sergeant. "Where's Will Johns? Isn't he here?"

The sergeant found a captain to ask. "This is Corporal Johns' mom. Can you tell me where he is?" he said. The captain looked blankly at me. Then it looked like something clicked in his brain.

"Oh my God, you didn't get the notification? Your son chose to stay behind for another three months so a married Marine could come home."

"Well, that's very nice of him to do," I said as calmly as I could." "Do you think you could arrange for him to call home so I could tell him I love him?"

"Yes ma'am, I'll make that happen for you by tomorrow."

So we packed up our welcome home signs, fresh baked cookies, got in the car, and drove home bawling our heads off. We were devastated.

> We know that suffering produces perseverance; perseverance, character; and character, hope."
> (Romans 53b–4)

Then in July, we went through the same routine, had the car painted, made signs, baked cookies. When we got to Camp Pendleton, I saw the same sergeant, captain, and chaplain who I had spoken with last time.

"Well gentlemen," I said, "I hope for the sake of all three of you, that William Johns is on that bus today." All three of the men marched up the hill to where the Marines were checking their weapons and each one asked for Johns. Marching back down shoulder to shoulder, they said, "We're happy to report that your son is in the armory."

This time, I cried tears of relief.

Prayer:
*Lord, turn my suffering into a stronger character;
fill me with hope for tomorrow.*

MAY 31

These Colors Don't Run

Deborah Johns, Blue Star Mom, Director of Military Relations for Move Forward America

MOM, DON'T they know we're doing a good thing over here?" William asked me over the phone during his second deployment to Iraq. Negative rhetoric about the war was spreading fast, and Cindy Sheehan had become an internationally known figure for her anti-war camp at President Bush's ranch in Crawford, Texas. "Please don't let us come home to what the Viet Nam vets faced," William continued. "Please tell them the good stuff."

"The press says it's all terrible, William. So tell me the good stuff."

And he did. That's when I got on radio stations and I began to tell their stories of progress, reconstruction, and hope, because the soldiers themselves were not allowed to. I made it clear in more than five hundred interviews that what Cindy Sheehan spoke negatively about military families—she was dead wrong. She didn't speak for all of us. Besides radio stations in the United States, I added my voice to the airwaves of the BBC, as well as stations in France, Germany, and Australia.

> "Act with courage, and may the Lord be with those who do well."
> (2 Chronicles 19:11b)

I had May 22 designated as Yellow Ribbon Day in California, and was the spokesperson for the bus tour called "You Don't Speak for Me Cindy," that crossed the nation and ended in a pro-troop rally in Crawford, Texas. Ten thousand people showed up outside the president's ranch to demonstrate support for the troops.

A year later, our second national bus tour was called "These Colors Don't Run" and showed support for General Petreaus and the troops. Another tour to honor heroes during the holidays collected 150,000 cards to send to troops. In all, we've rallied support with five national bus tours so far.

William and I have both come a long way from that bleak winter day at the recruiting office. He has completed three deployments in Iraq, and I am Director of Military Relations for Move America Forward, a non-profit organization supporting America's troops and their efforts to defeat terrorism. With the Lord's help, I found a way to not just survive my son's deployments, but to take an active role supporting him and other soldiers risking their lives for freedom.

Prayer:
Lord, take my fear and turn it into courage so I may serve you boldly.

Beginning at the End

Donna A. Tallman, daughter of a U.S. Air Force officer, screenwriter, regular contributor to The Christian Post

WHERE IS *John F. Kennedy's grave? What do OEF and OIF mean on a headstone? Where's the bathroom? Who's the oldest dead person buried here?*

A woman, who has answered the same questions for more than a lifetime, sits at a kiosk in the middle of the Arlington National Cemetery Visitor's Center patiently answering every question as if it's the first time she has heard it. People scramble about, filling water bottles, snagging tourist trinkets from the gift shop, and taking pictures . . . lots of pictures.

I take none. I'm not here to capture or preserve history; I'm here to experience it. Shortly after returning from our tour of duty in Spain in 1968, my family and I went to Arlington. We made the traditional loop up to the Kennedy graves where I saw carved in stone the reality of Senator Kennedy's assassination. That was almost forty years ago, and I have returned now as an adult, a grown up Air Force brat, a mother of three young men, a patriot.

> "'For I know the plans I have for you,' declares the LORD, 'plans to prosper you and not to harm you, plans to give you hope and a future.'"
> (Jeremiah 29:11)

A squad of uniformed military cadets enters through the southern door. The sea of people parts, and the corridor opens before the squad. The cadets walk smartly, heads up high, heels clicking on the highly polished floor, not one wrinkle among them. The squad never breaks stride in their cadence; nor bead of sweat on their brows, despite summer's oppressive heat. A holy hush follows them. They have come to Arlington to begin at the end.

In search of my own pilgrimage through America's history, I leave the majority of tourists behind and turn toward today's history found in Section 60. This section has been set aside for the soldiers of the Iraq and Afghanistan wars.

As I walk the empty access road, I am immediately engulfed by silence. Except for a lone gardener, I see no one. On this visit, I want to do more than travel through Arlington. I was not raised to be an American *tourist* who enjoys the benefits of liberty, but lives disconnected from the soldiers who have secured it. I want a commission.

Prayer:
Lord, make me an ambassador of hope to the soldiers who serve on the front lines of America's wars and to their families who await their safe return.

JUNE 2

Free Because of Sacrifice

Donna A. Tallman, daughter of a U.S. Air Force officer, screenwriter, regular contributor to **The Christian Post**

STEP BY determined step I walk on through Arlington Cemetery. A car passes on my left, then another and another. The procession of mourners drives by in slow motion making its way to the grave site. A color guard stands at attention near a freshly dug grave. A bugler waits for his call, and a squad of seven riflemen stands across the field for their moment of tribute. Cicadas hum just below the surface of unspeakable grief.

I hurry under a tree, not suitably dressed for a funeral nor invited by the family; but here by circumstance in my nation's field of honor. He is my soldier.

> "Greater love has no one than this, that he lay down his life for his friends." (John 15:13)

Beautiful in its simplicity, the military funeral proceeds with expected precision. A minister addresses the young crowd of mourners. The flag covering the soldier's coffin is folded and given to today's grieving widow whose two restless toddlers squirm next to her. She bows her head in anguished respect—uncertain the nation is truly grateful for her sacrifice, but so very proud of the hero her husband is. The riflemen give a twenty-one gun salute matched by twenty-one unexpected echoes from another burial in progress on the cemetery grounds. The shots of honor reverberate back and forth across the valley as if to emphasize the sobering cost of freedom.

The cicadas pick up their song again whirring louder and louder until I feel them pounding in my ears. Looking up through the tree, I see a helicopter has joined their cacophony giving tribute to this fallen hero. The bugler closes with the mournful notes of *"Taps,"* hanging onto the last note until it slowly dissolves into history.

The crowd disperses while I wait under the tree. Stillness returns. Slowly, I begin to walk the uniform rows of gravestones. The magnitude of what we have asked of our soldiers and the grief these families are going through comes quickly into focus. I realize that for the first time ever, I am standing in the graveyard of a war in progress.

Prayer:
Father, remind me that liberty never travels without its companion, sacrifice, and that sacrifice never travels without love. When I am tempted to forget the sacrifices of others on my behalf, remind me that even You paid the ultimate price for my freedom— the life of your only Son because You loved me.

JUNE 3

Yesterday's Widow

Donna A. Tallman, daughter of a U.S. Air Force officer, screenwriter, regular contributor to **The Christian Post**

A CAISSON moves by, and I leave to follow it to the next funeral. Just across the road a sign reads, "Section 61." It is a massive parcel of uncultivated dirt growing only two lone trees. As I wonder why an empty lot sits nearby, the top of the Washington Monument peeks above the small rise holding its breath, waiting for my realization.

"O God, the next war!"

I steady myself as waves of grief overtake me. Before I know it, I have taken out my camera, and am taking pictures so I never forget their sacrifice. I walk by the headstones of many highly decorated service members. There is a middle-age grandmother, a Marine who loves the Boston Red Sox, a team of five soldiers, and a grave marker for a Muslim. I stop to pray for these families and weep for their loss.

The cadre of mourners attending the earlier service has mostly disappeared. In its place a non-organized yet subconsciously synchronized, convoy of mini vans arrives. A woman gets out of her van, grabs a blanket, lawn chair, and a jug of water before slamming the door. Mounted on the back of her car is a sticker that reads, "Half my heart is in Heaven."

Another minivan arrives, and another. Each van carries a single woman armed with grief and memories.

Her home has betrayed her. It is no longer full of the life and hope of her husband's return, so she escapes to Arlington to reflect. The widow comes to say the things that she cannot say at home . . . to utter aloud the unspeakable agony of her heart. Surrounded by a field of dead strangers, the widow now feels more at home in a cemetery than she does in her own house. She is tired. She is lonely. She is broken.

> "He gives strength to the weary and increases the power of the weak." (Isaiah 40:29)

In the waning afternoon hours of what has become a typical day, the widow lies face down over her husband's grave aching to hold and be held. She whispers a prayer of surrender, and asks for the strength for just one more day. Despite the challenges she knows await her, yesterday's widow rises to conquer her own battle—the battle for her future.

Prayer:
*Lord, when I have expended all that I have, remind me
that your resources are limitless and you eagerly
desire to add your strength to my faith.*

JUNE 4

The Great Equalizer

*Donna A. Tallman, daughter of a U.S. Air Force officer,
screenwriter, regular contributor to* The Christian Post

GENTLY AND quietly he clicks the door shut on his sedan so that even the breeze is unruffled. He deliberately walks toward the oldest row of graves in Section 60. His perfect posture looks military-trained, while the lines on his face mark him as Vietnam era. Always focused forward, the eyes of the man in his sixties hone in on one of the markers at the far end. Finally, he reaches the right one and slowly kneels in the grass. The grieving father bows his head.

Some have said that hospital waiting rooms are the great equalizers of life—that injury and sickness recognize no social class, no ethnic divide, no age category. All are equally at risk. Cemeteries are even more equalizing than waiting rooms. None recover here.

The father does not tarry long at his son's grave. He's not really here to visit him. Instead, he has come to care for the living. While no one else dares interrupt a widow's vigil out of respect for her grief, the father does. This tender, caring man can approach where others never should. He is a fellow sufferer, a tempest traveler . . . one who knows firsthand the cost of war.

The father begins his rounds of visitation to the daughters he has adopted in the grave-yard. He knows each one by name and checks on their welfare. Over the months they have all visited Arlington to grieve alone together; this unlikely group has grown from being intimate strangers among the tombstones to caretakers of one another's sorrow.

> "He heals the broken-hearted and binds up their wounds." (Psalm 147:3)

While he knows that he cannot bring his son home from Afghanistan, the father seeks to heal the history that death attempts to write in each of their hearts. Rising above his own agony, he reaches out to care for those around him, and in the process, finds refuge for his own soul.

Yes, Arlington is a graveyard, a place of the dead. It is also a show-case for valor, a field of honor for America's most courageous soldiers. And for those knit together by the Iraq and Afghanistan wars, Arlington is a place of healing from war's ultimate sacrifice.

Prayer:
When life's raging tempest threatens to break my heart and my spirit, would you, oh Lord, step in with your authority and restore calm to the churning waves around me? Deliver me and bind up any wounds incurred by my sojourn here on earth.

Do I Make You Proud?

Donna A. Tallman, daughter of a U.S. Air Force officer, screenwriter, regular contributor to **The Christian Post**

AN ARMY soldier approaches the row ahead of mine. I try to main-tain my composure as to not disturb his expression of grief, but my tears come faster than I can breathe. The soldier kneels to pray. After a moment, he stands, salutes, and puts something on top of the grave marker. The soldier leaves quietly, returns; then leaves again. I stand motionless and uncertain sensing he may want to talk, but hesitant to interrupt. He comes one more time, so I join him.

"Was he a friend of yours?" I ask.

"Yes Ma'am, he was."

"Would you tell me about your friend?"

He and the corporal were close friends. They served together in Iraq and Afghanistan. The soldier before me had been deployed overseas six times, and was struggling with the loss of many friends. I met him saluting his friend who died in 2005, but he was here for another friend whose graveside service I just witnessed. That friend was a medic, trained to work on injured soldiers while in transit on helicopters.

> "Have I not commanded you.? Be strong and courageous. Do not be terrified; do not be discouraged, for the LORD your God will be with you wherever you go." (Joshua 1:9)

"Ah, the helicopter fly-over was for him."

"Yes Ma'am."

"What can we do for you?"

"Bring us home, Ma'am. Please, bring us all the way home."

We stand together in silence for a long time, two total strangers connected by the intimacy of honor. His countenance is beautiful. In spite of his grief, in spite of the horror he has seen—he is beautiful. As soon as he leaves, I regret not getting his name. I wish I'd been able to listen to his story. I wished I'd prayed with him. I wish I'd prayed for his healing. I also wish I had told him how proud I am of him and the many sacrifices he's made for my freedom. How I wish I had told him . . . but I didn't.

Several minutes later, I pick up the piece of metal he left on top of his friend's gravestone. It's a dog tag. It has an American flag on one side and the words to Joshua 1:9 on the other side.

Prayer:
Thank you, Lord, that this soldier has confronted terrorism first-hand so that I never have to. Bring rest to his spirit, Lord, and remove any terror that has taken up residence in his heart.

The Smallest Patient

*Colonel Jay A. Johannigman, Deputy Commander
of the 332nd U.S. Air Force EMEDS
(Expeditionary Medical Support), Iraq, 2003*

ALL RIGHT, WHAT *do we have here?* I wondered as I opened the back doors of the Red Crescent (Iraqi) ambulance. It was a nine-year-old Iraqi boy who had been wounded almost nine days earlier by unwittingly picking up an anti-personnel device. Iraqi surgeons did the best they could for Saleh, but told his father to prepare for his death. The boy's father bribed a friend who was a Red Crescent ambulance driver to drive his son to our base for another chance.

Once inside the hospital, we were horrified to see that his abdominal wall had been completely blown away, exposing the intestinal tract. His right arm which he had lost in the initial blast had not been treated in nine days; it had been bandaged once and it was covered in blood and pus from his draining wounds. The portion of his remaining left hand was mangled almost beyond recognition.

> "If you believe, you will receive whatever you ask for in prayer."
> (Matthew 21:22)

The Air Force medics and I operated on him nine hours that first day. *God show me the way*, was whispering in my head over and over. By the grace of God, he began to stabilize.

As a military medical corps, we were not designed to care for pediatric patients, but we arranged for some materials from our army brethren in Baghdad. Every day I emailed a pediatric surgeon friend for advice, and she arranged for a company in Britain to overnight express us all the equipment necessary to do what's called a wound vac.

This boy, Saleh, had just one hand left that was salvageable.

"If we take this other hand what kind of a life would he have left?" the orthopedic surgeon mused.

"Tell you what, Eric," I replied. "If I can figure out a way to keep his belly together, you figure out some way to keep that left hand on him." So that was a pledge. Eric had never reconstructed a hand, but he got on the Internet and started working and pinning and cleaning. Every time we were back there cleaning Saleh's belly, he was back there doing something he'd never been trained to do, but somehow this all worked out. We prayed a lot. One nice thing about a deployed base—the chapel is always open and the lights are on.

Prayer:
*Lord, give me the courage to overcome obstacles
to achieve the things you want me to.*

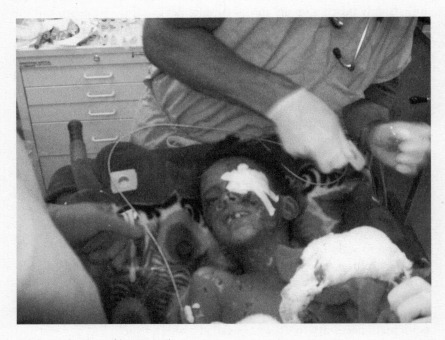

Saleh on the day of his arrival

Modern Medicine or the Hand of God?

Colonel. Jay A. Johannigman, Deputy Commander
of the 332nd U.S. Air Force EMEDS
(Expeditionary Medical Support), Iraq, 2003

TWO CHAPLAINS in particular prayed with us every day (Chappy Erikson and Thiesen), for which I was so grateful. As a deployed doc, the hospital is your chapel and God is everywhere with us. The chaplains were truly amazing—they helped get patients off the helicopter, ran blood back and forth, lifted patients onto the ambulance, said prayers at the sides of those soldiers we don't send back home. They were in the ICU as much for us as for our patients. And they certainly lifted us up as we worked on Saleh. They even held special prayer services for him.

> "For where two or three come together in my name, there am I with them."
> (Matthew 18:20)

It was amazing to see how the base was transformed with Saleh's arrival. We saw our soldiers, airmen, cooks, Security Forces, and our commanders come through and just lift the flap on the ICU tent to make sure Saleh was still there.

Throughout Saleh's stay with us, the entire hospital took care of that boy as we would our own son. But on his fifth post-operative day, Saleh was bleeding to death from his stomach. I had run out of medical options and I asked nurses to find the Chappy fast.

"Chappy Erikson, I have nothing left I can do." I said. "I've done all I can, I'm going to lose this kid. Will you come over and say a prayer?"

And Chappy did. He laid hands on this young man and lifted him up in prayer while Saleh was screaming and crying in Arabic, and his father was saying his prayers as a devout Muslim. All of us medics were standing there watching, crying—and when that happened that young man stopped bleeding. Was it medicine or God's hand? I know what it was. There was no more medicine to offer him. God spared his life that day.

Prayer:
Lord, let me never dismiss the power of praying with other believers.

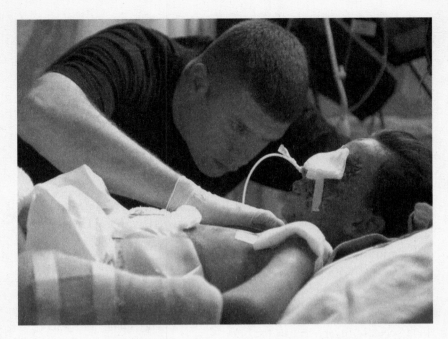

A USAF nurse caring for Saleh—the intensity needs no explanation

Just One Shot

Colonel Jay A. Johannigman, Deputy Commander of the 332nd U.S. Air Force EMEDS (Expeditionary Medical Support), Iraq (2003)

SALEH HAD done remarkably well under our care, but for a full recovery, this young man only had one shot, and that was to get him to the United States. Just as it is now, it was extremely controversial to do that—to take an Iraqi child, because "if you take one you have to take them all." I understand the politics of all that, but I was early in my experience. I told the boss that this young kid had to go to the United States.

If I had known then what I know now about how hard that was to accomplish, I would have given up a long time ago. But we didn't. We worked some back channels and were given some miracles. We got Saleh cleared to get on a C-130. The same anesthesiologist who was my first assistant was going to rotate home to California at the same time, and we found a pediatric hospital in Oakland who was willing to take care of him. So the anesthesiologist flew with this young man thirty-six hours all on Air Force aircraft.

Six-months later, my young friend Saleh was discharged from Oakland's Children's Hospital. They gave him all the care in the world without a penny being charged to him. I have a picture of Saleh and his cell phone. I know it works because I'm on his speed dial. And he will call me up. That was three years ago.

> "Be joyful in hope, patient in affliction, faithful in prayer." (Romans 12:12)

Today, he lives in Oakland, California. He has been mainstreamed, is in the sixth grade of a public school. He goes to school every day and his dad works in the hospital that has cared for him. They are both very grateful for what God has given them. This kid has got a resilient spirit that you would not believe.

Prayer:
Lord, when you show me the path to take, may I obediently respond no matter how impossible it may seem.

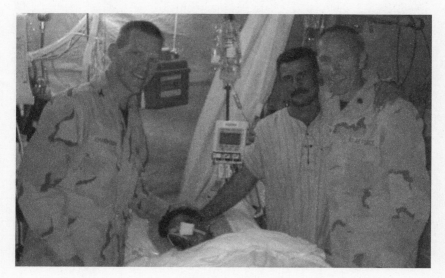

Chaplain Erikson with Saleh, his father Raheem, and Dr. Jay Johannigman

Last moments in Iraq—a prayer to God for a safe journey to the United States

Young Saleh with his American friends (courtesy of the *San Francisco Chronicle*)

Ninety Minutes

Colonel Jay A. Johannigman, Deputy Commander of the 332nd U.S. Air Force EMEDS (Expeditionary Medical Support), Iraq, 2003

MY GOD, this kid's in shock," the medic said after taking one look at a Marine corporal who had been hit with an IED.

"Sir, I've been in shock for the last hour and a half," that Marine responded. He then rolled his eyes to the back of his head and his heart promptly stopped. He went into cardiac arrest right there in front of those guys.

Immediately, they opened his chest and did something they never would have done in the United States. They pounded on his chest for more than ninety minutes. They did not give up. We stop in the United States after ten minutes. Ten minutes of that and if you don't have him back, that patient's dead. Those Marine doctors and medics worked on him for ninety minutes and they got him back. I don't know how they did that.

Then they packaged him up, said, "We've done everything we can, we're out of blood, out of juice, we're shipping him to you. Take good care of him." So that medical team sent him to our facility.

> "If any of you lacks wisdom, he should ask God, who gives generously to all without finding fault, and it will be given to him." (James 1:5)

He arrived at about six a.m. on a Sunday morning, an hour and a half before I started my shift. I walked into the room at seven thirty and it was eerily silent. Two of our surgeons were just passed out on the couches, still with blood on their clothes.

"What's going on?" I woke one of them up to ask.

"We got this kid last night and already put 110 units of blood into him," he said, "and I don't think we're going to save him."

So we walked over to the ICU to take a look at the patient together. The young surgeon was tormented. Sometimes we know we won't save a casualty and we have more coming in . . . so do we keep trying or are we kidding ourselves? After putting so much work and time, would we even have a patient that's salvageable?

Prayer:
Lord, when I am overwhelmed with tough decisions,
give me wisdom so I can see clearly which direction to pursue.

Father's Day

Colonel Jay A. Johannigman, Deputy Commander of the 332nd U.S. Air Force EMEDS (Expeditionary Medical Support), Iraq, 2003

WE ARRIVED at the Marine's bedside and found him asleep. The rhythmic sound of his breathing machine was a quiet but sobering reminder of just how fragile his life was at the moment.

"John, are you OK?" Andy, my colleague surgeon, grabbed him by the hand. This young Marine nodded his head.

"John, give me a thumbs up." With his one remaining arm, John gave a thumbs up.

We looked at each other and said, "Well, we're going to press forward. We're not going to give up on him." He was still bleeding, so we took him back to the operating room to wash out his wounds the best we could. We threw everything including the kitchen sink at him to try to make him stop bleeding. The chaplain was there every moment with us praying with us to give us the courage to do these kinds of things.

"As you know, we consider blessed those who have persevered." (James 5:11a)

It was Father's Day. Those of us who were fathers said we're not going to have his father remember Father's Day as the day he lost his son.

We didn't have enough stored blood for him, so we had soldiers lined up around the tent waiting to donate their blood for this young man because we were not going to lose him on Father's Day. He ended up needing 248 units of whole blood, but he survived Father's Day.

Thankfully, we were able to get him stabilized, packaged up, and flown to Germany. From there he made it back to Brook Army Medical Center in Fort Sam Houston, Texas, where his family joined him.

Unfortunately, in the third month of his recovery, he developed a severe infection that he was not able to recover from. So he passed away, but he did so with his family at his side, as God intended.

Prayer:
Lord, give me the strength to persevere to the best of my ability and leave the results up to you.

The Bigger Picture

*Carol Pinkerton-Ewens, mother of a fallen soldier
and three other army soldiers*

WE HAVE given the Army all four of our sons. Forrest died in the war already, and Oaken is fulfilling years of service as a West Point graduate. If I lose Oaken also, I not only lose him but also lose another part of Forrest, as they were identical twins. Our younger son Elisha had already served one year in Iraq, several months in Afghanistan and faces deployment again as will Oaken. Stephen enlisted into the Regular Army-Infantry shortly after Forrest was killed.

I remember when Eli was deployed, and how hard it was for me to face that he was going into an environment where other people would be trying to kill him. My sweet boy, who had never done anything to anyone, would be suddenly the unmarked, unknown evil occupier.

But my fears have never been limited to physical harm. I also feared for my son that his outlook towards this segment of humanity would become desensitized. I feared that the army would create an environment of survival which would breed dehumanization and Eli would look at the Iraqis as less than human. My greatest fear was probably that my sons would come home with their hearts hardened and changed, and unable to see God's essence in other people. I feared more for their spiritual health than their physical, as I believed their spiritual health is most vital to their physical health.

> "As the heavens are higher than the earth, so are my ways higher than your ways and my thoughts than your thoughts." (Isaiah 55:9)

I have a deep, simple faith that God has a plan for each of our lives and that our lives influence others in so many ways. I believe in what I call the "ripple effect," that you have the power to touch other's lives by the even simplest things you do. I believe that we have the potential for eternal effect, just like the ripples on a pond are initiated by a pebble being thrown in the water, and starts a concentric circle of movement that in turn will have impact elsewhere.

So during these times of deployments, my faith rested on the concept that God was using my children in a way that I may not be able to truly understand, but that God sees the ripples and eternal effect on the larger pond. I held onto this thought, trusting that God has his eyes on the bigger picture.

Prayer:
*Lord, when only being able to see parts of the whole throws
me into confusion, help me trust in your master plan.*

JUNE 12

A Mother's Prayer

Carol Pinkerton-Ewens

I'LL NEVER forget the day Elisha, not yet twenty-one years old, left for Iraq. Once he was on his way, I wrote these thoughts and prayer to the Lord, which I have continued to pray for each of my sons:

January 23, 2004

I watched Eli leave today, held him in my arms for the last time until we meet again, either in another year, or in our next life. He showed no fears, no worries, and only spoke to encourage me and lessen my fears. He has grown up so much, become a man in such a short time. I held my tears while saying goodbye, knowing that he was more worried about my feelings than his own, but inside, I felt those many months of separation looming and allowed each hug to settle deep in my memory.

> "So do not fear, for I am with you; do not be dismayed, for I am your God. I will strengthen you and help you." (Isaiah 41:10)

I just sent my son off to war, to the danger of losing his life from an enemy who hates him and wants him dead, my blessed affectionate caring son.

Blessed Be Your Name, Lord

I trust you to walk alongside my soldier son, Elisha, as he heads to a battle, not of his own making.

Bless Elisha's courage and stalwartness, as he continues to be more concerned about other's feelings and fears than his own.

I ask you to protect Elisha's heart, his mind, and his relationship with you. I ask you to be present with him on a daily basis.

214

Please allow Elisha to see you in the faces of all he meets, even those he fights against, and let him feel you beside him during times of danger and fear.

I entrust my son's heart to you. I ask you to be the guardian of his emotional, spiritual, and physical state, and his eternal life with You.

For I believe you are his Savior, his Protector, his Tower of Strength and Refuge in times of trouble.

Lord, bring peace to the troubled region and peoples of Iraq, Afghanistan and Iran, and bring this soldier safely home.

Prayer:
Father, remind me to pray the spiritual health of my loved ones at least as often as I bring their physical hardships before you.

JUNE 13

Stephen's Decision

Carol Pinkerton-Ewens

No, NO!" I cried, tears streaming down my face.

It was just a few weeks after Forrest's death when my youngest son, Stephen, announced his desire to enlist. I was still reeling in grief for one son. Stephen's decision absolutely floored me.

I experienced actual physical pain during any discussion of him joining up, but to no avail. He enlisted and left at the end of August 2006—six weeks after Forrest's death and just two days before we found out my father had terminal liver cancer.

Devastated by Forrest's loss, Stephen was driven to be part of the same thing that his big brother was. While he and the twins were always at odds growing up, in adulthood Stephen felt that Forrest was the only brother who really reached out to him during some of his hard times.

Watching all the attention given in the weeks after Forrest's death, Stephen, who had been rather lackadaisical about school, jobs, his life in

> "How long must I wrestle with my thoughts and every day have sorrow in my heart? . . . But I trust in your unfailing love; my heart rejoices in your salvation." (Psalm 13:2, 5)

general, suddenly saw something bigger than himself that he wanted to be part of. He saw that Forrest had achieved something honorable and worthy, and that others recognized it. I think he reevaluated his life and saw that he wanted to achieve the same.

Stephen had been offered a position in the Old Guard at Arlington National Cemetery, but turned it down to do his part in Korea for one year. Recently, he transferred to Fort Lewis and is now close to home.

How I cried when he tried to talk to me about enlisting. My pain was too raw from just losing Forrest, and to think my youngest, with whom I shared an incredibly close relationship, would defy me and leave me after being dealt such a blow, was unfathomable to me. It took me months—and still takes effort, to accept his decision.

Prayer:
Lord, show me how to echo David in Psalm 13 and rejoice in your salvation even as I have sorrow in my heart.

JUNE 14

Bravery

Carol Pinkerton-Ewens

ALL IN ALL, it has been a growing and painful process for me to accept my sons' decisions. If I had had my choice, my mother's heart would have had them all out of harms way, in school, working, or doing their part in a less violent way. But I have to accept that they are grown men, and cannot be held back by their mother's apron-strings. They must not live life with regret because they did not do something that they believe God would have them do. And so it is my part to somehow muster up enough strength and resolve to support them during these many upcoming years.

Sometimes I become angry that my children forced us to face more possibilities of injury and death. I look at the other families of fallen soldiers who I have come to know and see their living children rallying around them to support them . . . and yet my own head off into the same direction as their brother. Sometimes I question whether we were good parents. Are we not worthy of our children's compassion and protection? Or do they simply think that we are strong enough to handle the emotional and heart-breaking risks of losing another child? Should I be honored, angry, hurt?

"You're so brave," people often tell me. "I could never do what you are doing."

But where is the choice? Does not bravery mean you have *chosen* to do something to benefit others at the risk of your own harm? I have no choice in this matter, but have been forced to rely on God. Does that sound bad? The word "force" sounds like I think that is a poor choice, but I don't. Isn't it our human nature to rely on our own strength? In my case, I have been faced with my total weaknesses and inadequacies so sharply that I am forced to admit that without God, I would be a crumpled up little person in the absence of any hope. Presently and hopefully forever, I am content with relying upon God's strength, and trust that he will carry me through anything I will face.

> "It is God who arms me with strength and makes my way perfect." (Psalm 18:32)

Prayer:
*Lord God, arm me with strength and direct
my steps until I pass through this trial.*

JUNE 15

What I Didn't Know

Oaken Ewens, First Lieutenant, U.S. Army

WHEN THEY handed me the envelope I felt my heart sink. It was my job to hand-carry the dead soldier's personal affects as I escorted him to his final resting place. At that time I didn't know that one particular soldier had crawled on his hands and knees through the Afghan dirt until he had found all but the wedding band. I didn't know that this soldier knew exactly how much change the fallen soldier had in his pocket or that when he finally found his wooden cross it was hanging in a tree. I just knew that the package felt heavy and that the dead soldier was my twin brother.

When the funeral director opened the casket and left the room I didn't know that my little brother Stephen would straighten his life out—or that our childhood friend would give his life to Christ. I didn't know that there was a soldier in Afghanistan so impacted by Forrest that he refocused his life for Christ before dying a month later. All I knew was that there was lint on his bronze star. I gently removed it.

When the final bugle note faded and the crowd dispersed I found myself in a place I had never been before—a place of solitude before God. My twin brother, my constant companion, had gone on ahead of me to heaven. It was time for my faith to truly become my own in a way it hadn't before.

> "And we know that all things work together for good for those that love God." (Romans 8:28)

The two-year anniversary of that mountain ambush has come and gone and I feel keenly the lack of control for myself and my other two brothers who are in the Army. I have the same job as Forrest—the same rank. Will my life end soon as his did? Will my brothers? No matter the answer, we choose put our lives on hold while we serve our country.

Forrest once said, "Open your eyes and you will see, there is more to God than you believe." My faith sometimes feels blind, but I know Forrest was right. God is orchestrating more than I can even imagine, even if I can't see it.

Prayer:
Lord, help me to trust that you are using all things
in my life to somehow bring yourself glory.

JUNE 16

He Was Ready

Stephen Ewens, Specialist, U.S. Army

MY BROTHER'S death changed everything for me.

Before Forrest died, I wasn't going anywhere; I had no goals for the future. When he was killed, my eyes were opened to the value of life, and I knew I could do better with mine. After talking to all the soldiers that knew him I could see the pride and honor that they had in their work and that made me want to honor him by continuing his work. The army has allowed me to accomplish more than I could ever have done in the civilian world, and I am thankful for that.

It was difficult to see my mom in pain over my choice to enlist, but I had made my mind up. If anyone else was going to die in this war I would rather it be me.

Most of the time I block thoughts of Forrest's death from my mind because the pain is crippling. But when I deny his sacrifice, I feel that I am not honoring him enough. The fact that he died in combat makes me proud of him but also makes me terribly sad. Was his death instant or did he realize what was happening and that he was about to die? War is an ugly thing, it's not like the movies; these are real people with real families and real pains.

> "I have fought the good fight, I have finished the race, I have kept the faith." (2 Timothy 4:7)

Even though it has been two years, it's so hard to believe that he is not here anymore. I always think that I can just pick up the phone and call him, like he is on a long vacation. He was a great man, the most fun, loving, and exciting brother anyone could ask for. I always wondered why God took him and not one of his other brothers. It is clear now it was because he was the only one of us who was ready. He had run that race, fought the good fight, and lived a life full of dignity, honor, and pride. Knowing he was such a great man—now that helps with the pain.

Prayer:
Lord, help me strive to run the race in a way that pleases you so that I might be ready when you choose to call me home.

JUNE 17

Something Changed

Chaplain Col. Gene (Chip) Fowler, U.S. Army, Command Chaplain for Combined Joint Task Force 7 (the command and control element for all coalition forces in Iraq), 2004–2005

I WENT TO war on September 11, 2001. I don't carry the same kind of weapon that other soldiers do, but I went to war with them anyway. Something changed for our nation—a deep, penetrating soul-search. At the beginning of this war, I was called on to send some of my troops—chaplains and chaplain assistants—to serve the soldiers who would fight and die in this war. My heart burned as they left and I remained behind.

But in January of 2004, I finally found myself on the battlefield with them, sharing their depredations, fears, hopes, and faith. No one wants war less than the soldier who bears the brunt of its fury. They are a special lot—those who deem freedom worth the hardships and hazards of war—and I am so humbled and honored to serve with them. It's my job to help them strengthen their faith, but I find my faith being strengthened by them. I know that some question this war,

> "Blessed is the man who perseveres under trial." (James 1:12a)

but not the soldiers; they know what is at stake, for on September 11, 2001, something changed.

For the first time in six decades, we realized that we faced the sure extinction of the sweet water of freedom. And we realized that "whatever it takes, for as long as it takes," we must fight this war. Why? Because freedom is worth it. When we look at what life is like in the model "they" want to impose on the world, it is abhorrent to us. Freedom carries its pitfalls and excesses, yes, but freedom also gives us the power of choice. And choice gives us the opportunity to seek God in all his will and to enjoy life in all his glory. Something changed in 2001—we paid freedom's price. Now let us show freedom's power, "whatever it takes, for as long as it takes!" For we have been changed.

Prayer:
Lord, teach me how to sacrifice for that which is worth fighting for.

JUNE 18

The Agony and the Ecstasy

Chaplain Col. Gene (Chip) Fowler, U.S. Army,
Command Chaplain for Combined Joint Task Force 7

SEVERAL WEEKS during April and early May 2004 can best be described as "The Ecstasy and the Agony." The ecstasy came from the hope and joy experienced in remembering the central event of all history-the death and resurrection of the Lord of the Universe. On Easter Sunday morning, we had an absolutely marvelous Sunrise Service with so many people we could not count them.

The agony came from the senseless and sadistic murder of the four civilian contractors in Fallujah on March 31, and the heinous desecration of their mutilated bodies.

The ecstasy came from soldiers and civilians growing deeper in their faith and trust in the Lord Jesus.

The agony came from the attack on the convoy north of Baghdad where several were killed, and Tom Hamill was kidnapped and held hostage for three weeks.

The ecstasy came from his escape and reunion with his family.

The agony came from the highest total of soldiers killed and wounded in any month since the start of the conflict.

The ecstasy came from a wonderful and dynamic National Prayer Breakfast at Taji where soldiers and civilians gathered to ask God's blessings on our nation.

The agony came from the horrid rocket attack at that same base a couple of weeks earlier that took four lives, including a reserve captain whose civilian job was as a youth minister. As he lay there dying, he looked at individual soldiers saying, "Joe, I didn't see you at chapel Sunday; you know you need to go. Bob, I missed you at Bible Study."

> "Consider it pure joy, my brothers, whenever you face trials of many kinds, because you know that the testing of your faith develops perseverance." (James 1:2)

How does one deal with these ecstasies and agonies? Being able to handle the issues of life and death in the context of the eternal is the challenge. It is the work of chaplains and their assistants, and those whom they empower with a living faith. They take care of soldiers with selfless concern, imputing God's love and grace into the most difficult of situations. And then they take care of each other. May God continue to provide such servants to the military forces of our nation, nurturing their faith, strengthening their moral resolve, and lifting their souls toward heaven.

Prayer:
Lord, may my trials strengthen my faith instead of compel me to doubt.

Rising Up Against Evil

Chaplain Col. Gene (Chip) Fowler, U.S. Army,
Command Chaplain for Combined Joint Task Force 7

From an email newsletter dated June 11, 2004:

The abuses at the prison at Abu Gharib are obviously an embarrassment to all. The real hardship that is not known is that the soldiers currently assigned there are taking all the *heat* and scrutiny, even though they were not present at the time of the abuses last year and have been doing a good job. I have two chaplains permanently assigned there who are very strong in their spiritual leadership and encouragement, and are doing a marvelous job at helping their soldiers handle all the unwanted (and mostly undeserved) visibility. The alleged perpetrators are rightly being handled through the military justice system, but the actions of a very few will tarnish the reputation of the many who are honest and decent soldiers serving honorably.

Yet in light of this event, we were reminded of the nature of this conflict and our purpose for being here. The enemy we seek to stop has shown its true colors with the brutal and horrid decapitation of Nick Berg (added to the desecrations in Fallujah

> "Do not be overcome by evil, but overcome evil with good."
> (Romans 12:21)

in April, and many other examples). Debates will continue to be conducted over the legitimacy of this war, and history's story will be written. Yet God alone can determine its legitimacy. However, I cannot help but feel that God-fearing people, and humanity at large, must rise up against such evil as we see in this enemy. If not, then we all lose. As we reflect back sixty years ago to the largest single invasion of all of history at Normandy, we remember "the greatest generation" did precisely this. They knew not what they would find months later in the concentration camps; but when they saw the evil, they had a increased sense of their purpose and legitimacy. More and more, we are finding the same here.

Prayer:
Lord, may my life represent and honor Christ to all those around me.

U.S. Citizenship on Foreign Soil

Chaplain Col. Gene (Chip) Fowler, U.S. Army,
Command Chaplain for Combined Joint Task Force 7

IN OCTOBER 2004, we had a Naturalization Ceremony, where thirty-four U.S. soldiers from twenty-two nations became U.S. citizens. Until now, all Naturalization Ceremonies took place on U.S. soil by law. But President Bush signed a new law, effective October 1, 2004, which allows soldiers serving in a deployed location to be naturalized on the soil where they serve. Foreigners can join our military, pledging to support and defend (and die for) the Constitution of a nation not their own. Why would someone want to do that? Is it that in spite of our many frailties as a nation, we offer something that no one else does? From the stories of these soldiers, I believe so.

Undersecretary Aquirre, head of the U.S. Citizenship and Immigration Service, himself a naturalized American citizen, said in his remarks that because of the obvious increase of the threat of major violence against America and Americans worldwide, you'd think that immigration would have dipped in the last few years. We are being ostracized by "friends" and abandoned by "allies," but individuals are still streaming in ever-increasing numbers to join the hope, and to literally fight for the dream that America promises.

> "Love the brotherhood of believers, fear God, honor the King." (1 Peter 2:17)

To see the faces of those thirty-four soldiers; to hear the pride in their voices when they took their oath; to see the tears flowing down their cheeks—humbled me greatly. To hear the power and meaning in their words when they said the Pledge of Allegiance (including a lusty "UNDER GOD"), made tears flow down my cheeks. And I realized then and there, we still have a future, and God willing, we still have a bright future. The hopes and dreams that made America (out of a bunch of immigrants) two-plus centuries ago, is still here.

The country debates whether this war is worth it. I think the good I see happening, though hidden by the spectacular tragedies, makes me say yes. But when I see the power of purpose in the faces of new Americans in whom our future resides, then I know beyond the shadow of any doubt, yes—it's worth it. And I am proud.

Prayer:
Lord, help me appreciate more fully the great freedoms I have in America, but even more so, the freedom I have in Christ.

Scene Out of *M*A*S*H*

Chaplain Col. Gene (Chip) Fowler, U.S. Army, Command Chaplain for Combined Joint Task Force 7

IT WAS LIKE an episode of *M*A*S*H* when the evacuation helicopters landed. There were five casualties: four serious and one dead. I called for chaplain backup, and three more chaplains arrived shortly.

Chaplains are vital parts of the emergency medical team, but they have to know how to stay out of the way of the medical folks. Usually that means that they are positioned at the head of the patient where they can easily speak comfort to him or pray with him. The chaplain can also assist some of the medical procedures by getting things from the tray or holding something for the medics but mainly they keep focused on the patient.

> "Therefore encourage one another and build each other up, just as in fact you are doing."
> (1 Thessalonians 5:11)

My soldier had a seriously broken arm, a collapsed lung, and was covered in blood from the many pieces of shrapnel he'd taken. He was conscious, so I continued to engage him in conversation, including prayer, while the medics worked on him. He said he'd been hit twice. He was in his room when he was hit first. Bleeding, he went outside to get help when another round and hit him again.

We as chaplains have to maintain the peace of God in our own lives so that peace flows over to the ones we minster to so they're not as anxious. I felt that very strongly and that's what I was doing. There were about five or six times during that year where I was actively engaged in ministering to dramatically injured soldiers and in each case, I was the calming effect, not only to soldiers injured, but also the young soldiers who were the medics that were traumatized by all the ordeal. Some of these medics running the clinics were only eighteen to twenty years old. They'd been in college and were in a Reserve unit when their unit was called up. The aftercare was taking care of those folks. It was deeply rewarding ministering to them and helping keep them focused on the value that they give—the good they do in ministering to the broken bodies of soldiers.

Prayer:
Lord, cultivate in me a spirit which seeks to encourage others as they strive to serve you with their gifts.

JUNE 22

Sergeant Dima

Chaplain Col. Gene (Chip) Fowler, U.S. Army, Command Chaplain for Combined Joint Task Force 7

WITH THE ambulance gone, the majority of the medical team went straight to work cleaning the clinic—there was a lot of blood—and getting it ready to receive more casualties if and when another incident occurred. They must be ready twenty-four hours a day. What heroes they are.

> "Therefore my dear brothers, stand firm. Let nothing move you. Always give yourselves fully to the work of the Lord, because you know that your labor in the Lord is not in vain."
> (1 Corinthians 15:58)

The other few set about to process the remains of the one soldier killed. I assisted them. The soldier was Sergeant Dima, a Romanian who came to the U.S. a few years ago. He hailed from New Jersey and joined the Army Reserves after 9/11—a member of 411th Construction Management Section of the 420th Engineer Brigade. He became a citizen on October 3, 2004; was promoted to sergeant on the morning of November 13 and gave his life for his new country on the evening November 13.

Every soldier has a story; Sgt. Dima has become part of mine. There is something spiritual about kneeling and laying hands on the broken, bloody body of a soldier, praying for his soul and the three young children he was leaving in the care of his now single wife. It is somber and sobering to see the deep respect the medics have as they treat the remains of a fallen comrade. After we finished the preparation, I was honored to pull back the curtain and call the clinic to attention as the medics moved Sgt. Dima to a holding area, awaiting initial transportation to start his way back home. Every person was silent, prayerful, respectful. It takes people with some kind of moxie to do their job as medics, day in and day out, mostly taking care of our little aches and pains, but always ready for the worst. And when the worst comes, so does their best. I thank God that this is the ministry he placed in my hand. We gathered everyone in the clinic together, and I asked one of my Air Force chaplains to offer a prayer for these servants of health. It was well appreciated.

Prayer:
*Lord, thank you for your promise that our labor is
not in vain; help me trust you for the results.*

JUNE 23

Blue Fingers

Chaplain Col. Gene (Chip) Fowler, U.S. Army,
Command Chaplain for Combined Joint Task Force 7

THE SIGNIFICANCE of January 30, 2005, is summed up in inked-stained forefingers. This was the day Iraqis voted for themselves.

"The Iraqis who came out to vote did so to say thank you to the coalition," said our cultural advisor, Kadeem—an Iraqi ex-patriot from St. Louis who fled Saddam's revenge after Desert Storm. It was somehow a validating event for all the work, pain, and suffering of the soldiers here, and their families back home. Kadeem called his three brothers and asked them who they voted for; all three voted for someone different. And he said, "Never before has anything like this happened in Iraq, where people can determine their own future."

Yet such a thing comes at a cost—one that I will never forget, but will always honor. From February 1, 2004 to January 31, 2005 (the time I was in Iraq), we've suffered more than seven thousand wounded, almost seven hundred killed by enemy action and another nearly one hundred fifty who died from non-enemy causes—and those are just the U.S. military figures. There were many more when you include our coalition partners, civilian contractors, the friendly Iraqi security forces, and the many innocent Iraqi civilians.

"I don't understand why your soldiers die for my people," an Iraqi National Guard soldier told one of my chaplains. I hope Sunday's actions by the Iraqis begin to tell the

> "Though he slay me, yet will I hope in him." (Job 13:15a)

reason why. With blue fingers as badges of courage, a tidal wave of Freedom began that desperate terrorists could not stop as more than nine million free citizens voted.

Is this the dawning of a new age in human history? I don't know the answer to that. But it is a new age in the lives of Iraqis, and many other nations are looking to see what it means to them. For us as democratic freedom lovers, it gives hope that the incessant evil of terror is waning. The struggle against such evil as terror brings isn't over—the Devil doesn't give up easily. So we must persist and continue to pursue the objective of eliminating the demon of terror.

Prayer:
Lord, renew my hope in you above all else.

JUNE 24

What Can We Do?

Col. John Gessner, Army Corps of Engineers, Afghanistan, 2002

IT WASN'T part of their official mission in Afghanistan, but it was the most rewarding—Col. John Gessner and his Base Engineer Team sponsored an orphanage in nearby Charikar. This humanitarian project was going on when they weren't reconstructing the Bagram Air Base in support of Operation Enduring Freedom.

Orphans are part of the terrible cost of warfare, and in Afghanistan, this is particularly pronounced. There are more than thirty thousand orphans in the Kabul area alone.

When they arrived at the orphanage in Charikar the first time, about seventy-five children and staff hesitantly greeted these Americans in uniform.

"They were a little leery of us when we first met them but warmed to us in time," recalled Gessner. "What I first noticed was the lack of shoes and lack of glass in the windows in the sleeping rooms." Summer temperatures in Afghanistan reach higher than one hundred degrees but drop to the teens in the winter.

When we left the orphanage on that first day, a rather large Airborne Ranger sergeant major, nicknamed *Big Jim*, looked at me with tears in his eyes and asked, "What can we do to help these kids?" We decided to write a few letters home hoping that perhaps people would send us some donations.

The letters worked. The sergeant major's contacts sent numerous pairs of shoes. Jim Powers, a friend of Gessner's in Rockford, Illinois, mobilized his Kiwanis group to support the orphans. Powers also established a website for the orphans' plight and landed a front page story in the local paper. After the article in the paper, the orphans' website received more than four hundred hits the first two days. The donations began flowing in.

> "Religion that God our Father accepts as pure and faultless is this: to look after orphans and widows in their distress." (James 1:27)

"In three months, we received eight thousand dollars and three hundred fifty boxes of goods," said Gessner. "The first donation came from a friend's grandson who volunteered up his own shoes. While his grandma convinced him he needed his own shoes, he volunteered up his change totaling fifty-seven cents." Other significant donations included coats from J.C. Penney's and eighty hand-sewn quilted sleeping bags from a ladies' church group.

"I was asked by a reporter once what we had received from the orphans for our work," Gessner remembered. "My response was: 'A lot of hugs and the satisfaction of leaving the place a little better than we found it.'"

Prayer:
*Lord, instill in me a desire to give to others out of
the abundance with which you have blessed me.*

Col. John Gessner with orphans in Afghanistan

JUNE 25

Debunking the "Great Satan" Myth

Col. John Gessner, Army Corps of Engineers, Afghanistan (2002)

THE ANTICIPATION of distributing the donations to the orphans was contagious—especially on Sunday afternoons. This was typically the day Gessner's team of fourteen engineers plus some other soldiers helped with the deliveries. Civil Affairs officers and interpreters also escorted them on the forty-five-minute journey by armed convoy.

"Some of the soldiers who volunteered to drive the trucks for us had spent most of their time on base on engineer missions," Gessner said. "They were extremely excited about interacting with the kids and volunteered to go back several times. One told me it was the greatest thing he had ever done."

Initially, the orphans and staff were cautious around the Americans, because they had been told that Americans were "The Great Satan" and other stories that would soon be proven false.Interpreters explained why the Americans were there and that they had gifts for the children. After a few visits they got used to having us around.

Several of the kids picked out their favorite soldier and the soldiers had their favorite kids.

Donations included toys, stuffed animals, and candy along with school supplies, clothes, socks, shoes, underwear, and coats.

"One little girl used to run up and jump into my arms," said Gessner. "There was

> "A good name is more desirable than great riches; to be esteemed is better than silver or gold." (Proverbs 22:1)

never a loss for helpers to unload the trucks. One of the things that fascinated the kids was digital cameras. They could see the images immediately and the following week we would bring back copies of the photos we took." Some of the female staff members allowed the Americans to take their pictures, a very rare opportunity and honor in a Muslim country.

"When the Taliban or other terrorist groups return to recruit young people for their evil plans, I suspect the kids will remember the American soldier who brought those blankets, food, and kindness," said Gessner.

Prayer:
Lord, help me earn a reputation that is pleasing,
honoring, and glorifying to you.

JUNE 26

Home Improvements

Col. John Gessner, Army Corps of Engineers, Afghanistan (2002)

THE DONATIONS of clothing and toys were only the beginning. In the next three months the Americans rebuilt the orphanage kitchen, replaced the missing windows, provided funds for food, and purchased new kitchen utensils, cookware. and a one-month supply of firewood.

Not only was the staff thrilled, but the interpreter was so impressed at the support given to the children of his country that he purchased a one hundred-pound bag of rice for the orphanage.

Gessner turned over some of the cash he had received to a non-governmental organization (NGO) called the Knights of Malta, who developed a menu and purchased food for the orphanage on a weekly basis. "Rather than buying in bulk, this reduced the possibility of loss, waste or diversion of the food intended for the orphanage," said Gessner. "The Knights of Malta also outfitted three school rooms with desks, chalkboards and other supplies once we had repaired them."

With no water in the orphanage, the kids and staff walked to a nearby irrigation ditch and brought the water in by buckets. One day, while standing in the orphanage, Gessner noticed water running in through the back gate. The owner of the next property had already drilled through the dike and water was running freely on to his property.

> "Whatever you did for the least of these brothers of mine, you did for me." (Matthew 25:40)

"I asked the owner if we could put a spigot on the end of his pipe and let us run a water line into the orphanage," Gessner said. "He agreed and with a few hours work by the plumbers, the orphanage had running water for cooking and personal hygiene."

Several of the rooms in the orphanage had collapsed roofs and the windows and doors were knocked out. A local Afghan contractor initially asked for $4,000 to do the job but when Gessner told him he only had $1,000 to spend, he agreed to rebuild the rooms at that price for the kids. "It was one of the easiest contract negotiations I'd ever done," said Gessner. A few weeks later, the rooms were ready.

"You Americans are nothing like they [Taliban and Al Qaeda] said you were," the staff told Gessner. Then they placed their hands over their hearts and nodded in a gesture of respect.

"When we saw this," said Gessner, "we knew we had made an impression."

Prayer:
Lord, help me find joy in meeting the needs of others in your name.

Mission Accomplished

Col. John Gessner, Army Corps of Engineers,
Afghanistan (2002)

GREAT CATCH! Throw it here now, right here!"

On Sunday afternoons outside the orphanage in Charikar, English and Afghan voices rang in the air together as American soldiers and Afghan orphans played Frisbee, speaking and yelling in two different languages but laughing in the same. These times of interaction quickly became the highlight of the week for both soldiers and orphans.

While most of the conversation with the orphanage staff was through our Afghan interpreters, the soldiers interacted with the kids more through actions. "We communicated with hugs, smiles, or kicking a soccer ball," said Gessner. "Most of the kids just wanted to hang around us. Of course, having a pocket full of candy was always a help. The kids were always well-behaved."

> "A cheerful heart is good medicine, but a crushed spirit dries up the bones."
> (Proverbs 17:22)

When Gessner's unit passed out the stuffed animals, they took the opportunity to try to teach the English names to the kids. "In one case, they were having trouble with the word 'gorilla' so we settled on 'monkey.' The digital cameras were another great hit with the kids. For group photos, they liked passing around and wearing our hats."

Most of the children had picked out their favorite soldiers by the fourth week of the visits, though not everyone. One little girl didn't smile much despite the stuffed animals, candy, digital cameras, Frisbee, and soccer games. Gessner decided to make it his personal mission to brighten her day.

"I tried everything that worked with my own kids, including funny faces and wearing my hat backwards," said Gessner. "I even showed her how to smile by pushing the corners of my mouth up with my fingers. She did the same thing. After all of that, it was time to take the gloves off so I dove in amongst the girls and turned it into a tickle-fest. The smiles and laugher came out. Mission accomplished."

Prayer:
Lord, help me make it a priority to bring joy to those around me.

Mountain Supply Run

Col. John Gessner, Army Corps of Engineers, Afghanistan, 2002

COLONEL, WE'VE found about three hundred orphans sleeping in the caves in the mountains," an officer told Gessner. It was mid-December 2002, and Gessner's unit was just about to redeploy and leave Bagram Air Base and the nearby orphanage in Afghanistan.

The Americans discovered the children while on a military mission in Bamian, the area of the caves. The aviation unit told Gessner that they were flying a mission to this area and wanted to bring along some relief supplies.

"So we made a shopping list of blankets, food, and coats," recalled Gessner. "We estimated about two thousand dollars worth. The head of the aviation unit almost flipped when I pulled two thousand dollars from my pocket and handed it to him—the last of the donations we had collected for the orphans."

> "Defend the cause of the weak and fatherless; maintain the rights of the poor and oppressed." (Psalm 82:3)

The materials were purchased in the capital city of Kabul, which was experiencing a rebirth at the time. "Once the Taliban and Al Qaeda departed, the city came alive again," said Gessner. General Tommy Franks commented in his book about all of the city and street noise by saying it sounded like freedom. Restaurants, stores, and businesses began to reopen in the city.

A few weeks later, the helicopters flew to the mountains; it must have been close to Christmas time. When they landed, it was snowing. This year it must have seemed as though Santa's sleigh had been traded in for a U.S. Army helicopter. From the back of the helicopter ramp, the soldiers began passing out coats and blankets to the kids.

The "elves" who were responsible for providing the gifts for these orphans and those in Charikar were citizens, schools, churches, organizations, and clubs hailing from Illinois, Wisconsin, Washington, D.C., and as far away as Germany. Those who donated for the cause of these Afghan orphans may never know the extent of the impact their gifts had on these children (and other Afghan adult observers). But the kids will very likely remember the Americans in uniform who put down their weapons to make their winters a little warmer and their bellies a little fuller.

Prayer:
*Lord, keep me ever mindful of those less fortunate
than I am, and show me how to defend them.*

Soldiers and Orphans

*Col. Jim Powers, U.S. Army (Ret.); Kiwanis Club Webmaster,
Rockford, Illinois*

WHEN JIM POWERS, past-president and Webmaster for the Rock Valley Kiwanis Club in Rockford, Illinois, heard from Col. John Gessner about the needs of orphans in Afghanistan, he jumped at the chance to mobilize help by soliciting donations. It wouldn't be the first time he had lent a helping hand to the children of a combat zone.

Powers' first experience with homeless children and orphans came during his first tour in Viet Nam (1967–68). After sending pictures and writing to the parishioners at St. Patrick's Church, Rockford, about displaced war refugees in Saigon, support poured in. Day after day, packages arrived (clothing, supplies, toys), sometimes completely filling his office.

> "He who oppresses the poor shows contempt for their Maker, but whoever is kind to the needy honors God."
> (Proverbs 14:31)

Three months into his tour, Powers was transferred to Cat Lai, in a rural area about fifteen miles east of Saigon, where the members of his battalion took up a support role with a nearby orphanage. They worked off-hours on construction, played with children, and provided care packages from home.

"It seemed like an automatic response to their needs, such that it would have been unimaginable to not help," said Powers. "We have so much in our great country, and when soldiers go to a foreign land and witness so many with so little, it is a natural match. Also, I believe the helping behavior helps soldiers cope with the pain of being separated from loved ones back home."

Creating a website announcing the needs of the Afghan children was a natural both for Powers and for the Kiwanis Club, whose main focus is children. "If Americans are made aware of needs, particularly those of helpless children, they will pitch in. They need to be given information about the needs (the Internet being a perfect format) and then given the methods by which they can plug in. For me, the actions by all those who donated time, goods, energy and/or money demonstrated the wisdom of the late Mother Theresa: 'We don't have to do great things—only small things with great love.'" The donations collected through Power's efforts totaled thousands of dollars and hundreds of boxes of goods.

Prayer:
Lord, show me how I can help the needy in my own community.

JUNE 30

Ready to Go, Ready to Stay

Spec. Joe Olsen, U.S. Military Police, Iraq (2003–2004)

I SIGNED UP for the National Guard to pay for college. Not to go to war.

September 11, 2001, however, swept away all hope of being able to serve my years with the Guard peacefully.

Watching the news unfold on the television, my heart sank, and my stomach turned. This changed everything. Even as a soldier, war was not a reality to me until that day. But in that instant, the possibility of me going to war became inevitable.

My friends told me I wouldn't go anywhere. They were sure I wouldn't be pulled out of college, but I wasn't convinced. From that point on, I no longer could relate to my friends the same way I used to. They did not have to face what I was facing. Their lives would go on as scheduled, virtually unaffected by this act of terror. I had that sick feeling that as long as I was still in the military I would run a very high risk of getting deployed.

For the next year and a half my unit was regularly told that it was not a matter of *if* we would be deployed somewhere but *when*.

The stakes began to rise. By March 1, 2003, activation was now a certainty. If the United States went to war with Iraq, then my unit would

235

go in after the major combat mission was over and stabilize the country. Between September 11, 2001, and the time I was activated, I lived one day at a time: ready to go, yet ready to stay.

> "I will say of the LORD, 'He is my refuge and my fortress, my God, in whom I trust." (Psalm 91:2)

When the call came for my unit to be activated, I adopted Psalm 91 as my own. When I did, I immediately surrendered my fears to the Lord and in return, accepted the peace that surpasses all understanding, believing that he truly would deliver me from the snare of the fowler, the perilous pestilence, and any other harm from the enemy.

When I was twenty-one years old, I traded in my college textbooks and gym shoes for combat boots and weapons of war.

Prayer:
Lord, help me be ready to stay on this earth and live for you and ready to join you in heaven as I live day by day.

Worlds Apart

Spec. Joe Olsen, U.S. Military Police, Iraq (2003–2004)

LESS THAN four weeks after marrying Stephanie in the base chapel at Ft. Campbell, Kentucky, it was time to deploy. Saying goodbye to Stephanie was the hardest thing I have ever had to do in my life. However, I believed that God's protection not only covered me but also my wife back home and our marriage. I believed I would come home safely someday, and that Stephanie would be there waiting for me when I finally did get home.

After the goodbye, I set foot on the plane to Kuwait and set aside thoughts of danger in order to think about the adventure that lay ahead. I had the chance to sit in the cockpit with the pilots from time to time on the way to JFK airport in New York. Just before landing the pilot pointed out Ground Zero to me, certainly reminding me of why I was doing what I was doing.

As I was enroute to the Middle East, my wife was in cap and gown, marching to "Pomp and Circumstance" before being handed her college degree at her graduation ceremony. While at a layover at JFK, I called my cell phone, that was being held by my mother-in-law. I heard Stephanie's name called as she walked across the stage. It wasn't the same as being there in person, but at least I could be part of it in that small way.

> "'The LORD bless you and keep you; the LORD make his face shine upon you and be gracious to you . . . and give you peace."
> (Numbers 6:24–26)

The next day, upon stepping off the plane, the desert heat was almost unbearable. As soon as my boots hit the ground, I could feel my skin prickle with sweat and my mouth go dry—and we weren't even under the pressure of combat. I could not imagine being able to survive it but knew I had no choice.

Meanwhile, back in Tennessee, Stephanie woke up to a suffocating emptiness. She could not imagine being able to survive that ache of loneliness, either, but knew she had no choice. Just days ago, we had been together, a complete unit. Now we were worlds apart and digging in for the long road ahead.

Prayer:
Lord, remind me of your presence and grant me your peace today.

Spec. Joe and Stephanie Olsen on their wedding day, less than four weeks before Joe's deployment to Iraq in 2003

God with Us

Spec. Joe Olsen, U.S. Military Police, Iraq (2003–2004)

AFTER A MONTH and a half in Kuwait, we drove into the war zone that was Iraq, not stopping until we reached Baghdad. At each of these milestone steps, the need for protection that only God could provide became more and more urgent.

Following the initial invasion and downfall of Saddam, Iraq had no civil government, no police force, and no local military. Moreover, there were still Saddam loyalists along with Al Qaeda supporters in Iraq taking shape. Between roadside bombs, sniper fire, and rocket propelled grenades (RPGs), the situation we faced became far greater than the danger we originally expected.

Driving into Iraq was an unforgettable experience. We drove through rural villages plagued by poverty. From young boys to grown men, they all greeted us as heroes and called us friend. As we approached Baghdad, we began seeing signs of war. Abandoned or burned out military vehicles were seen frequently. Although I never felt any immediate danger on this trip, I will never in this lifetime know what dangers I may have been in on this convoy or any other.

When we reached our destination, the first thing we noticed was the constant sound of random gunfire off in the distance. On the night that Uday and Qsay Hussein were killed, the Iraqis celebrated by random gunfire, straight into the air, landing anywhere, including into our camp. As time went on, mortar and RPG fire added to the dangers.

Every night that I made it safely to bed, I gave thanks to God for his protection. We were all well aware of the fact that when we left camp that we were not guaranteed to return alive. We were not even guaranteed safety inside our camp. At any moment, anyone's "number could be called" and we would be standing before our Maker.

> "He protected us on our entire journey and among all the nations through which we traveled." (Joshua 24:17b)

For most people, this is where their faith either stopped or became compromised. But I had a quiet confidence from God: in a far away land that was permeated with evil, God was present in a very real way with me. He truly was Immanuel—God with us.

Prayer:
Lord, protect not just my physical well-being
but my mind, heart and spirit as well.

Close Calls

Spec. Joe Olsen, U.S. Military Police, Iraq (2003–2004)

A YEAR? TWELVE months? You're kidding, right?" I had to make sure the news I had just heard was for real. But it was no joke.

Upon arriving in Baghdad, we soon found out our deployment would be twice as long as the six-month duration we were originally told. One more year of trying to avoid roadside bombs, snipers, rocket propelled grenades, and the like. As the deployment went on, the violence escalated, but God remained faithful to me.

I made regular trips to Baghdad International Airport and Camp Victory that was next to the airport. One time we were late getting started on our mission, and as we got down the road we had to take a detour when the main road was closed because an IED was found. Had we been on time, my convoy may have been hit.

> "A thousand may fall at your side, ten thousand at your right hand, but it will not come near you." (Psalm 91:7)

When detouring around it, our lead vehicle led us into a marketplace. Instantly, we were surrounded by people both friendly and unfriendly— but of course, we couldn't tell who was who. The multi-story buildings all around provided plenty of places for snipers to ambush, but God delivered us safely out, and we returned to our camp without incident.

On another trip to Camp Victory, just before we were to leave to go back to our camp, we heard gunfire just outside the gate.

"Sniper fire," we were told. "Be alert." As we pulled out the gunfire stopped; once again, we returned to camp without a scratch.

Another time, our building took a direct hit from an RPG that landed on the roof in the very spot where I would talk on the phone when I had the chance.

These experiences were reminders of God's vigilance. I will never know in this lifetime if any IED's malfunctioned and did not detonate, or how close a sniper's bullet came to me, but I do know that any attempt on my life was foiled. We were scheduled to go home during the height of the violence, but instead we were extended for three more months. Despite all of these dangers, injury or death did not touch me.

Prayer:
Lord, help me trust you for all the details
of my life, both large and small.

JULY 4

Homecoming

Spec. Joe Olsen, U.S. Military Police, Iraq (2003–2004)

MY HEART was racing. I took a deep breath as I wiped my palms on my legs one more time. It was July 2004, eighteen months after I first deployed. Now, as the plane touched down at Ft. Campbell, I was nervous.

We marched into a building and stood for a short ceremony. And then I saw her—my young wife who had endured so much on the home front while I had been away. I wrapped her in my arms, relishing the reunion. This time I wasn't just home on leave; I was home for good. Seeing her again after so much time had passed didn't make me nervous.

The nervousness came from the reality that I would no longer be shielded from the battles of life itself. I had been on active duty long enough to become institutionalized in the Army. Suddenly I could no longer rely on the Army to feed, clothe, shelter, and pay me. I would have to go back to school and even back to work. I could no longer just be legally married. I would have to truly *be* married. When I hear of all of the cases of post traumatic stress disorder, divorces, and even suicides that this war has caused, I am humbled and eternally grateful for God's protection that I held so dear in war, and now has been extended to me years later.

After I arrived home, I realized just how radical God's protection of me had been. In the year plus I spent in Iraq, not only did I remain alive and uninjured, but I do not remember ever requiring so much as a band aid for a minor cut. I am not quite sure why God chose to protect me in such an extreme way, under such dangerous conditions. I certainly do not feel deserving of such protection, after so many soldiers just like me did not make it home safely. But he proved to me that he was with me, even to the ends of the earth.

> "If I rise on the wings of the dawn, if I settle on the far side of the sea, even there your hand will guide me, your right hand will hold me fast." (Psalm 139: 9–10)

Prayer:
*Lord, wherever I go, may I desire your
presence and favor above all else.*

JULY 5

The Day That Changed Us

Stephanie Olsen, wife of military police officer Joe Olsen

I HAD NEVER seen him look like that. Head down, hands in his pockets, lost in a world of his own. Our eyes met and we both knew this day was going to change who we were and what we were to each other.

It was September 11th and the whole world was changing. Buildings were falling. People were dying. America was gripped with fear. Our lives, like every American's, suddenly changed. For my then-boyfriend, Joe, it meant the very high possibility of active military duty. For a young man in the National Guard we knew it would take a homeland attack to force him into full-time duty. That day our worst fear became reality. For the first time in our relationship a separation, due to activation, would most likely be inevitable.

Throughout the day people continually asked Joe, "Have you gotten a call? Heard you anything yet?" All I wanted was for people to go away and leave us alone. It was one of the hardest days in our relationship. I realized that if I was going to make a life with this man, the road ahead of us was not going to be easy or predictable. Suddenly, all the things we wanted from life didn't matter. Tomorrow was questionable, our future was unsure, and our world and our security were being challenged.

We decided that day in the midst of all the horror, turmoil, and questions that we had each other, and we would face the world together. War was inevitable; that we both understood. Do we get married as we had been planning? Should we wait? How do we carry on in the face of an uncertain timeline? So many unanswered questioned were born that day. But one thing was for certain. We would choose to make it work. We chose to stay together. That day we committed to facing tomorrow together, even though tomorrow was so unsure. If God had called Joe to serve his country, and if God had brought us together, somehow he would see us through the unknown.

> "Even though I walk through the valley of the shadow of death, I will fear no evil, for you are with me; your rod and your staff, they comfort me." (Psalm 23:4)

Prayer:
Lord, where there is shadow, there must be light. Help me focus on your light to help me walk through my valleys.

The Wedding

Stephanie Olsen, wife of military police officer Joe Olsen

I WAS STANDING in an old army chapel in my white wedding gown. The room was quiet, the mood was somber, and we all knew the hard road ahead. All I could see at the other end of the aisle was a man, my man, in army green. Only our closest family and friends were gathered on the front pews, about ten people in all. At the end of a very long walk were my father, the minister who would marry me to Joe—the man I wanted to spend the rest of my life with. There was no beautiful music, no friends in beautiful gowns, no extended family, no photographer.

News of my fiance's impending deployment came two weeks before the war officially began and two months before our planned wedding day. All arrangements had been made. Every single detail had been finalized. And then it all fell apart. The war began, the word came, our lives changed.

Looking down the aisle at him, all I can remember thinking is, *This is not the way it should be; this is not our plan, but it was God's plan.* I was starting down a path that I had no idea how it would end. All I knew at that moment was that marrying him was right. I had no guarantees, no absolutes. For the first time in my life, there was no safety net. My future was wide open with many possibilities. I was fully aware that I may not like some circumstances that I was facing.

> "Trust in the LORD with all your heart and lean not on your own understanding."
> (Proverbs 3:5)

The uncertainty of the upcoming weeks, months, and years was in God's hands. We were only offered one choice: to trust God. Learning to allow God to have full control is not always easy and sometimes he takes matters into his own hands. For me learning to totally trust God came at a time when I had no other choice. Sometimes I think that is what it takes. He must remove the situation fully from my hands to show that I can trust him with the one that I love.

Prayer:
Lord, help me to trust you with the things and people I hold most tightly to.

JULY 7

The Goodbye

Stephanie Olsen, wife of military police officer Joe Olsen

WE STOOD in the darkness, there were no words to say. We had said all we wanted to say and some we didn't—mainly goodbye. The "what ifs", and the "just in cases"—no, we chose not to speak on those. It was our last night together. The next morning he would be on a plane headed for Iraq, and I would be walking across a stage to receive my college diploma. Two weeks married, and we were facing a long separation. Our lives were going in two different directions, literally. I was to begin my career, and he was leaving to fight a war.

The coming months held much uncertainty. We didn't know when we would see each other, touch each other, or even hear each other's voices again. We refused to consider the alternative that we might not ever do any of those things again. But somewhere, in the back of our minds—like the really terrible nightmare you hope you never have—we both knew this could be our last moment together.

How do I hold onto that moment? How do I turn my back on my life partner and walk away not knowing when or if I will ever lay eyes on him again? Somehow I turned and walked away. On my way home

> "He will keep you strong to the end . . ."
> (1 Corinthians 1:8)

I cried. I cried like I had never cried in my entire life, and I prayed like I had never prayed. The ache I felt was indecipherable. A huge gaping hole was now in my life. I tried to pull my thoughts together, forcing myself to keep going when every fiber in my being wanted to turn back and just hold him one more time. I would be strong. I would not fall apart. I would do it for him. I had no idea where his journey was leading, but that night I made the choice to be strong—but I knew that strength would have to come from some source outside myself.

Prayer:
Lord, be my strength when I am weak.
For your name's sake, sustain me.

The End of My Rope

Stephanie Olsen, wife of military police officer Joe Olsen

DAYS AWAY from our first wedding anniversary and more than ten months into Joe's deployment, we were looking forward to him being home soon. When the phone rang, I thought he was calling to wish me a happy anniversary.

I was wrong. He was being extended. Again.

Originally he was not to have been gone longer than six months. Six months turned into a year and now it looked like it would be even more than a year and half. How long? No idea. Troops were short. Nerves that were already frayed and worn snapped. I don't remember anything about the rest of that day or the coming days.

I had never felt so out of control in my life. At that moment all of the will and positive thoughts and faith seemed to come to a halt. I felt like I was at my rope's end—just dangling out over an abyss that I had no hope of crawling out of. My first year of marriage was an utter disappointment. I was so angry. I felt robbed and abandoned. It was the darkest time in my life. I had no way of knowing when I would ever again see the man I loved. Already he felt like a distant memory; holding onto him was harder and harder each day.

> "God has said, 'Never will I leave you; never will I forsake you.' So we say with confidence, 'The Lord is my helper; I will not be afraid . . .'"
> (Hebrews 13:5b–6)

That day a very hard lesson was learned. It was not about my strength, I had obviously failed. The motivation that kept me going had to come from somewhere else—anywhere else—because I was not able to supply needed strength any longer. It was during that time that I learned what it truly meant to rely on God. In the darkest, hardest, and most unsure moments, God was there. In the frustrations he was there. In the uncertainty he was there. And I lived through it because he was there.

Prayer:
Father, help me draw strength from you even in my most helpless state.

Our Story

Stephanie Olsen, wife of military police officer Joe Olsen

MANY PEOPLE ask me how it feels to be the wife of a former serviceman. I can sum it up in one word: personal. It's very personal because it's now our story, our sacrifice, our time lost. Joe's deployment to Iraq directly affected who we were and who we are today. Surviving the experience for Joe (physically and emotionally), and for me (psychologically and emotionally), taught us that living out our vows was overwhelmingly important and real. In good times and bad—I was his wife, and he was my husband. We held it together even though we were apart. While he longed to be home, I longed for him to return and bring with him my sense of home. He was where I belonged.

We stayed true to each other even in a long separation. Through every trial. Overcoming all obstacles. This is our story. Our legacy. Our history.

It is who we are. We can now truly say that we appreciate each other every day. We know what it is like to face the world without each other, and it'is not a way of life we ever want to face again.

I now understand the legacy that my grandparents and others of many generations gave us. The love of country, in good times and bad. The right to freedom of speech, even though we may not always agree with each other's words. The right to worship our God, even though he may not be someone else's god. My husband sacrificed so much so that our children will have a legacy to inherit. My family, friends, country and yes, God, are worth fighting and dying for. I want my children to grow up in a world where they have the rights and the freedoms to live their lives to the fullest extent of their efforts. Freedom is personal. Freedom comes at a high cost. While my husband didn't pay the ultimate price, we honor those who do. It is our right and our obligation. Freedom is not free!

> "For this reason a man will leave his father and mother and be united to his wife, and they will become one flesh."
> (Genesis 2:24)

Prayer:
Lord, help me show my appreciation for the sacrifices men and women have made to help protect freedom around the world.

Hero Missions

Sgt. Joseph Bills, Chaplain's Assistant, U.S. Army, Afghanistan (2004-2005); Iraq (2006-2007)

A KNOCK ON my door jolted me awake at 2 a.m.

"Twenty minutes, sir!" a voice announced.

I rolled out of my cot and shook the sleep from my mind and body. The unexpected wake-up call meant more U.S. soldiers had been killed. It was time for another Hero Mission—time to get on the helicopter and collect the remains somewhere in northern Iraq.

As a chaplain's assistant, it was my job to go on these Hero Missions almost as soon as the soldiers were killed, day or night. As the helicopter landed, blades still running, I'd hit the ground and collect the remains and make sure everything ran smoothly. We'd do a ceremony for them, and transport them down to a bigger air base to prepare them for the ramp ceremony so they could fly home.

> "The race is not to the swift or the battle to the strong . . . but time and chance happen to them all. Moreover, no man knows when his hour will come."
> (Ecclesiastes 9:10–12)

What I saw, smelled, and touched on these Hero Missions was pretty bad, but I had to do it. Even though I didn't know the soldiers personally, I felt like I did. I thought about their families back home and the buddies they left behind. I just wanted to do the best I could to honor them.

During the fifteen months in Iraq, I flew more than three hundred flight hours for close to eighty Hero Missions—and there were multiple remains each time. I recognize that nothing is promised. Soldiers in combat died, but guys who would just be walking to the mess hall would be killed by a mortar, also.

It all goes back to the Lord Jesus Christ, just putting my life in his hands. That's the only way I dealt with it. I still struggle, at times, sleeping, as I think about those soldiers we picked up. I probably will for the rest of my life. It was hard, but I also felt honored to be able to minister in this special way.

Prayer:
Lord, when confronted with the atrocities of war and other injustices of the world, show me what I can do about it, and what I need to leave in your hands.

Face to Face with the Taliban

Sgt. Joseph Bills, Chaplain's Assistant, U.S. Army, Afghanistan (2004-2005); Iraq (2006-2007)

YOU'VE GOT *to be kidding me,* I said to myself when I understood what was happening.

The chaplain and I were making our rounds within a U.S. Army hospital as part of our usual responsibilities during my twelve-month deployment in Afghanistan. We would minister to casualties and the medical staff alike. We had seen charred flesh, broken bodies, missing limbs, every kind of combat injury one can imagine.

But we had never seen this.

In one corner of the hospital, past all the U.S. soldiers suffering injuries, our medical team was diligently working to try to save the life of an Afghani Taliban guy who had inadvertently blown his arms and legs off with his own Improvised Explosive Device (IED). It wasn't a suicide-bombing—this guy had just screwed up and blown himself up.

Blood was everywhere. It seemed like quite a lost cause to me. Yet our doctors were trying to help him, even though this guy had prepared a bomb to blow us up. A known enemy that we knew would gladly kill us all if he got the chance.

> "So God created man in his own image."
> (Genesis 1:27)

What's the point? I thought. *If he dies, that's one less person we have to worry about hunting in the future.* Those things go through your head. It's kind of hard to have compassion for a terrorist who hurts himself.

But the doctors were operating from a different principle: they were dealing with a human life, and all human life has value. If they could possibly save that life, no matter who it was, that was their duty—to use their skills to help and not harm. And one has to realize in the overall big picture that these Taliban were just ignorant and had no idea exactly what they were fighting against.

The doctors worked on that armless, legless Taliban terrorist for a long time. They just couldn't save him.

Prayer:
Lord, let us not forget that you created all men and women in your image and that each life has worth and dignity.

JULY 12

Operation Flying Start

Sgt. Joseph Bills, Chaplain's Assistant, U.S. Army, Afghanistan (2004-2005); Iraq (2006-2007)

THE IRAQI children's eyes shone and their smiles just radiated unspeakable joy. You would think we had given them something unbelievably grand, something they could never ever imagine owning. You'd think we had just handed them they key to a better life. Maybe we did.

We gave them pencils. And they gave us an emotional payback of satisfaction that is difficult to describe.

The exchange was just one of many through a program our battalion (mainly our chaplain's office) put together called Operation Flying Start—and Operation Flying Start was just one of many similar humanitarian missions we did in Iraq. We contacted churches and organizations back home, and they gathered school supplies, soccer and sports equipment, etc., so we could distribute them here to orphanages and schools.

> "He who oppresses the poor shows contempt for their Maker, but whoever is kind to the needy honors God." (Proverbs 14:31)

As our convoy vehicles prepared to take all this stuff to the Iraqi people, we did it along with the Iraqi Army because we wanted to push them out front to make relationships. At that point, the average Iraqi citizen was scared of the Iraqi Army. They thought if they talked to the Iraqi soldiers, that others would kill them. So by having the Iraqi army help us distribute these supplies, we intended to teach the kids not to be afraid of them. We wanted to help them realize there's a different way of life—and that America is not bad; we were there to help.

To see how the children reacted to the gifts of basic, simple necessities gave us a greater appreciation of what our being over there was all about. Someone can have a conversation about whether or not we should be there—but there's no denying that these are still people who have suffered a lot—they are an oppressed people. It's just horrible. There's no way life should be like this.

Prayer:
*Lord, show me where I can help in my own community to
lift a burden from the oppressed and poor.*

Meeting Christ in the Desert

Sgt. Joseph Bills, Chaplain's Assistant, U.S. Army,
Afghanistan (2004-2005); Iraq (2006-2007)

MIGHTY IS our God . . . *Mighty is our King* . . . Camouflage-clad soldiers playing guitar, keyboard, and drums belted out songs of praise and worship from the front of the modest chapel that we built in the desert of Iraq. As the music drifted out of the building and over the sand, U.S. soldiers and contractors continued to file in, along with people of the Muslim faith who were either curious or just enjoyed the music. Either way, they heard the gospel.

> "If we confess our sins, he is faithful and just and will forgive us our sins and purify us from all unrighteousness." (1 John 1:9)

Plenty of people had said it couldn't be done. "You can't build a church," they had said. "You don't have the wood and the supplies. It's impossible."

But God made a way; we built that church, and he met us there. We had multiple people come to Christ in Iraq. As one can imagine, there were people coming to church who never would have under any other circumstances. Many of these people were dealing with family issues separate from (but perhaps complicated by) the stress of their deployments. When they decided to seek answers from God, the church was there for them, and so were the chaplain along with many other believing soldiers.

The same thing happened in Afghanistan, too. Some Afghanis that had been checked out and cleared were allowed on the base, and at least one of them, after coming to church, became a born again Christian. It was so incredible to be a part of God's work on the other side of the world. At these services, people would come to the Lord and want to be baptized. So we would have baptisms right there in Afghanistan and Iraq. We're not going to let a combat zone stop that.

I would never say God makes a war happen so he can draw people to himself. But I can say that even during war, amidst the casualties and death, he still brings new life to those who call on his name. The enemy may take the body, but the Lord saves the soul. I count it a privilege to have been a witness to that.

Prayer:
Lord, open my eyes to where you are working,
and show me how to be a part of it.

Saddam's Remains

Sgt. Joseph Bills, Chaplain's Assistant, U.S. Army, Afghanistan (2004-2005); Iraq (2006-2007)

SERGEANT BILLS, grab the chaplain, let's go." It was 6 p.m. on December 30, 2006. My colonel seemed urgent to get on the helicopter—but then, we considered all Hero Missions urgent, so I didn't think much about it. I just moved.

"We have to go now," he said again. We flew in two different birds to Baghdad in case anything should happen to one of them.

> "Surely God will crush the heads of his enemies, the hairy crowns of those who go on in their sins." (Psalm 68:21)

After landing on one of small bases there, I noticed secret service men walking around. *Okay, what's going on?* I wondered.

I soon learned that the remains we were about to collect were not those of a hero at all. We were picking up the remains of Saddam Hussein, hanged that morning, and to be delivered back to his hometown of Tikrit. We got the mission because we transfer remains, and we were in charge of the north where Tikrit is.

The officials in Baghdad had wanted to bury him in an unmarked grave there in Baghdad and keep its location a secret. But his family was there, pleading with them to be able to take the body home for a burial. After eight hours, the officials gave in.

Finally, around 11 p.m., we were ready to go. The family wanted to verify the identity of the body, so they unzipped the body bag. We all stood around staring into that face. Here was the dictator that had so oppressed his people. Here was the tyrant America had spent years fighting. At least, here was his body.

The magnitude of the scene was not lost on me—I wanted to somehow document the moment, but snapping a picture of his body was out of the question. Instead, once we were back in the helicopter, I took a picture of myself just to capture the date and time. It may look like an ordinary picture to anyone else, but when I see it, I'll always remember—that was the moment after I had seen the face of evil, and had seen that he had met justice once and for all.

Prayer:
*Lord, thank you for delivering the Iraqi people
out of the hands of Saddam Hussein.*

Dust Storm

Sgt. Joseph Bills, Chaplain's Assistant, U.S. Army, Afghanistan (2004-2005); Iraq (2006-2007)

SWELTERING. Blistering. Withering. Scorching. It was summertime in Iraq, the temperature hit 130 degrees. It was in this heat that we learned there was another Hero Mission to do. One problem—an intense dust storm along the way meant we couldn't fly out to pick up the soldier.

This was a big deal. It's not good for a body to just sit in the heat like that, as one can imagine. And these soldiers, his friends and comrades, were out there with him. Not only do we want to get him out of there as quick as possible out of respect for the dead, but in order for his teammates around him to get their heads straight. They can't be sitting there with their friends decomposing in the back of a Humvee—can't function. That's why we were such a fast reaction team.

> "Pray continually."
> (1 Thessalonians 5:17)

We were paralyzed to do our duty because the dust storm stubbornly refused to ease up. It looked like we wouldn't be able to take off all day. We were helpless to control the situation, except for one thing: prayer.

Lord, the chaplain and I prayed together, *we need to get this soldier on home. We really need to get our guy out of there. Calm the winds, settle the dust, clear the skies. Make a way for us to fly.*

Within an hour—and against the meteorological odds—we were getting on the bird and going to pick up that soldier. We got him through God's grace so he could be taken care of properly. And his fellow soldiers, though still keenly aware of his loss, were better able to focus on the rest of their mission.

Sometimes the Lord answers prayer so directly, so quickly, that it can only be credited to God (as in this case). Other times, what we pray for isn't given to us for reasons we can't ever hope to understand. I've learned to make my peace with that. The important thing is to keep on praying, and trust God for every outcome.

Prayer:
Lord, help me remember to take all things to you in prayer,
believing you will answer according to your wisdom.

The Lord is My Strength

Sgt. Joseph Bills, Chaplain's Assistant, U.S. Army,
Afghanistan (2004-2005); Iraq (2006-2007)

HERO MISSIONS wasn't the only responsibility I had in Iraq, but it was the most challenging and the most rewarding, hands down. For all the counseling that the chaplain and I gave to other people, sometimes I wished someone would ask me how *I'm* doing. We try to bear the burden as best we can, but it's a lot for anybody.

At times I'd come home from a mission and break down and cry. I tried to give it to the Lord, asked God to be with that soldier's family. One soldier had a one-year-old son, but he will never see his dad. Maybe that son was born while his dad was gone, and all he'll have is a picture.

All of these soldiers' deaths have affected me. I think about the ones that weren't married. I'd sit there and think about their mom or dad getting this news right now. When I picked up their son, they didn't even know yet. We were on the spot so fast that thoughts of their loved ones flashed though my mind: *Wow. This is going to tear their hearts out.*

> "Because you are my help, I sing in the shadow of your wings. My soul clings to you; your right hand upholds me." (Psalm 63:7–8)

Sometimes people wonder how, with my job, I could remain positive and upbeat and keep a smile on my face. The only reason I could do that is because of the Lord. Everything else just kind of falls into place. I don't worry as much about danger, something happening to me. I don't do stupid things, of course, and put myself in harm's way by careless mistake. But once I do give myself over to the Lord, it's a relief. It takes a lot of stress and burdens off of me.

My time in Iraq was the hardest experience I've ever had for a number of reasons, but the Lord sustained me—and I would do it again in a heartbeat.

Prayer:
Lord, sustain me and be my strength through
each day and stage of my life.

Significance of Life

Lt. Kevin Hamilton, U.S. Army, Iraq (2003–2004)

THE AIR crackled, sizzled, and smoked with gunfire and rockets hell-bent for American soldiers. A platoon of 82nd Airborne troops had just been ambushed outside Fallujah and had taken several casualties. As my team and I came closer to the scene just minutes later, a sniper team in the area came on the radio with a warning.

"There's a group of thirty to forty men in the middle of the road about a mile away with guns and RPGs," he told us. It was the ambush team. My vehicle and two tanks raced towards the area.

When we arrived on scene, all of the men scattered in vehicles. One truck pulled out and blocked the road so that we could not pursue. Shots rang out from the tank, warning the truck to move. With that, the truck recklessly sped towards the tank.

> "For the wages of sin is death, but the gift of God is eternal life through Jesus Christ our Lord." (Romans 6:23)

The tank commander fired a few shots into the cab killing the driver; the truck rolled to a stop and four men burst out and took off running. The tank commander shot them all.

Afterwards, I had to secure the area and clear the bodies of any weapons. That's when I saw him . . . one of the men who had tried to escape on foot and had been shot. We tried applying first aid but it was pretty obvious that he was not going to make it.

That whole night stands out to me as a paradox. We shot them and then tried to save them. My emotions went from rage over the fact that they had killed some of our soldiers to compassion and sadness. *Here is a man about to enter the gates of hell,* I thought as I watched him die. It was pretty rough, and I will never forget it for the rest of my life.

It really brought home the greater significance to taking a life. I realized that whether I liked it or not these terrorists needed Jesus just as much as my soldiers did. And no matter what uniform a person dies in—be it dress uniform or tattered robes—if they do not know Christ as their savior, their eternal fate is the same.

Prayer:
Lord, give me a heart for people's souls.

255

Kevin and Kristen Hamilton

Lt. Kevin Hamilton

My Times Are in Your Hands

Kristen Hamilton, wife of Kevin Hamilton,
U.S. Army, Iraq (2003–2004)

MY HEART was heavy. I desperately missed my husband and longed to be with him. I could only imagine just how lonely, scary, and disconcerting it would be to be sent halfway around the world to risk his life in uncomfortable conditions with people that he had only known for a matter of months. I wanted so badly to fly to him and "take care" of all his needs. Kevin is a strong, independent man—certainly more than capable of taking care of himself. Still, I would lay awake and wonder: *Who's encouraging my husband when he feels down? Who's ministering to his spirit when he needs a friend? Is anyone praying with him?* In the end, I felt like no one could replace me in looking out for my husband.

Then I read a book called *The Hand of God* by Alistair Begg. What an incredible blessing—the book follows the life of Joseph. In chapter four Begg drives home a key point that I felt was written directly for us: Joseph was a long way from home and everything familiar to him, yet he was still hemmed in "behind and before" by God.

It pierced my soul because I realized that I could so easily replace Joseph's name with Kevin's. Begg writes that God's presence was the source of Joseph's protection. What a relief. My burden was lifted when I understood that there was nothing that my presence could do that God's presence wasn't already doing. In fact, God's presence was all that Kevin needed. His circumstances could have been a thousand times worse, and still God was with him, and God was sufficient. I didn't have to be burdened with anxiety or concern. My amazing God was taking care of my amazing husband in ways well beyond my capabilities. From quiet, possibly lonely nights in his cot in the barracks to riding in the military vehicles on patrol, to helicopter rides to Baghdad, he was surrounded and secured with the power of God. What was left to worry about?

> "My times are in your hands; deliver me from my enemies and from those who pursue me." (Psalm 31:15)

Prayer:
Lord, thank you for remaining in complete control of all my days, and those of my loved ones.

JULY 19

Preparing to Deploy

Sgt. Shane Klein, Iowa National Guard, Iraq (2008–2009)

AS A MAN with a wife and four children preparing for a year in Iraq, we prayed for my physical safety. But what is more of a miracle? To save the body or the soul? God has delivered my soul from death. Not only does this show his love for me, but also shows his power. He has rescued me from eternal death to eternal life by going there himself and fetching me out.

Sgt. Shane Klein with his wife Sara and children just before his deployment to Iraq (courtesy of Catchlight Imaging)

God does not promise that I will never suffer bodily harm, but by already giving me new life in Christ he has demonstrated his power to save to the uttermost. Since he loves me enough to sacrifice his only Son on my behalf, I know that he will always do what is best for me. I don't know if that means physical safety, but I know that he is capable of keeping me safe in the midst of danger.

I know that my Lord will go anywhere that I am. If the very constraints of death itself cannot hold him back from what the Father has purposed, certainly on this earth there is no obstacle he cannot overcome.

Feeling the assurance that my Heavenly Father will never let go of me and being comforted in the knowledge of his spiritual and emotional provision for me, still I am surprised that a prevailing anxiousness builds on the horizon.

> "Be at rest once more, O my soul, for the LORD has been good to you. For you, O LORD, have delivered my soul from death, my eyes from tears, my feet from stumbling, that I may walk before the LORD in the land of the living." (Psalm 116:7–9)

I know that I am heading into a test of my faith; my greatest fear is that of failing. I fear the possibility that my thoughts and actions might soil the name of the One who called me by my name and forgave me. But I know that my God has delivered my feet from falling in the past and will again. I know that he is watching every step I take. I will walk before my Lord in the land of the living.

Prayer:
Lord, keep my feet from stumbling as I walk the path
you have set for me as a follower of Christ.

A Meeting with the President

Lt. Col. Mark Murphy (USAF), 354th Maintenance Group Deputy Commander

IT WAS AN event Eielson Air Force Base (Alaska) will never forget: a hangar full of airmen and soldiers getting to see President Bush up close while we hosted his refueling stop as he traveled to Asia on August 4, 2008. Air Force One landed at Eielson on time—to the minute; however, when he left less than two hours later, the president was fifteen minutes behind schedule. Here's why.

On December 10, 2006, our son, Shawn, was a paratrooper deployed on the outskirts of Baghdad. He was supposed to spend the night in camp, but when a fellow soldier became ill, Shawn volunteered to take his place on a nighttime patrol. As the turret gunner in the lead Humvee in the convoy, Shawn was in the most exposed position. He was killed instantly with two other soldiers when an IED ripped through their vehicle.

> "Show proper respect to everyone."
> (1 Peter 2:17a)

After the president's speech, I felt a tap on my shoulder and turned to see a White House staff member. She asked me and my wife to come with her, because the president wanted to meet us.

Stunned, we grabbed our two sons that were with us and followed her back into an empty conference room. A short time later, the Secret Service opened the door and President Bush entered, walked up to my wife, pulled her in for a hug and a kiss, and said, "I wish I could heal the hole in your heart." He then grabbed me for a hug, as well as each of our sons. Then he turned and said, "Everybody out." Not even a Secret Service agent remained.

"Come on—let's sit down and talk," he said. He slumped down in a chair, completely relaxed, smiled, and suddenly was no longer the president; he was just a guy with a job, sitting around talking with us like a family member at a barbeque. For the twenty minutes, he put everything and everyone on hold to meet with the family of a Private First Class who gave his life for his country. The President shared his private self with us in the process.

What an incredible lesson on service. We weren't on the itinerary and Air Force One was late because of it. If the president of the United States is willing to drop everything on his plate to visit with a family, surely the rest of us can do it. No one is above serving another person, and no one is so lofty that he or she can't treat others with dignity and respect.

Prayer:
Lord, show me where I fall short of
showing others the respect they deserve.

New Perspective on Service

Lt. Col. Mark Murphy (USAF), 354th Maintenance Group Deputy Commander

FOR THE NEXT twenty minutes, President Bush talked with us about our son, Iraq, faith in God, convictions, his family and his feelings about nearing the end of his presidency. He asked each of our teenaged sons what they wanted to do in life and counseled them to set goals, stick to their convictions, and not worry about being the "cool" guy.

He said that he'd taken a large amount of heat during his tenure and was under considerable pressure to do what was politically expedient, but he was proud to say that he never sold his soul. Sometimes he laughed, and at other times he teared up. He said that what he'll miss most after leaving office will be his role as Commander in Chief.

He thanked us for the opportunity to meet, because he felt a heavy responsibility knowing that our son died because of a decision he made. He was incredibly humble, full of warmth, and completely without pretense.

We couldn't believe how long he talked to us, but he seemed to be in no hurry whatsoever. In the end he thanked us again for the visit and for the opportunity to get off his feet for a few minutes. He then said, "Let's get some pictures." The doors flew open, Secret Service and the White House photographer came in, and suddenly he was the President again. A few pictures, more thank yous, a few more hugs, and he was gone.

> "Serve wholeheartedly, as if you were serving the Lord, not men." (Ephesians 6:7)

The remarkable thing about the whole event was that he didn't have to see us at all. But he put everything on hold to meet privately with the family of a Private First Class who gave his life in the service of his country.

You often think of service in terms of sacrificing yourself for someone in a higher position, but how often do you remember that serving someone below you can be much more important? If you're in a leadership capacity, take a good look at how you're treating your people, and remember that your role involves serving the people you rely on every day.

Prayer:
Lord, cultivate within me a spirit of service for everyone regardless of their social or professional status.

JULY 22

Ambush at Roberts Ridge

Capt. Nate Self, Army Ranger, Afghanistan (2002–2003); Iraq (2003–2004)

AROUND THREE a.m. on March 4, 2002, Army Ranger Nate Self and his thirteen-man Quick Reaction Force were sent to recover a fallen Navy SEAL in Afghanistan, a place teeming with hundreds of al-Qaeda fighters.

"There was no place on earth more hostile to U.S. soldiers and no place would my team rather be," Self recalled. "We were there because we were Rangers, and we had a creed to uphold: Never leave a fallen comrade!"

Self and his team weren't told that helicopters that had been sent to the mountain (later named Roberts Ridge) had come under fire. When the

Chinook helicopter was shot down in an ambush, a fifteen-hour firefight ensued.

Bullets whizzed past Self, rocket-propelled grenades ripped through the air around him. Self began to plan a counterattack on the high-caliber machine-gun bunker, even though he was bleeding from a shrapnel wound in his leg.

Hours of fighting dragged on as Self and his men tried to stabilize the area enough for helicopters to come in and evacuate the wounded. In the meantime, fellow soldiers lay bleeding in the snow all around them as they fought off the enemy at such close range they could see their faces.

Self and his men found the fallen SEAL who had been killed with a shot to the head, and also located the body of a dead U.S. serviceman from the first failed rescue attempt. Three of Self's men were killed in that day-long battle on the mountain. But if not for Self's clear thinking and strong leadership, the casualties would have been even more.

> "How long must I wrestle with my thoughts and every day have sorrow in my heart? How long will my enemy triumph over me?" (Psalm 13:2)

Senior officers back at the base heaped praise upon Self and his team for being able to get off the mountain and kill the enemy without sustaining greater losses—especially since they had been caught unaware.

For Self, the battle resulted in a Silver Star for valor, a Purple Heart, and later, a position of honor as President Bush's guest for the 2003 State of the Union address. To those watching, Capt. Self represented strength, resolve, and success of the military.

But Self didn't want to be honored. In fact, by 2004, he wanted to die.

Prayer:
*Lord, when I feel ambushed by uncontrollable circumstances,
give me wisdom and guidance to make the right decisions.*

Invisible Battle

Capt. Nate Self, Army Ranger, Afghanistan (2002–2003); Iraq (2003–2004)

SEVERE POST-TRAUMATIC stress disorder had delivered a near-fatal blow to this war hero; he left the Army in late 2004, cutting short a would-be military career. Vivid nightmares, anxiety, anger, and self-destructive behavior took hold of him.

"I just hated myself," said Self. "I felt like I was somebody different. And since I didn't feel like I could be who I was before and hated who I was now, I wanted to kill the new person. I felt like I had messed up everything in my life. The easiest way, the most cowardly way to escape was to just *depart*."

Though he never asked for help or told anyone he was contemplating suicide, Self's parents intervened to direct him to the help he needed. Christian Army chaplains trained in PTSD provided counseling, and he went to group therapy sessions at the VA. But he also joined a small group for vets with PTSD at his church, First Baptist Church in Belton, Texas. The leader was his chaplain counselor.

> "Three times I pleaded with the Lord to take [the thorn in my flesh] away from me. But he said to me, 'My grace is sufficient for you, my power is made perfect in weakness.'"
> (2 Corinthians 12:8–9a)

"At the VA small group, we talked about symptoms, but we were never allowed to talk about our experiences because they were afraid it would trigger us. But it was those experiences we needed to talk about the most. At the church, we got into God's Word, bathed all sessions in prayer, told our stories, wrote about and shared our experiences and that was extremely therapeutic. We looked at spiritual solutions and examples of warriors in the Bible. Turning my PTSD into Christian service has helped me get past to the other side of it."

The writing that Capt. Self began at church developed into his memoir, *Two Wars: One Hero's Fight on Two Fronts—Abroad and Within* (Tyndale House, May 2008). Self also helps train churches from New York to San Diego on PTSD by sharing his testimony through Bridges to Healing.

"There are many things in life we go through that God allows for specific reasons," said Self. "We can be hurt by things over which we have no control. That doesn't mean it's not fair, but neither does it mean that God needs to take it away, God can use the thorn in the side—the anguish is there for a reason."

Prayer:
*Lord, help me allow you to shine through my
weaknesses so people will see your glory.*

Not in Bondage

Capt. Nate Self, Army Ranger, Afghanistan (2002–2003); Iraq (2003–2004)

TODAY, CAPT. Self's PTSD is much less severe, but some symptoms still remain. He still has haunting dreams most nights, intrusive thoughts, and certain problems with anger. He still feels somewhat emotionally numb. While he used to wonder if complete healing was possible, he has since decided that answer doesn't matter.

"I don't know if it's right to say, 'I want to be healed from all this,' because it's a very humbling thing to be in this position and know that I'm being held in grace," he said. "It equips me for better ministry and service. To wish away this thorn in my side would remove a significant portion of my testimony. It's not that I have to be in bondage to PTSD. What matters is, now that I have it, what am I going to do with it?"

> "Then Job replied to the LORD: 'I know that you can do all things; no plan of yours can be thwarted.'" (Job 42:1–2)

Self now works as a consultant on officer-training materials for the Army and is active in his own church's military ministry, which serves one hundred military families in their three thousand-member church.

When Self was experiencing darker days with PTSD, members of his church reached out and listened to him. Now, he's passing it along. "When soldiers come home, I'll take them to breakfast or lunch as soon as I can," he says. "They need people to be interested, to show that they care. If people think that the VA hospital will solve all the problems, they'll overlook the greatest source of healing in any situation—Jesus.

The majority component for recovery is a spiritual solution, more than any secular clinical answer."

Even as Capt. Self works toward healing, he realizes that his symptoms may never go away, and he has a peace about that. "Look at Job," he said. "All that stuff happened to him, he did not deserve. He kept asking God why until God said, 'Look, don't ask me why until you understand why I laid the foundations of the earth. You need to be comfortable with my sovereignty.'"

Prayer:

Lord, teach me to be more interested in your character and sovereignty than I am in securing comfort for myself.

Safety in God's Hand

Vanessa Peters, wife of Capt. Dave Peters, U.S. Air Force

MOST FOLKS of my parents' generation remember exactly where they were when they heard the news that JFK had been shot. For my generation, we remember where we were on September 11, 2001.

I sat in a roomful of women where we had gathered for Bible study. The church secretary interrupted our meeting to tell us what had happened and to ask us to pray, which we did immediately. Unaware of the extent of the attacks, we simply prayed for God's providence to prevail, and asked him to comfort those affected by acts of terrorism.

> "The LORD will watch over your coming and going both now and forevermore."
> (Psalm 121:8)

Being a newlywed and rookie military wife, my first thought went to my husband. He had just become mission qualified, and was on his first long temporary duty trip (TDY) as a pilot on the C-5 Galaxy. He told me that he was in Egypt, and the crew carried ravens (military police officers) "just in case." I hadn't heard from him in a couple days.

I left Bible study, and raced to a nearby friend's house to turn on the TV, where I saw images of Egyptians dancing in the streets and celebrating the demise of Americans. This was where my husband's first mission had taken him.

Capt. Dave Peters, U.S. Air Force, prior to his deployment to Iraq in 2003

I took a deep breath and whispered a silent prayer: "Lord, keep my husband from danger or harm. Bring him home safely. I'm not ready to be a widow. Yet, not my will, but yours be done."

As I drove home, a large line of cars lined the highway nearing the exit to the base. Military police were searching vehicles and thoroughly checking ID's, even to get into base housing. As I waited, my mind began to wander. Was he on the ground? In the air? Could he contact me?

When I arrived, the answering machine light blinked to indicate that I had a message. Thankfully, it was my sweet husband, telling me that he had been in the air en route to England when the attacks occurred. "Thank you, Lord." I exhaled as I praised God for this good news. God had known my husband's location all along— safely in the palm of His capable hand.

Prayer:
Lord, keep me safely in the center of your will,
even if dangers surround.

267

Dave Peters and
his wife Vanessa

Good News From Baghdad

Capt. Dave Peters, U.S. Air Force

A S I WATCHED the news coming over Armed Forces Network (AFN) in the dining hall on April 9, 2003, I saw the old statue of Saddam Hussein being toppled in the city square in Iraq. It was another "routine" day for me in Moron, Spain—a convenient stopover for the C-5 Galaxy in Europe. We were carrying materials to support those men who were accomplishing the seemingly clean sweep through Iraq. It was business as

268

usual, a sunny stopover, but this bright day had a little more shine on it with the good news from the front and an opportunity to write my wife:

"Looks like some good news from the front with Baghdad falling and statues toppling . . . I am proud that I got to contribute to the effort and even more grateful to my lovely, wonderful wife who supports me so much - you really do make my job easier knowing that you have a great attitude and want to support me however you can . . . I thank God for you and hope to be back home soon . . ."

Only eighteen days before, the victory was no sure bet. Our mission that night had us bound for Kuwait to drop off some support equipment for the 101st Airborne. From our vantage point above the Red Sea, we could see Naval vessels kicking off the "Shock & Awe" campaign by launching Cruise Missiles into Iraq. Once we arrived in Kuwait, we made several rushes to the bunkers, donning chemical defense gear, and anxiously awaiting the sirens to silence. As the threat dropped, we quickly prepared the aircraft for a return flight to Spain and left the theater uneventfully, wondering if more uncertain nights were on the horizon.

> "Rise up, O God, judge the earth, for all the nations are your inheritance." (Psalm 82:8)

As it turned out, that is as perilous as my encounters with the enemy were. The long hours flying across the oceans and continents, constant uncertainty of alert schedules, and many days apart from family posed the more challenging threat. My exposure to the thorny battlefields in Iraq was brief and distant, mostly from miles above the action. But my satisfaction in playing a role in our nation's war was no less sure than the soldier who patrolled the streets of Fallujah.

Prayer:
Lord, be sovereign over the nations; may your will be done in the governments of the earth.

"We've Got to be a Target"

Capt. Tom Joyce, U.S. Navy (Ret.)

SEPTEMBER 11, 2001 started off just like any other day. As a Deputy for Naval Aviation, I arrived to work at the Pentagon in Arlington, Virginia, around 5:30 a.m. so I could have Bible study and prayer time before the day got going. Forty-five minutes later I immersed myself in working on budget figures for Congress, because we were trying to request some new aircraft and weapons systems.

"Captain Joyce." I glanced at the clock as a Navy commander came by my desk. Two hours had passed already. "You need to come take a look at this airplane that just hit the World Trade Center," she said.

"It's probably just a small Cessna that had taken off at one of the regional airports there, maybe lost its way in the fog and ran into one of the towers," I said, not giving it any second thought.

"No, you need to come take a look at it," she responded.

So we went to the office next door, and watched the aftermath of the first plane that hit the first tower. We watched it until we saw the second airplane hit the tower.

"It's a coordinated attack," the guy next to me blurted out. As an aide to the admiral,

> " ... there is terror on every side; they conspire against me and plot to take my life." (Psalm 31:13)

his military mindset kicked in. He picked up the phone on the desk and immediately dialed to a friend of his who was on watch at the National Military Command Center in the bowels of the Pentagon. The NMCC is the place from which wars are run.

"What do we got?" he asked.

In a coded message, the response came back: "We've got other planes that are hijacked. We're under attack. We don't know from who."

Looking at each other in that fifth floor office of the Pentagon, we said, "We've got to be a target." We knew it was only a matter of time.

Prayer:
Lord, let me not forget that even in times of war and terror, you have not relinquished your sovereignty.

This Is It

Capt. Tom Joyce, U.S. Navy (Ret.)

I'VE GOT TO *clear my head,* I thought as I stared out my office window toward Arlington National Cemetery. I had watched the news until I could no longer watch the replays. Now it was time to think.

We knew there would be other attacks. We were up there on the fifth floor, most likely in harm's way, but what do we do? We don't leave our post. We continue to do our job and see who needs help. All the admirals who worked at our office were gone for a meeting, which made me the senior guy in my office. I wasn't about to run away and seek my own protection.

I called my wife, Deshua, who was teaching at the time and told her what was going on. "You might want to let the principal of the school know," I told her. "And people should start praying."

Turning back to the window, I tried to focus my thoughts on what might happen and what our responses should be in various scenarios. I didn't need to imagine the possibilities for long.

Moments later I saw the fireball coming toward the window.

This is it, I thought. I watched a big bright light rushing toward me and thought it was a bomb. It happened all at once, but at the same time everything seemed to slow

"My times are in your hands; deliver me from my enemies and from those who pursue me." (Psalm 31:15)

down. And while one eye was focused on the fireball, my right eye was focused on a bag of Doritos I had put on my desk to eat later. I was watching this fireball thinking, *I'm about to die,* and looking at the Doritos thinking, *I guess I'm never going to eat those.* Then, before I knew it, the floor buckled, lifted me up, and threw me back. The plane had hit the building directly beneath me.

Prayer:
Lord, give me the courage to be where you've placed me, even if that means being vulnerable to any kind of attack or inconvenience.

The World Just Changed

Capt. Tom Joyce, U.S. Navy (Ret.)

I SCRAMBLED TO my feet and grabbed another guy. "You and I are going to be the last ones out of here," I told him. "We have to make sure we get everybody out."

There were about one hundred people in our office to evacuate. Some we dragged out, some were carried out. The pressure from the explosion blew cinder blocks across the office, hitting some people squarely, splitting their heads wide open. We knew we had to get them to first aid pretty quickly.

By that time the fire was starting to consume our office. We picked our way across the floor on hands and knees through debris and glass to stay beneath the thick black smoke. Someone pointed out, "That's got to be aviation fuel, look at the way it's burning." We were all aviators, so that's when we realized it was a plane that had hit us.

Meanwhile, an intelligence officer from my office had been in the Navy Operations Center on the first floor directly below us calling up information to us when the plane hit, instantly killing forty-two people and blowing this officer completely out of the C-ring where he had been. He went back into the fire four times to pull four people out. He saved their lives. So many different people responded with acts of heroism that day.

> "Since you are my rock and my fortress, for the sake of your name lead and guide me."
> (Psalm 31:3)

Back upstairs on the fifth floor, our time was running out. The area we were in was completely on fire, which turned all the exits into dead ends. We were walking down the escalators (all power had been knocked out), and ended up finding an exit on the other side of the building—completely on the other end of the world, we used to say. It took us the better part of forty-five minutes to get out of the building.

As one can imagine at the Pentagon, there was no problem with people taking charge. But other than those that were giving specific directions, nobody else spoke as we filed out. It was silent—and really eerie. Everybody knew the world had just changed.

Prayer:
Lord, as the world changes and leaves me with nothing to rely upon,
may I constantly come back to you for guidance.

Chaos

Capt. Tom Joyce, U.S. Navy (Ret.)

ONCE WE GOT outside, many of us broke into a dead sprint to get to the other side of the Pentagon to see who else we could pull out of the building. We didn't know the first responders were already there—all we knew was that a large number of people were hurt. We could hear them yelling and moaning, but we couldn't get to them because of the fire. It was chaos. And we didn't think it was over.

Is the same thing going on at the White House? My mind raced. *What other facilities have been attacked? What about my family? If these people are doing this to innocent people on airplanes, they could be setting down nuclear weapons right where my family is.*

Nobody could reach anybody. Most of the phone circuits were overloaded, even for cell phones. My oldest daughter saw the news in her high school classroom and thought for sure I was dead. It was two to three hours before I was able to connect with my family.

An hour later, we were told there was another plane inbound—Flight 93—that crashed in Shanksville, Pennsylvania. So they

> "When I am afraid, I will trust in you." (Psalm 56:3)

had us all scurry away and take cover under the overpass on Interstate 395 for awhile. Every couple minutes, F-16s flew about fifty feet over the Pentagon.

Finally somebody told everyone to go home, watch the news, and be ready to report back to work tomorrow. Nobody could get in and out of the parking lot, so fifteen thousand of us walked on the shoulders of I-395. Many cars coming out of Washington pulled over and offered rides.

The fellow who helped me evacuate our office and I were picked up by two guys. When Dan Rather said something on the radio about "crazy Islamic fundamentalists," these two guys started yelling at the radio in Arabic, pounding on the dashboard, swearing out the window.

What in the world did we get ourselves into? we thought. We quickly jumped out of the car in the slow-moving traffic and walked to a subway station. Two hours after I had left the Pentagon, I finally made it home.

Prayer:
Lord, when things don't make sense, help me keep my focus on you.

What Now?

Capt. Tom Joyce, U.S. Navy (Ret.)

I KNOW WHAT you've been through today, Tom, but one of our men has been reported missing." It was one of the pastors at the church where I served as an elder calling me that evening. "We think he's gone. Will you come with me? I want you to break the news to the family."

I knew exactly where this man's office was. I saw that wreckage, and there's no way he would have made it. We checked all the hospitals to be sure, but I wasn't surprised to learn he wasn't at any of them.

Sharing the news with his wife, fifteen-year-old daughter, and eleven-year-old son was the most difficult thing I've ever had to do. I still see the daughter's eyes periodically when I wake up at night. *Who's going to walk me down the aisle?* they seemed to say. *Who's going to interview my prom date?*

Completely exhausted emotionally and physically, I returned home that night around 10 p.m. When my oldest son Ryan, a junior in high school, saw me, he jumped up out of his seat, and threw his arms around me.

> "I urge you to live a life worthy of the calling you have received."
> (Ephesians 4:1)

"Dad, I'm so thankful that God spared your life today," he said.

After a few minutes, he dropped his arms, stepped back, and looked at me. "Dad, I gotta ask you a question. For some reason God spared your life today at the Pentagon. What are you going to do now with the rest of your life?" He repeated the question, said "I love you Dad," went upstairs and went to bed.

It was the most penetrating question anyone's ever asked me. It was just like God said to Ryan, "Challenge your dad and go to bed." It was that clear.

September 11, 2001, was a wake-up call for me. I had already been considering going into ministry after retirement, and on that day, I felt like God was saying, *I want you to make a decision. I spared your life. I want you to do something a little more valuable with it.*

Two weeks after my Navy retirement ceremony in 2003, I was sitting at a desk at Immanuel Bible Church as the new Pastor of Discipleship and Family.

Prayer:
*Lord, help me fulfill your purpose
for me in a way that honors you.*

Filling Up

Cdr. Mark D. Waddell, SEAL,
U.S. Navy, Iraq (2003–2006)

MARCH 19, 2003, Iraqi Border. It was the first day of the invasion, and Navy SEAL Commander Mark Waddell was outfitted in his chemical suit and armed with chemical/biological/nuclear gear in anticipation of a possible chemical attack.

"You know," he told another officer who was with him, "today is also my birthday . . ." The conversation stopped cold when the night sky lit up from a Marine Corps CH-46 helicopter exploding. The helicopter was carrying some British troops into combat, and they were all killed instantly.

"And that's the way I started my birthday that year with the rocket that the Iraqis were shooting at us," remembered Waddell. "They sounded like big jets flying over our heads, and chemical alarms were sounding, and it was very confusing in the fog of combat as we were attacking them."

This was not the first time the twenty-year combat veteran had witnessed a violent end to human life, but it would prove to be the start of a year that would overwhelm him. "My life was full of seeing human tragedy," he explained. "So in 2003 there was more human tragedy, there were more people killed, there were more uncertainties, there were more paradox situations that I had to deal with, and very intense emotional trauma. I was just full."

> "O LORD, the God who saves me, day and night I cry out before you. . . . for my soul is full of trouble." (Psalm 88:1, 3a)

Waddell and his wife, Marshele Carter Waddell, compare the experience to a scene in the film *Titanic* where a handful of men are arguing about whether the ship would sustain the blow or sink. "And then the engineer steps forwards and says, 'If only three or four compartments had been affected, we would be okay. But it has spilled over into a fifth compartment, and she will sink.' And that jumped out at me; that was my husband. Too many compartments had been affected and filled up, and therefore the weight was going to pull him down," said Marshele.

Prayer:
Lord, when I begin sinking, lift me up with your mighty hand.

275

Vacation Backfire

Marshele Carter Waddell, author of Hope for the Home Front *and co-author of* When War Comes Home: Christ-Centered Healing for Wives of Combat Veterans

WHEN MARK came home from his first combat deployment in Iraq in early May 2003, Marshele and their three children were ready. Before his homecoming, Marshele had picked up free tickets to Disney World that had been offered specifically for military families as a way to "support the troops" and show appreciation for their service.

"Subsequently I made these plans so when he arrived home we could go to Orlando and enjoy Disney World to honor him and have fun as a family," said Marshele. "And it turned out that that was probably the worst place we could have gone."

The crowds pressed in around them. Giant Disney characters got in their faces. The air was thick with the explosions of fireworks and the screams of people on rides.

"That whole trip was awful," said Marshele. "It was awful for me. It was awful for the kids. That was one of the first times I could tell that something had changed for Mark."

> "My eyes are dim with grief. I call to you, O LORD, every day; I spread out my hands to you." (Psalm 88:9)

Normally, Mark—and the entire family—would have enjoyed this type of vacation as a chance to escape daily routines and concerns and bond with each other while making special memories. But this was not a normal time for Mark. He was miserable.

He was having physiological responses to the sites, the sounds, and the smells around him. He was in a sweat all the time. His heart raced, and he fought to keep panic at bay. The kids were all excited about being there, but he was so consumed with his reactions to his surroundings that he couldn't engage with them like he wanted.

"He was trying desperately to have fun," said Marshele. "But he was exhausted. He didn't need Disney World. He needed something much different."

Prayer:
*Lord, supply us with that which we truly need;
you're the only one who can.*

The End of Me

Marshele Carter Waddell, author of Hope for the Home Front *and co-author of* When War Comes Home: Christ-Centered Healing for Wives of Combat Veterans

A FTER LEAVING the chaos of Disney World, things didn't get much better for the Waddells. In fact, things got worse.

"Everything was hard," said Marshele. "Everything was difficult because Mark was no longer Mark. About one year later I reached a breaking point where I went through a lot of different emotions—confusion, anger, guilt. I had the feeling that maybe this was my fault. Maybe I wasn't being a good enough wife. Maybe if I took on more responsibility around the house. Maybe if I did everything for Mark and kept his world balanced then he would get past whatever it was he was in."

By this time, Mark had assumed the position of Director of Operations for all the East Coast SEAL teams, which meant several trips back and forth overseas, in and out of combat zones. Even when Mark was home, he was busy training and preparing himself and others to deploy again. So without a sustained amount of time to really address the problem, the situation could not improve.

> "My soul is in anguish. How long, O LORD, how long?" (Psalm 6:3)

"When the men come home—whether it's for two weeks of rest and relaxation and going back to the war front or maybe they're coming home for six months—they're trying to avoid the conflict," said Marshele. "They're trying to reconnect and have a life. Spouses don't have time to address these huge problems or even avoid them. A year after Mark had come home in May 2003, I had reached the end of me."

As a veteran military wife, Marshele had been able to categorize and file away everything for awhile, but she got to a point where she couldn't do it any more. "I was saturated with what had been our military life experience. I told him that whether he went with me or not, I needed counseling. I had to go find somebody objective that could tell me I wasn't going insane."

Prayer:
*Lord, help me surround myself with people
who will speak truth and wisdom to me.*

277

Secret Struggle

Cdr. Mark D. Waddell, SEAL, U.S. Navy, Iraq (2003–2006)

WHILE THE Waddell family felt like they were crumbling on the inside, on the outside, they still seemed picture perfect. Yellow ribbons hugged the trees in their yard and flags waved proudly overhead. Friends of their high school son were in and out of the house all the time. There was no indication that anything was wrong and that's the way Mark wanted it.

"I was kind of glad Marshele got counseling if that's what she needed, but then I was also a little worried about my career if people found out," said Mark. "We had been a community pillar of strength and faith, and I didn't want to show that our faith had been shaken or that we were at risk as a couple, because it would have made a farce of everything we had said and stood for."

As an officer in special operations, Mark's response to the nagging sense that something was wrong was to just carry on.

"[SEALS are] used to suffering," said Mark. "We're used to enduring and doing without." So alone, Mark dealt with nightmares, emotional numbness, distressing and vivid daytime flashbacks. He saved his tears for when he was alone.

> "Create in me a pure heart, O God, and renew a steadfast spirit within me."
> (Psalm 51:10)

About a year and a half after Marshele started counseling, Mark admitted that he needed help, also. But he didn't want to talk about it with Marshele; he just wanted her to know that he recognized there was a problem that he was struggling with and needed help.

"I saw my marriage unraveling," said Mark. And then I thought to myself, *All this sacrifice and I'm about ready to be here on earth with nothing left. My wife, my children, and everything I had fought for and was willing to die for I was about to lose because of my response to the people that I was supposed to love.*

"Is there anything that you wouldn't do to save our marriage?" Marshele asked him.

278

"I would do anything," Mark responded.
"Would you go talk to a doctor? Would you just go see your doctor?"

Prayer:
Lord, when life seems to fall apart around me, speak to my
heart and create in me a steadfast spirit to wait upon you.

AUGUST 5

I Was One of Them

Cdr. Mark D. Waddell, SEAL,
U.S. Navy, Iraq (2003–2006)

WHEN MARK decided to talk to a doctor, he chose one with whom
he had already developed a deep respect for: Dr. Dan Sutton, a
SEAL team doctor, a regular physician. When there was a mass casualty
in Afghanistan, the largest loss of SEAL life in history, Dr. Sutton and
Mark were intimately involved when the bodies were brought back
through Dover, and their remains returned to the families.

"Doc Sutton went to Dover and was
with everybody that returned," said Mark.
"As a result he more fully understood what
combat stress was all about—he knew the
symptoms of post-traumatic stress and its
disorder."

> "Have mercy on me, O
> Lord, for I call to you all
> day long." (Psalm 86:3)

Mark was also watching people coming back, including the wounded,
the remains, and those who had no visible injuries to their bodies. "I
understood that there were post-traumatic symptoms going on within the
field community and with the guys returning from combat," said Mark.
"There were just an incredible number of deaths that happened in
Afghanistan. The smells of rotted flesh still clung to the equipment that
came back."

Mark knew that Dr. Sutton had been doing a lot of reading on PTSD
and comparing notes with what he observed in the troops coming home.
"I told him that I would like him to start informing us on what he was
seeing, so that we could keep our commodore, the guy in charge of all the

SEAL teams on the East Coast, informed. We had a great working relationship with each other," said Mark.

Another instrumental player in Mark's life at that time was the Group chaplain, Cory Cathcart, who had also been doing a lot of reading and research about the effect of combat stress.

"So through what I learned from the chaplain and the doctor, and by Marshele getting counseling, I realized that I was one of them," said Mark. "I was one of the thousands of service members with PTSD."

Prayer:
Great Physician, heal us of the pain of our yesterdays and our todays.

AUGUST 6

You're Not Going Crazy

Cdr. Mark D. Waddell, SEAL,
U.S. Navy, Iraq (2003–2006)

I WAS PRAYING without ceasing," said Mark. "I was afraid of breaking. I thought I was going crazy."

When Mark vulnerably described to Dr. Sutton how he was doing emotionally with all the trauma that he had experienced, Dr. Sutton said it was ordinary human capacity trying to adapt to abnormal stress.

"Mark, post-traumatic stress and post-traumatic stress disorder are not mental illnesses," Dr. Sutton told Mark in his office. "You're not going crazy. All this stuff that's going on right now is not your fault."

Mark agreed with Dr. Sutton to go get counseling, but only as long as it was faith-based. "The only thing I was hanging onto was my belief in Jesus as a Christ-follower," said Mark. "If I didn't start off with faith-based counseling, then it would be a futile endeavor."

> "Praise be to God, who has not rejected my prayer or withheld his love from me!"
> (Psalm 66:20)

As soon as he began his series of counseling, Mark noticed a positive change. "That's because with Dr. Sutton I had an emotional breakdown, and then the confirmation that *I wasn't going crazy* from someone who studies the mind, the psyche, and PTSD," said Mark. "It was so reassuring to learn that all these circumstances of this trauma weren't my fault. All these feelings that I was having were a normal response to extraordinary trauma."

Mark was also told that PTSD is the only clinically diagnosed anxiety order that's directly associated with a known cause. "These were landmark things for me because when I thought I going crazy, when I thought I was losing everything, and then I hear the diagnosis, I knew there was hope," he said. "There was hope for recovery—not only some recovery but complete recovery, to go back to feeling again, to loving again, to establishing relationships again."

Prayer:
Lord, thank you for the hope we have because
of your mighty power and grace.

AUGUST 7

Next Steps in the Journey

Marshele Carter Waddell, *author of* **Hope for the Home Front** *and co-author of* **When War Comes Home: Christ-Centered Healing for Wives of Combat Veterans**

THE BEST news my counselor told me was that everything I was feeling was normal. She helped me understand my husband's crisis," said Marshele. "She helped me understand his mind, his heart, and the reactions he was having to his life experiences."

Mark's willingness to go to counseling was another huge step for the couple. "When he tried to be so strong for so long, it was good to see him be vulnerable and open with me," said Marshele. "I know it was really hard for him."

The journey toward complete healing isn't over yet, Marshele said. "But there are greater signs of healing now. The monsters that raise their heads are getting smaller, and the victories are becoming bigger over time. I think that time is such a huge part of this prescription. We just have to wait. We have to keep doing the right things, keep loving one another, and keep believing that faith, hope, and love will endure—and they will undergo anything if given the chance."

The Waddells are more able to talk openly in the moment of rising tension, or within a couple of hours of the incident. Reconciliation is taking place much more quickly than before.

In 2007, Mark and Marshele began sharing their story with other churches through Bridges to Healing, the PTSD ministry branch of Campus Crusade for Christ's Military Ministry. Marshele also speaks directly to women who share their experiences in her book, *When War Comes Home: Christ-centered Healing for Wives of Combat Veterans*, co-authored with Reverends Chris and Rahnella Adsit.

> "He heals the broken-hearted and binds up their wounds."
> (Psalm 147:3)

"When families go through these combat deployments and especially when dealing with PTSD on a moderate to severe level, everyone close to the situation goes through a faith crisis: *Where was God when all this happened, where is he now? Why do I feel like I knock and the locks are bolted?*" said Marshele.

"In those times, as long as you don't give up, you will grow. God hears all of it, and eventually he responds, he stirs, and you will know he's present in it. It just seems like forever in those long dry spells."

Prayer:
Lord, give me the discipline to stay faithful to you even in the dry spells.

AUGUST 8

Going to War

Capt. Stuart Zeigler, U.S. Army, Afghanistan (2007–2008)

WE'RE GOING to war!"

I will never forget those four little words that were spoken by an ROTC instructor at Temple University in Philadelphia, Pennsylvania. It was September. 11, 2001, and we both sat speechless before a tiny 12-inch black and white television screen watching a third plane crash before our very eyes into the Pentagon.

Five years later it had seemed that those words had indeed come true for every soldier serving in the U.S. Army, except me. Having received my commission as a second lieutenant in the army in 2003, virtually every one of my fellow ROTC classmates had one or two deployments in support of the "global war on terror" in Iraq and Afghanistan. As of September 2006, I had none.

After several deployment notifications that fell through, I became convinced that it was my destiny to remain a commissioned officer in the Army Reserves, working stateside as a specialist in homeland security. This non-deployment affected me in an adverse way. It seemed that everyone else was doing their duty or deployed overseas *Why am I lucky? Why do I get to stay behind?* I wondered. I was single yet watched as many of my friends with wives and children were called up to go serve while I stayed behind. *It's not fair that they have to leave their families and I still haven't gone once,* I thought.

> "Why, you do not even know what will happen tomorrow."
> (James 4:14a)

It came as little surprise when in September of 2006 I received my latest warning order from the army that I might yet again be deploying overseas. I chalked it up to another "boy who cried wolf" scenario and went about my daily life. In the two weeks between my latest alert and when I was required to report for soldier readiness processing, my life would change forever.

Prayer:
*Lord, as I make plans for the future, remind me
that you are ultimately in control.*

A U G U S T   9

Love and War

Capt. Stuart Zeigler, U.S. Army, Afghanistan, 2007–2008

ON SEPTEMBER 24, I was introduced to Amanda through mutual friends. We instantly bonded. Six days later Amanda and I went on our first date. In between the day we met and our first date, I received the official notice that I was indeed going to be departing in late December of 2006 for pre-deployment training at Ft. Riley, Kansas, followed by a twelve-month tour in support of Operation Enduring Freedom in Afghanistan.

"Do I still follow this love?" I asked God repeatedly. With each and every date and moment spent with Amanda I felt more assurance that this woman was not only special, but a woman with a heart for Christ and a woman of encouragement. I specifically remember one evening several weeks into our relationship asking her "not to forget me when I am away." She promised me she wouldn't.

Then the two of us shared a moment that I had never shared with a woman before. We prayed together. Then suddenly, one of us began to slowly and very softly sing a familiar hymn. The other quietly joined in. The two of us sat there holding, praying, and singing praises with each other. How do two people find true love and then cope with the separation of that love in such a short period of time? The impossible is accomplished and expressed through intimate prayer, and unending songs of praise to a God whose plan is far greater then we could ever hope or imagine. Thanks be to God that his thoughts are not our thoughts and his ways are not our ways. Never in a million years would I have imagined God would bring my future wife to me before sending me overseas in his service. Little did I know that day that it would be through song and prayer that God would draw me closer to Amanda, but more importantly, closer to him.

> "'For my thoughts are not your thoughts, neither are your ways my ways,' declares the Lord." (Isaiah 55:8)

Prayer:
*Lord, help me not be so intent on my own plans that
I fail to see the better path you have for me.*

AUGUST 10

Mighty Fortress

Amanda Zeigler, wife of Capt. Stuart Zeigler, U.S. Army, Afghanistan (2007–2008)

GOD TRULY became the focus of the year 2007—the year Stuart was deployed—because the Lord was all we had to cling to. Stuart was completely in his hands, and all I could do was pray (and pray, and pray more). There were some nights that I was too distraught to do anything but read my Bible in search of comfort and peace. Psalm 77 was good for the nights I felt like I was coming apart.

Stuart always said he could feel my prayers, especially during the first days that he arrived overseas. Knowing that Stuart was lifted reassured me immensely. I prayed for him every day, usually many, many times. It was also comforting to know that the God of my mundane suburban existence was the same One who had created the spectacular mountains of Afghanistan, and the barren scrub terrain that became the backdrop for Stuart's daily life. I remember thinking how the human spirit can adapt rather quickly to sudden life changes and great emotional turmoil.

Stuart would often remind me that "God knew what he was doing" when he brought the two of us together, and that what God brought together, no man would separate. We knew we were being challenged, but we had a great Helper on our side, holding me when I was lonely and afraid and sheltering Stuart in the face of danger. I also came to see God as not just a

> "But I will sing of your strength, in the morning I will sing of your love; for you are my fortress, my refuge in times of trouble." (Psalm 59:16)

passive do-gooder who was amiably blessing us from above, but one who at any point could defend my soldier from scores of Taliban, stop an IED from detonating, and could shield him from any "terror that stalks by night." The children's rhyme leads us to believe Jesus is "meek and mild," but the Jesus that I experienced was truly a strong and mighty fortress.

Prayer:
*Lord, I praise you for being our shield and
protection for body, mind and spirit.*

AUGUST 11

Future Grace

Capt. Stuart Zeigler, U.S. Army, Afghanistan, 2007–2008

FOR SEVERAL months during my tour I was assigned to a remote outpost along the Afghan/Pakistan border. I was assigned to teach, coach, mentor, train, and advise the leadership of the newly formed Afghan National Border Police.

I found myself several miles from Pakistan on a remote outpost with thirty-five border police soldiers living in conditions of no running water, no electricity, and very little contact with the outside world. For a period of time I was very lucky to be able to use our satellite phone for a five-minute phone call once or twice a week. It was during these times that I learned to rely on prayer to see me through. Feeling very much helpless I learned to lift up Amanda in prayer on a daily basis.

Throughout my deployment I chose two verses (Romans 8:18 and Romans 8:28) to recite when I was down and looking to encouragement. I would pray them and draw upon them for strength.

Romans 8:18 states, "Yet what we suffer now is nothing compared to the glory he will reveal to us later."

It is simply amazing when I pondered and reflected upon the future grace that our Lord and Savior would eventually pour out upon us. No matter how many bad days there were in Afghanistan, no matter how down I felt emotionally, no matter how much pain I experienced physically . . . all that was NOTHING compared to what good things were to come my way. As a believer in Christ, I believed that my suffering was nothing compared to the joy, grace, and love I would experience in a lifetime to come with Amanda as my wife and the love of my life. I took comfort in these verses on a deeper level. I used them to give me courage. If God decided to call me home during that year of service in Afghanistan, all the suffering I endured would be nothing compared to the promise of future grace and glory that is promised to me through faith in Christ Jesus.

> "And we know that in all things God works for the good of those who love him, who have been called according to his purpose." (Romans 8:28)

Prayer:
Lord, when my shoulders droop with the weight of suffering,
keep me steady with the promise of future grace.

Back on the Home Front

Amanda Zeigler, wife of Capt. Stuart Zeigler, U.S. Army,
Afghanistan (2007–2008)

DURING THAT year of deployment, I struggled when friends would complain about missing their husbands or boyfriends due to work or some other minor inconvenience. *How can you be so inconsiderate knowing all the while that I would give anything just to be able to call Stuart?* I thought as I stared at them in disbelief.

The hardest overall period of time was the weeks immediately following his arrival in Afghanistan. I was a wreck. I lived alone, had lost my job, and now felt like I had lost my other half. Adding to despair and confusion was the hard fact that I'd only known this man for a matter of months.

What if he really isn't the one I'm going to marry? What if I still have feelings for him when R&R comes around, and he's not in love with me anymore? What if he no longer thinks I'm pretty? What if I'm not a good enough Army girlfriend, and don't send enough letters and care packages? All the questions wandered through my mind.

Of course none of this actually happened, but the feelings were real. I would alternate between consuming all the news I could find, and isolating myself from every media outlet, convincing myself that if I didn't know about the bad stuff, it would not happen to Stuart. One time, newscaster Stone Phillips, commented on how the approaching spring was going to be a violent one for Afghanistan and the troops, with the Taliban promising a spring offensive. I stared defeated at the TV, and then let my imagination get the best of me, resulting in what felt like a panic attack. It was awful.

> "Wait for the Lord; be strong and take heart and wait for the Lord." (Psalm 27:14)

Another challenging time was in early spring when Stuart was sent to a remote outpost on the Afghan-Pakastani border. We went weeks and weeks without any communication. The only phone contact we had came from a SAT phone. He called me on Easter Sunday, and we talked for four minutes. Those four minutes made my week. Thank God for technology. Oftentimes I would marvel at how far we've come since just Desert Storm, nineteen years ago. How wives managed in World War II, I will never know.

Prayer:
Lord, grant me patience when my heart screams out for immediate deliverance.

287

The Storm and the Safety Net

Amanda Zeigler, wife of Capt. Stuart Zeigler, U.S. Army,
Afghanistan (2007–2008)

FOR ME THE deployment was a tumultuous storm raging beneath me, threatening to swallow me whole. But during the storm, I was held up by a safety net. Yes, the water would splash on me, and get me wet, yet I would never be pulled under—I would never drown. In my mind, God was the safety net protecting me and holding me day in and day out.

God comforted me through many different sources. Sometimes all it took was an encouraging conversation with an acquaintance, and other times it would be a timely Bible verse, just when I needed to hear it. I read Psalm 91 (The Soldiers's Psalm) over and over again. I also read Song of Songs, and found hope in how the male lover is reunited with his female lover—when "the season of singing comes" after the winter. Lastly, some of the great hymns of the faith were instrumental in uplifting us. Stuart and I loved "How Firm A Foundation." The lyrics, "Fear not I am with thee oh be not dismayed for I am thy God and shall still give you aid." This verse was such a relief to me when Stuart returned to Afghanistan after R&R (when we got engaged).

> "Trust in him at all times, O people; pour out your hearts to him, for God is our refuge."
> (Psalm 62:8)

Yes, there were days that were bleak, scary, lonely, but in the end, I was never overcome. My friend once described the feeling of being prayed for as being "unnaturally buoyed." That is absolutely true, and in a way, it was such an exciting thing. We needed God, and he was there. God answered our prayers for Stuart's safety, and the safety of his team for which I'm still grateful to this very day. Our raw dependence on him was vital to making it through. In a way, I feel sorry for people who never get to experience their faith in such a throbbing way.

Prayer:
Lord, make me dependent upon you no matter
how comfortable my life already is.

A Good Friday

Lt. Paul Brian Kim, Chaplain, United States Navy

I'LL NEVER forget that day—what I heard, the miracle I witnessed, and its effect the Marines in my care.

Paul, make a U-turn, I heard in my mind.

Knowing it was the voice of God, something I've learned to listen to over the years, I immediately turned my car around.

I had been driving inside Al Taqaddum Airbase, which is between Ramadi and Fallujah. It was Easter weekend, 2006. My job was to serve as a chaplain to fifteen hundred Marines. Their jobs were dangerous. Many of them searched for improvised explosive devices. The enemy hid them in potholes, dead dogs, and any place they could.

Shortly after turning my car around, I saw a makeshift hospital. A corpsman ordered me to stop my car and explained the situation. Fifteen marines had been hurt by rockets in an attack in Fallujah, but only one was in critical condition.

I quickly parked and went into the tent where the doctors and nurses were doing all they could to save the Marine's life. Soon his heart monitor flat-lined. A doctor declared him dead.

One of my prayers for my deployment was that none of the Marines in my care would die. However, when someone dies, a chaplain's duty is to be available. A medic read his dog tag and announced he was Catholic. They called for the Catholic chaplain, who came and began issuing the last rites.

> "Jesus called in a loud voice, 'Lazarus, come out!' The dead man came out, his hands and feet wrapped with strips of linen, and a cloth around his face. Jesus said to them, "Take off the grave clothes and let him go.'" (John 11:43–44)

I heard the voice of God speak to me once again, as clearly as he had when I made the U-turn. *Pray for resuscitation.*

I began to pray, explaining to those around me that God had called me to pray for resuscitation.

"Revive him, Lord. Resuscitate him," I prayed over and over again.

Others began to pray with me. Ten minutes later, the heart monitor suddenly started beeping. The Marine was alive. The medical personnel began their feverish work on him again. Soon everyone was crying tears of joy. Several began shouting, "This is a miracle." The medical team stabilized the Marine, and he was flown to a hospital in Germany.

As I drove back, I was awestruck. I praised God for what he had done. Then the significance of the date hit me. It was Good Friday, the day of our Lord's death. The Lord brought back to life a Marine on Good Friday. He answered my prayer. All of the Marines in my care came home alive.

Prayer:
You are a God of miracles. Thank you for revealing yourself in marvelous ways and may I keep my eyes open to what wonders you have planned for me.

AUGUST 15

Baptism

Lt. Paul Brian Kim, Chaplain, United States Navy

THE STORY of that's Marines resuscitation spread quickly. The corpsman and the people in the tent began to share what happened. I talked about it as I led patrol prayer, a time of devotions before Marines went out on patrol.

My attention quickly turned to the upcoming Easter Sunday service that included baptism. Something I discovered is that the spirituality of the Marines is truly deep. They are hungry for God and his presence in their lives. As a result, I led five Bible Studies, not including Sunday service, each week. I wanted to give those who were interested an opportunity to celebrate Easter, and for some Marines and a few Iraqis to have a chance to express their new-found faith.

There was one problem. I had to figure out a way to create a baptistry in the desert. The task was not easy. I dug a deep hole, covered it with a plastic liner and poured eight hundred gallons of water into it. It took me all day.

That Easter service was amazing. The hundreds who attended, worshipped God for the resurrection of his Son, Jesus Christ, and praised him for bringing the Marine back to life two days earlier. When it came time for the baptisms, I lifted the cover off the hole.

I was shocked, all the water was gone. Apparently a hole in the plastic liner had drained the water.

I explained what had happened to those attending the service.

"Let's pray and see what God does," I suggested.

Thirty minutes later, a water truck came out of nowhere. Here we were in the middle of war zone, and an Iraqi water truck was just passing by. We stopped it. The truck had a special pump on it that filled the hole in less than a minute. What took me eight hours the day before took this truck only seconds!

> "Then Jesus said, 'Did I not tell you that if you believed, you would see the glory of God?'" (John 11:40)

"Man, God is alive! God is working overtime," I heard some of the Marines say. "First a man came back to life and then God provided water for baptism in the desert."

It was a very special moment. There were no dry eyes in the audience that day as thirty were baptized. God filled our hearts with his presence in a momentous way on Easter Sunday.

God continued to use the miracle of the Marine's resuscitation. Over one hundred accepted Christ as their savior, including some Iraqi Muslims and even some Buddhists, something I could relate to.

Prayer:
Thank you God meeting my each and every need.
Thank you for the strength of your presence.

Paul the Evangelist

Lt. Paul Brian Kim, Chaplain, United States Navy

CHAPLAIN PAUL, you're too evangelical," another chaplain complained to my commanding officer.

You can fire me now, I thought.

The United States Military respects the faith background of its members. No one is required to see a chaplain. But when people are faced with their mortality, they need someone who can answer their questions. Depending on their background and styles, chaplains approach their work differently.

"I know that my life is short, and I know I need to live my life for something that will last forever," I often explain.

I was born and raised as a strong Buddhist in South Korea. Becoming a Christian was the farthest thing from my mind when my family came to America. My great-grandmother was the only Christian in my family. She prayed for me, but I rejected her over and over. Then one day I was driving past a church.

The thought, *Paul, why don't you pray?* suddenly entered my mind.

I didn't know how to pray or respond to what I now know was the voice of God.

"I don't know who you are, but thank you for a good day," I replied.

I started praying every day, especially when I caught a glimpse of the cross on that church's steeple. My heart became softened by those prayers.

One day my mom and I agreed to go to church with my great grandmother. My dad and two sisters decided to attend another church that day.

At the end of the sermon I was crying uncontrollably. I felt God's presence. It was a package deal. That same week, my mom, dad, two sisters, and I all came to Christ.

I went on to attend Georgia Tech. Instead of becoming an engineer, I attended seminary. After that, I served as a missionary for fifteen years in Africa and the Middle East. Then I became a chaplain.

"Bless me, yet the Lord loves me so much he sent me to Iraq and not Hawaii. He sent me to Fallujah and Ramadi," This is what I tell people about my six-month deployment.

> "Then Ananias went to the house and entered it. Placing his hands on Saul, he said, "Brother Saul, the Lord—Jesus, who appeared to you on the road as you were coming here—has sent me so that you may see again and be filled with the Holy Spirit." (Acts 9:17)

"My goal and vision is clear—Jesus Christ didn't die for things, he died for people. Chaplains are there to help those Marines and sailors realize there's something deeper than what they're experiencing," I explain.

My commanding officer respected my perspective that day. "Chaplain Kim is doing a great job" he told the other chaplain. The matter over methods was settled.

Prayer:
Thank you God for being my commanding officer, one who knows me intimately and understands my gifts and abilities.

Meant to Be a Chaplain

*From the blog of Jessica Alley, wife of Chaplain (Capt.)
Will Alley, Iraq (2008–2009)*

WHEN WILL was first deployed, I remember feeling as though my world was falling apart. However, we both had a feeling that God would reveal his future plans for Will during this "wilderness" time.

Will had been deployed for only a month when a friend asked about Will's future plans.

"I think he'd make a really good chaplain," I heard myself say. My words startled

> "For I know the plans I have for you,' declares the LORD."
> (Jeremiah 29:11a)

me so much I jumped in my seat. That thought had never run through my mind before. Suddenly, I thought, *That's it! He's meant to be an Army Chaplain!*

When I got home I emailed him with my revelation. You can imagine my excitement the next day when I got this email from him in response:

Wow! I prayed last Friday that if this was really what God wanted me to do that he would put it on your mind as well. That's amazing. I haven't wanted to share any of this until I was more sure about what God wanted me to do, so I have been praying about his purpose for me and that he would speak to your heart as well. I wanted him to speak to you so that I could get a confirmation that it is his will.

As for being a chaplain , I knew the army was short of them, but it didn't hit me until I was in a unit that was deployed and hadn't had a chaplain for a couple of months . . . that's just not right. So, I decided that when our chaplain does arrive that I would ask him questions about being a chaplain without telling him or letting him know that I have been thinking about being one. The more he would tell me about what his job is and what kind of things he does, the stronger I felt about the call.

Isn't that crazy? This was in the fall of 2003. When he came home in March of 2004, we started planning. He departed the army in the summer of 2005 and began his three-year seminary tour.

Prayer:
Lord, open my eyes to see the next steps you
want me to take in my own life.

Seven Days to Deployment

From the blog of Jessica Alley, wife of Chaplain (Capt.)
Will Alley, Iraq (2008–2009)

DECEMBER 6, 2008.
Will leaves one week from today for his second deployment. I choose to look at this as just a speed bump in the road for us. Will may be able to email me every day and hopefully, won't be gone more than sixteen months. The bottom line is that the deployment is Will's job and God's will. How can I argue with that?

Will has an amazing opportunity to minister to soldiers who desperately need him. Since he was called to the ministry in the fall of 2003, he has been waiting for this moment. As a wife, few things are better than to watch your husband fulfilling God's purpose for his life. He can't wait to get his boots in the sand and start his mission.

> "Be joyful always, pray continually, give thanks in all circumstances, for this is God's will for you in Christ Jesus."
> (1 Thessalonians 5:16–18)

With that said, looking forward to deploying does not mean Will is looking forward to leaving us. He has said many times how much he is dreading our final goodbyes. As most of you know, he and Carlee Scott are the best of buds. It stings his heart when he realizes that she'll be almost four and a half-years old when he returns home. To think that Owen will be over two years old and walking and talking just baffles him.

I could not be prouder of him as a father, as a soldier, and as a servant of God. But while I may be happy for him, no wife ever wants her husband to leave for over a year. Knowing that I will be raising two small children alone while carrying (and delivering) a third is overwhelming. Even today, I'm not sure I'll be able to do it. But I'm going to try. This is the road that has been chosen for me, and I will travel it proudly.

Although I will have many fearful moments, I can't reside in fear. I won't be ignorant and think something can't happen, but instead I will recognize it, pray for safety and peace, and move on. I will not allow the enemy to hold me captive in fear.

Prayer:
Lord, help me travel well the road you have set before me.

AUGUST 19

Shock

From the blog of Jessica Alley, wife of Chaplain (Capt.) Will Alley, Iraq (2008–2009)

DECEMBER 19, 2008.

On Wednesday afternoon, I dropped the kids off at Heather's and went alone to the hospital for my ultrasound. While I was waiting for the OB doc to review the results of the ultrasound and come back in, I saw the still shot on the screen. It was the most perfect little baby, in early pregnancy bean-like form. I was in love and SO excited. When the doc came in, however, he was concerned.

> "The LORD upholds all those who fall and lifts up all who are bowed down." (Psalm 145:14)

"How much have you been bleeding?" he asked.

"Uh . . . none," I replied.

"What I am seeing is a lot of bleeding around the baby. What I am not seeing is a heartbeat."

After several moments of utter disbelief and questioning, he confirmed the truth: my baby had died. I proceeded to experience the greatest sadness of my entire life. I have never missed Will more than I did in that moment.

Finally, at 9 p.m., Will called from Kuwait. "So how'd it go?!?!" he asked, completely unaware.

I delivered the news. It was terrible. He was so devastated. He began grieving the loss of our baby as well as wrestling with the thoughts of me going through this grief alone and being without him at night.

I spent most of the night being either numb or sobbing. It's a pain I've never experienced before. My emotions are frail, but I have been surrounded by the kind of support you could only dream of in a crisis. My constant tears have dried up, and I have clarity and peace. I long to see this sweet angel and I know one day I will. He/She is in heaven, whole, and complete with Jesus.

I never thought I would watch my husband deploy and then five days later be told that our unborn baby has died. If it happened to someone else, I would have thought that I could never handle such blows. Through it all—the pain, the sadness, the anger, the frustration—one thing is clear. **God is Sovereign.** He still reigns. He still loves. He still comforts. I *will* praise him in this storm.

Prayer:
Lord, in times of trial, may I cling to the truth that you still reign.

Men Down

From the blog of Jessica Alley, wife of Chaplain (Capt.) Will Alley, Iraq (2008–2009)

FEBRUARY 9, 2009.

I knew this day would be coming but I had no idea it would be this bad.

From the Associated Press:

> A suicide car bomber struck a U.S. patrol in northern Iraq on Monday, killing four American soldiers and an Iraqi interpreter in the deadliest single attack against U.S. forces in nine months.

Yes, these were soldiers from Will's battalion.

My stomach turned. I knew this meant that Will would be thrust into the most difficult challenge of his life so far. I knew the weight he would have to bear for the almost 1100 soldiers in his battalion would be heavy. I wanted to hug him. My stomach turned for the families. My stomach turned for the unit. Later in the day, Will emailed again and said that he watched the fourth soldier die in the hospital with his own eyes.

I spent Monday in a daze. I searched desperately online, trying to find more details and more information. Before bed, Will had written me to tell me about the ramp ceremony (where they load the remains on to the airplane for travel back to the U.S.). I knew he was involved in that, and I ached for him. He was exhausted and drained, which I could tell by his emails. There was more work to be done, so our e-visit was quick. I wanted to hug him again.

> "We wait in hope for the LORD; he is our help and our shield." (Psalm 33:20)

On Tuesday, he sent me the news that left me speechless . . . breathless. One of the four killed was his battalion commander—the leader. *OH MY. . . . NO!* All four of the soldiers' lives were precious and not one is valued more than the other. But the leader? I cannot believe it happened. I knew this guy and he was an amazing leader. This battalion has been rocked to the very core. How can I be consumed with trivial things like laundry or runny noses when such tragedy has just occurred? How is it possible that I am sitting in my beautiful, comfortable house when my husband is in the midst of crisis so far away? Oh, why can't I be close enough to hug him?

Prayer:
Lord, when life doesn't make sense, help me wait on you.

AUGUST 21

Men Down Part 2

From the blog of Jessica Alley, wife of Chaplain (Capt.)
Will Alley, Iraq (2008–2009)

FEBRUARY 9, 2009.
Then I learned more. Will was the one who identified the bodies at the hospital. This threw my stomach in turns again. My sweet husband's beautiful brown eyes were the ones that saw these damaged bodies of his

fellow soldiers, his brothers. Such a horrific sight cannot possibly ever be forgotten. I wanted to turn back time, erase this pain, remove such sadness and grief from his mind, from the entire battalion, and from all the families.

Then I learned that he almost went on that convoy that killed our heroes. He wouldn't have been in that same vehicle, but likely the one behind it. He said it was a very frequently-traveled road. Reality has set in for me.

I asked about the ramp ceremony. In his own words:

I led the whole battalion information to the ramp of the aircraft, positioned myself front and center of the ramp, and waited for everyone to get into position. Once the 4 FLAs (Field Ambulances) positioned themselves and the pallbearers unloaded the transfer cases, I marched out to meet them halfway down the run way. Once they got close to me, I did an about face and led the procession through the "honor corridor" (made by a split battalion formation on either side) to the ramp while reading Psalm 23 out loud. Once we got to the ramp, I paused for them to get into position, and then moved into the belly of the aircraft. The caskets then came one by one up into the aircraft and I said one last prayer for our fallen comrades. Then I called the pallbearer detail to execute a salute, facing movement, and then forward march out of the plane. After that, the CSM called the battalion to gather around and gave a pretty inspiring speech. Then I closed out with one last prayer/blessing to those there. We concluded the ceremony by me leading the formation off of the tarmac. It was pretty moving, and I think we carried it out close to perfection.

I have been proud of Will many, many times in my life. However, I have NEVER been more proud of him than I am today. He has performed his chaplain duties with such patience, comfort, and compassion. He is empty, drained, exhausted, and mourning . . . but Christ is his rock and because of that, Will is being a rock to his brothers.

God is the same today as He was before Monday. He is still good. He still reigns. He is with us and with them. Good CAN come out of such a tragedy.

Prayer:
Lord, thank you that your goodness and sovereignty never change.
Help me see your purpose in the midst of pain.

Only Six More Months!

From the blog of Jessica Alley, wife of Chaplain (Capt.)
Will Alley, Iraq (2008–2009)

JUNE 26, 2009.

Military life is all about counting down. Either you are counting down to the next deployment, to the homecoming, to the R&R, or to the end of R&R. There always seems to be some sort of countdown. Well, one of my countdowns ended today when the kids and I dropped Will off at the airport. Our R&R had ended.

There are so many thoughts going through my head right now. I am not even close to being as emotional as I was when he left back in December, but I am still pretty bummed. We had the best two weeks! Having him home 24/7 for two straight weeks was awesome. We had such quality family and couple time.

I am incredibly thankful that Will's battalion will not be extended, and that we only have six more months to go. We are halfway done with our year. Some of you reading this are laughing, thinking "ONLY SIX." Some of you think there is no way you could go without your husband for so long. Let me reassure you, you can.

I miss my husband terribly, and he is not even out of country yet. However, I am even more convinced than ever that Mosul is God's will for him. Being in the center of God's will is an extremely peaceful thing, and Will and I have both learned that such peace is precious. We rest in knowing that we are obeying God and fulfilling his plan. It's not always easy or enjoyable, but it's right. As always, we are thankful.

> "Jesus Christ is the same yesterday and today and forever."
> (Hebrews 13:8)

When thrust into a situation like this, we are forced to rely on the only thing not influenced by emotion . . . that is our faith in God. Regardless of how happy or sad we are, God remains the same. He is unchanging and we find our strength and stability in Him.

Prayer:
Lord, help me place more trust in your unchanging character
than in how I feel with my own changing emotions.

Parting Gift

Leah and Sgt. Christopher Dubree, Iraq (2006–2007),
Afghanistan (2009–2010)

MORE THAN anything else, Leah and Chris Dubree wanted a child. They dreamed of growing their family and bringing a precious new life into the world. In April 2006, after three years of trying to conceive, they learned that Chris would soon be deployed to Iraq, so they decided to put their plans for expanding their family on hold until he returned. God had other plans.

On June 7, 2006, Chris was sitting in his office when the phone rang.

"Criminal Law South Specialist Dubree speaking, how may I help you sir or ma'am?" he answered.

"Hi Daddy," Leah said with a smile.

Though this timing wasn't what they had planned, Chris was ecstatic.

"I lost all control of myself. I looked like a little kid who had just found his missing, most favorite toy in the whole world," said Chris. "I knew that this was a sign from God. He had placed me on a path that may not bring me home, so he wanted to fulfill our wish of being parents."

> "Many are the plans in a man's heart, but it is the LORD's purpose that prevails."
> (Proverbs 19:21)

By the time the Dubrees discovered they were expecting, the baby was seven weeks along—which meant that the little life was already growing by the time Chris and Leah decided to stop trying until after deployment.

"I had so many mixed emotions about this because my husband was leaving and would miss so much," said Leah.

On August 23, Chris headed for Iraq. "I kept as close a contact as I could throughout the pregnancy. Leah sent LOTS of pictures for me to see how she was growing with our miracle inside growing as well," he said.

Chris and Leah did not choose for Leah to be alone for her pregnancy. But they recognized that if this was God's plan for them, then he must also have a plan to help them through it. God often interrupts our lives with unplanned circumstances. However, if we look closely, even trials can be avenues of God's blessing.

Prayer:
Lord, show me the blessings you have in store
for me through the situations I did not choose.

It's Time!

Leah and Sgt. Christopher Dubree, Iraq (2006–2007), Afghanistan (2009–2010)

CHRIS HAD scheduled his R&R leave around the baby's due date, January 21, 2007, to make sure he was there for the birth. This time, it was the baby girl who had other plans. On January 3, Keesley (which is the Celtic female form of Christopher) decided it was time to move.

"My whole family was there and everyone was excited, except we were missing someone really important," said Leah. "I kept telling my family that I missed Chris and couldn't do this without him, but my mom just kept telling me that God would help me through this."

Meanwhile, on the other side of the world in Iraq, Chris was on edge. "I called about every fifteen minutes, anticipation and adrenaline coursing through my body," he said. "Finally, on the fifth phone call, I heard the enthusiasm in the air before I actually got the news: I was a father now as of 1:56 a.m. January 4, 2007."

Ten minutes later Chris received his first picture of Keesley via email. "When I saw the picture for the first time I started to tear up of course, and all my friends could say was, 'How can that be? She is beautiful, but she looks just like you.' They were trying to get me out of my emotional phase, but I was too deep into the miracle God had given my wife and me."

> "'For my thoughts are not your thoughts, neither are your ways my ways,' declares the LORD." (Isaiah 55:8)

When Leah and Chris finally got to talk that evening, they cried tears of both joy and sadness together on the phone. "He told me that he was proud of me, and I answered him with, 'I need you home!'" said Leah. "We were both so happy with having her and being parents."

Sometimes God's timing doesn't make sense to us. It isn't what we would have chosen, or how we would have planned it. During these times, may we simply trust in God's sovereignty rather than dwell on what we cannot control ourselves.

Prayer:
Lord, grant me the courage to trust in your plan for my life.

Love at First Sight

*Leah and Sgt. Christopher Dubree, Iraq (2006–2007),
Afghanistan (2009–2010)*

WHEN CHRIS stepped off the plane and saw the tiny bundle in his wife's arms, it was love at first sight. Keesley was eleven days old.

"I remember it as if it were yesterday," Chris said. "The first thing I did of course was give quick hugs and kisses to the adults, and then it was strictly baby time. I stole her away and held her as if I had held a hundred children before her."

Completely oblivious to all the strangers in the airport smiling at the scene, Chris only had eyes for Keesley. "All I could focus on was that the little life I had in my arms was biologically mine, but I knew then and will always know that she is God's child. I am just blessed to raise her for him."

While Chris was home, Keesley was having trouble sleeping because she had tummy pains. After trying everything from gas drops to switching formula, nothing seemed to help—except her daddy.

"I was in the recliner with her and I started to nod off and then I realized she was asleep," he said. "So we found a solution to the fussy nights with gas build up. I would sleep with her on my chest in the recliner, which worked perfectly."

> "Because you are my help, I sing in the shadow of your wings."
> (Psalm 63:7)

When it was time for Chris to return to Iraq, he left a worn T-shirt of his with Leah to put in her crib. The scent of Keesley's daddy seemed to help soothe her, even after he was gone.

Saying goodbye again after his R&R was one of the hardest things Chris and Leah have ever done.

"I know that God made my child for me," said Chris, "and he also realized that I would have such a difficult time being away that he gave me ways to cut through those hard times."

For Chris, those "ways" were emails, phone calls and pictures sent back and forth. What are the ways God has provided for you to get through your own difficult circumstances?

Prayer:
*Lord, give me the strength I need to shoulder
the burdens you've allowed me to have.*

Home Again

Leah and Sgt. Christopher Dubree, Iraq 2006–2007, Afghanistan 2009–2010

TEN LONG months later, November 8, 2007, Chris's deployment to Iraq was over. He officially moved back home to be with his wife and daughter.

"My unit marched into the field house and waited while a few people said some words," said Chris. "I cannot remember what was even said; I was too busy staring at my wife and now, ten month-old daughter. Keesley was being loud, of course, throwing her snacks and being a normal ten month-old. All I could think was, *Wow, she is ours. I helped to create her.*"

The formation released, and Chris made a bee line toward them. At first, Keesley was a little unsure of who Chris was. "As soon as I spoke, though, I saw something click in her eyes," said Chris. "I took off my hat and I saw something else click. It would have taken more power than any person in the world had to keep her from coming to me. Of course I cried some more and then we went home."

Back in their own home, they set Keesley down, and she started to walk away. When Chris turned around, there was Keesley taking her first steps, walking right toward her daddy. "All I could do was stare open-jawed at the little bundle that had chosen to wait to show that she could walk until I came home," said Chris.

Even though Keesley didn't remember her dad from his two-week visit when she was a newborn, she recognized his voice from all the phone calls and recognized his face from the pictures. She took her first steps to follow him because she knew him, even though he had been physically absent.

> "I am the good shepherd; I know my sheep and my sheep know me . . . My sheep listen to my voice; I know them, and they follow me." (John 10:4, 27)

In the same way, Jesus calls himself our shepherd, and says in John 10 that if we know him, we will follow him, too. Though we never lay eyes on Jesus while on this earth, we can learn to recognize his voice and follow his call.

Prayer:
Lord, help me discern your voice out of the many I hear each day, and give me the grace to follow you.

Another Daughter, Another Deployment

Leah and Sgt. Christopher Dubree, Iraq (2006–2007), Afghanistan (2009–2010)

ON CHRISTMAS Day 2007, one special gift for the Dubrees outshone everything else under the tree. They discovered that they were once again expecting.

"I knew that God was giving me back the things I had missed with our first daughter," said Chris. "I was able to see the entire pregnancy firsthand, the birth, and the first eight months of Nikayla's life which is what I had missed with Keesley."

When Nikayla was just two months old, Chris learned he would be deployed to Afghanistan in 2009. "It was very hard for me after having another child knowing that he would be leaving us again, but I knew that God was on our side, and he would get us through this just like the did the last deployment," said Leah. "I was so upset and hurting for my Chris, because he was going to miss so much once again."

> "And we know that in all things God works for the good of those who love him, who have been called according to his purpose." (Romans 8:28)

Determined to do what she could to foster that daddy-daughter relationship, Leah began working with Nikayla to say her first word. Finally one day, she said it to him: "Da da!"

"The look on his face was so priceless and I knew that was a moment he would carry with him always," said Leah.

When Chris left for Afghanistan, he said, "Keesley was exactly twenty-seven months and twenty-three days, and Nikayla was exactly seven months and twenty-eight days. Currently, I am missing with Nikayla what I have seen with Keesley, but I get updates on a daily basis."

In the meantime, Leah talks to Nikayla about her daddy and Chris talks to her on the phone. "I continue to pray for his safety and that Nikayla will remember him," said Leah. "Things aren't as hard as I thought they would be, and I know that's because I have grown in Christ. God is so wonderful!

My daughters and I miss Chris so much. Each day has its ups and downs, but we know that everything will work out in the end because God is our savior."

AUGUST 28

Preparation

Kerri Hartwick, wife of Chief Warrant Officer
Michael Hartwick, Iraq (2005–2006)

MICHAEL AND Kerri Hartwick were high school sweethearts. They married during their senior year of college and then decided together that he would join the military.

"His dream was always to fly," said Kerri. "He loved airplanes, anything that flew. I was supportive."

Mike served in Bosnia, Kosovo, Albania, and Iraq as an Apache helicopter pilot for the Army. In November 2005, one month before he would deploy a second time to Iraq, he arranged a "powwow" with Kerri.

"We each took a day off of work, and the kids were in school," remembered Kerri. "He'd been deployed before and knew the risk factors. We should have done this before; maybe this was a God thing. But he made sure we sat down together and talked about everything we needed to discuss in case he would not return—from finances, to who he wanted to be pallbearers, who he wanted to speak at the funeral, and where he wanted to be buried. We talked about where the kids and I would live, his thoughts on me remarrying. We discussed everything. It was hard. He put all our finances and insurance information in a binder for me. I didn't know then what a blessing that would turn out to be for me."

When Mike deployed, Kerri prayed the same prayer each night: "Lord, if you bring Mike home safely I will praise you for keeping him safe. If you have other plans for him, you need to prepare my heart because I won't be able to do it alone."

"I didn't have a premonition," she said. "But God put that in my heart that I needed to pray that way."

In speaking to their children, seven-year-old Tanner and ten-year-old Haley, Mike never promised he wouldn't get hurt. He said he'd do his best to stay safe.

> "Many are the plans in a man's heart, but it is the LORD's purpose that prevails."
> (Proverbs 19:21)

Prayer:
Lord, prepare my heart for whatever you have in store for me.

April 2, 2006

Kerri Hartwick, wife of Chief Warrant Officer Michael Hartwick, Iraq (2005–2006)

SUNDAY, APRIL 2, 2006, dawned clear and bright in Belton, Texas. Kerri and the kids were looking forward to the battalion Easter egg hunt planned for that afternoon when the phone rang.

"Kerri, have you heard anything about an Apache helicopter crash?" It was Mike's stepdad in Missouri.

"No, I haven't," Kerri told him. "If I hear anything, I'll let you know."

Kerri and the kids went to the egg hunt as planned, then to church before heading home. It was 5:45 p.m. when they pulled in the driveway. While Kerri and Tanner stayed outside chatting with some neighbors, Haley ran into the house.

"Mom," she said, rushing back outside. "There's a message on the answering machine that said, 'Kerri, I'm sorry to hear about your family. I'm on my way down.'"

Instantly, Kerri knew. Pulling her neighbor aside, she said, "Can you take the kids into your house and shut the blinds?"

"Why?"

"I'll explain later. Please take the kids."

Once Kerri's neighbor returned from getting the children settled in the house, she inquired again about what was going on.

"Was there a car in front of my house today?" Kerri asked her.
"Yes."

"There was a helicopter crash and Mike has been killed."

Five minutes later, the notification team was in Kerri's home, confirming what she already knew: Mike had been killed in action the day before. She fell to her knees, in shock.

"One thing I had prayed was: 'Lord, if Mike gets killed, I pray my children won't be here when I hear it. I don't want them to see me or to remember the men in the green suits.' Because God answered that prayer, I was able to walk over to my friend's house after I gained my composure and tell Haley in a loving way what happened to her dad.

> "But as for me, it is good to be near God. I have made the Sovereign LORD my refuge; I will tell of all your deeds." (Psalm 73:28)

Then Tanner came in, Haley held him and I told him, too. Even though it was the worst day of my life, I said 'God is so good because he answered my prayers.'"

Prayer:
*Lord, help me see your goodness even
when my vision is clouded with pain.*

AUGUST 30

Untouchable Soul

Kerri Hartwick, wife of Chief Warrant Officer
Michael Hartwick, Iraq (2005–2006)

THE NEXT day, Kerri received a mysterious phone call from the detachment.

"Please do not watch TV or go on the Internet," the officer told her. "We need to come out and see you."

Kerri agreed. *What could this possibly be about?* She thought. *I wonder if they screwed everything up and it's not even Mike who was killed.*

When the detachment came, they asked her to sit down.

"I'm sorry to tell you that there's a terrorist-created video of them pulling someone from a helicopter," they said. "It's all over the Internet and television." The footage was so unclear that viewers could not identify the face or even if the man was wearing an American uniform. Still, there was a chance it could have been Mike.

They searched her face, bracing themselves for any number of emotional reaction, but they weren't expecting Kerri's response.

She laughed. "Is that it?" she asked.

"Yes maam, it is."

"Mike's soul has already gone to heaven," said Kerri. "I don't agree with what they're doing, but if that was Mike, it was just his body. They're not bothering him any little bit."

When they were gone, Kerri mused, *Funny—I was up all night searching the Internet and never saw that video*. Still, she banned her kids from the TV and Internet for two weeks to make sure they wouldn't see it either.

> "Finally, brothers, whatever is true, whatever is noble, whatever is right, whatever is pure, whatever is lovely, whatever is admirable—if anything is excellent or praiseworthy—think about such things."
> (Philippians 4:8)

Kerri and the wife of the other co-pilot who had been killed agreed that they would not say anything about it, not acknowledge it on TV during any interviews. "If you respond to that video, you would give glory to what is evil," explained Kerri. "Glory is to go to God." The two wives asked TV stations to pull the footage from their programs, and they agreed.

To this day, Kerri has not seen the video and the kids are not aware of it, either. "God protected me from seeing those images, and I'm not going to go looking for them," she said.

Prayer:
Lord, help me dwell on your goodness rather than the world's evil.

The Funeral

Kerri Hartwick, wife of Chief Warrant Officer
Michael Hartwick, Iraq (2005–2006)

AS MIKE'S funeral date approached, Kerri had more on her mind than just honoring her husband's life. She had three specific prayer requests on her heart, which she shared via a mass email: 1) safety for the hundreds of people traveling, some from around the globe; 2) good weather to allow for the Apache helicopter flyover as planned; and 3) that if a group of war-protestors crashed the funeral as they had planned, that they would either go home quietly or that Haley and Tanner would feel more support from the attendees than anti-war sentiment from the protestors.

God answered.

The day of the funeral, April 14, was a beautiful day, and everyone arrived safely, including family, friends, 198 patriot guards, and emergency vehicles from five counties who participated to pay tribute to Mike's service. The protesters came, saw how many supporters there were, and decided to go home.

> "Yet the LORD longs to be gracious to you, he rises to show you compassion. For the LORD is a God of justice. Blessed are all who wait for him!" (Isaiah 30:18)

"God tested my faith with the threat of the protestors, but ended up providing," Kerri said. "I could have gotten ugly and argued about it on the Internet, but God took care of it in his own way."

When Kerri, Tanner, and Haley arrived back home in Texas after the funeral, another blessing was waiting for them. As Kerri pulled the mail from the mailbox, a glimpse of familiar handwriting made her heart stop and the tears begin to fall. Stuck between bills and catalogs were two postcards addressed to Tanner and Haley, written by their dad on April 1, 2006—the day he was killed.

"On Saturday, April 1, we had been hoping for a call from Mike but didn't get one," said Kerri. "The kids wondered why he didn't call. With these postcards I can show them that their Dad was thinking about them the day he died. God is so good. I just bawled when I pulled these postcards from the mail. How could someone question whether God was present?"

Prayer:
Lord, thank you for showering us with
blessings that demonstrate your compassion for us.

Reaching Out

Kerri Hartwick, wife of Chief Warrant Officer Michael Hartwick, Iraq (2005–2006)

FIVE MONTHS later, Mike's good friend prepared to deploy. Kerri promised to take care of his wife if anything happened to him.

On February 2, 2007, he made the ultimate sacrifice with his life while serving in Iraq. Now it was Kerri's turn to reach out and provide the support that she once needed; she spent two weeks with the new widow.

"I had to watch her struggle with who should be pallbearers, where she should bury him, whether she should have the funeral on post or in a church," said Kerri. "God showed me how blessed I was to be able to know I honored Mike in the way he wanted me to."

During the first year after Mike's death, Kerri spoke on a monthly basis to casualty assistance officers, sharing her story of how her first casualty assistance officer mishandled her case, but her second casualty officer went above and beyond to help her. In the local community, she helps civilians learn how to help military families now that parents were being deployed every other year.

Currently, Kerri volunteers and speaks to soldiers about how to prepare families in the face of tragedy. She is also the military ministry chairperson for her church, First Baptist in Belton, Texas. She keeps track of all military families in church and checks on them to see how they're doing and where they are in the deployment cycle. She's coordinates Military Family Nights Out, during which the church provides dinner and child care for children so the parents can get out. She also works with Veterans Fellowships, where soldiers and veterans of all ages get together. Both ministries are open to any active duty families in the community.

> "Praise be to the God and Father of our Lord Jesus Christ, the Father of compassion and the God of all comfort, who comforts us in all our troubles, so that we can comfort those in any trouble with the comfort we ourselves have received from God."
> (2 Corinthians 1:3–4)

"People ask me how I can still be in the military community, serving them," says Kerri. "After fourteen years in, you can't just leave. This is my family."

Prayer:
Lord, show me where you want me to minister using the experiences and insights you've given me.

Knights of Heroes

Maj. Steve Harrold, U.S. Air Force

IN NOVEMBER 2006, U.S. Air Force Major Steve Harrold, then stationed in Colorado Springs, lost a good friend who was killed in an F-16 crash in Iraq. He left behind a wife and five children, two of which were sons the same ages as Harrold's boys: seven and nine years old. Harrold felt called to do something for these boys and others like them who had lost their fathers to the war.

Partnering with Journey Chapel Pastor Eric Eaton in Monument, Colorado, a one-week camp was born in June 2007 called Modern Day Knights—later named Knights of Heroes. Sixteen boys from five states came to spend time together. He paired them with a mentor so they could spend their days kayaking, rock climbing, camping, and doing other outdoor adventures. The camp pays for all expenses,

> "Don't let anyone look down on you because you are young, but set an example . . ."
> (1 Timothy 4:12)

including airfare for those who come and hotel stays for the moms and siblings.

The camp teaches the boys principles from the book *Raising a Modern Day Knight* by Robert Lewis: 1) reject passivity, 2) accept responsibility, 3) lead courageously and 4) expect the greater reward. In the final camp session, Pastor Eaton rides in on a white horse dressed in knightly armor and challenges the boys to rise up to the challenge of authentic manhood. Each boy is "knighted" by Eaton's sword and receives a special gift to take home.

First-year campers receive a family crest to emphasize the importance of carrying on their father's legacy. Second-year campers are given a King Arthur replica dagger to hang on their wall, symbolizing that the camp is arming them for battles they'll face as they grow. In June 2009, third-year campers were given a shield with their family crest hand-painted on it to signify that they can defend themselves against whatever life throws at them.

"We give the boys tools they can use for the rest of their life," said Harrold. "I've seen their confidence increase. We challenge them in every single way physically and watch them face their fears. I've noticed a big change in the manner in which they accept demanding tasks. We challenge them to take responsibility for all of their decisions. And to see their faces after they accomplish something they' didn't think they'd be able to—it's amazing."

Prayer:
Lord, guide these young men without fathers
and help them find godly role models.

SEPTEMBER 3

Not the Only One

Maj. Steve Harrold, U.S. Air Force

MAJOR STEVE Harrold, founder of Knights of Heroes, says he didn't expect the impact his camp would have on the boys' mothers who accompany them to camp.

"It's the friendships they develop with other widows," said Harrold. "To come here for a week and share their stories, talk about challenges they're facing, and get advice, is really big. It means a lot for them to see that other people care about what they're going through. It's important to know they're not alone and not forgotten."

> "A father to the fatherless, a defender of widows, is God in his holy dwelling." (Psalm 68:5)

Nine-year-old Tanner Hartwick has attended Knights of Heroes since it began, and in September 2008, chose to write a school assignment about the experience:

I'm Not the Only One

One evening mom says, "Do you want to go play at the neighbor's house?" My sister and I said yes! So we played at the house and then my mom asked Haley to come here. When my sister came out, she was crying so hard that she couldn't talk to me that well. But then I went in and said, "what did you say to her?" My mom said, "Son, your dad died." At that moment I thought I was in a dream and ran home like a cheetah! When I got home, I ran into my mom's room and looked at a picture of my dad. I remembered the last words he said to me were I love you and I said I love you too. My mom came in and hugged me.

A couple of months later my mom heard on the radio about a camp in Colorado called Modern Day Knights (now Knights of Heroes). I went to the camp. When I saw all the boys that lost their dad too, in my mind I knew that I wasn't the only one without a dad. That week I made a lot of friends and it was cool! I was out camping in the woods and doing lots of boy things. It was more fun then going to Disney World and made me feel better to know that I wasn't the only one. My mom and sister had fun doing girl things too. I wait all year for camp time to come again. This year will be my third year.

Prayer:
Lord, show me how to support those who feel forgotten.

SEPTEMBER 4

Haley's Testimony

**Thirteen-year-old Haley Hartwick gave the
following testimony at a Fields of Faith Rally for
Fellowship of Christian Athletes in October 2008:**

IN DECEMBER 2005, my father left for Iraq on his second tour. I didn't realize it would be my last goodbye. On April 2, 2006, my mom, my seven-year-old brother, and I received tragic news that my dad had been killed in action while on a flight mission the day before. We were all brokenhearted. All I could do that night was cry my heart out. Friends and our church family came for comfort. I stayed locked up in my room. I was asking God why he had done such a dramatic thing to me. *Why me Lord? Why such a great man?* At the time it was so hard to glorify and understand the Lord, but my mom always said to praise the Lord through the good and bad. My mother was such a great role model through this time. She led us strong with encouragement.

> "I tell you the truth, anyone who will not receive the kingdom of God like a little child will not enter it."
> (Mark 10:15)

God was testing our faith for him. When God gives you a situation you have to try your hardest to praise him and make it. A few months after his death, this wonderful organization (Snowball Express) gave us a trip to California with other Gold Star Families. I came home from the trip overwhelmed by how much God has really blessed me by having ten years of memories to cherish. I knew my dad loved me and I know my Heavenly Father up above loves me. As long as you have faith you'll be good, because faith is like a muscle. The more you use it the stronger it gets.

I honestly believe that everything rides on hope and faith.. I can do all things through Christ who strengthens me if have faith, trust, and love the God almighty. I know for sure I'm going to see my dad and God someday in heaven. Are you?

Prayer:
*Lord, grant me child-like trust and faith in you,
even when life isn't what I expected.*

SEPTEMBER 5

Prelude to Deployment

Sara Horn, wife of BU1 Cliff Horn,
U.S. Navy Reserves, Iraq (2007–20008)

SARA HORN spent her twenty-sixth birthday aboard the Navy aircraft carrier USS *Harry S. Truman* off the coast of Iraq, among 5500 sailors and Marines waiting for a declaration of war by the Commander in Chief. On Sara's birthday, March 19, 2003, they got it.

Though her husband Cliff was in the Navy Reserves, Sara saw herself more as a journalist than a military wife. Sara's mission during her ten-day stay on board was to find and report stories for *Baptist Press*. She wasn't disappointed. She met a fighter pilot who prayed for his leaders and clothed himself with the armor of God (Ephesians 6) along with his flight gear. She even witnessed the first baptism take place on board using a joint direct attack munitions (JDAM) crate filled with water. "This is normally used to end life, but we're using it today for the beginning of life," the chaplain had said.

In November 2003, Sara traveled to Baghdad to cover more stories for a book she wrote with Oliver North, *A Greater Freedom*. There she talked with an American sniper who, six hours after recommitting his life to Christ in Baghdad, encountered fire on a mission. While taking cover behind a metal gate, Sara recalled what the soldier had told her. "He distinctly felt God tell him, *You're not safe, you need to move.* So he did. When the firefight was over, he went back to that gate. The sides were riddled with large bul-

> "The LORD your God is with you, he is mighty to save."
> (Zephaniah 3:17a)

let holes. But where his chest had been, there were thirteen dents. He told me, 'I put myself in a place to die but God pulled me out.'"

The trips were life-changing for Sara. "Faith is so important in life and death situations," she said. "God is all you have sometimes. And when it comes down to it, God is all we need. That trip was a real wake-up call for me."

It was also the beginning of Sara's call to minister to military families, especially through the written word. In addition to *A Greater Freedom*, Sara has written dozens of articles for military wives and authored the book, *God Strong: A Military Wife's Spiritual Survival Guide* (Zondervan, 2010).

"War serves as a reminder that we need God," said Sara. "A lot of people have forgotten that."

Prayer:
Lord, remind me how much I need you; help me depend on you alone.

Wives of Faith

Sara Horn, wife of BU1 Cliff Horn,
U.S. Navy Reserves, Iraq (2007–2008)

WHEN SARA'S husband Cliff was scheduled to deploy to Iraq in 2007, she realized another benefit her trips to Iraq provided.

"My experience in Iraq helped me so much to be able to share and explain things to other military wives," said Sara. "They ask, 'Why does he have to leave and help these other people?' I can tell them I've talked to Iraqis and know how thankful they are.'"

Sara understood that she needed more than that insider perspective to get through the upcoming deployment.

"God made it very clear that I must have other women to connect to during my husband's absence," said Sara. But she was four hours from Cliff's drilling base and she knew no other military wives in her town.

> "By this all men will know that you are my disciples, if you love one another."
> (John 13:35)

Before Cliff deployed, an army wife living in Nashville—while her husband was deployed—saw a newspaper article about Sara and contacted her. The two met for lunch.

"We had the best time talking and laughing and realizing that neither of us were crazy; we related to what we were going through," said Sara. "We wondered, *Is there someone else in Nashville who would enjoy this fellowship too?*"

Within a month, Sara created a website and an email address with the intention of finding other Christian military wives in Nashville. It worked. In December 2006, ten ladies from all branches came for their first meeting and began meeting monthly. Wives of Faith was born.

Soon, other military wives across the country heard about Wives of Faith and modeled their own groups after Sara's.

"We have ladies who contact us all the time about starting chapters," said Sara. "I'm in the process of putting a lot of content on the website (www.wivesoffaith.org) to help them along the way."

Military wives have emailed Sara for help with marriage, family, and deployment struggles. "So many times all I can do is pray for them and point them in the right direction," said Sara. "But when I walk beside another military wife, I am making a difference in ways I might not realize."

No matter what challenges God allows us to face, we can all use those to support and encourage others in the same situation.

Prayer:
Lord, help me see my trials and springboards for ministry to others.

The Right Promises

Sara Horn, wife of BU1 Cliff Horn,
U.S. Navy Reserves, Iraq (2007–2008)

WHEN CLIFF Horn, a Seabee, went to Iraq and was assigned to a special task force working with a special forces unit, communication between Caleb and his daddy all but ground to a halt.

The pictures stopped coming. The Web cam no longer brought Cliff back into Caleb's world. When Cliff was able to call home, it was always late at night when the little boy was fast asleep.

"Kids see how we react and handle things," said Sara. "I tried to be positive around Caleb about the deployment, but the first month that Cliff was in Iraq was really hard on him."

> "God has said, 'Never will I leave you; never will I forsake you.'" (Hebrews 13:5)

In those first thirty days, Sara noticed that Caleb had two major meltdowns. He would cry despondently. "I finally sat down with him and asked if he was upset about his dad being away. He told me he had a bad dream that Daddy had been shot."

Sara debated about what to do to make her son feel more secure. "The biggest tendency is to say, 'Daddy is safe, he's not going to get hurt.' But you can't guarantee that. I always said, 'We know that God is looking out for Daddy, God is watching over Daddy."

The next time Cliff called, Sara told him about Caleb's dream and asked if there was any way he could send a picture of himself doing his job that wasn't combat but construction. So Cliff got a photo approved by the unit of him in a bulldozer and emailed it home. Sara printed it out and had it ready when Caleb came home from school that day. Once he saw that picture, the nightmares stopped.

"We prayed for Cliff every night, but I had to be careful that I didn't make promises I that I questioned if I could keep," said Sara. "We're at war. It's a great time to emphasize the importance of prayer and trusting God, knowing God is in control no matter what."

God doesn't promise his children that life will be without pain, either. But he does tell us he won't let us go through it without him.

Prayer:
Lord, help me find comfort in your promises.

SEPTEMBER 8

Happy Independence Day?

Sara Horn, wife of BU1 Cliff Horn, U.S. Navy Reserves, Iraq (2007–2008)

ON THE FOURTH of July, 2007, Sara Horn did not feel like celebrating. She sat on the couch alone, curtains drawn, while Caleb played outside. She stared blankly at the turned-off television in front of her, which stared just as blankly back.

I can't go on, she thought. *I am so done. Tired. Spent. This is too hard. I can't do this by myself.*

> "I can do all things through Christ who strengthens me."
> (Philippians 4:13)

"It was the lowest point of the deployment for me," Sara remembered. "Our close friends had disappeared. They didn't check on me or email Cliff anymore. It was getting hard to do the ministry of Wives of Faith because I got caught up in my own struggles of deployment."

But on that Independence Day, God told Sara she didn't need to try to be so independent: *You aren't supposed to do this by yourself,* she could almost hear him say. *You have been trying to do this by yourself for the last seven months. But you need me—and my strength is sufficient for you.*

It was a turning point for Sara. "I realized I needed to turn it over to God and let him provide the strength I needed instead of me doing it all

319

myself," That's something that I'm trying to share with other wives, also. I think we have it in our heads (because it's drilled into our culture) that we have to be strong for everybody, but often we can't be. We just can't. But God is the strongest when we are the weakest. That's what we have to remember and focus on—we're not supposed to have it all together."

The Horns are expecting a second deployment in 2011, and Sara is hoping to use what she has learned so far. "God has taught me so much about leaning on him and finding strength," she said. "I haven't learned it all, but if I can just share what I'm learning with someone else. It makes it all worth it. God put us here to share our struggles and help each other."

As Americans, we pride ourselves on having a can-do attitude, but may we remember that without Christ, we can do nothing.

Prayer:
Lord, don't let me pride and self-sufficiency
prevent me from relying on your strength.

Encouraged by Community

Benita Koeman, wife of Chaplain (Capt.) Scott Koeman,
Iraq 2003; Qatar/Afghanistan (2005–2006)

NEW YEAR'S EVE, 2002. Friends from our church snapped a photo of my husband Scott and me together as we prepared to toast in the New Year. And what a year it would be. God was calling Scott to full-time ministry in the U.S. Army as a chaplain, and we were somewhat excited about the new military adventure that lay ahead. But things were heating up in Iraq and our New Year's celebration was tainted with a bit of anxiety as we faced impending deployment and many unknowns.

While Scott served in the National Guard, I was accustomed to him being gone one weekend a month, and one month in the year, but the army? I knew nothing about the army. *How long would Scott be deployed? Would there be chemical weapons involved?* One thing I was certain of

"Carry each other's burdens, and in this way you will fulfill the law of Christ."
(Galatians 6:2)

was that in three months I was going to be delivering our third child, and my husband was not going to be present.

My mother-in-law kept me occupied on the day of Scott's departure. On the second day of deployment, one of our church friends brought us lunch and stayed to eat with us. Evidence of God's provision continued to show through his children: prayers, meals, companionship, childcare, and other gestures of support and encouragement.

In mid-March the invasion into Iraq began, and with parting words of love, encouragement, and prayers for my husband, I wrote "Know that we will be fine . . . don't worry about us. You know that so many people are caring for us here."

I was raised to be independent and help myself, so it was awkward to receive the extra attention. Being on the receiving end was hard to swallow. I did not want to be portrayed as needy or helpless. But when I look back at our first deployment, I fondly recall what it truly feels like to experience Christian community. We were surrounded by people who loved us and cared about us. God used his church and our family to tangibly embrace us during those uncertain months.

Prayer:
*Lord, help me be humble enough to allow
others to serve me when I need it.*

SEPTEMBER 10

Operation We Are Here

*Benita Koeman, wife of Chaplain (Capt.) Scott Koeman,
Iraq 2003; Qatar/Afghanistan (2005–2006)*

IT WAS JULY 28, 2005. The kids and I arrived home from dropping Scott off at the airport to a driveway littered with his residual attempts of packing for Qatar. Two years prior, our family left this civilian community for our new military installation. We had returned home for Scott's second deployment, counting on the support we expected from the people who knew us best.

I adopted a genuine, "I can do this" attitude about the deployment. But I couldn't do it alone, and most good intentions to help, from the people we loved fell by the wayside. As I struggled to take care of our young children (ages two, four, and six years old), I felt alone and abandoned. At one point I bordered depression. I tried my best to smile, to fake like all was okay, and to convince myself it was. But it wasn't.

Upon my husband's return we PCS'd (permanent change of station), I carried residual hurt and anger. Many nights I would lie awake and ask God, "What do I do with this?" and "Where do I go from here?"

As time passed I heard other military wives share their stories of hurt and disappointment because of the lack of support from their churches. I realized that our churches and others who loved us do not intentionally forsake their support—they just don't understand our struggles. To create an awareness of the challenges of the military home front, the website *Operation We Are Here* was born. This became a site to offer practical suggestions, support, and encouragement.

> "Lord, You have assigned me my portion and my cup, and have made my lot secure."
> (Psalm 16:5)

Over time, God removed my hurts and redeemed a very painful year for His glory. I was committed to honor him despite my circumstances. I learned by experience that people (even those who love us) will disappoint us and that our circumstances hold no guarantees. But importantly, I was reminded that God will not abandon me. He is good, and I continue to put my hope and my trust in Him.

Prayer:

Father, when life is tough and just doesn't make sense, help me to take my eyes off of myself and lift my gaze to You, for only You can satisfy.

SEPTEMBER 11

Brave Face, Tender Heart

Sonja and SFC Jason Mannarino, Iraq (2006–2007)

NO ONE ever told Sonja Mannarino that deployment would be easy. But no one told her it would be this hard, either.

Her daughter was fifteen and her sons were eleven and four years old when her husband of sixteen years deployed. While Jason encountered enemy fire in Iraq, Sonja felt like the home front was under attack as well.

Her four-year-old son cried for days after saying goodbye to his daddy, especially at night because Jason always tucked him into bed. Her eleven-year-old son went through depression and gained a lot of weight, eating to fill the void where his dad had been.

"It was hard for him. He was Dad's helper working on cars or in the yard together," said Sonja. "He had a lot of anger too and took it out on me verbally. I had to sit down with him and say, 'What you're doing is not right.' It tore my heart out because there was nothing I could do."

Every day Sonja put on a brave face and tried to be strong for the children. But every night, after the kids were in bed, she was the one crying to her Heavenly Father for comfort. "At night, I felt alone," she said. "I was trying to smile for my kids, but the pain was still there with Jason being gone. As time went on, things got easier but it was still hard, especially on certain days like Father's Day, Christmas, and the first day of school."

> "Fear not, for I have redeemed you; I have summoned you by name; you are mine. When you pass through the waters, I will be with you. . . . "
> (Isaiah 43:1b–2a)

The Bible is full of heroes who faced fear even as they took the path God had set before them. Joshua had to be told four times in Joshua 1 to "be strong and courageous." In the psalms, David cries out to God many times in fear for his life. Queen Esther feared for her safety as well. Following God's will doesn't mean we will not fear, but it does mean that God will walk beside us every step of the way.

Prayer:
Lord, turn my fear into confidence in your power, not mine.

SEPTEMBER 12

Secret Weapon

Sonja and SFC Jason Mannarino, Iraq (2006–2007)

AS SONJA held down the fort, she quickly saw the need to go on the offensive against spirits of fear, worry, resentment, anger, and bitterness. Instead of waiting for discouragement to invade and occupy her home, she countered this obstacle at every turn by wielding the Sword of Truth: God's Word.

Her tactic was simple: she printed Scripture verses off from her computer and stuck them all around her house with Scotch tape so God's Word would constantly be before her eyes and the eyes of her children.

> "For the word of God is living and active. Sharper than any double-edged sword, it penetrates even to dividing soul and spirit, joints and marrow; it judges the thoughts and attitudes of the heart." (Hebrews 4:12)

Taped next to her bathroom mirror: *Be exalted, O Lord, in your strength; we will sing and praise your might* (Psalm 21:13).

Taped inside her kitchen cupboard: *Even though I walk through the valley of the shadow of death, I will fear no evil for you are with me* (Psalm 23:4).

Taped above her dresser: *He will have no fear of bad news; his heart is steadfast, trusting in the Lord* (Psalm 112:7).

Taped in her living room: *But as for me, it is good to be near God. I have made the Sovereign Lord my refuge; I will tell of all your deeds* (Psalm 73:28).

The result was powerful. Instead of dwelling on the unknown of the future, Sonja chose to dwell on what she did know—that God is good, and he's in control. Even after Jason returned from deployment the following year, Sonja left those verses hanging around her home.

"Without God, I couldn't have made it," she said. "I needed comfort and peace, and he gave it to me. That is just amazing. Jason and I prayed with each other through email. We would speak to each other about God and Scriptures to lift our spirits. God's presence was really strong."

Sonja was able to ward off attacks from the Enemy by claiming God's truths. Meditating on Scripture cleared her mind and heart of the swirling negative thoughts that threatened to consume her. You can do the same.

Prayer:
Lord, give me the discipline I need to study and memorize your Word.

SEPTEMBER 13

Danger and Protection

SFC Jason Mannarino, Iraq (2006–2007)

WHEN SFC Mannarino was stationed in Taji, Iraq, he could count on one thing—he would be fired upon every day.

"I didn't know if I'd live another five minutes let alone make it through the deployment," he said. "We got shot at, mortared, attacked constantly. It was a daily occurrence, two to four times a day. I wasn't in a great place."

One day, an 82mm mortar landed five feet from Mannarino—in the spot where he had been standing a moment earlier—and blew up in the air. "Mortars are designed to blow out, but it blew up, away from me," he said. "I felt the Holy Spirit protecting me."

Another day, two of his soldiers were hit with mortars and needed to be flown to Germany for medical care. Mannarino also witnessed an Iraqi security guard across the street get his face blown off from sniper fire.

> "Satisfy us in the morning with your unfailing love, that we may sing for joy and be glad all our days. Make us glad for as many days as you have afflicted us, for as many years as we have seen trouble."
> (Psalm 90:14–15)

These are experiences he didn't write home about to Sonja and the kids. In fact, he didn't even have time to process the danger and loss of life surrounding him on a regular basis. He knew his life was at risk, but he also knew God was watching out for him. Mannarino read Psalm 91 daily and left his Bible open to it even when he was not in his room.

"I became very desensitized, but now that I'm home, it does catch up to me," he said. "I've been back for two years. I still have moments where I'll talk to guys about Iraq, and I'll have to quit because it really brings back a flood of emotion that I never dealt with."

Soldiers like Mannarino may not come home with visible injuries, but their spirits might need some healing after what they've experienced. Jesus, the Great Physician, has the power to heal not only our bodies but our minds, hearts and spirits as well.

Prayer:
Lord, heal my troubled spirit and renew my soul again.

Finding Purpose

SFC Jason Mannarino, Iraq (2006–2007)

IN THE BEGINNING of his deployment, SFC Jason Mannarino didn't want to go on, but he did anyway. It wasn't his own hardship that was on his mind, however. It was his family's.

"I know Sonja and the kids had a tough time coping with the entire thing," he said. "I told her, 'There has to be a purpose. There's got to be a reason that this is happening to us in this portion of our lives. God's got a plan. I don't know what it is, but he has a plan.'"

The hardest part for Jason, he said, was knowing that his wife and children were having an extremely difficult time. "I thought about them every minute of every day. They were my drive to come home. They are what I live for."

Looking back on the deployment now, Sonja said the experience invigorated her marriage and brought them closer to each other and to God. "Before, we didn't have the greatest marriage," said Sonja. "We didn't hate or yell at each other, we were just kind of far apart. I see now that there was a purpose for this deployment; God opened up my eyes to see that I can make it through difficult times if I rely on him. My faith just got stronger. Jason and I are closer now to each other, and we're closer as a family."

> "Now we see but a poor reflection as in a mirror; then we shall see face to face. Now I know in part; then I shall know fully, even as I am fully known."
> (1 Corinthians 13:12)

God may have had other purposes for Jason's deployment that no one can see yet, but at present, Jason and Sonja say it's enough that it brought them closer together.

We all walk through valleys at some point in our lives. Some of us will be blessed on the other side with the understanding of why God took us down that road and how he plans to use it in our lives, but not always. Regardless, we are called to follow him daily, even though we can't see the big picture like he can.

Prayer:
Lord, help me follow you even when I can't see your plan.

Passion Fatigue

Starlett Henderson, army veteran, army wife, and military lifestyle writer

MENTION DEPLOYMENT to a friend or family member and questions like "How many times has he been deployed?" are asked. This late in the war, it's not uncommon to hear "three times" or "almost five years in the last ten." It's a shock sometimes, to me even, when I hear myself say it out loud.

I noticed this time I have a hard time minding the details of where David is and what he's doing. I see it like this: he's one of two places—here or not here. One thing is for sure: right up there with compassion fatigue is my own passion fatigue.

I wish for those early days of the war, when we were sure it was just and winnable. Lines have crossed and blurred now. Subsequent deployments haven't gotten easier with our multiplying stressors or the soldiers' changing enemy. In my darkest, lonely hours I cry, "If this isn't persecution, I don't know what is." It's not that I don't believe in what we're doing. I've long felt this is our family's duty, honor, and ministry. I just wish there were more soldiers in the fight.

> "And God will use this persecution to show his justice and to make you worthy of his Kingdom, for which you are suffering."
> (2 Thessalonians 1:5 NLT)

I sigh when I realize the similarities between the need for soldiers fighting to liberate the oppressed overseas and the need for Christian soldiers to disseminate the freeing Truth. There will never be enough of either and the work will not get easier. The fact of the matter is that the more persistent we are, the worse it will get, on earth. So I pull up those boot straps and focus on the Lord and what it all means. I focus on his promises of the rewards in Heaven and the knowledge that opposition (read: persecution) means we are striking a nerve with the enemy, and it isn't all for naught.

Prayer:
Lord, Thank You for our opportunity to serve You and our nation. Thank You for promising heaven and giving meaning to our suffering.

Something to Be Humble About

Starlett Henderson, army veteran,
army wife, and military lifestyle writer

IF YOUR HEART goes unchecked like mine, sometimes it may be puffed with pride. It doesn't take much: a few poignant lyrics, hearing the American flag snap sharply in the sky on a windy day, making it to another homecoming intact. For the most part, the country honors our service and sacrifice of a military family as a whole. Military spouses are elevated right along with service members.

I had one of these moments recently. A monument was erected atop one of the nation's premier ski jumps right in my in-laws' hometown. We went for a visit, and it was a site to behold. A garrison flag flies high and brick pavers bear the names of many who have served or are still serving. Inside is a time capsule that holds the DD214s of half the state's veterans. The time capsule will be opened in about one hundred years, 2106. My husband and I are veterans from the counties recognized. I was so proud.

My mind wandered to where my family would be in 2106. Who would be there to be proud for us? Would the children of tomorrow gain a sense of the full measure of patriotism as is one of the monument's stated

> "Humble yourselves before the Lord, and he will lift you up in honor." (James 4:10 NLT)

purposes? "I bet not," I thought. Already signs of vandalism were cropping up too close for comfort. I was indignant to think that one hundred years down the road, a ceremony might go unnoticed or veterans might be forgotten. I hope it won't be.

In that hope, I attached a prayer, but at the same time was gently admonished for taking credit for God's strength and maybe not caring enough that God is so often forgotten. In our three-day drive to the in-laws, we passed a few other sites to behold: crosses in the mountains, steeples seen from far off distances, a marble statue at least four stories high of Jesus with outstretched arms. Next time I'll do more than drive-by; I'll pray that one hundred years from now, veterans and military families will recognize God as the one who sustained them.

Prayer:
Father, strip me of these prideful feelings, for I know it's You, not us, who has the power. Forgive me for acting as if I'm the only one. It's Your grace and strength from which I draw my own. Thank You.

Faith, Hope, and Love

Starlett Henderson, army veteran,
army wife, and military lifestyle writer

Truth is that David had me from: "I prayed for you." But my interest was piqued even more from "I enlisted."

David and I have a long history. We were in the same circles since junior high. We dated in those circles, but we didn't really know each other. That became very apparent the day I started hearing rumors that David had enlisted via the delayed entry program.

"In the Army? Can he do that?" I questioned. He was seventeen. My own young life had been shaped by family members who served. I had a deep interest through the military instruction I received in JROTC classes. To me, the military symbolized—symbolizes still—selfless service, compassion for others, a level of personal responsibility. It was a world I deeply respected. This young man was put on my heart as "the one."

THUS MY journey with the military began by writing daily letters to David at Basic Training in 1989. He came home, we dated, and he told me one day that he prayed for me, as in he asked for me from God. The gifts just kept on coming.

Soon I was a soldier myself, then an Iraqi Freedom military spouse, and now Enduring Freedom spouse. This Army wife life brings the best and worst of times. I choose to reflect on the best experiences: a greater love, a life of service, and children who have learned what it means to be dedicated and selfless.

> "Three things will last forever—faith, hope and love—and the greatest of these is love."
> (1 Corinthians 13:13 NLT)

Without our children and me, I feel David would not have made it this long, this far. Without him and his brothers—he calls them—we would not have the free living we enjoy. We're a team. It's hard to feel that way, especially when we're apart as often as we are together. But we have our faith and hope—and bigger than enduring freedom—we have enduring love.

None of it would be possible except for my heavenly Father bringing our two loves together. His hand has carried us from that first hello through many good-byes, and he'll deliver us to our final reunion, whenever that may be.

Prayer:

Gracious God, I thank you for bestowing peace upon us. I pray for those military couples whose faith and love may feel less than enduring. I ask that you cover them and give them hope.

SEPTEMBER 18

My Army Wife Army

Starlett Henderson, army veteran, army wife, and military lifestyle writer

FOR ME, each deployment has had its own fresh challenges. Having to work was one of them, going to school was another, and being pregnant for part of another. The stressors mounted, particularly when we received orders for a back-to-back deployment that David could have opted out of, but, doing so would opt him out of the right career progression and leave his soldiers with inexperienced leadership. We prepared for the quick turn-around. I quit my job, graduated school, and moved in a short time frame. David was gone shortly thereafter, and I began struggling.

> "And since we know he hears us when we make our requests, we also know that he will give us what we ask for." (1 John 5:15)

I wasn't going to be able to leave the house to get this job. I didn't know anyone to babysit. I was fatigued from caring for an infant, and I wasn't in a military town. So I submitted a tall prayer to God. "*I want something I can do from home that will make use of my higher education and will make me lots of friends,*" I told him.

The struggle continued. I was eking out a living. My church friends, a very small FRG [family readiness group], were supportive and helped me remain faithful. But I still wanted what I wanted. Weary with need, I began a cursory search online—"Army Wife" or "deployment support"— may have been my search terms. My find was Army Wife Talk Radio in 2004.

What a Godsend. I found fulfillment there in sharing answers with other spouses and many friends who understand—all the while working from home. It's not where I saw myself twenty years ago. It may not be where I see myself twenty years from now, but it's just what I ordered to make it through Deployment I, II, and III.

God is using me and my involvement in the online talk radio realm, now Army Wife Network, to relieve the pressure. I'm only left with one more need lately and that is to have my husband home. But I am smart enough to know that if there was no Army, there would be no soldiers (with their spouses, fiancés, and families) to support. And no job for me. So, I'll be thankful he saw fit to provide just what I needed for the time it is needed.

Prayer:
My, how You fulfill my need. Your strategy is divine,
and I'm happy you intervene on my behalf.

Soldier Boy's Love Story

Starlett Henderson, army veteran, army wife, and military lifestyle writer

MORE THAN missing her son David, I imagine Grandma Mary Henderson struggles, knowing David's children miss him. There's Thomas, thirteen, and there is the granddaughter Mary never thought she'd have, Tara, five.

I had put the thought of another child out of my head. I just kept saying I was done, until I started to feel I wasn't. David was leaving for Iraq the first time, and we left it to God to settle the question. He answered with a resounding "*yes.*" Tara was born.

Just before David's third deployment, his mother described David's perspective on leaving his new daughter as if David were speaking:

As our eyes locked, I knew the meaning of "love at first sight."
She smiled at me as if she had known me her whole life. Her hand caressed my cheek like the whisper of a feather. My heart beat faster as I realized I had waited my whole life for her.

We have been inseparable for five months. We have cuddled and laughed late into the night. She has fallen asleep in my arms. She trusts me completely to protect her and love her always. As

331

I watch her sleep, I try to form the words to fashion a good-bye. How will she understand?

Sleeping so peacefully beside me, she is unaware of my turmoil. She is my love, my life; everything has changed since I met her. I watch her sleep; she must be dreaming pleasant thoughts. She will not understand why I must leave. How do I explain that I must serve a second deployment to Iraq? I lean over, needing to kiss her, but not wanting to disturb her.

> "Yet God has made everything beautiful for its own time . . . So I concluded there is nothing better than to be happy and enjoy ourselves as long as we can."
> (Ecclesiastes 3:11–12)

She smiles a lopsided grin...

I think my beautiful ten-month old daughter just murmured, "Da-da."

My questions were plenty. *Why must we separate again? Why did God allow this child to be born at this time?* We don't understand, but we have been enjoying our daughter for all she's worth.

Prayer:
Lord, we don't understand, but thank you for having a plan. We put our faith in you and resolve to revel in your wisdom and glory.

SEPTEMBER 20

A Prayer for My Country

Donna Tallman delivered this prayer on Memorial Day weekend, 2009

FATHER IN heaven,

We come before you, Lord, to thank you for America. Thank you that before the foundation of the world, you selected us to live here; to raise our families here, and represent you to those around us who've never met you. We are grateful for this privilege, Lord, and stop to give you praise.

Just as you selected men and women in Scripture to fulfill strategic roles in your plan for the nations, you also intentionally called us to live here in the United States in this season of time . . . for this hour.

Your destiny for us was to enter this nation's history during the twentieth century and lead it into a new era. We are Millennium Ministers assigned to take your unfailing and unchanging message of hope to a nation that has been captured by an insidious addiction to constant diversion.

John Winthrop, Puritan leader and governor of Massachusetts, desired that the New World become a beacon of light to other nations. He longed for this land to be the shining city set on a hill that Jesus referred to in Matthew chapter five. But we are not that. So we come to you this morning, Lord, and ask for your intervention. Return us to our foundation, to our heritage, and to your destiny for us as a nation and to your destiny for us as your church.

We can only become that shining city when the hearts of America's people turn to you. Help us see, Father, that it is not our productivity that you want. You don't want the work of our hands—our industry, rather you want the surrender of our hearts. Politics will not cure America's heart. Science, technology, law, or philosophy won't fix it either—only a revival sent from you for your church can restore America from within.

> ". . . A city on a hill cannot be hidden."
> (Matthew 5:14)

We are desperate for you, Lord. America will never fully shine from atop that hill until your church experiences the freedom in Christ you intended. You came to set us free, yet we have bound ourselves to our own culture's excesses and temptations. Forgive us, Lord, we come now in repentance and ask for your restoration.

A Prayer for My Country, Part 2

Donna Tallman

FATHER,

Remind us that liberty never travels without its companion—sacrifice, and that sacrifice never travels without love. When we are tempted to forget the physical sacrifice America's soldiers have made on our behalf, remind us that it was their blood that bought this nation its freedom. In the same way, remind us that it was the sacrifice of your blood that bought our spiritual freedom when your own son paid the ultimate price for our redemption . . .

And this you did because you loved us.

Lord, America's soldiers have become some of our greatest teachers. They teach us the significance of duty, honor, and sacrifice. They show us how to persevere in the face of extreme trial. We ask that you heal the hearts of our soldiers. Fill them with the assurance of your presence in their hours of fear, doubt, or even despair. Provide them with hope when they feel hopeless and peace when their spirits are in turmoil.

Father, this nation was founded on the work and character of many high-caliber men and women you selected to lead us. We ask that you again bless us with gifted leaders for our nation, our state, and our city. Grant us wisdom and discernment as we participate in the election process in the coming months. May our minds and hearts be attuned to your will for us in this hour.

> "If my people, who are called by my name, will humble themselves and pray and seek my face and turn from their wicked ways, then will I hear from heaven and will forgive their sin and will heal their land." (2 Chronicles 7:14)

When President Reagan said farewell to the nation he had served for eight years in January of 1989, he affirmed John Winthrop's prophetic call that America was to become the shining city on a hill that would serve as a beacon of hope to the nations of the world.

May we stop and remember those who desperately need freedom and consider what sacrifices we must make to procure it for them. May we remember those who hurtle through the darkness and step in with the

Good News that the Light of the World has come to light their way home —to true freedom found in Jesus Christ.

In the precious name of Jesus who desires to lead us all to freedom, Amen.

Danger in the Red Zone

Brandt Smith, PhD

THE RAPPORT of mortars being launched could be heard in the distance. The trailing whine ended in a large bang. The explosions were close tonight. Indirect fire is not often well aimed by the insurgents. On this night it again missed its mark landing in the residential area outside the Green Zone. It was the middle of the night.

It was a hot night. The lack of electricity made the flashes of light seem even brighter. Gunfire could be heard sporadically in the background. His teenage daughter held on tightly. The blasts brought fear and frailty to their home. A father holds a daughter and knows her heart.

The danger was real and ever present. It was mid-2006, and Baghdad was a violent place. Brandt Smith left the comfort of the United States to go to Baghdad, Iraq. He voluntarily went with his wife and daughter into a combat theater. Away from the relative protection of the Green Zone, they lived in the Red Zone, the real Baghdad. He and his family would remain in this 'dark corner' of the earth for over two years.

> "The angel of the LORD encamps around those who fear him, and he delivers them."
> (Psalm 34:7)

When you live in a city where terrorism is constantly battling against freedom, you learn that violence and chaos are commonplace. The list of friends lost to this violence brought Brandt deep pain. Yet amidst the turmoil God provided a refuge, sometimes through miraculous acts of protection, sometimes through the quiet presence of His love. Tonight, his daughter would have the reassuring words of her father speaking God's Word.

In the psalms he found a resting place. There are passages sprinkled throughout the psalms that illustrate God's compassion and grace for those in harm's way. David was a man of war, and he had insight into the brevity of life. He understood this and communicated it to God. In many of these passages, David conveys a hope that meets the needs of the soldier and the missionary—and their daughters.

The trembling began to subside. The noise faded to silence. And peace returned to their home.

Prayer:
Lord encamp around me. Teach me to fear you.
Thank you Father for delivering me once again.

SEPTEMBER 23

The Mission:
Return Safely to the Office

Brandt Smith, PhD

THE CAR rounded a corner and began to approach the government building. It was a scene eerily absent of normal daily activities. All quiet in Baghdad—hardly normal. It usually indicated that a curfew had been imposed; or something was about to happen, just happened, or was happening and you had not been informed.

As the car approached, gunfire pierced through the silence. Rounds coursed across the road all around them. Instinctively the driver began to pull the car to the side of the road. Brandt's assistant in the back seat

> "Morning by morning
> He awakens me."
> (Isaiah 50:4b)

screamed, "la, la, la, " translated "no, no, no!" in English.

The road in front of the ministry headquarters was lined with barriers and razor wire. There was nowhere to go. The driver stepped on the gas and drove through the firefight. The racket of gunfire and the crack of bullets passing by overwhelmed the senses. They made it to the other side. They were alive, but silent. Not a word was spoken as they completed the drive to the office.

They pulled into the office parking lot and got out to examine the car. Not one bullet had hit the car. Miraculously they had been delivered through the hail of bullets. The two Muslims looked in disbelief. It is not common for a Muslim to pray with a Christian, but his driver and assistant held hands with Brandt as he prayed, thanking God for His protection. Once in the office Brandt turned on the computer. An email had just arrived. One of the Christians praying for Brandt and his family had been awakened in their sleep with the sense that God wanted them to pray for Brandt. The email said, "I was just awakened to pray for you. I don't know what is going on in your day today, but I wanted you to know that I am praying."

We may never know why our heart is burdened to pray, but we must pray nonetheless. He is drawing us to himself co-laboring with him in his work, his will.

Prayer:
Father God, show me your heart and awaken me from my sleep to pray. I long to co-labor with you. May your compassion be my compassion, may my heart break for what breaks your heart. Thank you God for awakening me.

SEPTEMBER 24

Why Are We Here?

Brandt Smith, PhD

IT WAS NIGHTTIME. It was also the end of the fourth day of the curfew that kept them prisoners in their home. The heat of the day would never fully dissipate. Without the comfort that they were so accustomed to before coming to Iraq, Brandt's wife leaned over and asked, "What are we doing here?" Brandt would answer, "Well, we are following Jesus." She would reply with an affirming, "I know, but man . . ."

His wife would not be the only one to bear the strain, the hardship. Brandt waded through confusion. "Why are we here? Why did God ask us to be at this place at this time." Brandt and his wife, Gail, would sit together and read in Luke 9 where Jesus was speaking to his disciples and to the people. Luke 9:23 says, "If anyone wishes to come after me let him deny himself."

When you cannot do your own shopping; when you do not have freedom of movement, and you know there are evil people that would like to see you dead; you get a sense of what it means to deny yourself.

Jesus also said, "Take up your cross daily and follow me." On some days, Brandt would just ask, "Lord, how much do I need to deny myself? How heavy must my cross be? How far do I have to follow you?" The answer would come quietly and with clarity, "All the way." There it was; Brandt was the one who had bent his knee to God, God simply said, "This is what I am asking of you at this time in your life."

For Brandt, that was sufficient. It was a reminder that following him wasn't necessarily the easiest path but it was the best path.

> Then he said to them all: "If anyone would come after me, he must deny himself and take up his cross daily and follow me. For whoever wants to save his life will lose it, but whoever loses his life for me will save it. What good is it for a man to gain the whole world, and yet lose or forfeit his very self?" (Luke 9:23–25)

Whether in Baghdad or any other city in the world, we must ask if we are on his path. Complicated by personal sacrifice, discomfort and the constant threat of violence, Brandt found the sufficiency of Christ. Soldiers and missionaries alike find themselves denying their own personal comfort and desires. For them, life holds a far more significant purpose.

Prayer:
Father, teach me to deny myself and follow after you.
Save my life, let my gain be you and not this world.

SEPTEMBER 25

Living in a Besieged City

Brandt Smith, PhD

WHO ARE the Iraqi people? How are they alike or different from us?

Like us, they want stability in their nation and to raise their families in peace. They want to be recognized legitimately as a people that contribute to the world. They have a sense of humor not much unlike our own. They laugh at things we laugh at and cry at the things that cause us to cry. What sets them apart is that they have endured three wars in their

338

homeland, leaving their self-esteem torn and battered. Naturally, their emotional stability has become destabilized.

There were days that Brandt felt he was in a bad place. Violence and crime are a gnarly combination that can sour anyone's view of a location. But there were other days when Brandt would realize, "good grief I am stuck in traffic just like they are." They were both suffering. It is hot; engines are overheating. They are just trying to get home too; they were all in the same boat. There is something about the camaraderie of mutual suffering that levels the playing field.

Being stuck in traffic for hours at a time was not an uncommon experience. He would roll his window down and turn the car off. It was easy to carry on conversations with those stuck in traffic next to him. Inevitably his Arabic would run out, and others would ask, "Are you an American?"

> "Praise be to the LORD, for he showed his wonderful love to me when I was in a besieged city." (Psalm 31:21)

Brandt would say, "Yes, I am," and they would go on to tell him, "Oh, thank you for being in our country. We love America. Thank you so much. We love you. We love George Bush." They love freedom.

The violence, the mundane hardship of traffic jams, the lack of electricity—all define the unsettled city of Baghdad, a city at war. God knew exactly where Brandt was. God led him there. And throughout all the trials that he and his family contended with, God showed his wonderful love to them.

Prayer:
Father, while our friends and family are in war torn cities in foreign lands, show them your wonderful love.

Into the City of Mosul

Maj. John Croushorn, MD (retired veteran)

WE FLEW in low over the northern city of Mosul. Forward Operating Base (FOB) Freedom was just over four miles north of the downtown city center. Our southeastern approach would take us over the ancient gates of Nineveh, the city that Jonah traveled to around 760 BC.

The ruins were spread out all over Mosul.

At fifty feet above the ground the Iraqis could see our faces and we could see theirs. But traveling at a speed of 120 knots it did not give you much time to focus on anyone. Nonetheless, it was a peaceful flight in. We landed on the pad, shut down and walked to the dining facility while our helicopters were refueled.

FOB Freedom was set among several palaces. Their ornate beauty and landscaped lawns were in stark contrast to the poverty we flew over to get there. We entered the dining facility (DFAC) and enjoyed the hot meal.

After lunch we walked down to one of the palaces and took pictures of each other standing in front of large paintings of Saddam holding a child and standing with an old woman. I found it ironic that one of the most evil men in the world would be pictured standing with the most innocent.

We returned to the aircraft and began our startup procedures. Right on time our scheduled group of travelers arrived and jumped on board. We took off low and fast and moved beyond Freedom back over Mosul. Within minutes we were over the desert again, for our flight to Baghdad.

Several weeks later a man walked into the DFAC during lunchtime. He detonated the explosives, killing twenty-two and wounding sixty. In a moment, twenty-two human beings who were hungry and ready to eat lunch were no longer alive. Sixty individuals went from relaxing to agonizing from wounds both internal and external.

Life changes quickly, in a heartbeat. Whether by heart attack, automobile accident or improvised explosive device, life can change forever. To take for granted each breath of life is to waste the gift of it. God is good. He does not desire death even for his enemies. But death does come just as surely as life.

> "For I am convinced that neither death nor life, neither angels nor demons, neither the present nor the future, nor any powers, neither height nor depth, nor anything else in all creation, will be able to separate us from the love of God that is in Christ Jesus our Lord." (Romans 8:38–39)

Prayer:
Father, help me see each day for the promise it holds. You promise that there is nothing that can separate me from your love Abba.

Maj. John Croushorn
preparing for a flight,
September 2004, Balad,
Iraq

Marc's Last Letter Home, Part 1

Marc Alan Lee, SEAL, U.S. Navy

MARC ALAN LEE understood the cost and sacrifice that service defined. He single-handedly held off enemy fighters by creating an offensive diversion while his team rescued a wounded teammate from a rooftop. The firefight took place in Ramadi, Iraq August 2nd, 2006. Marc Alan Lee became the first Navy SEAL to die in Iraq.

"Glory is something that some men chase and others find themselves stumbling upon, not expecting it to find them. Either way it is a noble gesture that one finds bestowed upon them. My question is, when does glory fade away and become a wrongful crusade, or an unjustified means which consumes one completely?"

341

"I have seen war."

"I have seen death, the sorrow that encompasses your entire being as a man breathes his last. I can only pray and hope that none of you will ever have to experience some of these things I have seen and felt here. . . ."

"I have seen hate towards a nation's people who has sic never committed a wrong, except being born of a third world, ill-educated, and ignorant to western civilization. It is not everybody who feels this way, only a select few, but it brings questions to mind. Is it ok for one to consider themselves superior to another race?"

"Surprisingly, we are not a stranger to this sort of attitude. Meaning that in our own country, we discriminate against someone for what nationality they are, their education level, their social status. We distinguish our role models as multi-million-dollar sports heroes or talented actors and actresses who complain about not getting millions of dollars more than they are currently getting paid."

"Our country is a great country. My point of this is how can we come over here and help a less than fortunate country without holding contempt or hate towards them, if we can't do it in our country. I try to do my part over here, but the truth is over there, in the United States, I do nothing but take."

> "The King will reply, 'I tell you the truth, whatever you did for one of the least of these brothers of mine, you did for me.'"
> (Matthew 25:40)

"Ask yourself, when was the last time you donated clothes that you hadn't worn out? When was the last time you paid for a random stranger's cup of coffee, meal, or maybe even a tank of gas? When was the last time you helped a person with the groceries into or out of their car?"

Prayer:

Father, you are good; you are compassionate. Let me see your heart. Give me your compassion. Burden me with the cares of the least of these brothers of yours.

Marc's Last Letter Home, Part 2

Marc Alan Lee, SEAL, U.S. Navy

(Marc continues his thoughts on care and compassion for others)

THINK TO yourself and wonder what it would feel like if when the bill for the meal came and you were told it was already paid for. More random acts of kindness like this would change our country and our reputation as a country. It is not unknown to most of us that the rest of the world looks at us with doubt towards our humanity and morals."

"I am not here to preach or to say 'look at me,' because I am just as at fault as the next person. I find that being here makes me realize the great country we have and the obligation we have to keep it that way."

"The fourth has just come and gone and I received many emails thanking me for helping keep America great and free. I take no credit for the career path I have chosen; I can only give it to those of you who are reading this, because each one of you has contributed to me and who I am."

"However, what I do over here is only a small percent of what keeps our country great. I think the truth to our greatness is each other. Purity, morals, and kindness, passed down to each generation through example."

"Train a child in the way he should go, and when he is old he will not turn from it." (Proverbs 22:6)

"So to all my family and friends, do me a favor and pass on the kindness, the love, the precious gift of human life to each other so that when your children come into contact with a great conflict like that we are now faced with in Iraq that they are people of humanity, of pure motives, of compassion."

"This is our real part to keep America free!"

Marc died for these values. He was raised "in the way he should go." Even in the stress of combat he did "not depart from it." Marc loved by giving. On August 2, 2006, he gave the ultimate gift.

Prayer:
Abba, help me live by example and teach our children about your compassion. Father help me learn of your example. Your steadfast love and kindness never cease.

Love Must Overcome the Thugs in Iraq

Mike Meoli, SEAL, U.S. Navy, and Government Contractor

I HAVE BEEN one of the government contractors operating in Iraq that you may have heard about in the news. I work with many other contractors who, like me, are on Authorized Absence (or discharged) from either Special Forces, Marine Recon, SEAL Teams, and so forth.

Old ways die hard among thugs. And pure thuggery is what has ruled Iraq for more than ten years before Saddam Hussein under Al-Bakir. There are still a few thugs standing in the wings trying to vie for power because that's all they know. It doesn't matter what variation on Islam they are spouting—they are nothing more than mob bosses, and the Iraqi people, in general, are tired of it. Add some foreign terrorists to the mix and a liberal media in an election year and these thugs think they are going to win. I pray American voters see that we must finish this one the right way. If we walk away now, we will be responsible for a lot more than the two million Cambodians and every last Montainyard that was murdered the year after we abandoned Indochina. Here is the reality I see everyday.

> "For from within, out of the heart of men, proceed the evil thoughts, fornications, thefts, murders, adulteries."
> (Mark 7:21)

The Iraqi people as a whole love us. You read it right—love us. Terrorists may hate us and radicals in different ethnic groups within Iraq may hate each other. But in general, the common Iraqi people—Shias, Sunis, Kurds, Chaldeans, Turkomen—all have one thing in common: for one instant in time, they have hope for their future and the future of their children, and that hope is centered around one group of foreigners—you guessed it—Americans, the good old USA.

And there are dozens of coalition forces who help us. Young military people from most of the free countries in the world are here and willing to lay down their lives because America has led the way in spreading the good news of freedom and democracy to the oldest land on Earth.

We are all helping to train Iraqis to protect themselves with sound moral and ethical procedures. We know that teaching adults is important, but educating children is the key. So there is a lot of money going to rebuilding schools in Iraq and getting rural children to attend for the first time in history.

Mike viewed the images of friends mutilated and hanging from a bridge in Fallujah. The scene was horrific. What should be done?

He related three examples of how Americans dealt with indigenous people and their dead and prisoners we take. The missions took place in the two weeks following the Fallujah atrocities, just outside the gates of his Forward Operating Base.

Whether thugs attempting to steal freedom away, terrorists enacting barbaric behavior or the examples that Mike shares over the next few days, the truth of where these acts come from remains.

Prayer:
The acts result from the state of the heart. The inner man must be examined. Our thoughts and speech, as well as every act is an overflowing from the heart.

SEPTEMBER 30

Mission #1 Protection/MEDEVAC

Mike Meoli, SEAL, U.S. Navy, and Government Contractor

A TAXI FROM Baghdad approached our front gate. Unknown to the gate guards, he was carrying one of our translators. He was ordered to slow down. When he didn't comply he was forcefully ordered to stop and get out of his vehicle. In panic he floored his accelerator pedal thinking it was the brake causing his vehicle to lurch forward toward the gate. Appropriately, the gate guards fired eight 5.56 caliber rounds into the taxi.

The vehicle veered off into a field and came to a stop. Miraculously, no one inside was seriously injured by the gunfire. After the vehicle and both Iraqis were searched it was determined that the driver made a near fatal mistake but it was not deliberate.

If the guards were bloodthirsty, they could have continued to fire their weapons until they were sure that both Iraqis were dead. But they are professionals and they followed their current ROEs (Rules of Engagement) until the car was not a threat and then safely reassessed the situation.

But that's not the end of the story. After tending to some minor wounds of our translator, I noticed the elderly Taxi cab driver was holding his chest with a clenched fist. I gave our translator a series of questions to ask and found the man was experiencing severe pressure on the left side of his chest radiating to his left shoulder and arm. He had an irregular pulse. After putting him on our EKG monitor I found him in a potentially life-threatening heart rhythm and determined he was in the beginning stages of a heart attack. Because he was outside our gates there was no legal reason to treat him. If we had hatred in our hearts, we could have let him suffer for his mistake and die. But we were not on a dangerous convoy, and there were no hostiles approaching, and we do not have hatred in our hearts.

> 'Do not plot evil against your neighbor, and do not love to swear falsely. I hate all this,' declares the Lord.'" (Zechariah 8:17)

So we brought him into our compound and put him on oxygen, and I administered several doses of nitroglycerin, started an IV, and gave him morphine and other appropriate drugs based on his changing condition. And we packaged him for flight, and called in an American Dust-off MEDEVAC Crew. I flew with him to the closest Combat Surgical Hospital.

For twenty-four hours he received the same high level of medical care that any American soldier would have received. Eventually, the hospital staff turned him over to an Iraqi ambulance when he was stable, and he was given American medications to take home. Although it was completely his fault and our guards did exactly the right thing, an American Civil Affairs officer is tracking the cab driver to help him process his claim to get his taxi cab repaired or replaced.

One week later, he returned for his cab, and he made it very clear that he doesn't hate us either.

Prayer:
Father, let me hate what you hate and love what you love.
Give my heart your compassion and my soul your peace.

Mission #2: Civil Affairs

Mike Meoli, SEAL, U.S. Navy, and Government Contractor

IRAQ IS AN agrarian country where you find many farmers and shepherds. Most shepherds are nomads and live like the Bedouins who still roam between all Arab countries. Some own land and stay in one place. It is important for our own safety and theirs that we get to know all of our neighbors.

A few days ago, the son of a local shepherd came to our front gate and reported that the dogs had returned home but not the father. Subsequently they found some of the sheep outside a nearby abandoned Ammunition Supply Point (ASP). The ASP was not secure and is full of live unexploded ordinance (UXO).

Fearing the worst, the son asked us to help find his father.

Our officer in charge of security carefully considered the risk and asked our input, and we decided to form a search party to

> "The sacrifices of God are a broken spirit; a broken and contrite heart, O God, you will not despise."
> (Psalm 51:17)

find him in the ASP. We found the body of the shepherd directly adjacent to a small crater, which was obviously caused by the detonation of a relatively small UXO.

We used a technique to roll him onto his back from a remote location in case the body was booby-trapped with an IED (improvised explosive device). On close examination we determined that in addition to entering a dangerous restricted area, the shepherd had obviously been tampering with the UXO, which led to his own demise.

There were no morbid jokes. If we were callous and uncivilized, we could have left the body for the dogs and wolves. No one would know. If we were barbarians with hatred in our hearts we could have done things barbarians do to bodies, which perpetuates more hatred.

Because we are professionals, we carefully documented and retained his personal possessions for his family, and we contained his remains in a coroners pouch; and we placed that in an American body bag.

Because we don't have hatred in our hearts, we took our translator out to the family to notify them of the death and to provide grief support. They specifically requested to see the remains of their loved one. So we prepared them for what they would see and then we brought them in and respectfully showed them. Then we presented the intact right hand of the shepherd for them to touch and caress. We waited with them while they prayed Muslim prayers (even as some of us were praying silent Christian ones). Finally, the U.S. Army expedited the arrival of the local Iraqi Police authorities so that they could bury the remains before sunset, which is their tribal custom.

Prayer:
You know my heart God, and I know what you want of my heart. Teach me to be broken and contrite. Prevent hatred from entering the space I reserve for you.

OCTOBER 2

Mission #3: Interdiction Operation

Mike Meoli, SEAL, U.S. Navy, and Government Contractor

ON MARCH 31, 2004, the same day that the four Blackwater operators were murdered in Fallujah and their bodies were desecrated, I was activated to patrol with a Quick Response Force (QRF). We were summoned to the same ASP where we found the body of the shepherd except this time we had to go much farther in where the UXO was so thick it was like a carpet.

In past weeks in the same area we encountered handfuls of looters who either scrap for metal or ordinance, which they sell. When they sell intact ordinance it is used for only one purpose—the base charge for the IEDs (improvised explosive devices), which blow someone up everyday from here to Israel. In each of the previous instances we searched and detained the individuals and turned them over to the US Army.

On this day there were fifteen looters found, and then there were twenty, and then twenty more, and soon there were more than one hundred. We started with only eight of us "contractor" operators and three regular Army Infantry soldiers. Two of the Army soldiers found themselves isolated with over fifty looters. They asked for our immediate assistance, so we split off two three-man teams and patrolled in on foot.

From a distance across all the UXO at least two of the looters shot at us with AK-47s, which were extinguished by immediate suppressive fire.

Eventually, my team converged on the two soldiers in the middle of the ASP along with various other looters we apprehended on the way in. After adding our looters to the mix, we were then managing 148 looters.

Because we were carrying more than 250 rounds of ammunition each, we could have lined them up and shot every one of them. Or we could have forced them to walk back through a minefield or any number of unspeakably worse things that have been done in this country by their previous government. But that is not the American way, and that is not the model of behavior we wish to perpetuate here or take back home with us. So we kept firm order and discipline and carefully searched each of them. And then we placed them along a safe road out of the UXO.

> "But I say, love your enemies! Pray for those who persecute you!" (Matthew 5:44)

When we were sure that everyone was safe, and we knew exactly where the arriving U.S. Army would meet us, we formed them in disciplined columns and carefully marched them out of the ASP.

We returned that night to our FOB, and we heard the news of the fate of our brothers in Fallujah and saw films of their charred remains hanging on a public bridge and people screaming with jubilation.

Prayer:
Father, help me reflect your love in a place where
evil rejoices over death and turmoil.

OCTOBER 3

Daniel in the Lion's Den

Maj. John Croushorn, MD (retired veteran)

WE WERE returning from Najaf and headed to the Polish Base three miles north of Al Hillah to refuel. The flight day was half over. We would refuel and then fly north to Baghdad to conduct our last mission before returning to Balad.

We shut down once we landed. There were American MEDEVAC birds stationed there and a couple of large Polish helicopters. To refuel at most bases we would keep the engines running, here we had to shut all the way down. It was a needed break.

We walked up the hill to the left, past living quarters to the main road through the base. And there before us were the reproduction of the Ishtar Gates. They were tall and blue. This was the focus for the Polish division's drive from the south. While the rest went for lunch in the dining facility, I followed one of the pilots through the gates and into the courtyard beyond. We met an old archaeologist that offered to show us around.

As we walked I was struck by the history. "This is where Daniel was thrown in the lion's den. . . . This is the Street of Processions. . . . This is the Great Throne Room." It was amazing to be near the ancient history of our faith.

I was tired and hot; the nature of war kept us very busy. Sometimes that busyness precluded the time I longed for in my own thoughts and reading in the Bible. I would begin to feel distant from my faith in those times, but the reality of Daniel and his trust in God was made more real by this place. It was a needed encouragement.

I recorded stories and prayers for our children and would send them home from time to time. That night I read from Daniel 6:6–28. It is the story of Daniel in the lion's den. I then described what it looked like today. I want their faith to be as real as Daniel's.

"I issue a decree that in every part of my kingdom people must fear and reverence the God of Daniel. 'For he is the living God and he endures forever; his kingdom will not be destroyed, his dominion will never end. He rescues and he saves; he performs signs and wonders in the heavens and on the earth. He has rescued Daniel from the power of the lions.'" (Daniel 6:26–27)

Prayer:
Father, you are the living God and you endure forever!
Your kingdom will never be destroyed. Your dominion will
never end. You rescue and save! You are worthy to be
praised even when I fear the worst has come upon me.

An MH-60 Blackhawk from Task Force 185 Aviation takes off on a mission from Balad, Iraq

God Is a Strong Tower

Maj. John Croushorn, MD (retired veteran)

IT WAS LATE in the evening. It had been another hot long day, but one in which I was able to return to the relative comfort of my trailer. As I lay there, bright lights cast moving shadows through my window. The shadow of my blinds moved up the wall. Out the window I could see the flare floating down. It was not far away. I stepped outside to get a better look.

My trailer was behind tall Texas t-barriers that protected us from direct fire. The flare was just south of us. A second flare opened and began floating down. Then the obvious struck me. One reason flares are shot is to identify the enemy. We didn't see visible light flares much because of our night vision devices.

The flares should have been my warning. Suddenly fire erupted just over the wire. A firefight ensued. Tracers raced overhead. Two small explosions, automatic gun fire. Then as quickly as it began it ended. I was still standing there. I was surprised that I had not felt my heart racing or been overcome with the urge to run for cover. Perhaps it was because I was tired. Maybe it was because I knew I was behind the protection of those t-barriers. I went back into my trailer and crawled back in bed.

> "The name of the LORD is a strong tower; the righteous run to it and are safe."
> (Proverbs 18:10)

One thought came to mind. "Strong tower, He is a strong tower." Just as those t-barriers provided for a measure of safety, ultimately God is my strong tower, protecting me from the dangers this life holds.

Prayer:
Abba, you are my strong tower. I run to you in my fear and uncertainty. I know I am safe in your arms. Safe from my enemies, safe from myself.

Pilots and crew with Task Force 185 Aviation after landing in Mosul, August 2004

Author, Maj. John Croushorn, during a mission in 2004

OCTOBER 5

Explosions All Around

Maj. John Croushorn, MD (retired veteran)

IT WAS A beautiful night for a run. The sand in our part of Iraq was like talcum powder. You cold smell it in the air. It made for some spectacular sunsets. It was still too hot for a comfortable run, but after a few months of acclimating to the midday heat, the evening air felt refreshing.

I jogged down the road that paralleled our side of the airfield. It was a mile from where I lived to the corner where an Iraqi T-55 tank set. I would run down and turn around and run back. I was on my second lap having just turn around at the tank when I saw the flash.

It was big and beautiful. White Phosphorous (WP or "Willie Pete") burns without oxygen. It burns hot. The explosions are unique in that the fragments of white phosphorous arc away from the point of impact they glow brightly and leave white trails of smoke.

The most immediate thought I had was that the blast landed near my trailer. I'm the doc for that area, and I'm a mile away on foot. I ran harder and prayed that no one was hurt. Across the airfield I could see another explosion. It was distant but bright. Since when did the enemy start shooting WP at us?

The round had not injured anyone on our side of the base, but the round that hit the other side had scored a direct hit on one of our TOCs (Tactical Operations Center), and several guys were burned pretty bad.

Life is so frail. In the midst of a beautiful sunset, those rounds dropped in and wounded good soldiers. That night we returned to the fight. The TOC's operations were up and running within an hour. Life went on. War went on.

"As a father has compassion on his children, so the LORD has compassion on those who fear him; for he knows how we are formed, he remembers that we are dust. As for man, his days are like grass, he flourishes like a flower of the field; the wind blows over it and it is gone, and its place remembers it no more. But from everlasting to everlasting the LORD's love is with those who fear him, and his righteousness with their children's children— with those who keep his covenant and remember to obey his precepts."
(Psalm 103:13–18)

Prayer:
Father God, you are so good. Help me see how frail this life is. Help me remember that we are dust. Let me use my days to honor and fear you oh God. Keep your righteousness with my children's children.

Life Changes Quickly—
Faith Does Not

Col. Jim Phillips, Physician

I SAW MORE people killed in Iraq than in Afghanistan. Part of it was the role I played. Just seeing fresh casualties when they came in was a difficult thing. One night there were four guys that came in after an IED attack. They arrived at a typical random time—unexpectedly. Each of them probably died the instant the IED detonated, as terrible damage had been done to their bodies.

> "When this is done, I will go. . . . And if I perish, I perish."
> (Esther 4:16)

It is hard to describe how sudden and devastating the loss of four young men can be. They were all in the prime of life. We learned later that one had just been commissioned out of ROTC. They were here one day, driving in their vehicle. And then a moment later, they were gone.

I think the abruptness and non-subtle way that events transpired was an eye opener for me. These experiences did not weaken my faith but strengthened it. I wondered how others went through the experience without faith. It was a lot of emotion and mental tragedy to wade through. Faith provided protection that is difficult to describe. My faith did not provide a reason why bad things happened. It did allow me to get to the point of accepting that there are some things I will not be able to figure out.

Life and especially war will not always make sense. God doesn't promise that everything will make sense, or that he will be predictable. I do know that believing that God was larger than the events happening around me, gave me a sense of control. His control. It allowed me the freedom to have to trust God's control of what was happening around me.

Prayer:
You are the God of all comfort. Please give your comfort, solace, encouragement, joy, strength, peace and assurance to those still grieving the loss of a loved one, close friend, or fellow soldier.

Jim Phillips is a physician and soldier. In 2003 he led the 2nd battalion of the 20th Special Forces Group (2/20 SFG) to Afghanistan. He was the Battalion commander. He has also served in Iraq. There he worked as a physician with the 1st Cavalry Division. Both missions served important roles in the war on terror. Both experiences gave him a deeper perspective on war and faith.

I Pursued My Enemies

Col. Jim Phillips, Physician

IN AFGHANISTAN I played a war fighter role. We had Operational Detachment Alpha (ODA) teams spread out all over the country. The Afghanistan people are tough as nails. They appear to be unemotional. You could really understand how Alexander the Great lost there. They are also incredibly industrious. They can make anything out of everything. They are also pretty inscrutable, hard to read. One thing they do value is the humanity we brought. Although we pursue our enemies, we also care for those we liberate. It is the Special Forces motto, *de oppresso liber*. The English translation of this Latin phrase is "to liberate the oppressed".

> "I pursued my enemies and overtook them. I did not turn back until they were destroyed." (Psalm 18:37)

We had gone out to visit a forward operating base for one of the ODAs. A family had brought in a young child, approximately two months old. He had probably been sick for a while. The medic for the team had kept the kid alive until we arrived. He had done everything a pediatrician would have done without the benefit of labs. The medic had started an IV line and gave the child fluid and antibiotics.

We decided that nothing else could be done there, so we loaded the child on the Chinook and flew to the combat support hospital. I held the child on the way.

That was what we did. We were not just there to kill and destroy. The people are tough as nails, but they responded to the humanitarian side of what we did. Death and oppression are the enemies. Humanity is more than the ultimate end; it is also a great deal of the means by which we reach the end.

Prayer:
God of mercy, may we show your grace and mercy to those who are in need. Creator of all, may we show your love and compassion to everyone we meet.

Intestinal Fortitude Required

Col. Jim Phillips, Physician

ONE NIGHT in the Combat Support Hospital there was a stryker team that was brought in. Their vehicle had burned after being shot up while on patrol. There were a couple of guys with modest injuries. What made it worse was that it was a friendly fire incident. Two strykers out on patrol came close to each other. One didn't recognize the other and fired. It was just a bad circumstance all the way around. Thankfully, no one died.

They were sitting around the treatment area trying to sort it all out. There was a moment of silence and then they just all started laughing. It's hard to describe the camaraderie, the ability to take life and death encounters in stride. Most people would not be able to understand how these guys could laugh together and not be devastated by what almost happened to them.

> "Though the fig tree does not bud and there are no grapes on the vines, though the olive crop fails and the fields produce no food, though there are no sheep in the pen and no cattle in the stalls, yet I will rejoice in the LORD, I will be joyful in God my Savior."
> (Habakkuk 3:17–18)

In my experience, I wasn't impressed with any one individual more than the general rank and file's willingness to be there, suck it up, and complete the mission. It's a testament to our country's true strength that these men do their jobs, survive multiple brushes with death, and to ultimately find meaning in something of which a large part of our country fails to see value. Most Americans do not understand the quality of people that our country can put on the ground in foreign lands.

Most Americans also do not understand the intestinal fortitude required to go through life threatening events and laugh out loud. Soldiers face hardships and shoulder burdens that the average American cannot fathom. Yet, under the hardship a lot of true character is revealed. That night in the CSH, it was revealed in laughter.

Prayer:
Whatever happens in our lives, dear Lord, restore to us your joy, your love, your hope, your peace. Strengthen our faith when it's tested and tried. May we always stay true to you until the very end.

Calling Home

Maj. John Croushorn, MD (retired veteran)

OUR UNIT had set up morale, welfare, and recreation (MWR) tents around our area. Guys could call home for four cents a minute. You could get online, and some would even videoconference with loved ones at home. You would think that a place where folks phoned home would be a happy place, but that wasn't usually the case.

The nearest MWR tent was less than twenty yards from where I slept, just behind a wall of concrete barriers. It was open twenty-four hours a day. I would drop in to make a phone call before I went to work or left for a mission (if it was a reasonable time back home). Julie and I talked several times a week. Most of the guys would have their heads lowered to preserve as much privacy as possible while calling home. It was impossible to hide the struggles of keeping a family going from a thousand miles away.

What can you say, other than you love them and pray for them? You want to hear everyday details that help you feel as if things are all right at home. Your spouse doesn't generally have the time or energy to give a lot of those details. They are burdening the stresses of raising children and running homes by themselves. Julie blessed me by hiding her frustration most of the time.

> "But those who hope in the LORD will renew their strength. They will soar on wings like eagles; they will run and not grow weary, they will walk and not be faint." (Isaiah 40:31)

Connections with life at home were so important to all of us. Care packages would come and go, but for someone to collect and send the local paper meant the world. Highly valued items were personal notes from children, pictures of my own children, or the most treasured item: a tape recording of their voices. Feeling connected meant that I could focus on the mission. It was very empowering.

Prayer:

Dear Lord, when we are separated from loved ones, may we sense your presence in our lives. May we feel more connected than ever to our loved ones back home. May we sense your deep, abiding love. May we gain new strength, courage, and purpose.

Author, Maj. Croushorn with Maj. Conroy, one of the Task Force 185 battalion surgeons

My First Trip to Iraq Was As a Marine.

SPC James Maloney

I WILL NEVER forget the morning of November 22nd, 2005. I was a Marine Lance Corporal and my boots had just hit the ground in Rahmadi. I had been in the Marines for two and a half years by this point. I had undergone every training situation and course that the Marine Corps could offer me. This was my first deployment. Before that morning I always considered my self a man of faith. Up until that time I had only gone to church occasionally. I still said my prayers and went about my life.

I stepped out of my bunk area. The sun was bright, brighter than I could remember any other morning. It was about 0800 hrs. I proceeded to walk down the road toward my HQ to report for duty. I was alone with my thoughts and the surreal feeling of being in a combat zone when all of a sudden, BOOM, an RPG slammed into the wall about one hundred feet behind me. I stumbled for a moment and pulled up my weapon. The guard towers began to engage immediately, but all I could think was "this was it" my body was shaking and heart was pounding harder and harder as I took a knee behind a wall and regained my composure.

> "You will keep in perfect peace him whose mind is steadfast, because he trusts in you." (Isaiah 26:3)

The quick reaction force (QRF) rushed past by me in a hummer, and once I saw the situation was under control, I picked myself up and ran back to my HQ with my gear. I told my staff sergeant the story, and he thought it was a good idea that since I was there to send me and two other Marines to go and brick up the wall. We did, but I will never forget my instant reaction when the RPG impacted that wall. I remember saying the prayer and being calmed by it. I am Roman Catholic, but I think a man of any faith could appreciate the sense of calm that prayer brings. I was scared but still ready to do my duty.

I am currently an army reservist serving with a transition team in Iraq. I still have the same dog tags with the same medals only now I wear a gold cross around my neck and read from religious and inspirational books.

I look back at my first trip here, and I can see so much progress. I can say I lived to see change in the people and the country. I chose to put my self here in service to my country and remind myself every day that God is with me and watches over our families and us. I know with certainty that no matter what happens I am safe. The U.S. military provides a blanket of security for the nation as God provides security for us.

Prayer:
Dear Lord, please replace our fears with faith, our anxiety with peace, our dread with joy, and our questions with courage.

Soldier's Creed

Maj. John Croushorn, MD (retired veteran)

I WAS, "THE OL' man" at airborne school. Thirty-four years old was almost twice the age of the average student. Ft. Benning in October was not bad at all, but the mornings could be a little cold. We gathered in formation before 5 AM. Shorts and short sleeves were the standard uniform for morning Physical Training. We stood there shivering as the Black Hats drank their coffee inside. Then, slowly at first, they came outside and checked each line to account for all the students.

The formation was brought to attention. The accountability reports were called off and then one of the black hats began to yell out the Soldier's Creed. Everyone joined in by the third word . . .

> I am an American Soldier. I am a Warrior and a member of a team. I serve the people of the United States and live the Army Values.
> I will always place the mission first.
> I will never accept defeat.
> I will never quit.
> I will never leave a fallen comrade.
> I am disciplined, physically and mentally tough, trained and proficient in my warrior tasks and drills. I always maintain my arms, my equipment, and myself.
> I am an expert, and I am a professional.
> I stand ready to deploy, engage, and destroy the enemies of the United States of America in close combat.
> I am a guardian of freedom and the American way of life.
> I am an American Soldier.

To hear three hundred men yell this out in unison was awesome to behold. Everyone there had different backgrounds; some had different political beliefs and religious convictions, but they were drawn together in that creed. This is a clear representation of the American soldier. These principles, defined in blood by generations past, enable soldiers to do incredible things during times of exceptional trials and stress. It is a source of strength.

> "You armed me with strength for battle; you made my adversaries bow at my feet."
> (Psalm 18:39)

This is repeated every morning across our nation as young men and women prepare for their day. The author of strength has been faithful to provide all we need when facing our adversaries.

Prayer:
Father, arm me with your strength. Allow me to remain true to you and to those that rely on me.

OCTOBER 12

The Warrior Ethos

Maj. John Croushorn, MD (retired veteran)

IN THE MIDDLE of the Soldier's Creed are four lines that are referred to as the warrior ethos. It is central to the character of a soldier. It elevates cause above person. Selflessness and service are its underpinning. It further motives the soldier to do what must be done even if all appears to be lost.

I will always place the mission first.
I will never accept defeat.
I will never quit.
I will never leave a fallen comrade.

The Bible states that we are made in the image of God (Genesis 9:6). Images of angelic paintings with flowing white garments are hard for a soldier to relate to. At times we don't feel angelic, and I have yet to see a clean uniform outside the wire.

The Lord delivered the Israelites from Egypt in one of the most dramatic ways that could have been imagined. Moses stretched out his hand, and the sea parted. All the Israelites passed on dry ground, and then

> "The LORD is a warrior; the LORD is his name." (Exodus 15:3)

God looked down on the Egyptians from the pillar of fire and "threw them into confusion" (see Exodus 14). In the Egyptian's words, "The Lord is fighting for them against Egypt." The Egyptians tried to flee but when Moses stretched his arms out again the sea engulfed them. The escape from and defeat of the Egyptians were complete.

Exodus 15 records a new song that Moses and the Israelites sang to the Lord immediately following their deliverance. It provides a different image of God, one which warriors today can take strength in. We are after all made in His image.

Prayer:
God give me the strength to be a warrior. I know I am made in your image. By your example and by your name I have strength to fight. Give me, Father, the strength to show your mercy and grace when called for and the intestinal fortitude to complete my mission.

OCTOBER 13

The Desires of the Iraqi People

*Captain Skip Mahaffee, Law Enforcement
Trainer for the Iraqi Government (2005)*

I SPENT A lifetime in law enforcement. I retired from the Fairfax County Police Department, just outside Washington D.C., with twenty-six years of service. During my tenure I was the commander of our police academy. Training was a large part of my background. The U. S. Department of Justice needed trained peace officers to train Iraqis in law enforcement after the military took control of the government in Iraq. Saddam had plenty of henchmen but few law enforcement officers. We needed to train a generation of law enforcement officers to protect the newly found freedom of the Iraqi people.

I was there in January when the first interim elections were held. What an amazing experience to see the Iraqis going to the polls! The candidates were running for positions using the same system that we use—handing out flyers and putting up posters. For once, it wasn't a fixed election. Excited voters would come back to the training academy and say, "Mr. Skip, Mr. Skip, I voted! I voted!" Their enthusiasm was truly inspiring.

> "Look, there on the mountains, the feet of one who brings good news, who proclaims peace! Celebrate your festivals, O Judah, and fulfill your vows. No more will the wicked invade you; they will be completely destroyed." (Nahum 1:15)

We had a number of Iraqi policemen who had graduated from the program and had been asked to stay on to become trainers. They had to have completed the trainer program where we trained them to be instructors in western concepts of law enforcement. Sadly, one of my best Iraqi trainees was murdered right in his doorway. He was killed because he was working with Americans. This man was really loved by his fellow staff members and the students that he trained. Everyone pitched in to buy a huge black banner to honor him and placed it at the Academy. He was an amazing man who sacrificed everything for peace in his community.

The Iraqi people desire peace for the families just as we do. They long for democracy and liberty. They want to live life in a safe environment. What we are doing there is a worthy cause. It is something both my son and I believe in.

Prayer:

Our Father in heaven, comfort those who mourn. Our Savior who died, renew us by your resurrection life. Holy Spirit who indwells us, guide and lead us throughout our sometimes difficult journey here on earth.

Skip Mahaffee served as a law enforcement trainer for the Iraqi government in 2005. His mission was to train the Iraqi police in western law enforcement techniques. In 2006, his son Shane, an attorney/reservist, went to Iraq with a civil affairs unit. Unfortunately, Shane was seriously wounded in an IED attack and died about two weeks later. Skip has both served the cause of freedom in Iraq and experienced the ultimate cost of freedom in the loss of his son. His perspective reflects a painful truth that freedom is not free of sacrifice.

OCTOBER 14

Safety and Security for My Family

Captain Skip Mahaffee, Law Enforcement Trainer for the Iraqi Government (2005)

WE WOULD bring in a thousand Iraqi students every ten weeks. They received basic law enforcement training for eight weeks and then two weeks of officer survival training. We break them up into groups of thirty. I would be in a classroom with thirty to thirty-two police cadets, from ages eighteen to thirty-five. Saddam had terrorized Iraq for thirty-five years, so even the oldest ones in the course had known nothing but tyranny. No one remembered freedom.

I got to know them pretty well over the ten weeks. The last week right before they were to graduate you could sense how thrilled they were about their accomplishment. We did not graduate everybody. Many had trouble finishing their commitment. But for others, the sense of accomplishment was genuine.

Just before graduation I would go around the classroom and call them by name, and I would tell them that they may not be policemen their whole life. I would ask them what they wanted to get out of life. They would answer, "Mr. Skip all I want is safety and security for my family." They weren't looking to get rich. They weren't looking for retirement. They just wanted to be able to live their lives with security. I would tell them that in a democracy anything was possible. They may start a business or go to school. They had truly accomplished something, and now they were going to give back to their community.

> "I looked for a man among them who would build up the wall and stand before me in the gap on behalf of the land so I would not have to destroy it, but I found none."
> (Ezekiel 22:30)

The people over there have the same interest that we do with democracy and liberty. They want to live their lives in a safe environment. What we are doing over there is a worthy cause. We're helping them help themselves. The naysayers that say we need to leave have no idea of what we're doing over there.

Prayer:
Dear Lord, never let us forget that with freedom comes great privilege and great responsibility. Where tyranny reigns, bring freedom. Where oppression thrives, bring liberation and justice and peace.

OCTOBER 15

IED Attack

Captain Skip Mahaffee, Law Enforcement Trainer for the Iraqi Government (2005)

THE LEAD Humvee rocked violently. An IED ripped through the vehicle. Three of the four men inside were fatally wounded. Capt. Shane

Mahaffee was riding in that vehicle when it was hit. The driver sustained a devastating vascular injury to his leg. Shrapnel had penetrated into Shane's left lung. Shane jumped out of the wreckage and quickly took command of the situation. He directed the men in the remaining three vehicles to form a perimeter to prepare for any further attacks. Refusing medical care, he instructed his men to provide care to the others in his Humvee. After his soldiers had received the care they deserved, his men insisted that he too receive care.

> "I have fought the good fight, I have finished the race, I have kept the faith. Now there is in store for me the crown of righteousness, which the Lord, the righteous Judge, will award to me on that day—and not only to me, but also to all who have longed for his appearing."
> (2 Timothy 4:7–8)

A helicopter quickly arrived to take him to the Combat Support Hospital (CSH) in Baghdad. From there, he was taken to Landstuhl, Germany, where further surgery was required. His family was flown to be with him. Infection from the wounds ultimately took Shane's life. To the very end, he firmly believed in what he was doing. Even when he was hospitalized he said the mission was not yet accomplished. He instructed a friend of his to go back and tell his men that they needed to complete the mission.

His family was with him when he died. It was the day after Mother's Day, and his wife and mother were by his side. Three other soldiers died in the same IED attack. All four men are among the many heroes who have paid the ultimate sacrifice in Operation Iraqi Freedom.

Prayer:
Dear Lord, don't let us lose our way, neglect the truth you've given us, or fritter away the life we enjoy. Keep us faithful until the end of our days here on earth. How we look forward to eternity with you in heaven.

Shane Loved the Infantry

Captain Skip Mahaffee, Law Enforcement Trainer for the Iraqi Government (2005)

IN MAY 2007 we went to Fort Bragg, North Carolina, for a memorial service where Shane was remembered. A large man stood up and related a story about one night in Iraq. According to the story, it was around 3 a.m., and tension had filled the team during an operation. Suddenly this same large non-commissioned officer cut through the tension when he said that he had heard Shane's voice and he then knew everything was going to be okay. As this mountain of a man related his story at Shane's memorial service, it warmed my heart. The fact that my son and the sound of his voice calmed this man meant a lot to me. Shane had a command presence wherever he was.

Shane was called up from the inactive ready reserve. He had not seen a uniform for five years. He and I had talked a few years back. He said that his practice was going so well and that he just didn't have time to be in the reserves. We talked about it and I told him he had served his time and that he had completed his obligation honorably. When Iraq heated up, the military was stretched so thin that many reservists were called back into active service.

> "He has showed you, O man, what is good. And what does the LORD require of you? To act justly and to love mercy and to walk humbly with your God." (Micah 6:8)

When Shane was in the eighth grade I sat him down, and we laid out a five-year plan. I asked him what he wanted to do with his life. He said he wanted to be an attorney. So we talked to the counselors at school, and I told him he might want to think about being an attorney in the military. I told him if he did twenty years in the military as a JAG officer he could get out and hang his shingle anywhere and still enjoy a nice retirement check every month. I'm a former Marine. But I told him I thought the Army was the way to go especially concerning the legal aspirations. And that's how his time with the Army came to be.

When he went to college, he was in ROTC. He really liked the military environment; it suited him well. He was good at it. He liked the discipline and the structure. He became an instructor to other cadets. When it was time for him to be commissioned he had to put down his three top choices and one of them was the infantry. In 1997, I told him, "You're not in the JAG core? What happened to our five-year plan?" He laughed and said, "Dad, when I practice law five days a week and then I go to the reserve, the last thing I want to do is lawyering." His heart lay in the infantry. He loved the infantry. He never changed lanes. When he was called back up he went into a civil affairs unit.

Prayer:
Dear Lord, renew me in my inner man. May I act justly,
love mercy, and walk humble with you throughout this life.
And may I enjoy a wonderful welcome into heaven.

OCTOBER 17

Freedom Is Not Free

Captain Skip Mahaffee, Law Enforcement
Trainer for the Iraqi Government (2005)

R ONALD REAGAN once stated, "Freedom is never more than one generation away from extinction. We didn't pass it on to our children in the bloodstream. It must be fought for, protected, and handed on for them to do the same, or one day we will spend our sunset years telling our children what it was once like in the United States when men were free."

Address to the annual meeting of the Phoenix Chamber of Commerce March 30, 1961:

> I work with a lot of kids. My wife and I go to Washington D.C. every spring. We take school groups around Washington to see our great capital. Our theme is that freedom is not free. When we get to the Korean Memorial you'll see it written in stone, "freedom is not free." We don't want anyone to be killed in combat. Life is precious to us. Our serviceman's lives are precious as is every life in our country— babies, teenagers and adults. We value life. You can see the wheels turning in our student's minds. They seem to grasp the concept that life is precious. It is never okay to die. But sometimes it's necessary.

I enjoy the chance to explain to them our precious freedoms and how sacred the sacrifice paid for them is. There are many on this earth that would like to take it away from us. There's also a jealousy when others see what we have. It is often very different than what they have. There's also the unfortunate reality that sometimes we forget what was paid in sacrifice for these freedoms. It's great to be able to share the values that we have. Our family has sacrificed for those values greatly.

> "Who gave himself for us to redeem us from all wickedness and to purify for himself a people that are his very own, eager to do what is good." (Titus 2:14)

Failure is not an option. Ronald Reagan's wisdom is true for all democracies. It is only one generation away from extinction. In a matter of one generation, Iraq's democracy will fall if we just walk away and leave Iraq without a stable democracy.

Prayer:
Dear Lord, please make me holy, eager to do what is good and right and just and true. Please redeem many millions more, turning them from darkness to light.

OCTOBER 18

Army Values: Loyalty

Maj. John Croushorn, MD (retired veteran)

LOYALTY IS one of those unique words that brings clarity and focus to circumstance. It is an enabling word that can help me separate selfish and selfless motives and actions. In a moment that word can identify a gift or highlight an opportunity to give.

We are often motivated by deep values that define character. Loyalty is that for most people that serve. Service is in essence a byproduct of loyalty. We are loyal to our nation and its heritage. We expect it from others and we give it as well. Loyalty begets loyalty.

I used to think a great deal about the shared heritage we had with those who had fought in other great wars. I thought initially it was the shared burden of stepping into harm's way and the toil that separation from our families cost us. While that defines a part of that heritage there are some even clearer connections.

Do you remember how you felt the day the towers fell? Do you remember what it was like the next few days as people began to display American flags on everything? It was a culmination of all the emotions that come from seeing the true face of evil. It is that gut churning solemn state that arises from the horror of senseless death and destruction. That sense of the presence of evil is a part of a soldier's tie to heritage.

Whether walking through Fallujah or the European theater in 1944, the presence and effect of evil constantly surrounds the American soldier. To daily interact with people who are free who were once enslaved is a motivating thing. It is in part that intangible tie to heritage. It motivates us to continue to fight. We want to rid this small part of earth from the cancer of terrorism. There is no rationalization for its evil existence. It must be completely and utterly destroyed.

This is a part of what it means to bear true faith and allegiance to the US constitution, the Army, your unit and other soldiers.

In the Bible "the men of Zebulun" were singled out for their "undivided loyalty." What must have defined these men to be called out from so many great warriors? We know that they were experienced warriors and ready for battle. They were skilled with every type of weapon. Perhaps their greatest weapon was their loyalty.

Prayer:
Father God, help me remain loyal to you and those that have sacrificed so much before me. Impress on me the heart of the men of Zebulun. I want to be known as one with undivided loyalty.

OCTOBER 19

Army Values: Duty

Maj. John Croushorn, MD (retired veteran)

IT WAS A cold November night in 2003. Julie and I had not come to terms about my service, but I had already been commissioned and attended Basic Training in San Antonio and the Army's Flight Surgeon School at Fort Rucker, Alabama. We had a babysitter and in classic John and Julie fashion, our special date consisted of a light dinner and a walk in a local park. At the end of the first lap I told her the news that she never wanted to hear. "My unit is going."

She didn't say anything. She looked at me in disbelief. She turned and walked to the car and left. I didn't know if she was going to come back and pick me up or not. I just kept walking.

A couple of hours passed. She came and picked me up and we drove home. We went to bed without a word. A further split in the chasm.

I awoke the next morning with the kids. I fixed breakfast and played with them while Julie slept. Actually, I doubt she slept at all that night. You should know that my wife's faith has been very consistent. She has always had a close relationship with God. From time to time the way she would respond or relate to me would prove that it was not her emotions that spoke but rather the word she received from God. That morning, after the worst news she could imagine, she gave me a gift. She didn't have to, but she blessed me in a way that still is hard for me to understand.

She came out of the bedroom and walked in front of me to get her morning coffee. She returned to the living room, stood near the fire place and looked at me. She sat her coffee on the mantel and walked over to the sofa where I was sitting. With a slight grin she reached out her hands to my neck and said, "You know, I could strangle you."

> "But if serving the LORD seems undesirable to you, then choose for yourselves this day whom you will serve. . . . But as for me and my household, we will serve the LORD." (Joshua 24:15)

Duty involves a commitment to do what is right even when it leads to personal harm. Following through with my commitment to serve was a necessary part of duty. The act of stepping away from my family and promise of a good job was difficult but necessary.

Prayer:

Dear Lord, the cost of duty is so high. The cost is separation, lost opportunity, uncertainty. So often we give into the fear of the unknown. Remind us always that any cost is temporary for those who know and love you.

Remembering September 11

Vice Admiral Rich Carmona,
17ᵗʰ Surgeon General of the United States

I WILL ALWAYS remember where I was on September 11, 2001. It was a busy day. I was on a SWAT call in the middle of a hostage rescue. Earlier that morning the team was all on its way to a remote site in order to do mountain training. Half our team was already on the mountain. The other half was still at ground level. The page went out that we had a hostage rescue requiring immediate response. We were briefed on the way to the scene. Once we arrived we began to set up the perimeter. Just before 9 a.m. the dispatcher came over the radio and said that one of the towers had been hit by a plane. A few minutes later she came and told us it was deliberate.

We actually ended the hostage event very quickly. I was talking with the guy, telling him to go look at his TV. I told him, "The nation's being challenged. We are at war." I told him we didn't have time to deal with

> "Nothing can hinder the LORD from saving, whether by many or by few." (1 Samuel 14:6b)

him right now, and that we didn't have time to stay here while the nation was being attacked. I said that he needed to put that gun down or we would have to kill him. He was threatening to kill a child but what I said communicated the right thing. He came out and gave up the gun. We rescued the kid and returned to headquarters.

Once we were back, we set up a perimeter around the station. Then we started evaluating targets of opportunity. We looked at how to fortify everything. We called out to the airport to find out if planes were heading toward our area of responsibility.

I know exactly where I was on Tuesday morning, September 11, 2001, just before 9 a.m. It was just under two years before I became the U.S. Surgeon General.

Prayer:
Thank you, God that you never change. Your power, your presence, and your wisdom are limitless. You know the beginning from the end. Your purposes in our lives are clearly known to you. May we trust in your wisdom when we feel unsure.

Rich Carmona served as the 17th Surgeon General of the United States. He is also a decorated war veteran, having served with the Special Forces in Vietnam. Rich received a Bronze Star and Purple Heart among other military awards. Dr. Carmona has always been dedicated in efforts to serve his country and community. He has worn many hats to include, soldier, doctor, law enforcement officer, and SWAT team leader. He is both a soldier and the father of a soldier, as his son served in Iraq in 2005.

OCTOBER 21

Father's Love

Vice Admiral Rich Carmona,
17th Surgeon General of the United States

JASON WAS a twelve-year veteran noncommissioned officer of the reserve component when he received word that his unit was activated. As a father, I was concerned for his safety. He's a good kid. I know the amount of training that a reservist goes through. I knew that he would be seeing things in battle that he could not even dream of. I wondered if he would come home safely. As an admiral, I was also concerned about what our actual mission was there. These were questions that many of my colleagues at senior levels had. Is this a just cause? If so what is the strategic plan? Now it was more personal. What is the impact going to be on my kid and all the other kids serving over there?

I had the personal emotions of a father as well as the emotions of an admiral, and sergeant, who has also been in combat; who understood how difficult war is.

> "Don't let anyone look down on you because you are young, but set an example for the believers in speech, in life, in love, in faith and in purity."
> (1 Timothy 4:12)

I gave Jason many words of advice. The thing I stressed most was not to ever feel complacent or safe in a combat zone. Always be aware, looking around. When you're out on patrol or on a convoy, when things look good, and when it's quiet you always have to be thinking ahead. You have to be asking yourself what would happen if we got hit. What is the immediate action drill for a near ambush or a far ambush? You don't have time to think and react. You do it instinctively. I gave him a mini tutorial in combat. I didn't want to scare him. But I wanted to raise his awareness. It was one way I tried to prepare my son for war.

Having been a person who has dealt with emergencies it takes a lot to push my buttons. Whether being an operator, lifeguard, trauma nurse, or surgeon, emergencies have been a part of life. This was different. This time it was my son. I knew where he was. I would hear the battle reports from the day, and I would wonder how he was doing. Every few days we got a reassuring satellite call or an email that would say everything was fine. Having been in combat myself, you know about its uncertainty. The reality is that there is no certainty until that plane lands on U.S. soil and you're okay. As it got closer to his return you start thinking, *I hope it's not my kid that something happens to a week before coming home.*

Prayer:
May we wholeheartedly love, obey, and serve you, Lord, in our youth and as we get older. May we never become half-hearted in our loyalty to you, God.

OCTOBER 22

Liberating the Oppressed

Vice Admiral Rich Carmona, 17ᵗʰ Surgeon General of the United States

MY EXPERIENCE in special operations is much like many who are in combat now. You see the worse the world has to offer. When you see that, your faith is often challenged. You ask questions like, "Why did this happen? Why are all these children dead? Why are there suicide bombers?" All of us have those questions. With our mantra being to liberate the oppressed, you feel a sense of responsibility to make things better for people. We euphemistically call that doing the Lord's work. We are there to do what's right, just, moral and ethical.

Now that I was in an administration that set policy, my conflict was trying to align the role of liberator with the political challenges of being in a foreign country. Individually we are there for the right reason. When you're older and have been around long enough to reflect, you understand at some level we are simply the extension of political policy for our nation. That is where faith comes into, "Would God put me here if it wasn't right?"

"Freedom" is a word that conjures up a lot of images for us. For most of us it means freedom to worship, to go to school, to travel, to get an education. It means freedom to pursue life and to maximize your potential to benefit society. Those are things Iraqis have little knowledge of. Bringing freedom to others is a valiant struggle but it's also quite complicated especially with the political struggles these countries face. From a soldier's standpoint you feel a sense of righteousness, a moral and ethical drive that you're there for the right reason. When you get to the politics, it makes it more convoluted.

> "This is good, and pleases God our Savior, who wants all men to be saved and to come to a knowledge of the truth." (1 Timothy 2:3–4)

Freedom is a desired goal for most people. It's defined differently throughout the world. We need to fully understand the cultures that we're embedding ourselves in. Our vision of freedom is not always shared by other cultures.

Prayer:

Dear God, thank you that you so love the world. You don't desire any to perish. Instead, you want all to come to repentance. Please save men and women, youth and children from every continent, nation, and people group. We pray this for your eternal glory, honor, and praise.

OCTOBER 23

Families at Home

Vice Admiral Rich Carmona, 17th Surgeon General of the United States

I'M INVOLVED in a number of projects with the Department of Defense focusing on veterans and their families. Military families have just as much stress as the combatants. They worry everyday about the health and safety of their loved ones. They worry about their children not having mentors, leaders, fathers or mothers in some cases. They worry about keeping the family running. The family is very important. Soldiers in theater are worried about the environment their families are in. Are they safe and secure? Are their physical and emotional needs being taken care of?

It's a two-way street. When the family is cared for, the operator is able to stay more focused on the mission. Also, the family needs to feel that their loved one had the best training and is equipped with the best equipment to keep as safe as possible. This allows them to feel less apprehensive about their loved one being in combat.

> "Be wise in the way you act toward outsiders; make the most of every opportunity."
> (Colossians 4:5)

My advice to families is to spend time before the deployment period and talk through all the issues. Talk about combat. *How do we tell the children? How do we reassure them? How do we relate to one another over the next year? Who is going to watch over the family while I'm gone? How can I support you while I'm gone?* These are very difficult discussions, but they must take place. Soldiers must be mindful that their families will worry about what can happen. Their minds are filled with what if scenarios, "what if you don't come home?"

These issues cannot be ignored. The families that remain at home also must have a support network. They need to be connected to their community. The community easily recognizes a uniform, but it does not always recognize the family with a loved one deployed. It is important to share that burden with others. It is imperative if the soldier is to focus on the mission abroad.

Prayer:
Dear Lord, please give me opportunities to share your love with those who have a loved one deployed overseas. May I bless them as you have blessed me, and may you draw each one closer to yourself, God.

OCTOBER 24

Army Values: Respect

Maj. John Croushorn, MD (retired veteran)

EVERYWHERE WE stopped there were merchants trying to sell just about anything to Americans with U.S. dollars. They would strike a bargain and press continuously for an item that may only cost a dollar. Popular items were Iraqi bayonets, helmets, and uniforms from the old regime.

We had landed in Babylon to refuel. The crew shut the bird down and went to grab something to eat while it was being refueled. Several of us decided to go pay a visit to the merchants. There was a literal cardboard city set up near the perimeter of the base. There were rows of makeshift storefronts. Jewelry, games, knives, and medals at every stop. The merchants would literally follow you around offering various items, asking what we were interested in.

There was one merchant that sat with a smile on his face that didn't act as aggressive. These were usually the merchants that we enjoyed dealing with the best. He had handmade scarves, prayer caps, and other items. I noticed that he wore a patch over his right eye and that he was missing his right hand. I greeted him in Arabic, and a young man with him translated for us. He told me that the man had garments for sale for one dollar each. I asked the young man if I could ask the older gentleman how he received his wounds. He told me that the old man had refused to be a Baathist and that Saddam's officials had his right eye gouged out and then cut off his right hand. Before that he had been an official in the government.

> "And this is love: that we walk in obedience to his commands. As you have heard from the beginning, his command is that you walk in love." (2 John 6)

I bought a scarf and a prayer cap from him. I paid him, placed my right hand over my heart and thanked him for his time and then extended my right hand. He shook it and with a smile on his face replied in kind. I don't know if his grin was over the sale or the respect I paid him. Respect was something that he had not received from his own country, but would receive from countless of Americans, Polish, and El Salvadoran soldiers that would pass by his booth.

Leaders honor the individual worth of every person with dignity and respect. When this is communicated in action and word it empowers individuals. Respect is core to the military. Whether between teammates, both commissioned and non-commissioned officers, and their men, or with the local population we are trying to serve and protect, it is a vital component and mission enabler.

Prayer:

Dear Lord, with the world at our doorstep, including many who have been oppressed, help us walk in love. Please give us opportunities to show love, concern, and respect to them. Fill us, Holy Spirit, with your comfort, solace, and love.

Army Values: Selfless Service

Maj. John Croushorn, MD (retired veteran)

ONE OF THE hardest parts of going to war is preparing to go. It is a private, introspective process that involves the finality of preparing as if you might not return. To share that part of the preparation with your loved ones would cause a great deal of heartache and more emotional burden for them. They have enough of that already. There is something liberating though in taking those steps. You must examine your motives for serving. If you are going reluctantly, in opposition to the overall mission, you do yourself and your team a disservice. You cannot fully commit to or focus on the individual mission if you resent the reasons you are there.

Of all the motivations that is core in the Army's value system, selfless service is a connection to heritage that binds generations of soldiers. For me, the idea of serving was wrapped up in my family. I was serving for them. I wanted to protect them. This was difficult to communicate with Julie early on. Rational thought would also argue that I would serve my family best by being with them instead of a thousand miles away in war.

> "Place me like a seal over your heart, like a seal on your arm; for love is as strong as death, its jealousy unyielding as the grave. It burns like blazing fire, like a mighty flame."
> (Song of Solomon 8:6)

Acts of service along with motivation that is not self-serving provide the basis for many good works. When the human heart is motivated to serve others, then teamwork, self-control and discipline are easier to achieve. Faith is central to this. Faith and a belief that God is sovereign allow us the freedom of putting the interests of others above our own, including that of our own personal safety.

Prayer:
Holy Lord, please give us the words or images to express our heart emotions to those we love, especially those serving in the armed forces. May we rest secure in your mighty name and everlasting love.

A Mother's Prayer

Linda Croushorn

As I [John] prepared to go to war my wife and children tried to continue normal life in a new city. There is nothing normal when a family is separated by deployments. There is no point at which things become easier. Few can understand the depth of the trial. As you reflect back on the stories from this week remember those at home who have the hard task of keeping the home together and dealing with all the daily struggles alone. The following was a journal entry from my mother as I left the mobilization site heading for Iraq.

Wednesday, July 28, 2004
"Older women are to . . . teach what is good, so that they may encourage the young women" (Titus 2:3–4)

FATHER GOD, this morning I pray for John and Julie. Julie is struggling so very hard with John's decision to join the Army National Guard and all that has resulted from that decision. She is grieving his leaving for Iraq and dreading his being away from them for seven months. Please give her strength and hope, peace and grace. Help me be an encouragement to her. Father, I pray for contentment and joy to fill her life. Help us know best how to support her while John is away.

> "They devoted themselves to the apostles' teaching and to the fellowship, to the breaking of bread and to prayer." (Acts 2:42)

Bless John too, Father. I know his heart is heavy with concern for Julie and with missing her and Caleb and Katie. Thank you for the love they share—for each other and for you. Please keep him safe, Father, as he leaves Ft. Bliss this weekend and flies to Kuwait and then on to Iraq. Bless him in every way, every day. Keep him surrounded with your angels who will "guard him in all his ways" (Psalm 91:11). Thank you for your Word that promises: "Because he loves me, says the Lord, 'I will rescue him; I will protect him, for he acknowledges my name. He will call upon me, and I will answer him; I will be with him in trouble, I will deliver him and honor him. With long life will I satisfy him and show him my salvation'" (Psalm 91:14–16).

Bless John right now, Lord. Lift his spirit. Lift Julie's spirit. Restore their joy in their relationship. Bless Caleb and Katie. Protect and bless this little family, Lord I pray. Thank you for them. Thank you for being near us all during this time. Thank you for your love and grace and for getting us through difficult times. Thank you for your faithfulness, Father God. Be with all my loved ones this day, I pray.

Prayer:
May we draw ever closer to you, Lord, when separated from those we love. May we cling to your Word, may we walk in your ways, and may we seek your will each step along the way.

OCTOBER 27

Leadership

Col. Bradley Macnealy

MISSISSIPPI COLLEGE gave me a chance to tryout as the team's kicker, The coach allowed me but one kick for my tryout. Fortunately, my kick went eight yards deep in the end zone. It was a sixty-eight yard kick, the longest kick I made in my career. Football was one of my first experiences with teamwork and leadership.

People asked what made me an effective leader in Iraq. To be honest, I was scared to death on the inside, but just like the old saying goes I wasn't going to let anyone see me sweat. Early on I was unsure that I would be able to actually do what everybody wanted me to do. I knew I needed to ask the Lord to help me do the right things to take care of

> "For God did not give us a spirit of timidity, but a spirit of power, of love and of self-discipline." (2 Timothy 1:7)

my people. Throughout the experience I grew to trust my instincts that I believe were formed from my experiences and my faith in God to show me the way.

It was a difficult situation when I had to make a decision and my gut told me one thing and the people around me told me something else.

Another thing that defined my leadership was my staff. I have always felt that I must surround myself with the best people and then empower them. Effective leadership is a lot easier when the people around you do a great job.

We had six battalions working for us. Each one had its own commander and sergeant major. While most military organizations had higher-ranking officers in headquarters that wanted to run the battalions, we didn't. We let the battalion commanders and the sergeant majors call the shots.

I don't believe we needed to exert command authority, but rather we must give them the opportunity, show them the way, and empower them to do it. My management style is to not be a micromanager.

Prayer:
When we are weary, God, please renew us physically,
emotionally, mentally, volitionally, and spiritually.
When we feel exhausted, Holy Spirit, please fill us.

OCTOBER 28

We Didn't Lose a Single Soldier

Col. Bradley Macnealy

LEADING MEN and women in combat strengthened my faith. We topped out at around three thousand soldiers under my command. Before we left I had a meeting with all the families. I asked them what their biggest concern was. Their top concern was that their loved ones would come home alive. Secondly, they wanted to be able to communicate with their loved ones while we were there. They also wanted the leadership to keep them informed of what was happening.

It was confirmation that God was telling me our number one priority was to bring everybody home. We were not going to go over there to be heroes, we were going to do our job and not take extra risks that we didn't need to. We did take calculated risks and we mini-

> "When he came near the den, he called to Daniel in an anguished voice, 'Daniel, servant of the living God, has your God, whom you serve continually, been able to rescue you from the lions?'"
> (Daniel 6:20)

mized and mitigated the risk every way we could. We had twenty-six soldiers earn Purple Hearts but not one of these soldiers died. How many brigades operated over there and didn't lose a single person?

Once a week out I would send out emails and always remind families back home to continue to pray for us. I cannot emphasize enough how important that prayer was. When we got back to Jackson, Mississippi a news reporter asked me how, with three thousand soldiers, we operated for a year without losing anyone. I responded to him that it was divine intervention. It was a miracle that we actually brought everybody back to their families.

Prayer:

God of miracles, God of deliverance, God of salvation, thank you so much that you are the same yesterday, today, and forever. Please be our Rock, our Fortress, our Almighty King of Kings again today.

OCTOBER 29

They Are Just Like Us

Col. Bradley Macnealy

I HAD THE opportunity to meet with Iraqis at every level. The Iraqi people are really just like us. They want their kids to be raised in safety and to be successful. They do not want violence. They do not want terrorism. They want to build a peaceful life. Their biggest thing to overcome was to know whom to trust. They had a hard time trusting us because our folks would be in their village during the day and then go home at night. The terrorists would come in when we went home. And the people had a hard time trusting us because we wouldn't protect them. To make the situation worse, some of the mayors and local leadership were corrupt. General Petraeus's motto was: "Don't Commute to Work."

> "Do not seek revenge or bear a grudge against one of your people, but love your neighbor as yourself. I am the LORD."
> (Leviticus 19:18)

That was a change in doctrine. Our troops started living with the Iraqi military. They were living among the Iraqis, and it changed everything.

Living and working with the Iraqi troops allowed the Iraqi people to have more confidence in our troops.

Many people talk about the "surge." There were four parts to the surge. It was more than just increasing the numbers of boots on the ground. The Sunnis calling themselves the 'Sons of Iraq' started fighting the terrorists instead of the Shia. The Shia Muslims began fighting the terrorists instead of the Sunnis. The military began to move out of the bases and into the cities and living with the Iraqis. And there were increased numbers of troops in the problem areas. General Petraeus put our men and women out in the community, and the people were able to see who we really were. We were not oppressors. The terrorists were. They raped and stole from the people and destroyed the places they were at. We built up and healed. The contrast was too great.

The people of Iraq understand the cost of freedom. They want it for their children. They are just like us.

Prayer:
Dear God, I want to love you with all my heart, soul,
strength, and mind, and I want to love my neighbor as myself.
Please fill me and increase my love day by day.

OCTOBER 30

Top Ten Quotes in Iraq (Part 1)

Col. Bradley Macnealy

DURING MY time in Iraq I found ten quotes and phrases that define my view of leadership.

Number 10: "It doesn't matter who gets the credit." I hated hearing someone trying to take credit. It doesn't matter who gets the credit. That was one of the biggest differences between my peers and me. They were trying to take credit for everything. You should reward your people for initiative, bravery and ingenuity. Harry S. Truman once said, "It is amazing what you can accomplish if you do not care who gets the credit."

Number 9: " Respect is hard to get; you have to earn it.". It may be hard to get, but it's easy to throw away. You have to work at it every day.

The very first time a leader does something immoral or unethical that leader loses respect. You will earn respect by taking care of your people and keeping your word. It happens one day at a time.

Number 8: "Don't micromanage." Empower your people. Our pilots went out and did an amazing job. We let them make decisions. Many of the active duty organizations would require their people to call back to get permission to do anything. "Give a man a fish and you feed him for a day. Teach him how to fish and you feed him for a lifetime" (Lao Tzu, 4th century BC).

> "For the eyes of the LORD range throughout the earth to strengthen those whose hearts are fully committed to him."
> (2 Chronicles 16:9)

Number 7: "Take the initiative." Things will only happen that you make happen. It is incumbent on leaders to encourage their people to take initiative. Weak individuals sit back and let others do the hard work. If everybody took this approach nothing would ever get done.

Number 6: "Customer service." You have to have a customer service attitude. Many days we would get feedback that we screwed up a mission. I learned there are always two sides to every story. Instead of going down and chewing out somebody I knew the truth lay somewhere in between the two sides of the story and usually the first story is wrong.

Prayer:
*Dear Lord, please strengthen my heart and
please make me fully devoted to you.*

OCTOBER 31

Top Ten Quotes on Leadership (Continued)

Col. Bradley Macnealy

NUMBER 5: "Commanders in the field are always right, and the command pukes in the rear are always wrong." General Metz used to say this. Our helicopters had three different flare types to defeat the surface to air missiles the enemy was using to try and shoot down our aircraft. Our higher-ups at headquarters said that we only needed one type, but we had to say no. I went with the intelligence our guys had and sent it up to the General to sign off on the risk involved in not having all three flares. The general sided with the guys in the field, and we got our flares.

Number 4: "Force multipliers." The National Guard has multiple military operational specialties (MOS) per soldier. There may be only one military MOS but several civilian ones as well. When we applied what we knew in civilian life, our forces multiplied their capabilities significantly above the active duty's ability to conduct missions. We can make the operation more efficient.

Number 3: "The center of gravity in peacetime is operations but the center of gravity in war is aviation maintenance." It takes ten to fifteen hours of maintenance to fly one hour in a Black Hawk. We put the emphasis in supporting our maintenance guys. They kept us flying. We were able to fly twice the missions with half the helicopters in the first six months than the active duty element flew the entire year before us.

> "The LORD has sought out a man after his own heart and appointed him leader of his people." (1 Samuel 13:14)

Number 2: "Leadership is an attitude." My leadership philosophy used to be "competence and character," but now it is: "Leadership Is an Attitude." Whatever the attitude of leaders is, that is what the whole organization is going to adopt. What the leader portrays to his subordinates will be carried down throughout the organization. I believed in open and honest communication. That was a key component of how I wanted to define our organization.

Number 1: "A leader cares more about his troops than what his boss thinks." I saw many leaders that were more concerned about impressing their bosses and getting good evaluations than they were about genuinely caring for their troops. You always care about your troops; everything else will fall in place.

Prayer:
Dear Lord, may you make me a man or woman after your own heart.
May I lead others with your wisdom, power, and grace.

An IED at the Front Gate

Captain David Graves, Officer with a
Provisional Reconstruction Team in Iraq (2006)

I ARRIVED AT Forward Operating Base (FOB) Warhorse in March 2006. That was one of the more dangerous provinces since it was split 50 percent Sunni and 50 percent Shiite. When the tension grew between the religious factions the violence grew as well. FOB Warhorse was surrounded by major Iraqi roads on three sides. The Tigris River was on the other side and on the far side of the bank there were nothing but palm trees.

> "To him who is able to keep you from falling and to present you before his glorious presence without fault and with great joy—to the only God our Savior be glory, majesty, power and authority, through Jesus Christ our Lord, before all ages, now and forevermore! Amen."
> (Jude 24–25)

We were getting our stuff out after we arrived and I paused long enough to look up at the gate on the north side of the base and watch a convoy going by. There was an IED (improvised explosive device) that exploded on the convoy right in front of the base. The device had been planted at the front gate between the two guard towers. It hit an explosive ordinance truck and fortunately, no one was killed. But it shocked me that they could put an IED at the front gate of an American base between two guard posts.

When you feel like things are happening out of your control it is unsettling. Not only was it right under our noses, but it gave us the sense that no where was safe.

Prayer:
No matter what happens, Lord, I know all glory, majesty,
power and authority are yours. Please keep me from falling.
May I enter your glorious presence with great joy, knowing
I am completely righteous in your eyes because of the
ultimate sacrifice that Jesus Christ made for me.

Saved in the Bathroom

Captain David Graves, Officer with a Provisional Reconstruction Team in Iraq (2006)

WE HAD AN artillery unit of paladins on the base. They would fire outbound a good bit. Some of it was counter battery fire; some of it was indirect fire mission supporting our guys. Sometimes they were shooting illumination rounds around our base to help base security detect people setting up mortars or sneaking close to the perimeter. The base would get shelled a fair amount but until your ear gets finely tuned its hard to tell whether or not a round is coming in are going out. Both are extremely loud. The UAV runway strip was right next to where we slept, and that created a lot of noise as well. It was a hot refuel point for helicopters too. It was very loud.

> "You gave me life and showed me kindness, and in your providence watched over my spirit." (Job 10:12)

One night I was in my trailer winding down. We had just finished planning a mission for the next day. My roommate and I were sitting in our trailer talking. Suddenly there was a large boom. My roommate joked with me as he saw me flinch. He asked, "Don't you know what a paladin sounds like by now?" I had come out of my seat and gone down to one knee. He said, "Graves, come on man, that's the paladin shooting." I told him he was right and started to return to my seat, feeling embarrassed, when shrapnel started raining down on the roof of our trailer. I looked at my roommate and said, "When a paladin shoots, stuff doesn't land on our roof."

Then we heard screaming. A mortar round hit a trailer three buildings down and one over from us. We had sandbags all around our trailers about waist high to limit indirect fire casualties. This round landed about chest high through the wall and into a young man's bunk bed. Just before the round landed, the soldier had gotten out of bed to go and use the bathroom. He was sixty-five feet away using the bathroom when the round came in. His roommate was sleeping in the bed on the other side of the trailer and he was peppered by shrapnel. It didn't kill him, but it wounded him pretty bad. He was the one doing the screaming.

It was weird to think that the soldier's life was saved because of the nature call. It seemed entirely random.

Dear God, my life and the length of my days are in your hands. Please continue to keep those I know and love safe whenever they're in harm's way.

NOVEMBER 3

Heritage of Faith

Maj. John Croushorn, MD (retired veteran)

I REMEMBER THE Sunday worship our unit headquarters company would have during drill. It used to motivate me to hear the sound of all those men singing old hymns. That was amplified in sound and emotion when those hymns were sung in Iraq. They were truly battle hymns.

There was a tent the chaplains used to conduct services at Balad. It was one of the few tents on the airstrip side of the road. Because it was next to the runway it would be pretty noisy and that resulted in louder singing. As we sung worship songs, it was easy to appreciate the very real implications of God's grace, mercy and protection that filled the pages. I would think of the countless soldiers who have worshiped while deployed and that seemed to tie me to another aspect of the warrior heritage.

> "Therefore I will praise you, O LORD, among the nations; I will sing praises to your name."
> (2 Samuel 22:50)

The heritage of faith is strong in the military. Contrary to the old adage, there actually are a few agnostics in foxholes, but the realities of war and the proximity of death will cause the most hardened of men and women to consider the frailty of life and their own humanity. It was comforting and inspiring to sing those songs and pray with others who were of the same mind. We came from all over the country and were raised in many different denominations, but worship drew us together.

We bring back many life experiences: traumatic memories, fatigue, and discomfort, but the experience of faith practiced during war solidified my beliefs. The memories of worship and teaching, combined with the deep questions and prayer and the day-to-day encounters with the frailty of life are something that returned with me. My children and family benefit from that part of my experience.

Prayer:
I believe in you, Lord, and completely put my faith and trust in you. Move my heart to worship you again today.

NOVEMBER 4

Faith in God Is Important to Soldiers

Cdr. Robert T. Garretson

LIKE MANY others in America and around the world, I was profoundly affected by the events of September 11. Like so many I would ponder the depravity of the individual act, but also how it fit in with the theory of a just and loving God. For a man on the cusp of Christianity, these were tough questions to ponder. On that day, I was on deployment, and our carrier was just getting ready to enter the Persian Gulf. As events unfolded over the course of the following weeks, it became apparent that we would be going to war.

It has been said that there are no atheists in foxholes, and I certainly didn't intend on disproving the theorem. I began to ask myself such questions as, "Can I be a Christian and a military officer?" Without a good knowledge or foundation in the Christian faith, I was unprepared to answer such a question. I also had no idea how war fit into the personal crisis of faith. I had trained and instructed in tactics and operations for over eleven years. I knew that I was mentally and operationally ready for the actions of warfare, but where was I spiritually?

> "Don't be afraid," the prophet answered. "Those who are with us are more than those who are with them." (2 Kings 6:16)

Of my own accord and through my own morality, I had already arrived at my personal "Just War" theory. Remarkably, in hindsight, it seemed to mirror the theory that Cicero developed in the first century BC. "There must be just cause, there must be formal declaration of war by the constituted authority, and the war must be conducted justly."[1]

Throughout our involvement in Operation Enduring Freedom, I had time to dwell upon the stirring spirituality and burgeoning faith that I was beginning to feel. On a six-to ten-hour combat flight there was ample time to ponder life's greater meaning. I was also beginning to understand that the journey along the road to faith did not have to be a solitary one; I could stop and ask for directions.

At this point I began to speak with the chaplain. I figured after thirty-three years of self-study with no results, it was probably best to consult with someone better spiritually equipped than I was. The chaplain did two great things for me that day. First, he recommended that I take the time to look at the Bible. Second, he brought me to realize that I had to make the decision to accept Christ not just by myself but also for myself. It would be a decision that would take me well over a year to make.

Prayer:
Dear Lord, I think of those who haven't put their faith and trust in you yet. Please cause them to start asking questions and looking for answers in your Word, the Bible. Bring a godly chaplain across their path. Lead them to yourself, I pray.

1. Ferguson, John. War and Peace in the World's Religions. Oxford University Press, 1978. p.104.

Commander Robert T. Garretson was deployed with a Navy F-14 Fighter squadron, VF-213, "The Black Lions" as a part of the USS Carl Vinson carrier battle group. They were among the first into combat after September 11, 2001.

A Just War?

Cdr. Robert T. Garretson

TEN MONTHS home from deployment, I was asked to give a presentation to a group of students. The topic was to cover my involvement during the war in Afghanistan. In preparation for my lecture, the students had sent me a number of questions that they hoped to have answered. One of the questions had to deal with religion and the justification of war. It was a topic that I had not actively thought about since my return to the United States.

I knew that there had to be something in the Bible to answer this question. Time and time again I was steered by readings and theology to

Romans 13:1: *"Everyone must submit himself to the governing authorities, for there is no authority except that which God has established. The authorities that exist have been established by God."*

From my own personal moral convictions and my rather rudimentary study of the scripture, I was able to come to a "Just War Theory" that was reminiscent of the works of Calvin and Locke.

> Both in theory and in historical statement, then, the key thesis of the just war theory is that on the basis both of Scripture and natural law, government (and only government) has the right to use armed force, and then only in the defense of peace and justice and with severe limitations on both the ends and the means adopted. In as much as Christians participate in government and serve as government's official agents, then, they may—however regretfully and with however much moral caution—fight.[2]

2. Holmes, Arthur F. "The Just War." *WAR: Four Christian Views* (Winona Lake, IN: BMH Books), 1986. 130.

"Everyone must submit himself to the governing authorities, for there is no authority except that which God has established. The authorities that exist have been established by God. Consequently, he who rebels against the authority is rebelling against what God has instituted, and those who do so will bring judgment on themselves. For rulers hold no terror for those who do right, but for those who do wrong.... Therefore, it is necessary to submit to the authorities, not only because of possible punishment but also because of conscience."
(Romans 13:1–5)

Prayer:
I thank you that those in authority are servants of your kingdom, Lord, whether or not they know you. Please cause them to do what is right and what will bring glory to your name.

Beginning My Bible Study

Cdr. Robert T. Garretson

FOLLOWING MY initial spiritual awakening during deployment, one could say that my road to spiritual growth was paved with good intentions. I started to regularly attend church and Bible study with my wife, but I still had not had an illuminating moment of Christian conversion. I purchased a Bible and a devotional study guide designed to lead me through the entire Bible within a year. Despite carrying both books across the country numerous times, I failed to ever take the time to actually sit down and begin to study.

> "The word is near you; it is in your mouth and in your heart," that is the word of faith we are proclaiming: That if you confess with your mouth, "Jesus is Lord," and believe in your heart that God raised him from the dead, you will be saved. For it is with your heart that you believe and are justified, and it is with your mouth that you confess and are saved. As the Scripture says, "Anyone who trusts in him will never be put to shame."
> (Romans 10:8–11)

By October 2002, I was fully entrenched in the day to day toils of being a department head in a fighter squadron. I was responsible for ten aircraft and the leadership of approximately three hundred people. It was a time of great stress and great reward, but I seemed to be unappreciative of the opportunities.

The squadron was on detachment to Fallon, so my workload as the Maintenance Officer was on the rise. Yet again away from home, I was reminded that for the first eighteen months of my young son's life, I had been separated from him for the combined total of almost a year. For almost ten months I had been battling a foot ailment which, despite the best efforts of the doctors, made it difficult to even wear a boot. I had reached a point where I was feeling stressed, homesick, and melancholy.

On October, 30, 2002, I awoke in my room at the Bachelors Officers Quarters like any other day. Arriving at the squadron to brief the Commanding Officer on the status of the jets, I discovered that my daily flight had been cancelled. Normally, this meant the opportunity to get caught up on paperwork, or maybe head back to the 'Q' for a good workout or a little bit of TV.

I'm not sure what it was that finally prodded me to pick up my Bible and study guide. The devotional is set up in a manner that provides a contextual preview, assigns a specific scripture reading, and then has a personal application. The passage in the scripture reading that day would forever change my spiritual life:

Prayer:

Please continue your good work of drawing thousands more to faith in Jesus Christ, their Lord and Savior, Fortress, and King.

NOVEMBER 7

Putting Christ First

Cdr. Robert T. Garretson

EVEN WHEN I was home, I was consumed with work. While I thought I was doing a pretty good job of playing the action hero/tough guy, inside I was crashing. I felt lonely, stressed, depressed, and those who knew me best would later tell me they could see a shortness in my temper.

Finally, while the squadron was away from home again on a training detachment and received the word that we were going to war again, I began to recognize that I was losing altitude fast. I literally fell to my knees and asked the Lord, "God, I need you in my life, what do I need to do to save myself?" The answer He gave me was to reengage my spiritual life and get back into the fight. It was time to apply many of the things I had learned flying jets to my faith.

> "Above all, you must understand that no prophecy of Scripture came about by the prophet's own interpretation. For prophecy never had its origin in the will of man, but men spoke from God as they were carried along by the Holy Spirit."
> (2 Peter 1:20–21)

For example, I had to **apply flight control corrections.** To stop my descent, I had to take action and pull out of my dive. I had to actively accept and pursue a personal relationship with Christ

I had to **check my instruments**. In the jet, if you're out of control and only focus outside the cockpit, you fail to recognize what's really happening. During these times, you have to get inside the cockpit and focus on your instruments. The instruments don't lie, they give a true reading of our attitude and altitude. They let us see where we're at and where we need to be. In my spiritual life, the instrument is God's Word. I need to listen and apply God's Word in my life and get into God's Word through daily devotions as Chaplain Mike shared.

I had to **find my wingmen**. In military aviation, the wingman is special. We trust our wingman with our life and he trusts us with his. In a time of crisis, he provides support from a detached but understanding point of view. At the same time we support him. Every one of us need to fly through life with wingmen who we can connect with, who are in the same stage of life—someone to provide understanding and mutual support.

Prayer:

Please use the instrument of the Scriptures, Your Word, to give me a true reading of where I'm at and where I need to be spiritually. And please bring another wingman into my life, who will provide understanding and support through life's ups and downs.

NOVEMBER 8

Becoming a Transformational Leader

Chaplain (Lt. Col.) Gary Hensley Command Chaplain, Combined Joint Task Force 101, Regional Command East, Bagram Air Force Base, Afghanistan (2008–2009)

AN OLD CHINESE proverb says, "If you want five years of prosperity, grow grain. If you want ten years of prosperity, grow trees. If you want one hundred years of prosperity, grow people."

I believe leaders are both naturally gifted to lead and developed and mentored to lead. We must work to grow leaders for our future. To do this we will need a transformational leadership style. Transformational leadership requires one on one, knowledgeable investment in people. It finds ways to grow junior leaders for future challenges and demonstrates a vital personal connection between the leader and lead.

Why is this important for us? To become a transformational leader takes an intentional, time-invested approach to developing subordinates. This is not easy. It is a challenge in the present, fast-paced operational environment. Much is required from our leaders during war. We must accomplish more with less. We must work within the system in which we operate.

Let's define leadership.

In *Army Field Manual* (FM) 22-100, "Army Leadership: Competent, Confident, and Agile," there is a process that could be simplified as "Be, Know, Do." To quote from the field manual, "Leadership is influencing people—by providing purpose, direction, and motivation—while operating to accomplish the mission and improving the organization."

Harry Truman once said, "Leadership is the art of getting people to do what they don't want to do and like it."

Napoleon was known to say, "Leaders are dealers in hope."

Even Attila the Hun understood the focus of leadership, "Chieftains who meet their Huns needs, even at their own expense, are honorable leaders."

Who is the one person who has most influenced your life? Was it your dad, teacher, coach, non-commissioned officer (NCO), commander, friend, or someone else?

Jesus the Nazarene was a world-class leader. He provides the spiritual premise for true leadership. Mark 1:17 says, "Come, follow me! And I will make you fishers of men." In 1 Corinthians 4:11, Paul wrote, "Follow me, as I follow Christ."

> "This Ezra came up from Babylon. He was a teacher well versed in the Law of Moses, which the LORD, the God of Israel, had given. The king had granted him everything he asked, for the hand of the LORD his God was on him. Some of the Israelites, including priests, Levites, singers, gatekeepers and temple servants, also came up to Jerusalem in the seventh year of King Artaxerxes." (Ezra 7:6–7)

Jesus displayed all the attributes of a transformational leader. He developed his followers into leaders and role models for others to then follow. Leaders raise future leaders and invest themselves in those they are responsible for.

Prayer:
Dear God, please make me like Ezra, well versed in the Scriptures and bold to seek the favor of those in authority in order to do your will. By the power of Jesus Christ within me, please make me a transformational leader.

The Components of Transformational Leadership

Chaplain (Lt. Col.) Gary Hensley Command Chaplain, Combined Joint Task Force 101, Regional Command East, Bagram Air Force Base, Afghanistan (2008–2009)

YESTERDAY, WE began talking about leadership that produces generations of leaders. The next two days I want to discuss the focus of transformational leadership. This is the leadership style that invests in subordinates to create others-focused leaders that our military and nation need.

There are four components of transformational leadership: charisma, inspiration, being individually considerate, and intellectually stimulating. We'll discuss the first two today.

Transformational leaders are charismatic. Their followers seek to identify with their leaders and emulate them. This doesn't happen by accident. Leaders model leadership. They lead by example. In a real sense they are excited and enthusiastic cheerleaders for their subordinates. They speak with words and act with deeds that are admirable, appreciated, and highly esteemed. The more selfless the act, the more charismatic they become. They use words and actions that encourage determination, persistence, and "stick-to-itiveness." They speak and act with integrity that gains trust, confidence, as well as healthy dependence and reliance from their subordinates.

> "After I looked things over, I stood up and said to the nobles, the officials and the rest of the people, 'Don't be afraid of them. Remember the Lord, who is great and awesome, and fight for your brothers, your sons and your daughters, your wives and your homes.'"
> (Nehemiah 4:14)

Jesus asked his followers to follow him, learn from him, and emulate his actions. He instructed them to watch him and learn. He was the example of charisma.

Transformational leaders are inspirational. Leaders inspire their followers with challenge and persuasion. They provide meaning and understanding. They build a sense of vision and purpose in their subordinates. When you are with your subordinates remember these keys to being inspirational:

Be Enthusiastic—Get excited about what you are trying to accomplish. This is a contagious behavior even amidst difficult circumstance and fatigue.

Be Optimistic—Find the positive in all things. Your subordinates will focus on your optimism when circumstances discourage them.

Be Encouraging—Build up your people. Find the good and praise it.

One of Jesus' best known teachings focused on transforming the inner self. When he finished the 'Sermon on the Mount' (see Mathew chapters 5–7) it's recorded that the people "marveled at him." People long to be around transformational leaders. Their charisma and inspiration are rare in our society.

Prayer:
Dear God, please make me like Nehemiah, carefully assessing the situation and boldly calling others to follow me in doing the right thing. By the power of Jesus Christ within me, please make me an inspirational leader.

NOVEMBER 10

Characteristics of a Transformational Leader

Chaplain (Lt. Col.) Gary Hensley Command Chaplain, Combined Joint Task Force 101, Regional Command East, Bagram Air Force Base, Afghanistan (2008–2009)

TRANSFORMATIONAL leadership holds the key to growing great leaders for our military and our nation. Yesterday we looked at two attributes of these leaders, charisma and inspiration. Today we will look at the other two key components of this leadership style.

Transformational leaders are individually considerate. They provide their followers with support and focus on individual needs. These leaders recognize that each subordinate is unique and requires individual attention to develop into a mature leader. The leader takes on the role of a mentor and a coach. How do they accomplish this?

- find the individual's strengths and maximize them
- know their weak points and strengthen them
- see each individual as unique, having value that can be utilized for the benefit of others

Jesus found value in every person. He often focused on the weaker, less gifted in the crowd. Even those who were rejected by the crowd held value in his eyes. He empowered them to see that value and bless others.

Transformational leaders are **intellectually stimulating.** They are able to expand the follower's use of their own abilities. They find ways to stimulate their efforts to be innovative and creative. Whether by providing opportunity or challenge, their subordinates grow in their abilities and confidence. The following suggestions may help in this regard:

> "Rend your heart and not your garments. Return to the LORD your God, for he is gracious and compassionate, slow to anger and abounding in love, and he relents from sending calamity." (Joel 2:13)

- Applaud creativity. Those who are able to cast a problem in a new light and reframe circumstance to provide new perspective are truly creative.
- Ensure followers are included in the process. The leader is not always the answer provider. True leaders draw the answers out from their subordinates. A follower that feels they are apart of the solution is truly enabled.
- Restrict public criticism of mistakes or ideas. This not only works against the individual but the team as well. Criticize and correct in private.

Jesus' teaching was strong and demanding but he fostered a gentile approach to his disciples. He was approachable, and they identified with him.

In conclusion, to become a transformational leader, you must be willing to change your thinking. You must be willing to change your behavior. You must be willing to change your model. Christ is the great agent of change. Not only can he make us new creatures, he can give us a new disposition.

Prayer:
Dear God, please make me like the prophet Joel, turning my heart toward you, confessing and repenting of any known sins, and seeking to follow you wholeheartedly. By the power of Jesus within me, please help me to seek a positive example for others to imitate.

Do What Is Right

Brig. General (ret) Paul Casinelli, MD

MY EXPERIENCE starts as a sense of duty. General Robert E. Lee said, "Duty is the most sublime word in our language. Do your duty in all things. You cannot do more. You should never wish to do less." Andrew Jackson stated, "The brave man inattentive to his duty is worth little more to his country than the coward who deserts her in the hour of danger."

> "Now all has been heard; here is the conclusion of the matter: Fear God and keep his commandments, for this is the whole duty of man."
> (Ecclesiastes 12:13)

We have a duty to God our Creator to do what is right. If you believe in both the sovereignty and the providence of God, then he has you placed in positions and during times where you can see what that duty is. He opens your eyes so you can see what you need to do. It is one reason that I volunteered in the first place. It was very obvious to me that he had a very specific path for me to follow. My original reason for joining the guard was so that if I deploy I would be going with my hometown unit. I just didn't know my hometown unit would be in Mississippi.

I started on the ground floor, setting up the unit's medical section incorporating my experiences from Desert Storm and Kosovo. I helped develop their Standard Operating Procedures (SOPs). The commander, Colonel Brad McNealy, was outstanding. He was very supportive and simply told me to take care of his troops. The men and women of the 185th were professional citizen-soldiers. It was a great team to be a part of. The 185th Aviation Group was a great unit that shared my sense of duty.

Prayer:
Please strengthen my sense of duty to fear you, keep your commandments, and fulfill the duties you have called me to fulfill.

Brig. General (ret) Paul Casinelli (MD) served as the command surgeon for Task Force 185 Aviation (a Mississippi National Guard Unit) in 2004 during Operation Iraqi Freedom. At that time he was a colonel and the state surgeon for the Connecticut Army National Guard.

Flying to Meet the Needs of Others

Brig. General (ret) Paul Casinelli, MD

I FLEW OVER 190 combat hours during my deployment to Iraq. Besides the fact that flying is the fun part about being a flight surgeon, it is a requirement of the job. The physicals and sick call fill most days, but flying—it's what you love to do. It was exhilarating. Flying fifty feet above ground at 140 knots with the doors open was an experience of a lifetime and one very few people have the privilege of experiencing.

> "A wise man has great power, and a man of knowledge increases strength; for waging war you need guidance, and for victory many advisers." (Proverbs 24:5–6)

I did not, however, fly in combat for the fun. Being the flight surgeon I was one of the sets of the eyes and ears of the commander. My job is to see, feel, and report on the stress experienced by the crews. The only way that I can know that is to be familiar with the stresses they experiencing by flying with them. I have to be on the internal communications system (ICS) so I can hear them communicate. There are also duties associated with flying as crew. I am an extra set of eyes looking for the enemy. I am an integral part of the crew when I fly.

After a while when they get used to me being on the flight, they start talking to each other about certain things, but I understand they are not just talking about things to one another. They are communicating things to me because they know I'm listening. They might say the flying schedule is too grueling. Things they would not come to me and say. But they will know I'm listening. *The chow hall doesn't have a midnight ration. The way the flights are scheduled and the challenge scheduled we just missed supper.* I can bring those things right to the commander. And that's something he can do something about.

My friends would ask why I flew so much. I didn't fly because it was fun. I flew because it was a part of my duty. War does not have workweeks and weekends. We push soldiers to the limit. We have to make sure that they are not driven to go too far. Taking care of our soldiers is a part of waging war. It is a part of good leadership.

Prayer:
Dear God, please help me to listen to others, discern their needs, identify how certain needs can be met, and then take decisive action to help meet those needs.

Anti-Aircraft Fire

Brig. General (ret) Paul Casinelli, MD

SURFACE-TO-AIR fire was a part of army aviation during the Iraq War. That was just another aspect of flying. There were times when small arms or rockets were used against us. A lot of the time the enemy was firing rockets blindly at the sound. I remember we were concerned early on about people shining headlights up at us.

I do remember one episode about six miles south of Baghdad. We were flying south. It was a flight of two CH-47 Chinooks. I was in the trail bird. In the back of the lead bird there appeared to be a column of smoke. We looked down and it looked like there was someone firing a roman candle at us from the ground. And then all of a sudden it dawned on us that it was anti-aircraft fire, and then the streaks of light began coming at us. We just had never seen anti-craft fire before. The pilot did something with a helicopter I didn't know the helicopter could do, and we began to move away. At the same time he started yelling over the intercom system to return fire. The first Chinook began to put down fire as well and within a few seconds the anti-aircraft fire stopped. There were never too many dull moments.

> "Be strong and let us fight bravely for our people and the cities of our God. The LORD will do what is good in his sight." (2 Samuel 10:12)

War is not a safe environment, but to worry about the outcome of combat will only create an ineffective soldier. Whether by firefight or random indirect fire, life can end in a moment. If you thought about it too much you might wander at night whether you would wake up or not. The only way to be sane was to understand your faith is in the Lord and you would lie down in peace then whatever would happen would be his will. You had to accept that. And not so much that you had to accept it but that you needed to accept it with joy.

It was an aspect of duty. You will not add one second to your life doing anything differently. God is sovereign. Those of us who understood that then could more effectively perform our duties. It was an essential philosophy of Stonewall Jackson.

Captain, my religious belief teaches me to feel as safe in battle as in bed. God has fixed the time for my death. I do not concern myself about that, but to be always ready, no matter when it may overtake me. Captain, that is the way all men should live, and then all would be equally brave.

—*Speaking to Captain John D. Imboden (24 July 1861), as quoted in Stonewall Jackson as Military Commander (2000) by John Selby, 25.*

Prayer:
Dear God, I know you already know the day I will die. May I live boldly and courageously, never shirking back when duty calls.

NOVEMBER 14

Helping the Iraqis Face Life

Brig. General (ret) Paul Casinelli, MD

WE ALL FACE death. It comes without warning for most. Life can be over in a second. What some would call a misstep or an accident can also be described as a circumstance that is under God's complete control. We are truly frail creatures. We are built in a complex way, and we try to understand the process of life and death. The only way that I understand it is to see that we are walking miracles. From the time of conception until we die it's a miracle of grace and mercy. The body is so complex a creation that only one thing going wrong inside will affect the whole system and put a person out of commission.

When something sudden happens, most of the world would say you were in the wrong place at the wrong time. I would say that you are at the exact place at the right time and right place. That's my understanding of God's sovereignty. We're so dependent upon the Lord's good pleasure. Like the grass, we are here one day and gone the next. Ecclesiastes 1:2, "Everything is vanity." The next second we could be gone, but you cannot dwell on that. If you do then you couldn't live.

> "Consider the voice of the singers at the watering places. They recite the righteous acts of the Lord, the righteous acts of his warriors." (Judges 5:11)

The Iraqi people understood this. They were in many ways like any other people. They were family oriented and generally lived amongst family. We met with the sheik of the local village. He was a true leader. The people welcomed us into their homes and shared what they had with us generously. They were very clean and polite. They were quite hospitable, and their kindness always appeared to be genuine. They were interested in what we could do to help them—not to line their pockets but to help their community and their children.

We worked to help them in many ways. We had been bringing medical and nonperishable supplies and providing labor to restore a local clinic. One of the things that struck me when we went into schools was that the girls were afraid of us at first. The boys were not afraid of anything. The girls didn't really know what to make of us. The teachers had to let them know that we were not there to cause them any harm. We were there to help them and give them school supplies. It was one of the more human things we did. To reach out and help the Iraqi people in very real and practical ways was important. It allowed us to experience the sincere appreciation of the people.

Prayer:
Dear Lord, may you help our country's soldiers to act righteously in Iraq and Afghanistan. Please use their righteous acts to lead many Muslims to see your good hand in their lives. May they give you praise.

Developing My Faith

Brig. General (ret) Paul Casinelli, MD

IT HAS BEEN said that war is a mix between short moments of excitement and long periods of boredom. You had to have discipline and a plan for the "down time." There are always books to read or exercise. When you go to war you should have a plan for what to do with that extra time. Reading through the Bible or studying the Bible is a wonderful way to do this. The Officer Christian Fellowship program (http://www.ocfusa.org/) or other Bible study tools are wonderful for this purpose as well.

I would sit down at the computer and type out the passage of scripture I was studying, and I would comment on it and send it by email to my sons. I felt connected to them when I sent my thoughts on Scripture. I felt like I was still leading my family from afar.

One of the verses that always hit me while I was there was Isaiah 40:31: "But those who hope in the LORD will renew their strength. They will soar on wings like eagles; they will run and not grow weary, they will walk and not be faint." This verse was appropriate for me in so many ways. I was a colonel then, and an eagle symbolizes this rank. 'Waiting on the Lord' seemed appropriate given the time I spent alone. Not 'growing weary' was a constant effort. Psalm 23 also played a role in my deployment, with the idea that I could not rest but rather that the lord would cause me to 'rest in green pastures.'

"I always thank my God as I remember you in my prayers, because I hear about your faith in the Lord Jesus and your love for all the saints. I pray that you may be active in sharing your faith, so that you will have a full understanding of every good thing we have in Christ." (Philemon 1:4–6)

All of these experiences led to a growth spiritually that I had not experienced before. What surprised me was not only the amount of growth and confidence that developed in my faith, but also the depth that has remained over the last five years since my return home. The growth of my faith was one of the realities of my deployment. It was as constant as the never-ending routine and tutti-frutti ice cream at every dining facility.

Prayer:
Dear God, I'm thinking of a soldier serving you in Iraq or Afghanistan or now back from his tour(s) of duty. Cause that soldier to grow in faith, share it with others, and come to a full understanding of every good thing we have in Jesus Christ.

NOVEMBER 16

Explosions

Sergeant Major "Ted," special operations medic (name changed for security reasons). As a senior assault medic, he deployed more than a half dozen times to the war.

THE BLAST was incredible. I heard nothing. I felt everything. I was looking at the observation point (OP) outside of Kandahar, about to drink my first cup of coffee just after daybreak in December of 2001—then there was a flash, and suddenly we were physically not there anymore. The shockwave was like being hit by a wave in the ocean. It took our breath away. We were only sixty meters from the impact point. No one could hear anything after the explosion.

> "Just as man is destined to die once, and after that to face judgment." (Hebrews 9:27)

My sergeant major was standing to my left outside the building in front of a door. When the blast occurred it blew him through the door and on the pile with the rest of us. To put it in context, that amount of explosives was approximately one quarter to one third of what was used in the Oklahoma City bombing.

There were people standing close enough to the explosion to get flash burns on their eyes and second-degree burns on their chest from the actual heat and flash of the explosion but were otherwise relatively un-injured. Yet people far away were literally cut in half. There were people well within the lethal circle that were not killed. When the OP was hit directly, one soldier was simply gone and another was blown forty feet and only had a few scratches. The disparity of who gets the worst injury and where they were in relation to the explosion repeated itself over and over again.

It defies what we would assume to be logical. We think all those that are inside the lethal circle should be dead or seriously injured but that's not the case at all. It's very diverse what happens to people.

What we don't understand about explosions is related to what we don't understand about life. There is a time and a place where each person is going to die. At that point they'll be accountable for what they've done in this life.

Prayer:
Lord, lead us to the conclusion that we have just one life to live and that life will soon pass. May we live with the understanding that only what is done for you during our lives will be of lasting importance. Amen.

Casualty Collection Point

Sergeant Major "Ted" is a special operations medic.

INITIALLY, WE were unaware that it was a bomb. All we knew was that we had been hit. We were ready to defend our position when the call came down that Americans were down the hill and we needed to take the hill. Running outside, I encountered the masses of casualties: close to one hundred people were wounded or killed in that immediate area.

The shrapnel pattern from the 2000 pound JDAM bomb went down in front of and behind the observation post. There were a lot of Afghan forces in front of the observation point watching the bombing and they were hit too. Our small special operations force was now the only force defending the position. There was no other force in the area that could lend assistance; and for all we knew the Taliban had scored a direct hit and were beginning an attack.

The casualties were easy to identify but sometimes difficult to find. Some got blown under vehicles, others were buried, some laid in heaps. There was a village nearby and they began to come out after the explosion. They were curious but some were looting the wounded and dead. This furthered the chaos and absolute anarchy of the situation. We established a Casualty Collection Point (CCP) in between the two buildings. There were munitions preset in the OP to defend the position and they began to detonate and send ordinance directly at us. When this began to happen we had to move the CCP to a point better shielded from this incoming fire.

There was only one other medical provider capable of working initially and we split up the work at hand. Everybody was doing what they

> "I lift up my eyes to the hills—where does my help come from? My help comes from the LORD, the Maker of heaven and earth. He will not let your foot slip—he who watches over you will not slumber; indeed, he who watches over Israel will neither slumber nor sleep. The LORD watches over you—the LORD is your shade at your right hand; the sun will not harm you by day, nor the moon by night. The LORD will keep you from all harm—he will watch over your life; the LORD will watch over your coming and going both now and forevermore." (Psalm 121)

could and there was a constant stream of casualties coming into the CCP. Despite the chaos and confusion everyone was focused on the tasks required to secure the position and save lives.

We think it's difficult to keep focused when bad things happen, but sometimes the stress sharpens our responses and we push past physical discomfort and overwhelming tasks to do what needs to be done.

Prayer:
When chaos and confusion abounds, give me the ability,
O Lord, to focus on the tasks at hand.

NOVEMBER 18

Needing Help

Sergeant Major "Ted" is a special operations medic

AS I AM there on my knees, treating an injured soldier, someone poked me in my back.

"Leave me alone!" I shouted, not looking up.

Another poke, this one more forceful and into the back of my head. Turning around, I see an Afghan fighter with a large belt-fed RPK machine gun pointed at the back of my head with his finger on the trigger. He pointed at the empty bottles of antibiotics on the ground and then pointed the weapon back at me, putting his eyes behind the site of the weapon as if he was going to shoot it. Over the last hour he had seen us administer antibiotics to American soldiers, according to our protocol; he was clearly upset and wanted more antibiotics for the Afghan casualties.

> "The LORD will keep you from all harm, he will watch over your life; the LORD will watch over your coming and going both now and forevermore." (Psalm 121:7–8)

I quickly scanned for someone who could help me but I was alone. With my weapon slung on my back I was not in a position to discuss anything and I needed to act.

Grabbing some old needles, syringes and a small bag of IV fluid, I drew as much left over antibiotics as I could, injected it into the IV fluid, and gave all the Afghan casualties a shot in the arm of this antibiotic solution.

I can't even see anyone else from my unit, I thought as I was administering the antibiotics under gunpoint. But every once in a while I could hear a fifty caliber machine gun going off and I realized that our soldiers were still out there doing what they had to do to protect the position from being overrun by the Taliban. "I lift up my eyes to the hills, where does my help come from?" I recited Psalm 121 in my mind. "My help comes from the Lord, the Maker of heaven and earth. He will not let your foot slip, he who watches over you will not slumber. . . . The LORD watches over you, the LORD is your shade at your right hand; the sun will not harm you by day, nor the moon by night."

Finally, the Afghan fighter and his friends who had threatened my life just moments ago seemed satisfied.

Prayer:
Father, I know you promise I will never be alone. You will always watch over me and care for me. You will keep me from harm and watch over my life. Thank you Father.

NOVEMBER 19

Overwhelmed

Sergeant Major "Ted" is a special operations medic.

I WAS TIRED. My hands had begun to swell. They had been injured in the blast and working with my hands had not helped. I was thirsty. Someone had stolen my water and I was becoming dehydrated.

It was at that point when one of my guys came down and asked me if I was okay.

"No I'm not," I told him. "My hands are jacked up, I'm dehydrated and I have no security." He stood there, protecting me, so I could wash my hands and drink something for the first time that day.

Sitting in the shade of my friend, I was able to recuperate enough strength to continue. I wasn't even halfway done at that point. He gave me water, he gave me comfort, he gave me shade, and that may not seem like much but at the time it was a lot. I was working on people over and over and over again and used my hands constantly. And now I was having problems using my hands at all. He gave me water to wash all the blood off of them. I worked through having other people's blood coagulate and stick to your hands. To be able to wash all the dried blood off my hands, if only for a few minutes, made a big difference. For five minutes I did nothing but rest and drink. He gave me Gatorade and a power bar. He moved a vehicle into position to overwatch my area.

Just knowing that someone is watching you allows you to get down on your knees and turn your back and do what you have to do. To deal with the chaos and do what is needed for so many wounded takes all your attention. It took hours to figure out what everyone needed. At about five and half hours into the ordeal we were told that helicopters would be coming in, but it would only be for Americans. That presented problems. We had to have security and we had to move the American wounded to a different location. Thankfully they sent more helicopters and we were able to evacuate the Afghan wounded too.

> "For the eyes of the Lord are over the righteous, and his ears are open unto their prayers: but the face of the Lord is against them that do evil." (1 Peter 3:12)

Prayer:

Almighty God, remind us that you watch over us and that you hear our petitions. When we know the righteous are never alone, we are strengthened in our faith and emboldened to stand firm against the fiery darts of the evil one. Thank you, Lord, for this reassurance. Amen

NOVEMBER 20

Always Move Forward

Sergeant Major "Ted" is a special operations medic.

IT WAS THE largest aeromedical evacuation of casualties during the war. As I looked at some of the injury reports it's pretty amazing who lived and who died. Everyone has a time they will leave this earth. You have a choice to make the most of this life while you are here.

Initially in combat, everybody's afraid. You probably only see about 25 percent of what is happening because the entire experience is sensory overload. Many times people don't even hear bullets because they are so overwhelmed by the self-preservation instinct.

You shouldn't be here, run away, your brain tells you. But you have to move forward. The more experience you have with combat and the more you're exposed to the disparity between who lives and who dies, the easier it becomes to simply move forward.

You begin to understand that you cannot control whether you live or die. You'll act tactically sound and make good decisions and not take undue risk, but you have to let go of the fear of death. You have to be concerned and focused on the mission and on others around you.

A great soldier once told me that the Army was about soldiers taking care of soldiers and this is very true in my experience. If you're a leader on your team or the lowest ranking guy, your purpose is to take care of others and focus on the success of the mission. Being a part of that is something very special.

> "Therefore I tell you, do not worry about your life, what you will eat or drink; or about your body, what you will wear. Is not life more important than food, and the body more important than clothes?" (Matthew 6:25)

Surround yourself with the best people, the best tactics, the best equipment and techniques and no matter what, commit to making the mission successful. When you do this and let go of worrying, then there is nothing left but to move forward. As Robert Frost said, "the only way round is through." Christ said, "Who of you by worrying can add a single hour to [your] life?" and the reality is you just can't. Focus your attention on helping others and on accomplishing the mission and let go of trying to control the outcome through worrying. Tap into your faith for the peace that comes only from God—he has a plan for you.

Prayer:
*Lord, help us focus our attention on others
and the mission you have for us. Amen.*

NOVEMBER 21

Relying on the Lord

Sergeant Major "Ted" is a special operations medic.

PEACE AMIDST turmoil comes from faith. If you don't rely on God or have faith in his sovereignty, then it's all up to you, and that is absolutely fatiguing. You have to figure it all out and lean on your own understanding. Your hands will fail at the critical moment, and there's nothing you can do about it. You have very real physical and mental limitations. Simply put, without faith you will fail. Faith allows you to persevere. You will continue to do what you must do, knowing that God is the one in control of what happens.

During that incident outside of Kandahar, I felt like I was completely alone. But I wasn't ever alone. Even the people who trained me contributed to that success. The men who were not trained medically but were performing medical tasks because I was yelling instruction at them contributed directly to saving lives. There was a lot of noise and a great deal of chaos. But through it all there was an underlying peace that is difficult to explain.

> "And the peace of God, which transcends all understanding, will guard your hearts and your minds in Christ Jesus." (Philippians 4:7)

I have been on a few assaults that have lasted many hours. Those situations, just as the tragedy of December 5, simply call for persistence, all the way to the end. You can't just stop when you meet resistance. Persistence requires faith.

If we found ourselves assaulting a well-defended position, we would use what we had to reduce the target and reduce the threat. Fortunately, we have a lot of combined arms technology, which we can leverage to our advantage. At the end of the day somebody has to go on and occupy the ground. It's not until you're there that you can say the enemy no longer owns the objective. To move forward through the barriers and instinct to stop requires more than human initiative can accomplish. And through those times of conflict and struggle in your life, peace is still present if you believe.

Prayer:
Lord, help my unbelief. Help me to move forward through the barriers of life. Help me not to trust my human strength but depend solely upon your strength.

War Is the Domain of Friction and Violence

Sergeant Major "Ted" is a special operations medic.

UNDERSTANDING the commander's intent is very important to success on the battlefield. In life, we have our Commander's intent laid out in the Bible. Unfortunately, we are focused on ourselves and have moved away from the commander's intent: to have the free will to glorify him instead of ourselves.

The great military thinker and strategic theorist, Clausewitz said that "war is the domain of friction and violence." Not only war, but also the fabric of our life exists in friction. In your daily life, you are in a war of expectations and trials. We talk about periods of peace but there's never a true world peace. When one area of sovereignty bumps up against another it creates friction. It's true at the international level and the individual level.

> "The thief comes only to steal and kill and destroy; I have come that they may have life, and have it to the full." (John 10:10)

We have friction because we have free will. If you put free will into the military context it doesn't work well. Everybody cannot make up their minds about whether or not they shoot back at the enemy or engage in combat. We have to bury the idea of free will to have the unity required to accomplish the commander's intent and survive as a unit.

The winning strategy lies in applying our force and resources in a coordinated way to accomplish the bigger mission. It involves having our free will inline with the commander's will and committing to the success of the team above our own glory or survival. Don't lose yourself, your ethics or your honor by losing sight of the commander's intent. It wasn't a part of God's intent for you to focus on yourself or become self-reliant. Success is measured by your commitment to each other and your commitment to the commander's intent.

Truly we have a war without end now. And it's an issue of conflicting ideologies. The fight we are in is a big one. So all the little things matter, like how you prepare, how you pray, and how you conduct yourself. Understanding the creator's intent is the key to your success. He intended for you to have peace regardless of what is happening to you or around

413

you in this world and he wanted you to not only have life, but also to live it more abundantly.

Prayer:
Prepare us, Lord, for spiritual warfare. Embolden us. While we are in battle, grant us the peace that passes understanding. Amen

The War Comes Home

Terry Mitchell, Senior Editor, University Communications, Whitworth University

FORREST AND Oaken Ewens, identical twins, were students in my discussion group at Whitworth University in fall 2000. When I asked them if they really wanted to be in the same group, they were resolute: "We like being in the same classes," one said. "It's never been a problem."

During that semester, one—I can't remember which one—consistently turned in better papers than the other. Neither cared about that. There was no one-upmanship. The twins rarely spoke up in class, but their occasional comments and their papers reflected strong convictions, heartfelt beliefs, and love of God, family, and country. Their companionship was easy and supportive; their bond was tight.

> "a brother is born for adversity."
> (Proverbs 17:17)

Perhaps that bond expanded a bit when Oaken left for West Point and Forrest stayed on at Whitworth, helping to lead the track-and-field team to a conference championship and learning everything he could about history and his other passions. Other tests came as the young men pursued their military careers, first in ROTC, at the U.S. Military Academy, and then in the U.S. Army.

But nothing would break the bond; not even Forrest's death in Afghanistan's Pech River Valley on June 16, 2006. He was leading his men on a mission to distribute medical supplies when a roadside bomb went off. At barely twenty-five, Forrest was gone.

Two weeks after his brother's death, Oaken wrote in an online memorial, "I prayed so hard that God would stop my heart the night I heard."

Saying that he was "beyond tears," Oaken continued, "I miss you and I am so very proud."

Everyone who knew Forrest echoes that last sentiment. Though none of us can know the depth of his twin's anguish, nor the pain and pride of the rest of his close-knit family, all of us can join with another young man who wrote in Forrest's guestbook—a PFC who'd served under Forrest in Afghanistan. His final words were both an inspiration and a knife through the heart to those of us who went to the Web looking for comfort and camaraderie after Forrest's death: *"Climb to Glory, Sir!"*

Prayer:
Lord, may your glory be seen even in suffering.

NOVEMBER 24

A Special Thanksgiving

Capt. Amy Malugani, United States Marine Corps

(Excerpt from an email that Captain Malugani sent to her friends and family, November 30, 2005)

THE THANKSGIVING holiday was an opportunity to take time out to give thanks for all the blessings of my past, the present, and the ones to come. We had a memorial ceremony for the Marines who were killed in Operation Steel Curtain. I can't think of a better day to celebrate the lives of these young men, and give thanks for their courage and sacrifice. The sun shining, tears running behind sunglasses, and undoubtedly, God was present. Profound and sincere words were shared: life is precious—a gift—and one's spirit touches so many in such a short amount of time.

Later that day, I went running with a friend and we shared gratitude lists to pass the time. The first list—the people we are grateful for in our lives. The second list—gratitude for our bodies. The third list—gratitude regarding the deployment. We used the alphabet to guide us. I was amazed at the length of my list, considering many challenges throughout the deployment and homesick many times. After the run, I view my current situation differently. The lists were evident reminders that I am exactly where I need to be. There is such comfort in accepting this perspective.

When I returned from Iraq last year (March 2005) I was uncomfortable—overwhelmed—with the daily life in the states. The simple life—deployment—seemed so comforting, safe, and easy. Ironic, considering I spent a significant period of time outside the base, and our base received incoming fire more times than I would like to remember. However, there was a sense of safety in the simple life. After several weeks in the states, I realized it wasn't the deployment, but the people in my life and the choices I consciously made on a daily basis. I can have a simple life anywhere in the world, and I can ask God for help from anywhere—for where I am he is there too.

> "He who regards one day as special, does so to the Lord. He who eats meat, eats to the Lord, for he gives thanks to God; and he who abstains, does so to the Lord and gives thanks to God."
> (Romans 14:6)

A chaplain shared with me, "Instead of the simple life, how about a special life." I came into this second deployment anticipating and expecting the simple life. Unfortunately, I was confronted with everything but the simple life. The chaplain's words stuck with me. I don't have control over the daily pressures, demands, and expectations of the world but I do have control over the way I respond. I can make my life as special as I want—it's my choice.

Prayer:
*I choose to make today special, giving thanks
to you for the gifts you've given me.*

NOVEMBER 25

Army Values: Honor

Maj. John Croushorn, MD (retired veteran)

"What is life without honor? Degradation is worse than death."
—Lieutenant General Thomas J. "Stonewall" Jackson

THANKSGIVING in Iraq was a bittersweet event. It is hard to be thankful when you are away from home. However a warm meal, good friends, and a good mission is as comforting as any soldier could ask for. As we walked into the DFAC there was a familiar face behind the serving line. The Colonel and the CSM were serving everyone and smiling from ear to ear.

The contract workers were getting a kick out of it. The commander and CSM didn't miss an opportunity to thank each and every soldier that passed through the line. Later that evening, the Colonel and I were talking while puffing on a couple of cigars and I asked him if he enjoyed himself. He smiled and said, "You have no idea how thankful I am to be here, now, with these men and women. They're the best people I have ever served with."

> "The fear of the LORD teaches a man wisdom, and humility comes before honor."
> (Proverbs 15:3)

A man of integrity, a man known as intrepid—these terms are used by many to describe those who live in a manner above reproach. These are strong men and women with a moral bent for strength of character and justice. But beyond the public persona, the honor lies in their actions and motivations. The man with honor is seen for what he does for others and not for himself.

The Army values honor as a sacred virtue. Without it men are thrown by circumstance. Their decisions are based in self-centered vision instead of the outward concern for others. This is what makes a commander great in the eyes of his men. It is what motivates them to fight for him and sacrifice. It is truly a powerful thing.

Prayer:
Allow me to place others before my own interest. May my focus be on you, Father. Protect me from my own selfish pride, that through humility I may honor you by honoring others.

Take One Day at a Time

Col. Joe Wood, Chief of Clinical Operations for Multinational Corps Iraq

I WAS THE Chief of Clinical Operations for Multinational Corps Iraq (MNC-I). A large part of my job was establishing policy and procedures for the coalition from a medical standpoint. It did provide me a theater-wide perspective. I reviewed the security updates and battle reports

417

each day. But no matter how much perspective you have, at some point the war becomes personal.

It was 0500 hours. The sound was not what I remember most. The concussive blast seemed to take my breath away. The discomfort of awakening to the feeling of having the breath knocked out of you is a disheartening experience. I struggled to get my body armor as debris hit the sides and roof of my trailer. Then I had to consciously get up and out of the trailer. I remember thinking, "That was close; someone is probably hurt."

We had received a lot of incoming rocket fire that week. Only a few days before, fifteen rockets had impacted the living area. When the Quick Reaction Force arrived at the point of origination they discovered almost seventy more rockets that had not yet fired. I didn't know if more rockets were on their way, I just knew I needed to help if I could.

> "Let us acknowledge the LORD; let us press on to acknowledge him. As surely as the sun rises, he will appear; he will come to us like the winter rains, like the spring rains that water the earth." (Hosea 6:3)

I did not have an aid bag at the time. It would not have mattered for the soldier who was killed. The trauma was devastating. After the attack, the command directed that pre-positioned medical supplies be put in the living areas and other areas with large numbers of people. All I really changed was that I made sure I carried with me at all times a pressure dressing and a tourniquet, basic life saving items. I can recall numerous occasions in the past when I forgot to have those things on my person at times; I always had them after the attack.

I came away with a couple of lessons from that experience. You take one day at a time; and there's so much that happens that is outside of our control.

Prayer:
Lord, may I seek to know you better each day, not just when life goes well or life is hard. Lord, may I trust your sovereignty and control more each day, again whether life is going well or is hard.

Saddam Hussein—My Patient

Col. Joe Wood, Chief of Clinical
Operations for Multinational Corps Iraq

THE CALL came from the command surgeon for Multinational Forces Iraq (MNF-I). All detainees came under his authority, and there was one that needed a couple of specialists. I kept the list of where all the doctors were and what their specialties were. The MNF-I doc asked me to locate two specialists. One needed to be an endocrinologist and the other was a cardiologist. I told him he was in luck because I was the only endocrinologist in theater and I could get a hold of the cardiologist. When I asked what it was about I was told that I would have to be briefed in person.

> "The day of the LORD is near for all nations. As you have done, it will be done to you; your deeds will return upon your own head." (Obadiah 1:15)

In my briefing I learned that I would be seeing Saddam Hussein. I ended up seeing him as a patient several times. I diagnosed him with primary hyper-aldosteronism from an adrenal mass. It was a logistical nightmare to get the testing supplies and samples out of theater, but I executed the task I had been given. I remained his endocrinologist while he was a prisoner.

I was torn with the idea of providing care for someone who was so evil. I read the battle reports daily and could not help but feel that so much of the death and destruction was on this man's hands. It was hard to not let that emotional bias affect the way I treated him. It was difficult to reconcile internally, but I decided that I had to treat him as I would any other human. I had to be consistent in my approach even when dealing with such evil. It was ultimately empowering to my faith to know that I treated him no differently though he had given this country nothing but evil.

Prayer:
Dear Lord, help me never forget that every human being
is made in your image. Thank you for the assurance
that you are the ultimate judgment of every soul.

Saddam Hussein (Continued)

Col. Joe Wood, Chief of Clinical
Operations for Multinational Corps Iraq

PRIOR TO seeing Saddam, I wondered how I would feel since he was one of the most notorious dictators in our time; it was a curious thing to ponder. When I actually saw him I went into what I think of as "doctor mode." It almost surprised me to feel pretty much as I always do when I see a new patient for the first time. I treated him as any patient, my duty was to listen and assist in any way I could.

One specific time when I did a thyroid exam, it really occurred to me that what I was doing was pretty incredible; .

Read Psalm 112

I do the exam standing behind the patient and palpate the thyroid with both hands encircling the patient's neck so I thought, I wonder how many people have ever had their hands around his neck and lived to tell about it! I recall also thinking when I saw him that his change in status was pretty incredible (dictator to prisoner); going from a position of absolute power and incredible wealth to being a caged human. I worked in one of his palaces and saw some of his other palaces so I had an idea of his wealth.

We spoke some, but primarily through an interpreter and always about strictly clinical matters. He did cooperate with my exams, however there was a period when I was performing the cranial nerve exam where I had him puff out his cheeks, grimace, etc. It seemed he thought that I was perhaps trying to make him appear silly or something because he gave me a kind of stern look like *Why are you asking me to do this.* I explained to his interpreter and Saddam then looked at me, smiled, placed his hand over his chest and extended his arm as to gesture "go ahead."

Prayer:
"Father, draw me close and allow me to be someone that fears you, and takes great delight in your commands. I have seen that the wicked man wastes away and his longings have come to nothing. I pray that I would seek out compassion and righteousness and conduct my affairs with justice."

Danger in the Air

Col. Joe Wood, Chief of Clinical
Operations for Multinational Corps Iraq

I INITIALLY FLEW into Baghdad from Ali AL Salem Air Base in Kuwait. I recall the ride out to the plane and boarding and having feelings of "well, this is finally it; all these years of army training and now doing the real thing, going into a combat zone." It was a somber and reflective time on the flight into Iraq. I remember hoping that everything would be fine on the flight.

One of the pilots of the C-130 asked if I wanted to fly up front in the cockpit. I remember looking down from high above Iraq thinking how bleak the desert looked and why humans ever inhabited this part of the world. Once we got close to Baghdad, the pilots put on their body armor and directed me to do the same. One of the crew was looking out the windows for surface to air missiles, and the plane went into a combat flight mode and dropped like a rock out of

> "My Spirit remains among you. Do not fear." (Haggai 2:5)

the sky. The descent was pretty rapid and in a tight banking maneuver that generated some significant force. I tried to take some pictures but it was difficult due to the gravitational force of the maneuvers. Seemed a bit like a roller coaster ride.

In my role, flying was required for longer distances. Once, flying back to Iraq from a conference in Kuwait, our C-130 was locked on and fired at from the ground. There were explosions and sparks; it looked like fireworks. I could see light briefly from the windows out each side of the aircraft as the flares were deployed. Thankfully, not every flight was as memorable as that one was.

Prayer:
Dear God, please fill me today with your Spirit.
In place of fear, please give me your courage and love.

Selfless Service

Col. Joe Wood, Chief of Clinical
Operations for Multinational Corps Iraq

I WAS IMPRESSED by the selfless service of those I served with. They put their lives on the line and remained dedicated to each other and the mission even if there were political decisions behind the mission they did not necessarily support. The self-sacrifice and service was present at many levels. It was inspiring to see selflessness in the face of hardship and physical danger. Firefighters and law enforcement live in a service role and understand the strength and honor that comes from service and sacrifice, but the average citizen misses the benefits of service for the most part.

> "Not so with you. Instead, whoever wants to become great among you must be your servant, and whoever wants to be first must be slave of all. For even the Son of Man did not come to be served, but to serve, and to give his life as a ransom for many." (Mark 10:43–45)

I believe any time that we participate in some act of selfless service we draw closer to God's plan and experience his strength while working through adversity. This is most true for those at home. Our families were the true unsung heroes. They were not afforded the recognition but paid the same price. They often do not choose the sacrifice but bear the burden of both the loved one in harm's way and the weight of keeping the family and home running in our absence. With the uncertainty of not knowing when or if their loved one would return, I believe they showed as much strength and courage as anyone deployed.

I emailed my wife a couple of times a week and called home usually once a week to speak to her and my daughter. I also usually called my parents a couple of times a month. People did reach out to help my wife doing various things around the house and helping out with our daughter. I was struck by the warm outreach of family and friends with whom we had not previously had much contact; their letters, gift packages and other kind gestures comforted me and left a lasting impression upon me. I recall thinking if we each reached out to an acquaintance with the same kind of kindness, what a better world we would live in.

Prayer:
Thank you, Lord, that Jesus was willing to give his life as a ransom for many. By shedding his blood, our sins were forgiven. By his wounds, we were healed. By his resurrection, we have the assurance of eternal life.

Situational Awareness

Maj. John Croushorn, MD (retired veteran)

M ARK TARGET." The comment came over the internal communication system from the other crew chief. We were always scanning the environment for threats, and he found something. It was a large weapon with two barrels hidden beneath the palms. Though only a glimpse, it was enough for him to identify what appeared to be an antiaircraft gun. With those words the pilot pressed a key and recorded the GPS location of the gun emplacement. We continued on our mission, and the location was relayed to higher headquarters. An unmanned aerial vehicle was dispatched to the location to reconnoiter and verify. The call came back to the helicopter about twenty minutes later that indeed it was an AA gun emplacement and though unmanned appeared to be operational.

> "Be self-controlled and alert. Your enemy the devil prowls around like a roaring lion looking for someone to devour." (1 Peter 5:8)

It was destroyed, but it highlighted how vulnerable you can be if you're not aware of the situation or circumstance you are in. The helicopter had flown right over it. We were all scanning, yet only one in the helicopter saw it.

First Peter 5:8 calls us to be alert. However being alert in our society for most people means simply to be awake. That is not what is being communicated in the passage of this verse or the intent that God has for us as people of faith. Situational awareness captures that concept better for me. It is not complicated. Situational awareness is being aware of the situation that you're in. It's a simple concept. It involves knowing what risks are around you, your circumstances, your capabilities, and resources that you can bring to bear if that situation changes, and an unspoken intensity of focus on each of those factors. Situational awareness is to an extent, hypervigilance—it's not just being awake. What an indispensable concept for a soldier, especially one who is a Christian!

To have situational awareness in a convoy means you are visually and mentally engaged. Your eyes are constantly scanning for threats and resources. If something happens to change the situation, then your awareness of that situation will help you survive. I'm scanning, looking for threats both big and small. They can be intentional threats, such as people trying to hurt us, or they can be unintentional threats such as a pothole in the road, telephone wires that we might fly into, children nearby that we would have to avoid if they darted in front of us suddenly, or a brewing disturbance or distraction. Situational awareness allows me to focus my energy at preserving my role in the mission.

Prayer:
Father, help me to be aware of my circumstance. May my focus be on you instead of the situation. Help me not to be distracted from noticing what you are doing around me and when and where I should act.

DECEMBER 2

Army Values: Personal Courage

Maj. John Croushorn, MD (retired veteran)

ON NOVEMBER 12, 2004, a Blackhawk helicopter from the 1/106th CAB was shot down in one of the first aerial ambushes in Iraq. The right side pilot was hit by an RPG and lost her legs and had a severely damaged arm. The two crew chiefs were both wounded. The left side crew chief was wounded when a round came up through the floor of the aircraft and penetrated his seat and hitting his buttock. The AK-47 round did not penetrate his pelvis but it did crack it. The right side crew chief lost a portion of the bone in his lower leg.

The only one not to be wounded in the initial flurry of explosions and small arms fire was the left seat pilot in command, Dan Milburn. In the disarray that followed the initial explosion, his mind switched over to the training and years of experience that instinctively told his muscles what to do. Blackhawks without hydraulics are very hard to control, and he was losing hydraulic pressure fast. In a miraculous feat the warrant officer guided the falling rock out of the kill

"Therefore, since we are surrounded by such a great cloud of witnesses, let us throw off everything that hinders and the sin that so easily entangles, and let us run with perseverance the race marked out for us. Let us fix our eyes on Jesus, the author and perfecter of our faith, who for the joy set before him endured the cross, scorning its shame, and sat down at the right hand of the throne of God." (Hebrews 12:1–2) zone and landed the aircraft upright. Without communications, he was unable to initiate a call for help, so he reflexively got out of the aircraft and began helping everyone else out. His crew wounded, his aircraft destroyed he did not lose composure in the midst of the emergency. His personal courage and the ability to act despite fear saved the lives of his crew.

Personal courage is displayed in many ways and in many circumstances. Stories of courage while facing extreme personal danger are motivating examples of the inner strength we all hope to have. The hope is solidified when we face the stress and do the right thing despite the fear.

"Courage is resistance to fear, mastery of fear, not the absence of fear."—Mark Twain

"Courage is doing what you are afraid to do. There can be no courage unless you are scared."—Eddie Rickenbacker, World War I Fighter Pilot

Prayer:
Lord, I want to throw off any entanglements, fix my eyes on Jesus, and run with perseverance. Please strengthen and perfect my faith in the weeks, months, and years to come.

DECEMBER 3

History of PTSD

Frank Vozenilek, Viet Nam veteran, Point Man International Ministries

POST-TRAUMATIC stress disorder has a long history. Moses directed the commanders of the returning Hebrew warriors to encamp the army outside the Hebrew camp for the required cleansing period of seven days (Numbers 31:19). He also directed those who had slain or come in contact with a dead body to purify themselves according to the Hebrew laws on the third and again on the seventh days. Only then could these soldiers who had seen and tasted battle be allowed into the camp amongst their families once again.

Why? Not only because of the blood-borne disease they potentially came in contact with but, according to Jewish rabbinical clarification, it was because of the mental and emotional anguish the army had been put through in combat. God knew—and knows—the emotional pain soldiers feel when they see a comrade cut down before their eyes, or when they, who have been raised to respect human life, are now in a position to take life. These events traumatize the emotions and the psyche of the human being. God, in his wisdom, set forth the purification laws to counteract these traumas.

> "The LORD is close to the broken-hearted and saves those who are crushed in spirit." (Psalm 34:18)

Now fast forward to American military history. In the Civil War, the condition—*Soldier's Heart*—was recorded as shock-like symptoms along with mental and emotional symptoms. In World War I it was called *shell shock*. In World War II and Korea the problem was known as *battle fatigue*, and in Vietnam, *combat stress*. PTSD was finally recognized as a *mental/anxiety disorder* 1984.

Those with PTSD have severe problems trusting anyone and sharing that they have PTSD (if they even recognize it). But church laypeople can be trained to identify the outward displays and the internal feelings of a combat veteran. This basic training can be enough to help identify the problems:

- Get prayer support
- Make referrals to support systems
- Be able to support as a concerned layperson within the community.

Prayer:
Lord, make me more sensitive to the needs of returning veterans and their families; show me how to support them.

DECEMBER 4

Couples Facing Separation Is Tough

Don Richards, Psychologist Counseling Military Veterans

MARK RETURNED home in the spring. It was the end of his second deployment. He and his wife had discussed the toll on their young family, and he was exiting military service. Although they were both committed Christians, the deployment had been very difficult. He had been involved in combat operations in Ramadi and Fallujah. But the combat wasn't the only stress that tore at them. A year of separation and the stress of a young marriage and new baby were weighting both of them when he returned. There were signs that coming home would not be as easy as either had imagined. They expected the stress level to decrease, but instead it increased on his return.

Whether stress is combat or noncombat related, the signs are going to occur in the same way. The marriage relationship is often one of the first red flags. The husband may not feel needed. The wife may not be handling the return of the husband very well. For months she has handled the day-to-day needs of their family. There may be unique characteristics and a personality that was not present before he or she left, like temper outbursts or bouts of depression, anxiety symptoms, a pattern of withdrawal from social situations that were not there before the deployment. The couple may have difficulty connecting emotionally. If either spouse is having trouble adjusting to a return from deployment, primarily it becomes evident within the marriage relationship.

> "Wives, understand and support your husbands by submitting to them in ways that honor the Master. Husbands, go all out in love for your wives. Don't take advantage of them." (Colossians 3:18-19, THE MESSAGE)

If a person is unable to get through the adjustment and deal with the stress and separation as well as the stress brought about in war, then it is an issue (not a character flaw) that needs intervention. Be watchful for the warning signs and reach out for help. Without help someone who was highly functional becomes chronically less functional. The signs are not subtle. They are red flags snapping back and forth in the wind.

Prayer:

Dear God, please help me cherish, love, and respect
my spouse. Where there is strife, please bring peace.
Where there is hurt, please bring healing.

Don Richards is a psychologist that provides faith-based counseling to military veterans and has a history of dealing with combat veterans from Vietnam to Iraq and Afghanistan. He incorporates faith and counseling that focuses beyond the traumatic. America's wars have resulted in many mental and emotional casualties and men like Don are waging the fight to restore these men and women.

Families and Extended Deployment

Don Richards, Psychologist Counseling Military Veterans

PENDING SEPARATION is difficult; communication and preparation must take place. The shock of it all is often too difficult for most to deal with effectively.

One soldier shared with me:

> It was approaching Thanksgiving. Our unit had been notified of the deployment but we were not authorized to tell our families yet. It was a relief because most people did not know how to begin to give that news. Then without warning we were gathered together. The commander said, "The local news is going to release the story about our pending deployment tonight. If you don't want your family finding out that way, go home and tell them now." It was a gut-wrenching drive home. My wife and I went for a walk, and I broke the news. She was floored. Her worst nightmare had begun. How do you give that kind of news? How do you prepare to leave home?

There is no easy way to prepare for separation. Especially regarding deployment to a combat zone. There are numerous issues with fear, vulnerability, and shifting responsibilities. There is no easy way to begin that conversation. What is certain is that the communication must begin, and it must continue as deployment approaches.

The family needs a secure and strong support network. Those families who don't already have one need to be very deliberate in finding and establishing one. They need to be very dedicated until they develop this. They cannot let any of the personal struggles that they are experiencing get in the way of establishing a strong support group. A support group should include

> "Wives, submit to your husbands as to the Lord. For the husband is the head of the wife as Christ is the head of the church, his body, of which he is the Savior. Now as the church submits to Christ, so also wives should submit to their husbands in everything. Husbands, love your wives, just as Christ loved the church and gave himself up for her."
> (Ephesians 5:22–25)

some one who has experienced the same trial of separation or at least somebody who's been through something very difficult and who has had to lean on somebody else.

In addition to the work needed before the deployment begins, deployed soldiers should stay in contact and communicate as much as they can once they have left. Fortunately the mechanisms that exist today for communication back home far exceed those in past wars. Deployed soldiers have easy access to phones, and the lines of communication allow for speech, text, and video in many places.

Though technology has made it easier for military personnel to connect with loved ones, it is always difficult to communicate the personal struggles and trials of deployment with our families back home. The deployed soldier should avoid describing traumatic experiences. One must realize that the circumstance around our communication is anything but normal. The stresses on each person are so unique, and there is so much separation that families have a difficult time appreciating the stress of being thousands of miles away in harms person.

Prayer:
Dear God, when I must prepare to leave my spouse, whether for a day or year, please lead, guide, and direct my spouse and me. Keep our hearts knit together before we say our goodbyes.

DECEMBER 6

Dealing with Stress

Don Richards, Psychologist Counseling Military Veterans

ONE SOLDIER commented:

The quietness was uncomfortable. Only a few hours ago I was in combat. A man died; he was sitting in the place I was supposed to be. It should have been me. Life ends so quickly. Now I'm safe and they are preparing him to go home. I have to let my family know I am okay if the news reports anything. But how do you call home after an event like that? How do I let them know I am okay without scaring them?

Some people share everything with their families. I think that is a mistake. It is not their role to live the trauma with you. They are trying to survive a different stress, and those descriptions only add to weight they must carry. It is equally true that you shouldn't hide everything from them. After a while it will build such a barrier between you that nothing significant is shared.

> Husbands, in the same way be considerate as you live with your wives, and treat them with respect as the weaker partner and as heirs with you of the gracious gift of life, so that nothing will hinder your prayer."
> (1 Peter 3:7)

There is an advantage in discussing the possibility of this type of experiences prior to deployment. The weeks leading up to deployment are stressful, and many couples elect to not discuss anything related to the approaching separation. They fear that it will only lead to argument and distance. This just illustrates how stress levels increase dramatically even before the loved one leaves. Most people do not understand that level of stress. These issues require a support group, someone to facilitate the emotional groundwork required to make it through the deployment.

The deployed soldier can compartmentalize the stress given the relative simplicity of deployed life. (After all, cooking and laundry are handled for you.) Families at home have a much different environment in which to survive. Despite the day's traumatic events, milk and bread must still be purchased, dinner must be made, dishes and laundry must be tended to, children must be cleaned and fed and tucked in bed and then they struggle to get enough sleep to start it all over again the next day. This is done in communities that largely do not recognize them or the trial their families are going through. There is pitifully weak support in most of America for deployed families, and very few who understand the severity of the stress they endure.

Prayer:
Dear God, use the books like this one and Faith Deployed to raise awareness for the need to support the families of those serving in the armed forces in Iraq, Afghanistan, and elsewhere around the world.

Post-Traumatic Stress Syndrome

Don Richards, Psychologist Counseling Military Veterans

ANOTHER SOLDIER commented:

> I saw a lot of combat. Our unit took casualties in Najaf and Fallujah. I don't have to talk about it when I am around my guys, and I don't know how to talk about it when I am around friends from back home. I don't know if I have PTSD or not. When I am around my guys I feel fine; when I am around my family or friends they just don't understand. I can't relate to them. I struggle even to want to relate to them.

There is a saying that PTSD (now referred to as PTSS or Post-Traumatic Stress Syndrome), goes away when the victim is around other vets. Do soldiers stop suffering from PTSS around comrades or is it that the events are more understood and the stress reduced when they are with those who share the experience?

It is human nature to feel more comfortable around those who are familiar with our experience. That's true for PTSS regardless of whether it's from combat experience or sexual abuse. That's why we have groups for PTSS. There is a significant comfort that comes from not having to explain yourself or why an experience was traumatic.

> "Dear friend, I pray that you may enjoy good health and that all may go well with you, even as your soul is getting along well." (3 John:2)

Let me emphasize that someone should not base a decision about whether or not to seek help on the way he or she feels or behaves around others who went through the same experience. PTSS is the way those experiences effect a soldier outside that circle of comrades and friends. It is the way it affects his or her relationships with family and friends, coworkers, and supervisors. If those relationships are suffering or if one's ability to function in civilian life is affected by traumatic experiences then that person should seek help.

It's not how the veteran relates to other veterans but rather how he relates to his family and his obligations once he returns home, that is the question. This is one area the veteran should lean upon family. Trust their impressions. Comrades may be unable to tell whether or not a fellow soldier's experiences are affecting the ability to function. A soldier's family however, knows their loved one. Family members can more easily detect dysfunction and adjustment stress.

Prayer:
Please bring your healing to my loved one or friend or fellow church member who is suffering from PTSS. May he/she receive the professional and personal support that is needed.

DECEMBER 8

The Importance of Debriefing

Don Richards, Psychologist Counseling Military Veterans

ONE SOLDIER shared this story:

We hot-washed everything. Debriefing immediately after an action was a definite force multiplier. That meant when we returned from an operation we talked about what happened—the good, the bad and the ugly. It was essential that we not lose the value of experiences that we paid for with blood, sweat and a great deal of effort. There was another benefit though; everyone understood what happened more clearly. Those close to people who were wounded weren't allowed to sulk in personal pity. They realized they did their job and the injury wasn't due to their actions or inactions. It enabled them to get back up on the horse. Reality was we were going back out tomorrow and our heads had to be in the game, and not replaying yesterday's events."

Cognitive rehabilitation is the process of evaluating an event and framing it in a progressively more healthy way. It is one of the primary tools in treating Post Traumatic Stress Syndrome (PTSS). The reality is the earlier it is done the more profound the ability to deal with traumatic events. Units that advocate early debriefing with an emphasis on cognitive rehabilitation will see fewer PTSS casualties.

Early debriefing does appear to change the impact of traumatic events. I have seen this and try to incorporate it not only among my military experience but in the emergency department. If something bad happens it is very worthwhile to take my nurses and techs involved and let them know that they did everything right and they weren't responsible for something bad happening.

I would have to say that from my experience that early debriefing is the most valuable tool in preventing damage from traumatic events. I don't have the luxury of being with them immediately after an event. If early debriefing was done effectively I wouldn't be unraveling significant psychological issues and trying to break down defensive postures my patients have established over the years. Perhaps I would only be focusing on more practical issues of adjustment. If debriefing was done

> "I will stand at my watch and station myself on the ramparts; I will look to see what he will say to me, and what answer I am to give to this complaint." (Habakkuk 2:1)

well it would diffuse a great deal of distress and issues involved in post-traumatic stress syndrome.

Prayer:
Dear Lord, please help those in combat situations today to receive the early debriefing they need. Please protect them from PTSS.

Concern and Help So Necessary

Don Richards, Psychologist Counseling Military Veterans

THIS SOLDIER'S wife told her story:

Our neighbors were always nice to me. I do not believe they had any idea how hard it was keeping things going alone. The struggle was beyond what I thought I could bear. I did not know how to keep going. Occasionally someone would offer to help. At first I didn't feel comfortable accepting the help, but as the months passed by it became easier, especially from those who had gone through a similar situation. The help offered was inconsistent and although it was a nice gesture, it was brief, and rarely enough to feel like I had a real break.

It is important to initiate contact and reach out to families separated by deployment. They need time, and help with daily tasks, and often their responsibilities leave no time to call and ask for help. The contact can be as simple as a phone call, a loaf of pumpkin bread in the mailbox, a card on the door, ribbon on the house, mowing the grass without being asked, food on the doorstep. Anything that reminds spouses at home that they are not alone is support. If they have children, plan to entertain the kids, or get a gift certificate to a spa and watch the kids while they get pampered.

Many people ask how they can help? I tell them whatever you do for your family do for them. If you wash your car or your spouse's car then go and wash their car. If you cut the grass go and do that. If you cook then prepare a meal. Don't ask, just do. They will not tell you what they need.

One man from the church stated:

> "David replied, 'No, my brothers, you must not do that with what the LORD has given us. He has protected us and handed over to us the forces that came against us. Who will listen to what you say? The share of the man who stayed with the supplies is to be the same as that of him who went down to the battle. All will share alike.' David made this a statute and ordinance for Israel from that day to this.'"
> (1 Samuel 30:23–25)

It got to the point that I couldn't tell her I was going to cut the grass, because she would drop what she was doing and cut the grass before I arrived. I would wait until I turned on their street and then call.

Our churches also should support these families in the same way as it does when a member is undergoing severe trial. It's much the same as somebody who has a family member who is dying with cancer. Recognizing the trial and praying openly for them is very comforting and empowering.

During the observance of Veterans Day and Memorial Day, it's very important to emphasize the service and sacrifice of these families. They give a unique gift to our country and need to be recognized. The recognition is not for their benefit alone, it is also helpful to guide the focus of the fellowship and stimulate the support that is so needed by these families.

Prayer:
Dear God, please use me in my church to help raise awareness, support, and practical assistance for the families of soldiers serving overseas.

Looking to God

Don Richards, Psychologist Counseling Military Veterans

ANOTHER SOLDIER shared this insight:

"I do not know how guys get through the experience of combat without an anchor to reality like my faith provides me. I had heard the saying that there are no atheists in foxholes but I saw a different picture. Sure, most of those I was around professed belief in God, but those that didn't weren't convinced of his presence after combat, many were just shocked—they were numbed. The frailty of life is not lost on those who do not believe in God."

The deploying soldier should prioritize their time and take advantage of the faith-based resources the military offers while deployed. Chaplains are a part of the military and their heritage extends all the way back to our country's founding. They accompany troops on deployment and a vital part of the support base for soldiers deployed abroad. The enemy views them as morale officers. They do serve a vital function that effects morale, but beyond that they can also serve as the anchor to the faith that is so core to most of us.

Going into potentially traumatic events without a connection to your faith is no different than going into a combat zone without a weapon. You also wouldn't head into combat without body armor. An active pursuit of a relationship with God, including dealing with doubt and the fundamental questions that arise when you're in a situation like combat are as important as any

"Finally, be strong in the Lord and in his mighty power. Put on the full armor of God so that you can take your stand against the devil's schemes. For our struggle is not against flesh and blood, but against the rulers, against the authorities, against the powers of this dark world and against the spiritual forces of evil in the heavenly realms. Therefore put on the full armor of God, so that when the day of evil comes, you may be able to stand your ground, and after you have done everything, to stand. Stand firm . . ." (Ephesians 6:10–14) other preparation of battle. For you to return home safe and of sound mind you must be able to ask those kinds of questions and seek help to find the answers. How could a loving God allow things that happen in war to go on?

These are significant questions that we know arise in most people. The ability to point the individual to a sovereign God who truly is above and over the situation is enabling. The structure of having chaplains conducting worship services and Bible studies along with individual counseling is imperative for soldiers of faith who are in perilous circumstances.

Body armor obviously protects the body. The armor of God protects the soul, your faith, and sometimes your sanity.

Prayer:
Thank you so much for the countless thousands of soldiers who have truly committed their lives to Jesus Christ while serving in Iraq and Afghanistan. Please continue to bring thousands more to Christ. Give them Your full armor, God, so they can stand their ground against the Devil's schemes.

DECEMBER 11

Grenade Attack

Capt. David Graves, Officer with a Provisional Reconstruction Team

IT WAS AUGUST 31, 2006. We had gone down to Anbar, the same city they had found Saddam Hussein hiding in a hole. It's on the east side of the Tigris, about fifteen miles south of Tikrit. FOB Spiecher was on the north side of Tikrit so it was about a forty-five minute drive from the base. We made it down there by riding with another unit that I was not comfortable with. Part of our mission was to inspect the courthouses and determine whether or not they needed computers, a holding facility, or other infrastructure needs.

The insurgency was heating up all around us. Fortunately our convoy down to Anbar was uneventful.

After we arrived we began the meeting with the Iraqi judge in the courthouse. In the meeting was an Air Force JAG colonel I was working for, an interpreter, and a major from the unit that took us down there and myself. Outside, our guys were pulling security. After a while the security guys came up to remind us that we'd been there for about thirty to thirty-five minutes and said that we needed to be getting on the road. We wrapped things up and headed outside.

We were stepping back out to the vehicles to get ready to leave. The courthouse was set at one of the main intersections in the city. Here was a traditional Iraqi compound with a five-foot high concrete wall surrounding the courthouse complex. The guys had turned the vehicles around and were ready to head out. Another mission completed.

We had received a brief earlier that morning to let us know that there was another convoy approaching our area. It was a familiarization convoy to allow new unit commanders to see the area and get familiar with everything around them.

I opened the door to my truck to get into the Tactical Convoy Commander (TCC) position, put my weapon into the vehicle, and saw the first vehicle of the other convoy come through the intersection. As I put my gun down I heard what sounded at the time as a gunshot. In my experience in Iraq you would hear gunfire all the time. The police at times directed traffic by shooting AK-47s. Gunfire didn't really send up much of a red flag for us.

What had actually happened was an insurgent had thrown a grenade at us. The grenade hit the top of the wall around the compound. It sounded muffled in sound, like a gunshot to me. I don't know why it landed outside the wall instead of inside the wall. There was a lot that would happen that day I would not understand.

> "Yours, O LORD, is the greatness and the power and the glory and the majesty and the splendor, for everything in heaven and earth is yours. Yours, O LORD, is the kingdom; you are exalted as head over all. Wealth and honor come from you; you are the ruler of all things. In your hands are strength and power to exalt and give strength to all. Now, our God, we give you thanks, and praise your glorious name."
> (1 Chronicles 29:11–13)

Prayer:
Lord, thank you that in everything, even war, you rule over all.
Yours is the kingdom and the power and the glory forever. Amen.

David Graves was an officer with a provisional reconstruction team in Iraq in 2006.

More Grenades

Capt. David Graves, Officer with
a Provisional Reconstruction Team

AFTER THE grenade exploded, I grabbed my weapon and turned around and started looking. I couldn't find anybody to engage. It seemed like a typical insurgent attack. Fire and run. There was nothing to shoot at, so we went ahead and loaded up in the truck. I again set my rifle down and climbed in. What we did not know was that the grenade was used to try to flush us out and push us into the ambush. They had set up on the Main Supply Route (MSR) about a block down from us. By now the other convoy was coming through the intersection and the lead truck was about a block down.

> "When your people go to war against their enemies, wherever you send them, and when they pray to the LORD ... then hear from heaven their prayer and their plea, and uphold their cause."
> (1 Kings 8:44–45)

The insurgents threw hand grenades from the rooftops down onto the other convoy. There were two hand grenades that hit the last truck. These were not regular hand grenades. They were RPK-3 Russian antitank grenades with a shaped charge in the front end of the grenade. The first RPK-3 hit right in front of the Tactical Convoy Commander position and blew a basketball-sized hole in the top of the armored truck. It peeled the steel plate down with the full force of the blast and shrapnel going straight into the TCC's lap.

The second hand grenade hit right above the right rear tire. When the explosion happened I could see debris flying up into the air. That visually stuck with me as the most vivid damage from that engagement. I could not see the vehicle when it was hit. The building shielded it from our view at the time of the attack. I got on the radio and ordered the convoy to get out into the intersection and help these guys out. Then we pulled out into the intersection. The convoy commander had turned around and come back through the ambush and was sitting at the intersection. He and I did a quick frequency swap so that we could talk from inside the Humvees. He confirmed to us that he did not have contact with his entire convoy. They had lost their fourth truck.

The TCC's body armor and chest plate basically saved the life of the guy behind him. The explosion had knocked everyone unconscious. The truck went down to the end of the block and veered off down a side street and ran into the side of a building. The radios were dead. No one knew where they were. It was a scary ten minutes for their convoy commander.

I called back to the battalion headquarters at Spiecher to get the Apaches spun up. We needed some air support. The convoy commander went to help find his truck. We held the south part of the ambush site at the intersection. What was coming next? How coordinated was this attack? The minutes eased by, and tension didn't break.

Prayer:
In the worst of situations, Lord, please bind my heart to yours. Fill me, guide me, lead me, protect me, and fulfill your purposes in and through me.

Facing Death

Capt. David Graves, Officer with a Provisional Reconstruction Team

THE AMBUSH scene was chaotic. We held the south end of the site, while the other convoy attempted to find its guys.

After about ten to fifteen minutes they found the missing truck. While this was going on, we lost internal contact between the two convoys. Because we were sitting in an exposed intersection, with no one talking to us, we finally decided to move to the north part of town. When you lose communications, it gets very confusing very fast. I got my gunner to use hand and arm signals to get the other truck in the intersection to follow me. We pulled through the ambush site, found the rest of the trucks from the convoys, and loaded the wounded guys on to the truck.

We stopped and triaged the wounded to find out how bad their injuries were. It turned out that the other guys were suffering only minor wounds. About that time the Apaches arrived. We told battalion we didn't need MEDEVAC. We loaded up and drove for forty-five minutes back to Spiecher with Apaches giving over watch. We left the deceased soldier in the Humvee right where he was. The battalion commander from the infantry battalion came down and met us at the one bridge over the Tigris and led us into the base. Guys from the Combat Support Hospital (CSH) came out to remove the casualty from the truck and start processing the body.

Afterwards the guys told me that we were under fire the whole time. I remember being shot at, but it didn't seem like a large volume of fire, and it didn't appear to be very accurate fire. My memory only vaguely recalls that part of the engagement.

The tough part is the thinking about it after the fact. I'm filled with thoughts like *It should have been me. . . . Why did God spare me?* The guy who was killed was twenty-eight years old. He had a wife and two kids. It was his last mission. He was going home after that one mission. It was a difficult thing to swallow.

> "But Ruth replied, "Don't urge me to leave you or to turn back from you. Where you go I will go, and where you stay I will stay. Your people will be my people and your God my God. May the Lord deal with me, be it ever so severely, if anything but death separates you and me." (Ruth 1:16–17)

"Staff Sgt. Michael L. Deason, 28, of Farmington, MO, died on Aug 31, in Ad Dwar, Iraq, of injuries suffered when a grenade detonated on his vehicle during combat operations. Deason was assigned to the 3rd Battalion, 320th Field Artillery Regiment, 3rd Brigade, 101st Airborne Division, Fort Campbell, KY."

Prayer:
Death fills us with grief. God of all comfort, please give an extra measure of your comfort to those who have lost a loved one in combat in Iraq and Afghanistan and the broader war on terrorism.

DECEMBER 14

The Ultimate Sacrifice

Capt. David Graves, Officer with a Provisional Reconstruction Team

THE CONVOY was back on base, and the wounded were tended to. It was all over by about 1 p.m. We had DSN lines in the office that would allow us to call home free of charge. I called my wife that afternoon, but I didn't tell her what happened. I did tell her if she saw anything on the news to know that I am okay. We would watch a lot of the news while we were over there and saw information about how soldiers were killed in Baghdad or some other location. When the media reported where the casualty was based or where the engagement occurred, it can be really scary for the families. They watch every story, and the media didn't miss an opportunity to talk about a U.S. death.

Deason's death never even made the news. That really bothered me. It also surprised me. He didn't even make the news. I can't remember how many soldiers died in the month of August 2006. We were nearing a hundred soldiers killed a month. But the fact that this young staff sergeant, this hero that was on his last mission, the guy that was in ambush meant for me, sitting in my seat, the one that should have been me. . . . This should not have been ignored by the media.

> "'My name will be great among the nations, from the rising to the setting of the sun. In every place incense and pure offerings will be brought to my name, because my name will be great among the nations,' says the Lord Almighty.'"
> (Malachi 1:11)

We should never forget the service and sacrifice. Staff Sgt. Deason and his family made the ultimate sacrifice. We should always remember that.

Prayer:
Dear God, help me never to forget the names of people
I know who made the ultimate sacrifice while serving in combat.
Thank you that your name is great among the nations,
even those who haven't turned to you yet.

DECEMBER 15

Light and Honor

Gina Elliott Kim, daughter of Larry and Jean Elliott, missionaries to Iraq (2004)

WHEN MY parents came through Houston on their way to Iraq in December 2003, they visited my church and shared about the confirmation they received from Psalm 139:9–10 that Iraq was their "far side of the sea." Verses 11 and 12 continue to say, "Surely the darkness will hide me and the light become night around me, even the darkness will not be dark to you; the night will shine like the day, for darkness is as light to you."

Light and honor were two symbols that stood out to me during that Christmas. They also visited my church's Christmas Eve candlelight service. The whole church is dark, except for one little candle held by the pastor. From anywhere in the worship center, one can see this little candle's solitary light. Then that single candle lights another candle. Those two candles light two more and so on. Soon the whole church is lit from the light of one tiny candle. I remember looking at Mom. With tears streaming down her face, she turned to me and said, "That is Iraq! It is a dark, dark nation but we are taking in the light of Christ and we are going to light up that nation with the light of Jesus!"

> "But the word of God continued to increase and spread."
> (Acts 12:24)

And that is what they set out to do, lighting a few candles so those candles could light others, spreading God's word.

Also that Christmas, my family enjoyed our holiday tradition of sharing what the Lord had taught us in the past year and what we looked forward to in the coming year. Although my two brothers and I completely supported my parents' move to Iraq, we were more serious as we shared. My father felt our unspoken concern, and when it was his turn, he said he felt the center of God's will was the safest place to be and, for them, that was Iraq.

"Plus the worst case scenario," he said, "is that we get killed and we go to heaven with Stephen! What an honor we would consider that to be!"

Of course, we did not like hearing that, and no one really thought that they would be martyred like Stephen in the Bible. But what a comfort to know my father considered it an honor to be martyred. He considered it an honor to bring light to darkness no matter the cost.

Prayer:
Father, thank you for the honor of bringing light to darkness. Shine brilliantly through me today, casting your glow and spreading your hope.

Sending My Baby to War

Patti Smith, Mother of two Marines deployed to Iraq in 2005 and 2007, organizer of Operation Santa in the Midwest.

I WANTED TO fall apart right there at the airport, but something came over me. I gently grabbed my Marine son, Josey, by the chin and said, "Now you listen here . . . you come back to me alive and in one piece you understand?" For a brief moment he was my little boy again. His towering six foot six frame could not disguise his eyes filling with tears, lower lip quivering; he could only nod.

"Okay then," I said. "I will talk to you soon."

Surely this was the hardest thing I had ever done—send my baby off to war. My two sons are United States Marines and last year both were deployed at the same time. My youngest, Josey, was the first to go to Iraq.

Patti Smith with sons Josey (left) and Jesse (right) (Color Classics, Peoria, IL)

While home on his pre-deployment leave, I had tried to soak up and savor every moment with him. But now here we were at the Peoria, Illinois, airport. Before leaving America, he would return briefly to his base in California. My heart was breaking; I was so frightened of the unknown journey that laid ahead. I was silently pleaded with God to give me strength to be calm during the parting moments with my son.

> "Even though I walk through the valley of the shadow of death, I will fear no evil, for you are with me; your rod and your staff, they comfort me." (Psalm 23:4)

We hugged one last time, then my husband Greg and I went up to the observation deck and watched his plane take off. I gazed into the sky long after it was out of sight then collapsed on a nearby bench and wept bitterly.

"Please don't let this be the last time I saw my son alive," I begged God. For some mothers, it was.

For me, life began to be lived not one day at a time but rather one breath at a time. As Josey began the first leg of his journey, I began the first steps of my own through the valley of the shadow of death as I watched him fly off to war.

Prayer:
Father, Shepherd, help me trust in your presence today,
even though fear threatens to overwhelm me.

DECEMBER 17

Blessed Be the Name of the Lord

Patti Smith, Mother of two Marines deployed to Iraq in 2005 and 2007, organizer of Operation Santa in the Midwest.

MOM I'm getting ready to leave the States," Josey called to tell me.

"I'm in Germany," was the next announcement.

And finally, "Mom, I'm in Iraq."

With each phone call, I felt as though an elevator was slowly lowering me into the valley of the shadow of death. I would linger in that valley for many months to come.

444

Viewing the nightly news with its images of war and carnage, I would just shake my head. My son was in there somewhere, and I was absolutely powerless to help him. My total dependence came to be my faith in God; but oh how I wavered at times.

A couple of months later, the whole ordeal occurred again when my other son Jesse was deployed. This wasn't fear of the unknown; it was *sheer terror* of the unknown!

Although I have always been healthy, my physical body began to break down during this time. I was seeing a doctor; there was no apparent reason for my symptoms other than internalized stress. It was suggested I get on medication to cope but I refused. Sleeping through the night had become a thing of the past. Naps became my way of life. Awakened every night, I would pray and pray that the angels would protect my sons.

> "The LORD gave and the LORD has taken away; may the name of the LORD be praised." (Job 1:21b)

Car lights shining down our street at night would make me hysterical. I would run to the window to see if it was a government vehicle with two Marines coming to deliver dreaded news. If so, which son would it be?

One day I received an email from a friend and fellow Marine mom in another state. Her son was serving with Josey. It read, "Two Marines in dress blues just left our home. Our son Joe was killed yesterday. The Lord gives and the Lord takes away. Blessed be the name of the Lord." I screamed aloud when I read it.

Prayer:
Lord, strengthen my faith in you so that when tragedy strikes I may still praise your name.

DECEMBER 18

Reunion

Patti Smith, Mother of two Marines deployed to Iraq in 2005 and 2007, organizer of Operation Santa in the Midwest.

THOUGHTS OF my sons being in danger haunted me day and night. As president of our local military support group, I still had many responsibilities to carry on—meetings to conduct, support to give others, and service projects to complete.

During this time, I delivered two condolence books to mothers of fallen soldiers. After praying and crying with them, I would drive away from their home begging God, "Please don't let me be next." I felt the shadow of death as a constant dark weight over my spirit and body.

Finally, the day came for me to attend Josey's homecoming in Twenty-nine Palms, California, along with Kelly, his girlfriend at the time (now his wife). While we waited for his returning bus, the wounded from Josey's company walked among us. Some had limbs missing, were in wheelchairs, one was on crutches. The faces of handsome young men were scarred from burns. As they walked through the crowd, spontaneous applause broke out.

> "I will say of the LORD, 'He is my refuge and my fortress, my God in whom I trust.' . . .You will not fear the terror of night, nor the arrow that flies by day, nor the pestilence that stalks in the darkness, nor the plague that destroys at midday." (Psalm 91:2, 5–6)

Nearby on a table was a beautiful patriotic quilt. We all signed it for a family who's Marine would not be returning home, yet that family was there to support the rest of us. The look on their faces was haunting. How unfair it all seemed. While this family heroically supported the fellow Marines of their fallen son, I thought my heart would burst in anticipation of my own son's arrival.

The moment we were reunited paralleled only with the moment of his birth. I wanted to collapse from relief. I couldn't quit crying. We embraced and I sobbed, "Josey, I was so afraid I would never see you alive again."

"I'm home, Mom," he said. It seemed such a miracle to me.

And that was my turning point. My health began to improve. A few months later I would experience the victory of my other son's homecoming.

Prayer:

Lord, I praise you for being a trustworthy God, no matter what dangers and trials surround me and those I love.

Semper Fidelis

Patti Smith, Mother of two Marines deployed to Iraq in 2005 and 2007, organizer of Operation Santa in the Midwest.

TODAY, JOSEY is once again in Iraq. This past week the Peoria area has lost a Marine; I will attend those services, and deliver yet another condolence book. I will grieve with the mother of that fallen Marine and again ask God to spare my own son's life, like the persistent widow who never tires of making her case before the one who holds the matter in his control (Luke 18:1–8).

> "God, who has called you into fellowship with his Son Jesus Christ our Lord, is faithful."
> (1 Corinthians 1:9)

I'm not sleeping through the night again, but it's okay. The Lord awakens me to pray for my son's safety, and I'm happy to do it. In the dark and quiet hours when most others are deep in slumber, it's my privilege to trade the comfort of my bed for the honor of interceding on behalf of my son as he serves his country on the other side of the world.

Somehow it's better this time. Despair is not allowed to consume me as it once did. Although living through the deployments of my sons has been excruciatingly painful, I sense a deep strengthening has taken place. I still do not know what tomorrow holds . . . but I do know *him* who holds tomorrow—I place my trust in Jesus.

The first stanza of the old hymn classic "Be Still My Soul" says:

Be still, my soul: the Lord is on thy side.
Bear patiently the cross of grief or pain.
Leave to thy God to order and provide;
In every change, He faithful will remain.
Be still, my soul: thy best, thy heavenly Friend
Through thorny ways leads to a joyful end.

(http://www.cyberhymnal.org/htm/b/e/bestill.htm)

Let me ask you this. If you are not trusting in God, where will you go? To whom will you turn?

The motto of the United States Marine Corps is *Semper Fidelis*, which is Latin for *always faithful*. Let me encourage you to hold on to God and don't let go. For God is *Semper Fidelis!*

Prayer:
Lord, help me today to strive to be as
faithful to you as you are to me always.

DECEMBER 20

Operation Santa

Patti Smith, Mother of two Marines deployed to Iraq in 2005 and 2007, organizer of Operation Santa in the Midwest.

DURING JOSEY'S first deployment, instead of exchanging Christmas gifts, my husband and I agreed to outfit our son's platoon (forty Marines) each with a Christmas care package. Researching the internet for the best items to ship, a list was given to everyone I saw or knew along with a request for funds for shipping.

> "For we are God's workmanship, created in Christ Jesus to do good works, which God prepared in advance for us to do."
> (Ephesians 2:10)

The task seemed insurmountable. But enough came in for two hundred Marines— and we were just getting started. Operation Santa has grown to become the largest Christmas drive for the troops in the Midwest. Just three years later, by 2008, we shipped more than thirty thousand Christmas stockings to troops.

I serve as full-time volunteer for our beloved troops and veterans putting in fourteen-hour days working the telephone, Internet, and public speaking to raise awareness and funds. Operation Santa (www.operationsanta.info) is sponsored by Central Illinois Proud Families of Marines, a 501c3 organization which I co-founded, and for which I serve as president.

School children through senior citizens are involved with sewing stockings and writing personal notes. Businesses, civic clubs, veterans groups, families, individuals from all walks of life turn out to stuff the stockings. Our local Post Office comes to our location to pick up the

On behalf of my Marines and Sailors, I would like to take the time to thank you and everyone else responsible for the wonderful stockings. We truly appreciate this noble gesture because we can see that somebody took some of their personal time to make the stockings to include filling them. My men and women noticed this and were deeply touched by the kindness and generosity displayed. Gestures like these truly make everything we do worthwhile because it tells us that America cares about their men and women who are out here serving their country. Being away from our loved ones during the holidays is difficult, but we knew and understood the sacrifices we would be making when we signed on the dotted line. It truly is an honor and pleasure to serve our country. Once again, please thank every person who contributed to the wonderful stockings on behalf of the RED DRAGONS. We would also like to wish you and your families Happy Holidays and may God bless you all as well.

> "Greater love has no man than this, that he lay down his life for his friends." (John 15:13)

SgtMaj Diaz, Red Dragons

◆◆

Men and Women of the Central Illinois Proud Families of Marines, I received several boxes of stocking from your organization over the past couple weeks. Tonight I passed them out to my company. Needless to say, they were very well received. A small token from home goes a long way. For many of my Paratroopers, this will be their first Christmas away from home. For other Soldiers, like myself, it is yet another Christmas away from home (four years in a row I have spent Christmas in a new country!). For all of us, the stockings are a token demonstrating that there are great Americans back home who support us and make our daily sacrifices worthwhile. . .

Please continue the prayers as well, each one certainly makes a difference.

Respectfully, CPT Jeremy Riegel
Commander, HHC 173d Special Troops Battalion
Jalalabad, Afghanistan

It has been said "a child shall lead them . . ." and if it weren't for my sons' enlistment, this journey, although incredibly painful at times, would have never taken place. I have a depth that only comes through pain and sacrifice. My babies have become my heroes, and I cannot do enough for those who serve to defend the United States of America—the greatest country in the world!

Prayer:
Father, show me where I can be making
a difference in someone else's life.

Christmas Peace

Maj. Brandon Reid, United States Air Force

I HAVE NOT been back to Southwest Asia since I left in 2003. I have, however, spent many additional months on the road since then. During these times there is always this one constant in my mind: my wife and children who I miss, but God is always there to help me through the pain of longing for my family. They are my compass.

In December 2005 I was two and a half months into a four-month deployment to the Philippines in support of the Global War on Terror. It was Christmas night. Like most Americans, attending a Christmas Eve service has always been a central part of my Christmas celebration, whether at home or abroad. But this was the first time I didn't attend. I couldn't get myself into the Christmas spirit. As a matter of fact, I was quite bitter about the military, my surroundings, and life in general. Once self-pity sets in, it's easy to let it build and believe that you're the most pathetic person on earth. These beliefs aren't true, however once again God was there to bring me out of my misery.

> "I thank God, whom I serve, as my forefathers did, with a clear conscience, as night and day I constantly remember you in my prayers. Recalling your tears, I long to see you, so that I may be filled with joy."
> (2 Timothy 1:3)

I had taped a picture of my daughters in their Christmas dresses next to my cot. While I had been praying to God each day, they were often empty prayers. However, after talking with my wife on a satellite phone I went to sulk on my cot. Upon looking at the picture, I closed my eyes, started to say a few words, and stopped. I didn't feel like thanking God at all. After about thirty seconds, guilt came over me. I closed my eyes again. At that time the God's spirit came over me, stabilizing me. I felt a closeness that I hadn't felt in weeks. He was with me at my most troubling time. I felt refreshed and reassured that whatever the challenges of the next two months, the Lord would walk with me and see me through; I simply had to have faith and be assured of God's promise that he would with me no matter what was ahead.

Prayer:
*May I constantly remember those in my
inner circle, lifting them up in prayer to you.*

Christmas in Chaos

Chaplain Col. Gene (Chip) Fowler, U.S. Army,
Command Chaplain for Combined Joint Task Force 7

FROM AN EMAIL newsletter dated December 23, 2004:

The ancient city of Nineveh is in the news today. Modern day Mosul experienced the largest single coalition casualty event in the war we call "Operation Iraqi Freedom." An explosion in a dining facility killed more than twenty and injured more than sixty people. Many were U.S. soldiers; some were U.S. and Third Country National civilians. Every death is a tragedy as it reminds us of the price of the sin of Eden. To have so many die during the Holy Season of Christmas seems to deepen the pain of grief, but as the Command Chaplain for the Multinational Corps forces in Iraq, I was deeply satisfied at the response of our chaplain teams. Immediately, they arrived and began crisis ministry—taking care of wounded, giving Last Rites or Prayers for the dead, consoling the traumatized, and providing spiritual nurture and encouragement to all in the midst of tremendous chaos.

I can't help but wonder on a larger scale—isn't this the ultimate result of the Christmas story? God coming in the midst of human tragedy to provide loving care to wounded hearts, consolation to grieving souls, and abiding encouragement in the hope that there stands over the human drama of life a ray of light emanating from a star. A star that bodes for us all an ultimate peace in his love. A love so simple and pure as to find itself in the bosom of a Babe in Bethlehem. Out of the awful traumas of humanity, he is indeed the Hope of the world. May this Christmas carry more meaning for us as the Light of the World helps us see more clearly the hope that lies ahead—Peace on earth and goodwill among mankind.

> "For to us a child is born, to us a son is given, and the government will be on his shoulders. And he will be called Wonderful Counselor, Mighty God, Everlasting Father, Prince of Peace."
> (Isaiah 9:6)

Prayer:
Lord, in today's troubled world, may we look to you as
our Prince of Peace, the only source of true comfort.

Christmas in a Combat Zone

Capt. Stuart Zeigler, U.S. Army, Afghanistan (2007–2008)

ON CHRISTMAS Day of 2007, I once again found myself on a rather remote operating base in Southern Afghanistan. I woke up that morning very homesick and feeling far from my family and especially Amanda. I remember praying for some sort of worship opportunity to celebrate the birth of my Savior. The evening prior we were told that there would be no worship service due to the fact that we were too far from any major base and there weren't enough military chaplains to go around.

As the day started a fellow believer and I made plans to conduct our own worship later that afternoon. At about ten in the morning I walked to our Tactical Operations Center (TOC) to handle some routine paperwork when I noticed two helicopters appear on our computer tracking device about twenty miles away and heading toward our base. This struck me as odd because there were no scheduled flights in our area for that day.

Several minutes later a pilot came over the radio to let us know that the "chaplain bird" was inbound and that the chaplain would be on the ground for fifteen to twenty minutes to conduct Christmas worship. I instantly ran to find my fellow believer and the two of us practically ran down to greet the helicopters. Two UH-60 Blackhawk helicopters landed and out jumped ther other Army chaplains (one a Catholic priest and one a Protestant pastor).

So for me, Christmas Day 2007 was spent with a chaplain who had flown four hundred miles to conduct a fifteen-minute worship service complete with communion and seven other believers. God answers prayer. The helicopters circled the base for twenty minutes while the battlefield pastors worshipped and then picked up the chaplains and continued on to another remote base to conduct worship with more soldiers even further down range then we were. I will never forget Christmas worship with a rifle and helmet near a helipad in southern Afghanistan as evidence of God at work in a combat zone.

> "Therefore I tell you, whatever you ask for in prayer, believe that you have received it, and it will be yours."
> (Mark 11:24)

Prayer:
Lord, increase my faith that you hear and
answer prayer according to your good will.

Christmas Hope

Maj. Janis Dashner, Chaplain, United States Air Force

BECAUSE OF the danger that is still ever present here, I have not been able to see much of the area. The one sight that surprised me was the two signs in the airport pointing toward the Nineveh terminal and the Babylon terminal. Just for the record I didn't get here in the belly of a whale, but in the belly of a C-17, which in the dark of night on a blacked out runway could be mistaken for a whale," Chaplain Janis Dashner wrote in her Christmas letter to her friends in 2003. Although she had been deployed to the Middle East twice, she never expected to be deployed in Iraq.

> "This will be a sign to you: You will find a baby wrapped in cloths and lying in a manger."
> (Luke 2:12)

"My ministry here is more rewarding than I ever imagined. Nightly young troops come through our medical facility. Many have injuries that will change the way they live their lives forever. Some are critically injured, but with great skill, care, and prayer they are stabilized and flown out of this place to Germany, and hopefully home soon," she wrote.

Dashner considered it a privilege to spend time with these young men and women, noting that many hoped to return to their units.

"All of us will return home different people, I fear, and I hope," she continued.

Dashner understood the realities of the battlefield, the danger of injury and death. Yet she also knew the blessing—the power of God to transform hearts in the midst of war.

"Miracles abound here. Our base has been hit three times by missiles in the last two weeks and we experienced a ground attack the night after the announcement that Saddam was captured. Even still we have been safe and there is a feeling of security. In this austere setting, not too many complain about the long hours, port-a-potties and bad food," she noted.

"Everywhere there is an eagerness to bring hope and peace to this troubled, troubled land. Just when I am tempted to question the reason I am called to do this, I find a young person reaching for my hand and thanking me for a simple prayer and I am humbled by their faith." Dashner concluded her letter with a request. "During this Christmas season I ask you to pray for Peace that it might be real and swift in coming to this land and to the world," adding "with Christmas Hope."

Prayer:
Father, I pray for peace in the world's most troubled places today. I pray encouragement for those who are serving in our military in far away lands, who need comfort and strength.

Night Jump

Staff Sgt. Christopher Taffoya, U.S. Army, Iraq (2003–2004)

MARCH 26, 2003. It was the dead of night, but sleep was the furthest thing from my mind. The war in Iraq officially began just days ago, and my brigade and I were sitting at the airfield in Aviano, Italy, rigging up our rucksacks, preparing for a night jump. We were to open up the northern front.

It would be my first night jump. Rehearsing all the possibilities the next few hours held, I was scared out of my mind.

I suddenly remembered an elder from our church base saying once—read Psalm 91, the soldier's psalm. He was a Viet Nam

> "He replied, 'You of little faith, why are you so afraid?' Then he got up and rebuked the winds and the waves, and it was completely calm." (Matthew 8:26)

veteran and had told us that this psalm had gotten him through the war.

So as I'm sitting on my rucksack, waiting for time to go by, I must have read Psalm 91 a hundred times. Verses five and six stated, "You will not fear the terror of the night, nor the arrow that flies by day, nor the pestilence that stalks in the darkness . . ."

What does that mean to me? I wondered. Then it hit me. It seemed to tell me, *Do not fear what you're about it do, because you're going to be the terror of the night, and when day comes, you will be the arrow that flies by day. So what do you have to fear?*

After that, this unbelievable calmness came over me. It's like God was sitting next to me saying, *It's going to be alright.*

Sgt. Taffoya in
Kirkuk, Iraq

The previous ten jumps had always made me so nervous that I couldn't eat beforehand, consequently I was quite weak. This time though, I was able to eat right before the jump, and I even slept on the plane. When it was almost time to jump, I saw in the faces of the men around me the fear that I once had. But now I had overwhelming confidence that God was going to be there no matter what. God laid his hand on me and I knew it. I didn't see him, but he calmed my fears just like he calmed the Sea of Galilee with the disciples.

Prayer:
Lord, when I am afraid, calm my heart like you calmed the seas.

Sgt. Chrstopher Taffoya
at Arlington National
Cemetery

Grenade Attack

Staff Sgt. Christopher Taffoya,
U.S. Army, Iraq (2003–2004)

IN AN INSTANT, everything seemed to stop. I couldn't hear a thing. Dazed, I looked around and tried to make sense of the silent, bloody scene of confusion around me.

We had been on a foot patrol when an explosion from a grenade attack interrupted our progress. After walking another thirty yards, I looked down and saw that I was walking strangely. The blood on my leg was my own, after all.

Yep, I've been hit, was the thought that crossed my mind. For some reason I was about as concerned as I would have been if I had realized I was bleeding from a paper cut. I knew I would be okay, that God hadn't left my side.

I was taken out of battle at that point and went through five surgeries to remove shrapnel in my calf, ankle, and feet. I couldn't walk for at least a month since both feet were damaged, but I eventually healed up and talked the doctors into letting me go back into battle before they were planning to release me.

I returned to my guys and was back in the battle on Thanksgiving 2003. It was awesome. While nobody said it out loud, everyone was thankful on that day that I was back. That's where I belonged. I'm thankful for each little thing that happened in my life in Iraq. As I look back over it, I see where God had his hand. The grenade landed a foot and half from my feet. I'm still here today—if that's not a miracle I don't know what is.

> "Have I not commanded you? Be strong and courageous. Do not be terrified; do not be discouraged, for the LORD your God will be with you wherever you go." (Joshua 1:9)

Sometimes on our spiritual battlefield, we get wounded and end up not wanting to go back into battle, but we have to. We must allow our wounds to heal up with the help of others and get back where we belong—wherever it is that God has placed us.

Prayer:
*Lord, give me the strength and courage I need
to honor you in all my circumstances.*

Outnumbered

Staff Sgt. Christopher Taffoya, U.S. Army, Iraq (2003–2004)

KIRKUK, THE city in Iraq we were to take control of, was not just any city. It stands on the site of the ancient Assyrian capital of Arrapha, and was the battle ground for three empires—Assyria, Babylonia, and Media. The ruins of a five thousand-year old citadel are nearby. The history of this place reeked of war, bloodshed, victory, and defeat.

On the day we entered the city in April 2003, thirty thousand Iraqi army soldiers were there to defend it. There were less than one thousand of us.

Being out numbered thirty to one, we knew it would be tough and we'd suffer many casualties. But I was also confident we would win. As we approached the city, I claimed Psalm 91:7 again: "*A thousand may fall at your side, ten thousand at your right hand, but it will not come near you.*" We continued to march forward though the odds were not in our favor.

Upon entering the city, however, we were alone. The Iraqi soldiers, all thirty thousand of them, had retreated by the time we arrived. Not one was left. We took the city without incident or injury, and I praised God for his protection once again.

> "If you make the Most High your dwelling— even the LORD, who is my refuge—then no harm will befall you, no disaster will come near your tent." (Psalm 91:9, 10)

"What are we fighting for, anyway?" I can imagine the Iraqi soldiers asking each other before retreating. They served a tyrant. From the 1991 Gulf War until 2003, the former Iraqi government systematically expelled an estimated 120,000 Kurds, Turkmens, and some Assyrians from Kirkuk and other towns and villages in this oil-rich region. Meanwhile, the Iraqi government resettled Arab families in their place in an attempt to reduce the political power and presence of ethnic minorities. The Iraqi authorities also seized minorities' property and assets; those who were expelled to areas controlled by Kurdish forces were stripped of all possessions and their ration cards were withdrawn.

The reason why Americans have been as successful as we have in war is that we have something to fight for—something worth coming back home to. That's why I believe we would have held up in battle, even out-numbered as we were. But I'm still glad we didn't have to.

Prayer:
Lord, give me the courage and strength to march
forward into the unknown, knowing you are with me.

DECEMBER 30

Exposed

Staff Sgt. Christopher Taffoya,
U.S. Army, Iraq (2003–2004)

IT WAS ONE o'clock in the morning when a shot rang out above us. It was the night guard standing watch on the roof of our safe house in the middle of the city, warning us by firing his automatic weapon that our safety was being threatened either by the enemy trying to penetrate the property or attack us from any distance.

In a flash, our entire company of about one hundred and fifty men jumped out of bed, grabbed their weapons, and rushed outside to reinforce whatever was necessary. None of us had any clue what was going on—we had just awaken literally seconds ago. All of us were laying down and firing into the darkness. We were still in our pajamas, barefoot, and with no body armor on to protect ourselves. Nothing was between our feet and the rocky ground beneath them. Nothing was between our bare shoulders and the M-4s we steadied against them. And nothing was between our exposed flesh and the enemy fire that was aimed against us.

> "You will not fear the terror of the night, nor the arrow that flies by day." (Psalm 91:5)

That night the enemy fired seven rockets at us, each a little bigger than a baseball bat in size. One hit the roof and bounced off and the others didn't come near us. The Iraqis didn't have the technology we do that perfects aim, so they shot the rockets off in our direction from unstable launcher pods, just hoping that it would hit something.

When dawn came the next morning, there was nothing left to indicate what sort of casualties we may have inflicted on them. They either ran away or pulled all their men out. I'm sure that with so many of us firing in their direction, they changed their minds and turned tail to dodge the bullets. And none of the pajama-clad warriors were harmed

Prayer:
Lord, give me the confidence to do the right thing,
even if I feel vulnerable and exposed while doing it.

DECEMBER 31

Rebuilding Kirkuk

Staff Sgt. Christopher Taffoya,
U.S. Army, Iraq (2003–2004)

THIS WAR wasn't all about firing weapons. In fact, we spent 90 percent of our time not fighting the enemy, but doing reconstruction: fixing the hospitals and schools, reprinting school books, rebuilding streets, securing supplies, training their police force, getting the water and power turned back on. At Christmas time, our families sent toys for us to deliver to the children, and money for the adults so they could heat their homes and cook a little easier.

The children in general loved us, and we loved spending time with them, too. We spoiled the girls a little more than the boys and always gave our candy from our MREs to the girls. That, in itself, was hard for them to understand since females are considered less valuable in that culture.

One day I gave a pack of Skittles® to a little girl, and a little boy snatched the Skittles® out of her hand.

"Give those back to her," I told him as I grabbed his collar. I knew he didn't understand English, but after a few tries he got the message.

> "Turn from evil and do good; seek peace and pursue it."
> (Psalm 34:14)

He looked dumbfounded. *What are you doing? I'm a guy, I'm one of you,* his eyes seemed to say. But he handed them back to the little girl and looked at me again, this time with an expression of epiphany on his face. It's like a light went on in his head, as though he were thinking, *What if girls are important after all? Maybe we shouldn't treat them like we do.*

He walked away very slowly, as if he had a lot of thinking to do after that. I bet that was the first time someone stuck up for females in his life.

I'm sure we affected the children of that country more than we affected people my age and older. Adults are set in their perceptions, but when children saw us caring and giving people dignity, it might have been life-altering. When they grow up, they'll know Americans aren't evil; we just want everyone to get along.

Prayer:
Lord, help me be a peacemaker and
pursue true reconciliation wherever I go.

Acknowledgments

I CONSIDER WORKING on this book as a privilege and an honor. Our interviews with those who have sacrificed for this war have revealed new angles on history-in-the-making, and it's been an exciting journey. So to those people who have shared your stories with me, I thank you for giving us your unique perspective: Jessica Alley, Joseph Bills, Brian and Melanie Birdwell, Bill Butler, Christopher and Leah Dubree, Oaken Ewens, Stephen Ewens, Carol Pinkerton-Ewens, Gene Fowler, Kevin and Kristin Hamilton, Steve Harrold, Kerri Hartwick, Starlett Henderson, Sara Horn, Daniel and Wendy Gade, John Gessner, Jay Johannigman, Deborah Johns, Tom Joyce, Shane Klein, Benita Koeman, Jason and Sonja Mannarino, Carrie McDonall, Mark Murphy, Joe and Stephanie Olsen, Dave and Vanessa Peters, Jim Powers, Nate Self, Patti Smith, Christopher Taffoya, Donna Tallman, Frank Vozenilek, Mark and Marshele Carter Waddell, Andrea Westfall, and Amanda and Stuart Zeigler.

Sincere thanks and appreciation also go to my family for their support during this project: to my husband Rob for cheerfully watching our young children and settling for frozen dinners many times, to my parents Peter and Pixie Falck, to my aunt Carmen Ingham, and my cousin Carrie Christensen for all their help with childcare so I could focus on meeting deadlines. Thanks also to my neighbors Teresa and Christie Carr for the free babysitting when the pressure was on. My role in this book would not have been possible without you all.

Thanks to my agent David Sanford and Rebekah Clark for suggesting that I participate in this book project, and to God and Country Press/AMG Publishers for giving me the opportunity. To the AMG staff—Dan Penwell, Rick Steele, and John Fallahee—thank you for having a vision for this book and for bringing it to fruition.

Finally, thanks to my co-authors Jane Hampton Cook and John Croushorn. Together we have been able to produce what no one of us could have accomplished alone. Thanks for your partnership in bringing these stories to the rest of the world. —Jocelyn Green

• • •

Not everyone who serves on the battlefield believes they have a book's worth of insight to share. But many recognize that their experiences changed them or their loved ones so much that they must tell their story, even if what they have to say only fills a few pages. By telling of their experiences, they not only gain a deeper perspective on their own lives but they also encourage others as well.

What I love about this book is that it has given many people who have served in Iraq and Afghanistan or their loved ones the opportunity to share their unique perspective. These men and women have lived loudly for liberty on battlefields marked by extreme challenges while their families made quiet sacrifices back home. Former *Washington Post* editor Phil Graham once quipped that journalism is the "first draft of history." These eyewitness accounts are a final draft of journalism and the first pages of history documenting these never-before-told stories.

I want to thank each of you who shared your story with me: Todd Akin, Charles Baldwin, Will Brandon, Mark E. Braswell, Janis Dashner, Mary Ebersole, Mary Bass Gray, Matt Hamrick, Brad Head, Mike Hoyt, Michael Huntley, Gina Elliott Kim, Paul Brian Kim, Debbie Lee, Jim Lively, Amy Malugani, Sean McDougal, Daniel Nichols, Brandon Reid, Greg Rosenmerkel, Rob Thomson, Mark and Sandy Troutman, Robert L. Van Antwerp, and Mary Walker. You have inspired me by your service, courage, and strength.

I also want to express my heartfelt and sincere appreciation to my husband for your never-ending support as I pursue my passion for writing. I'm also grateful to Jonathan Clements and the Nashville Agency for continuing to believe in me as a writer and public speaker. Thanks also to producers of the FOX News Channel for giving me so many opportunities to provide historical insight into current events the past year.

Thanks to the God and Country/AMG staff: to Dan Penwell for acquiring this book, serving as managing editor, and for editing and proofing the book, to Rick Steele for editing and coordinating the publication, and John Fallahee for marketing.

Thanks especially to my co-authors Jocelyn Green and John Croushorn for your hard work and perseverance to make this book what it is—a kaleidoscope of faith and courage from those who have served their nation with dignity, respect, and honor. —**Jane Hampton Cook**

• • •

I have served with heroes, men and women that are larger than life. One would think from portrayals in movies and popular fiction that courage is anchored in bravado. It is not. In my experience it is usually anchored in simple, practical faith that emphasizes others more than self. This project has allowed much of this servant-leadership to be portrayed.

In interviewing those who have served and their families, I found a renewed respect for the cost of our freedom. The dreams and aspirations of great men and women were not merely put on hold but rather sacrificed for a greater cause. Their actions are directly related to their faith. Faith calls men and women to action when freedom is threatened, sometimes in dramatic ways.

Universally those that serve look to their families and friends for the support to withstand the hardship of deployment. It is however those that remain on U.S. soil that have the heavier burden. Sustaining life and home while a part of your family is away is difficult at best. The stress of not knowing what is happening to your loved one, seeing reports of conflict in areas they are known to be in, and at times dealing with the frustrations of a family pulled apart by deployment—these are common if not everyday trials these families go through. It is a trial my wife and children know very well. They are true heroes.

I would like to thank each of those who shared stories with me: Brandt Smith, Debbie Lee, Mike Meoli, Jim Phillips, James Maloney, Skip Mahaffee, Rich Carmona, Linda Croushorn, Bradley Macnealy, Joe Wood, Don Richards, David Graves, Rob Garretson, Gary Hensley, Paul Casinelli, and Ted. You and your families have given to this country in ways some will never be able to fully understand. Thank you.

Special thanks go to David Sanford and Rebekah Clark for introducing me to authorship. Their always-encouraging emails sustained me through many long days and nights. Thanks to Dan Penwell, Rick Steele, John Fallahee, and all those on the God and Country/AMG staff for their undying commitment to quality.

My co-authors Jocelyn Green and Jane Hampton Cook deserve special recognition. I am not a natural author, and their encouragement and motivation enabled me to complete this project. Their professionalism and passion appear on every page.

I must also recognize the true hero in my life. She went through the hardship and frustration of deployment, cared for our children and ran our household for what seemed an endless time. Her love and faith have preserved our marriage and enabled me to be the man I am today. Julie is the love of my life, and a true believer in all that is right with this world.
—John Croushorn